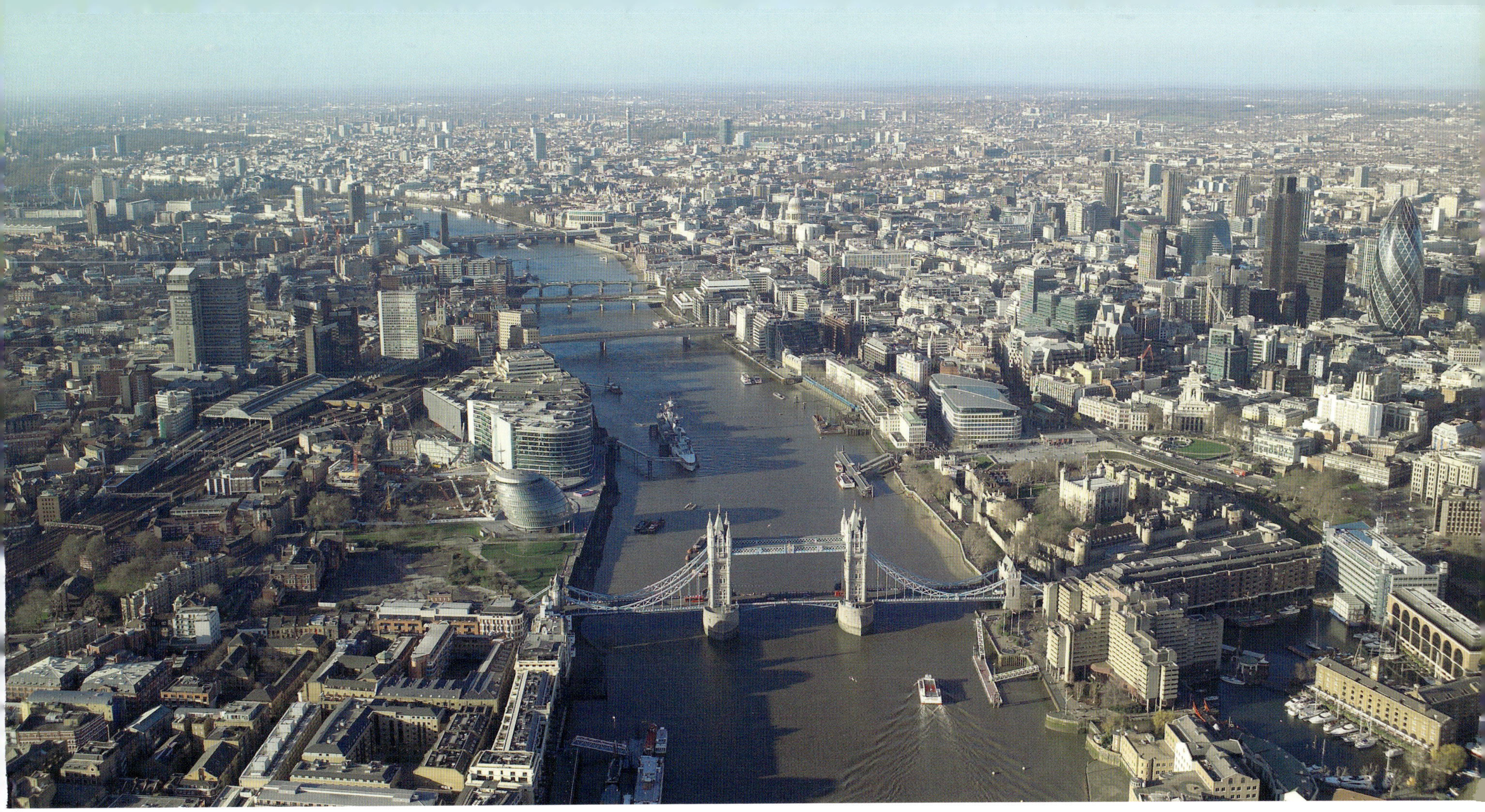

SOUTH-EAST ENGLAND
from the air

Ian Hay

Text by

Hilary Ellis

MYRIAD

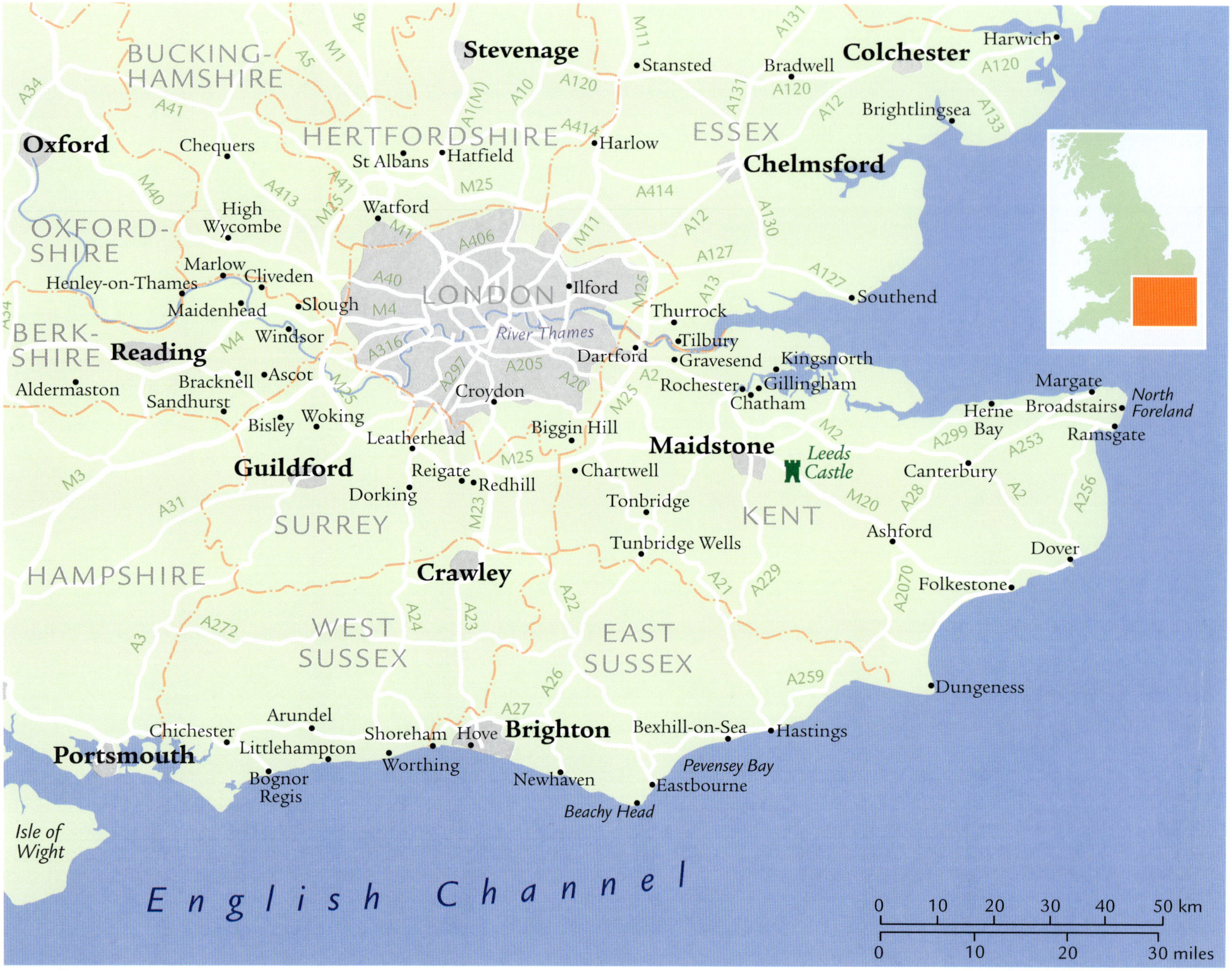

First published in 2010 by Myriad Books Limited, 35 Bishopsthorpe Road, London SE26 4PA

ISBN 1 84746 334 7 EAN 978 1 84746 334 0

Designed by Jerry Goldie Graphic Design

Printed in China

Introduction

The view from above gives an exciting new perspective on the south-east – Britain's most densely populated region. Yet despite the millions of people that live in or near to Britain's bustling capital city, the south-east is well known for its picturesque woodland and breathtaking coastline. The region's varied scenery ranges from nature-rich marshland bordering the Thames estuary, to soaring chalk cliffs along the Sussex Heritage Coast and expansive shingle shoreline at Dungeness in Kent. London is itself a very green city with numerous parks and gardens maintained for the enjoyment of the urban population and promenades along the banks of the river Thames.

The region's most famous tourist attractions are a delight when viewed from the air, particularly the royal residences at Windsor, Hampton Court and Buckingham Palace, where formal gardens complement the historic architecture refined over the centuries. Other stately homes and country retreats paint a picture of the aristocratic lifestyle of old. Certainly the region's many seaside resorts and spa towns are a reminder of how pre-occupied the wealthy Georgians and Victorians were with their good health. Eastbourne, Brighton and Bognor Regis all became fashionable when the royal family discovered the delights of fresh air and sea bathing, and photographs taken from above show some of the neat Regency architecture that still stands today.

London's steady expansion and the arrival of the railways has seen the fast growth of commuter towns beyond the capital's green belt. Modern-day residents can enjoy some of Britain's best sporting events at major venues for tennis, golf, football, rugby, sailing, cricket and horseracing. And while London is of course the nation's cultural capital with a wealth of museums, theatres and restaurants, the south-east also provides shopping on a grand scale at Bluewater and Lakeside Thurrock, as well as entertainment at the region's major music and community festivals, amusement parks and pleasure piers.

The south-east has had its fair share of invaders and this can be seen in some of the ancient monuments visible today. Important Roman sites at Chichester, St Albans and Colchester are found close to Norman castles built by William the Conqueror following his victory at the Battle of Hastings. Strategically important ports and dockyards along the coast, such as those at Dover and Chatham, were protected by fortifications and towers scattered along the shore. The region is also the site of some of the earliest Christian churches in Britain with Canterbury Cathedral becoming a major destination for pilgrimage; today it is a UNESCO World Heritage Site.

All in all, the wealth of dramatic and diverse perspectives in this book shows why the south-east is Britain's most visited region.

Hilary Ellis

Contents

CHAPTER ONE
London 4

CHAPTER TWO
Kent 36

CHAPTER THREE
Surrey 60

CHAPTER FOUR
Sussex 72

CHAPTER FIVE
Berkshire & the Thames Valley 94

CHAPTER SIX
The Northern Home Counties 108

CHAPTER SEVEN
Essex 116

London

One of the world's great cities, London is Britain's capital, its seat of government, a major financial centre and the home of the royal family. Millions of visitors are drawn each year to its remarkable buildings and museums, great green spaces, ceremonial pageantry and fascinating mix of people. The city's attractions include many of Britain's most historic buildings, such as Buckingham Palace and the Tower of London, and some of the most exciting and modern, such as the London Eye and the "Gherkin". The West End is renowned for being the theatre capital of the world, while many of the UK's greatest sporting venues are in London. Over 200 years ago, Dr Johnson wrote the words that still hold true today: "When a man is tired of London, he is tired of life; for there is in London all that life can afford."

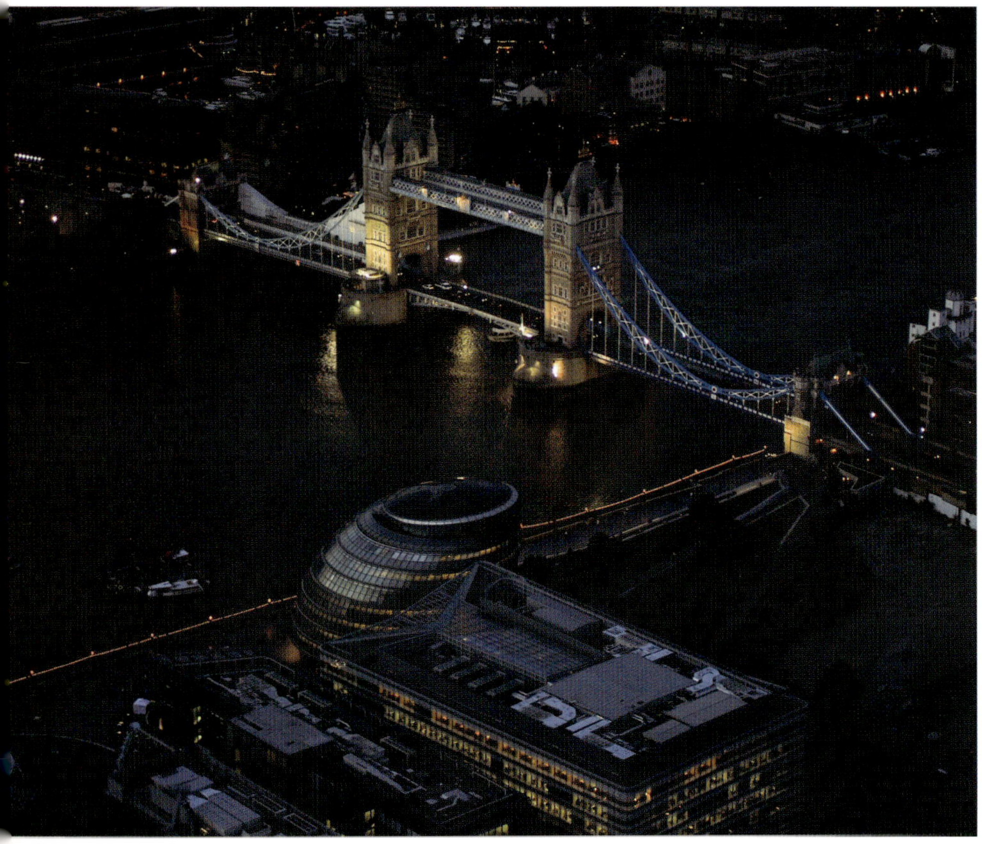

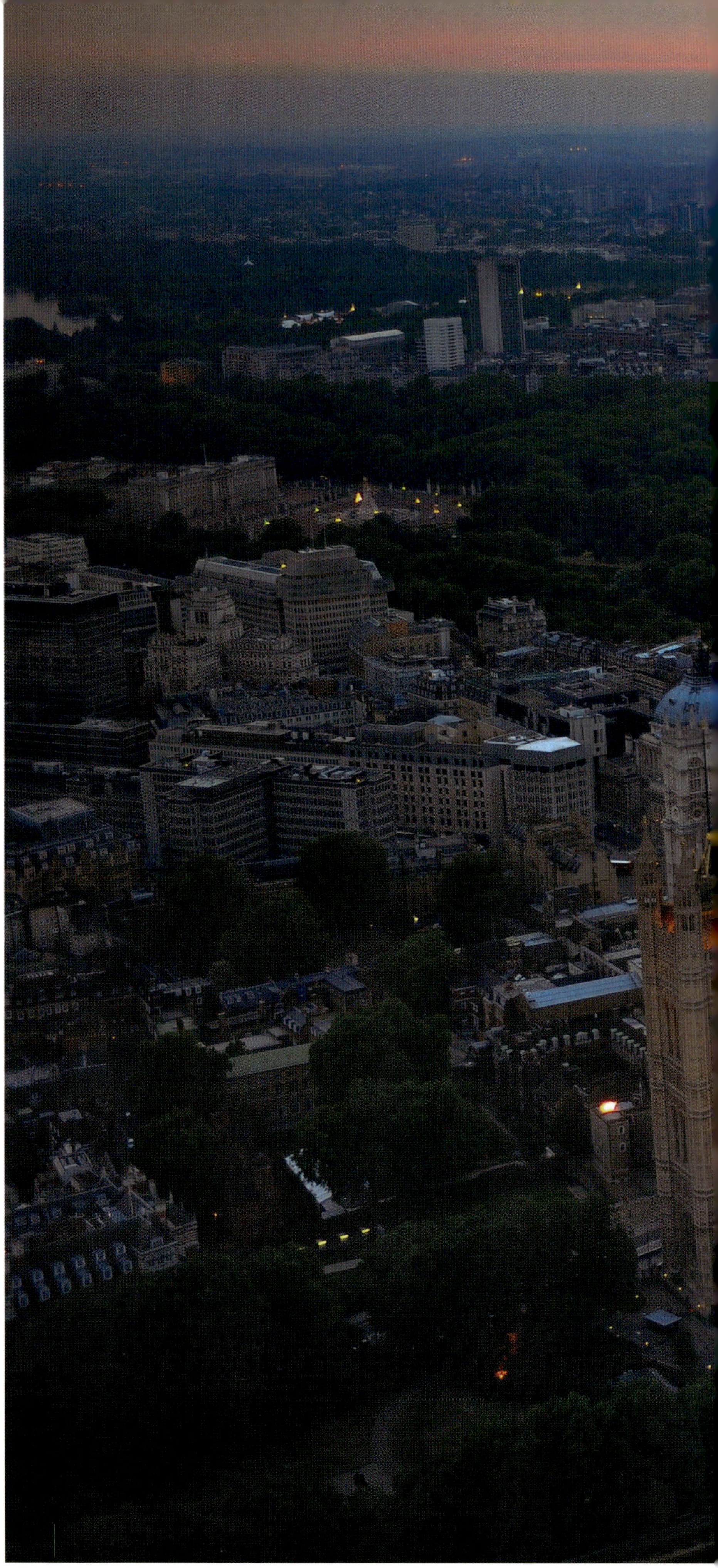

Skyline at night

The river Thames flows through the heart of London and is overlooked by world-famous landmarks such as Tower Bridge (above) and the Palace of Westminster (right).

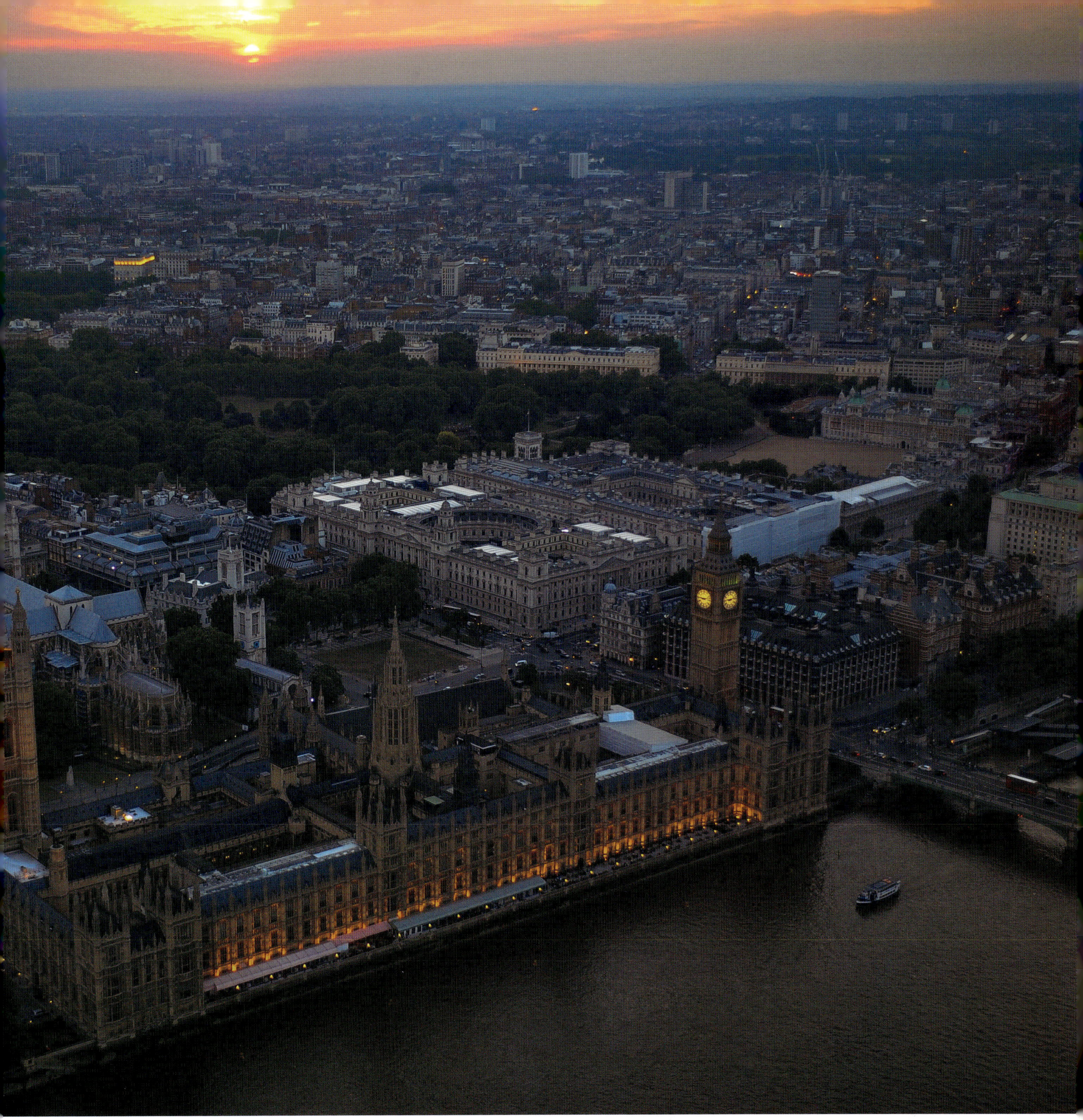

Westminster

On the north bank of the Thames lies Westminster, an area named after the Abbey or West Minster around which the settlement grew. Now home to a wide range of historic and prestigious buildings, Westminster is best known as the heart of political London and home to the seat of government. The Palace of Westminster, a UNESCO World Heritage Site, stands proud beside the river and is home to the UK parliament and Big Ben, the famous clocktower. The Old Palace, a medieval building complex destroyed by fire in 1834, was the royal residence of the Kings of England until 1512, before becoming the home of Parliament. The New Palace was designed by the architect Sir Charles Barry, assisted by Augustus Pugin, in the Gothic Perpendicular style and incorporated some features from the Old Palace spared by the fire. Running north from Parliament Square is Whitehall and its government buildings. Downing Street leads off Whitehall and is home to Number 10 Downing Street (seen to the right), the Prime Minister's main residence.

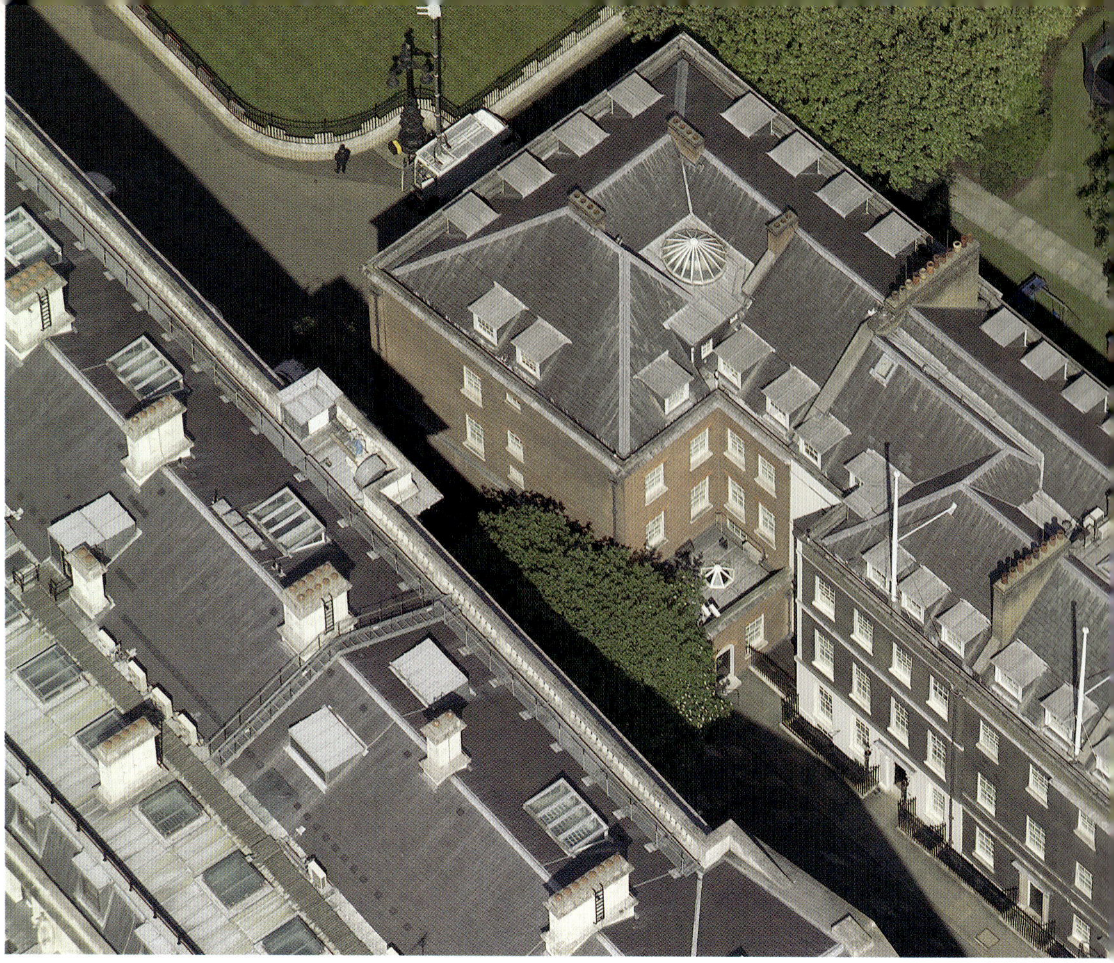

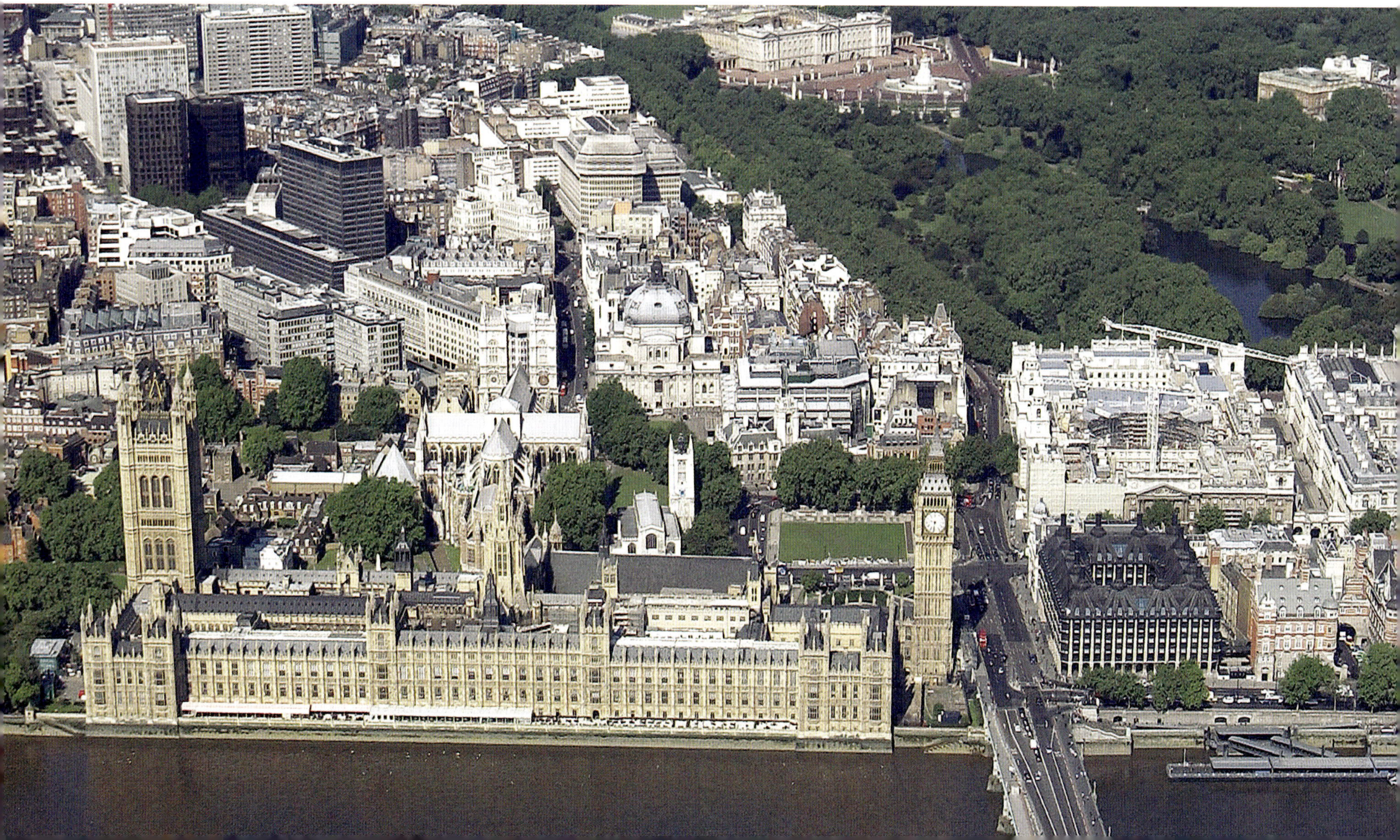

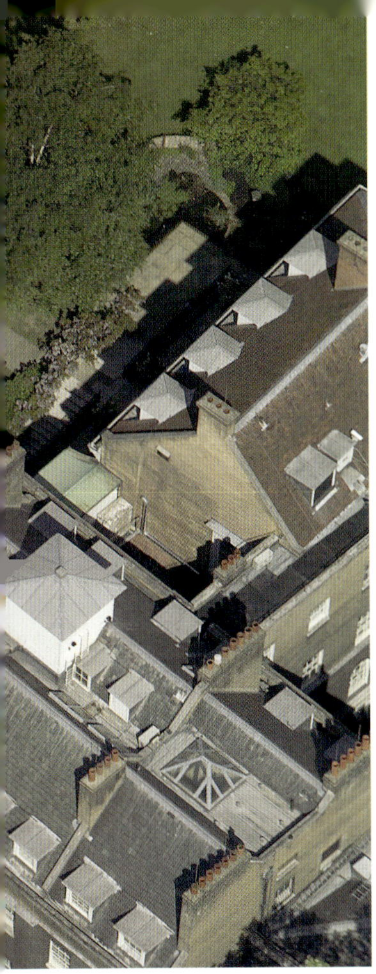

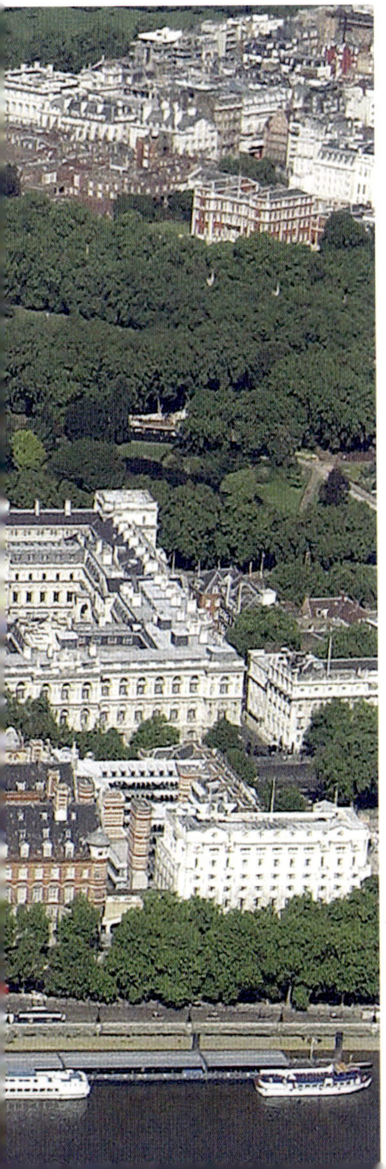

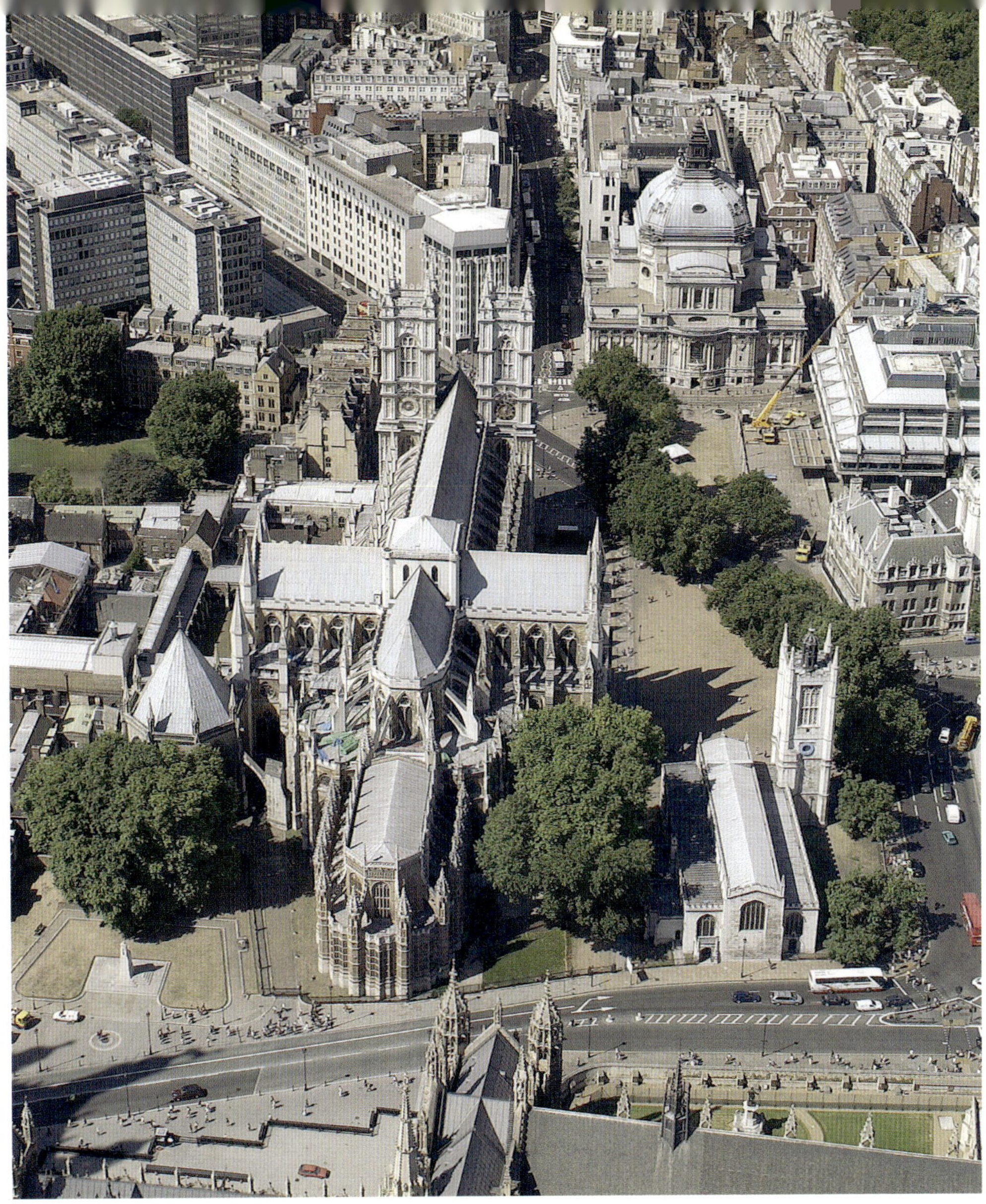

CATHEDRALS

Westminster Abbey (left), a magnificent 13th century Gothic church, is the final resting place for 17 monarchs and many famous Britons such as Geoffrey Chaucer, Isaac Newton and Charles Darwin. A coronation church since 1066, the Abbey was built on the site of worship of 10th century Benedictine monks and contains a medieval shrine of an Anglo-Saxon saint. Westminster Cathedral (below), the Roman Catholic Cathedral of the Archbishop of Westminster, is famous for its mosaics, marble and music. Built in a Byzantine style to a design by John Francis Bentley in the 19th century, the cathedral was completed within a very short time.

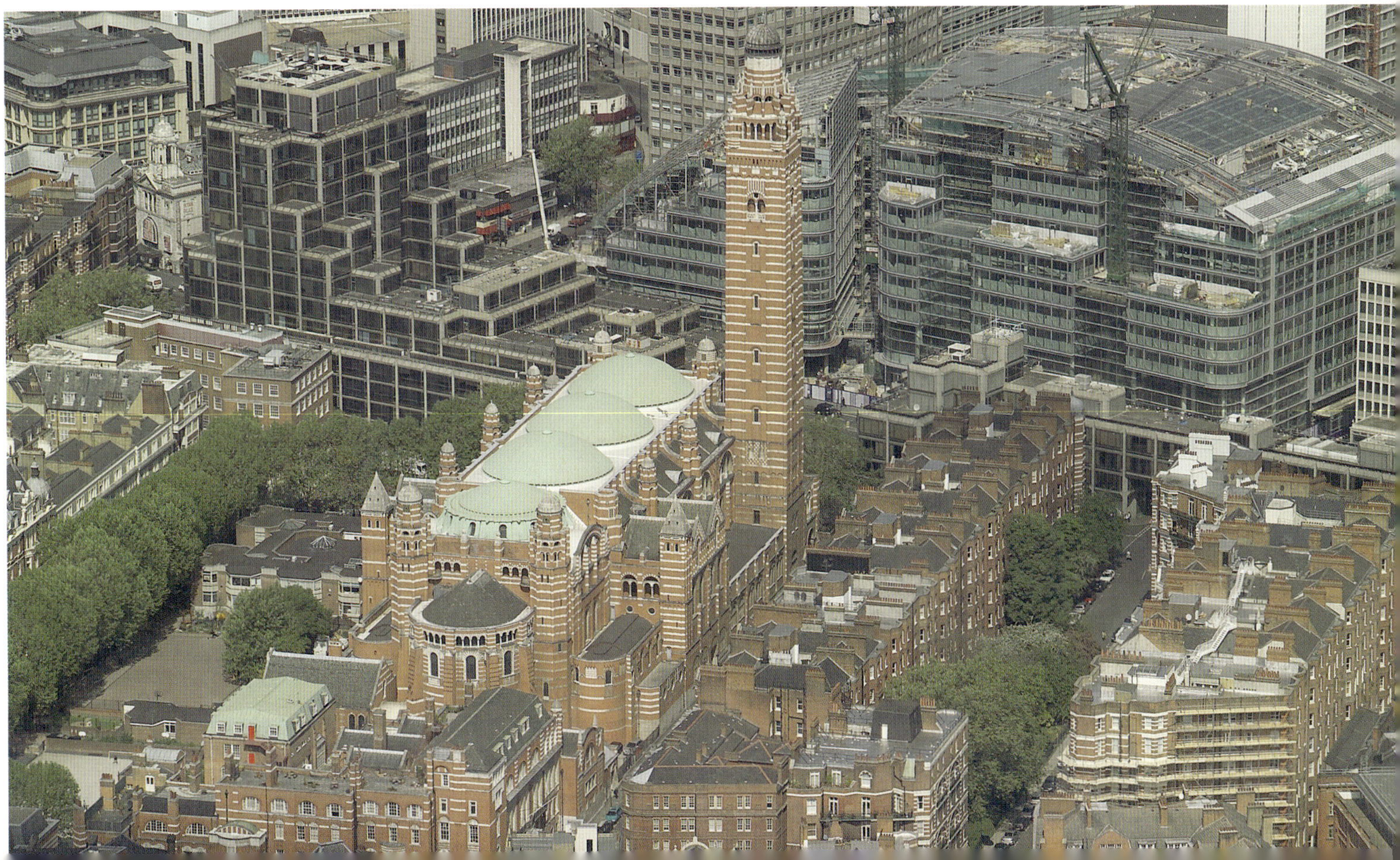

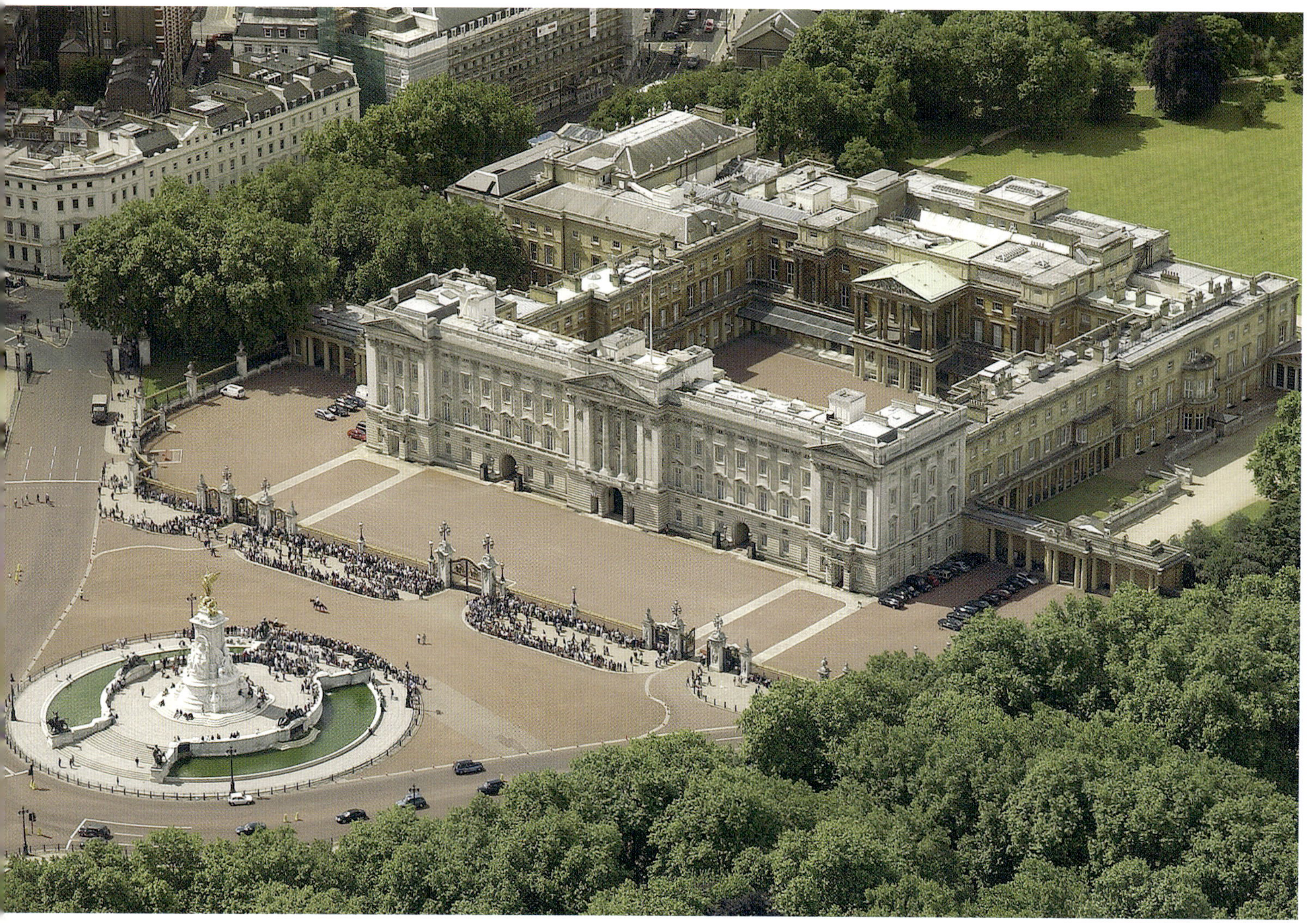

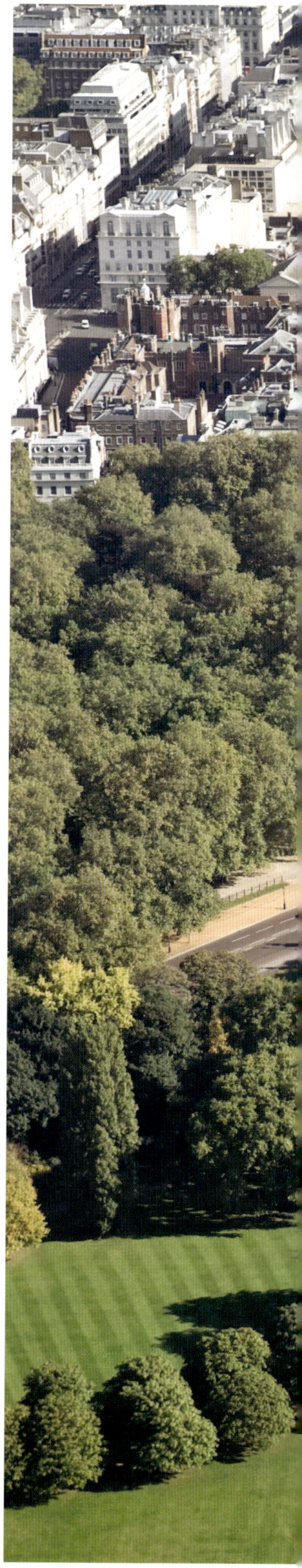

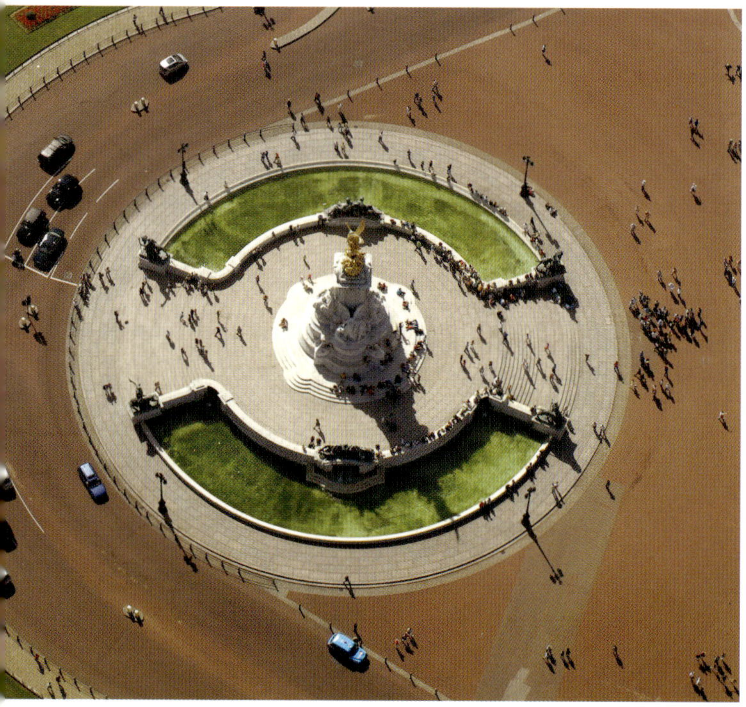

Buckingham Palace

Set at the end of the Mall, a grand avenue designed by Charles II, the imposing facade of Buckingham Palace overlooks the 1911 Victoria Memorial and includes the famous balcony from which the royal family greet crowds. In the 19th century, Queen Victoria made Buckingham Palace her royal residence, and since then all monarchs have followed suit. One of London's biggest tourist attractions, Buckingham Palace is also the heart of the monarch's administration and houses the offices of the Royal Household, the staff that support the activities of the Queen and her immediate family. Each year the palace hosts more than 50,000 guests, who attend banquets, lunches, dinners, receptions and garden parties. The building has 775 rooms and is furnished and decorated with works of art that make up part of the Royal Collection. The ceremony of the Changing of the Guard takes place in the forecourt of the palace each day during the summer and every other day in the winter unless it is very wet. For most of the year, guard duties at the Palace are performed by soldiers of the Household Division. A band from the Wellington Barracks accompanies the new Guard as they march to the palace forecourt to take over from the old Guard.

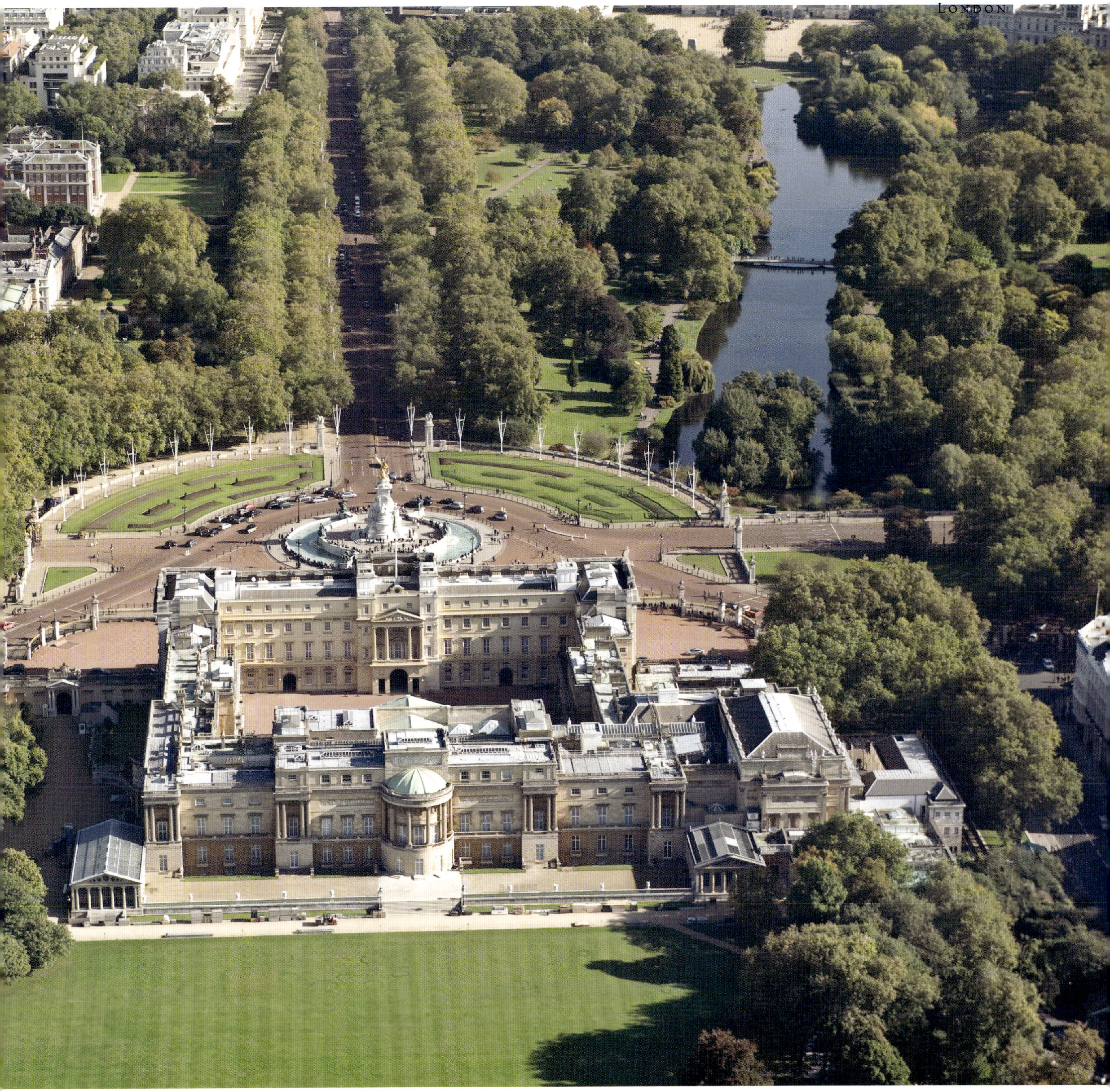

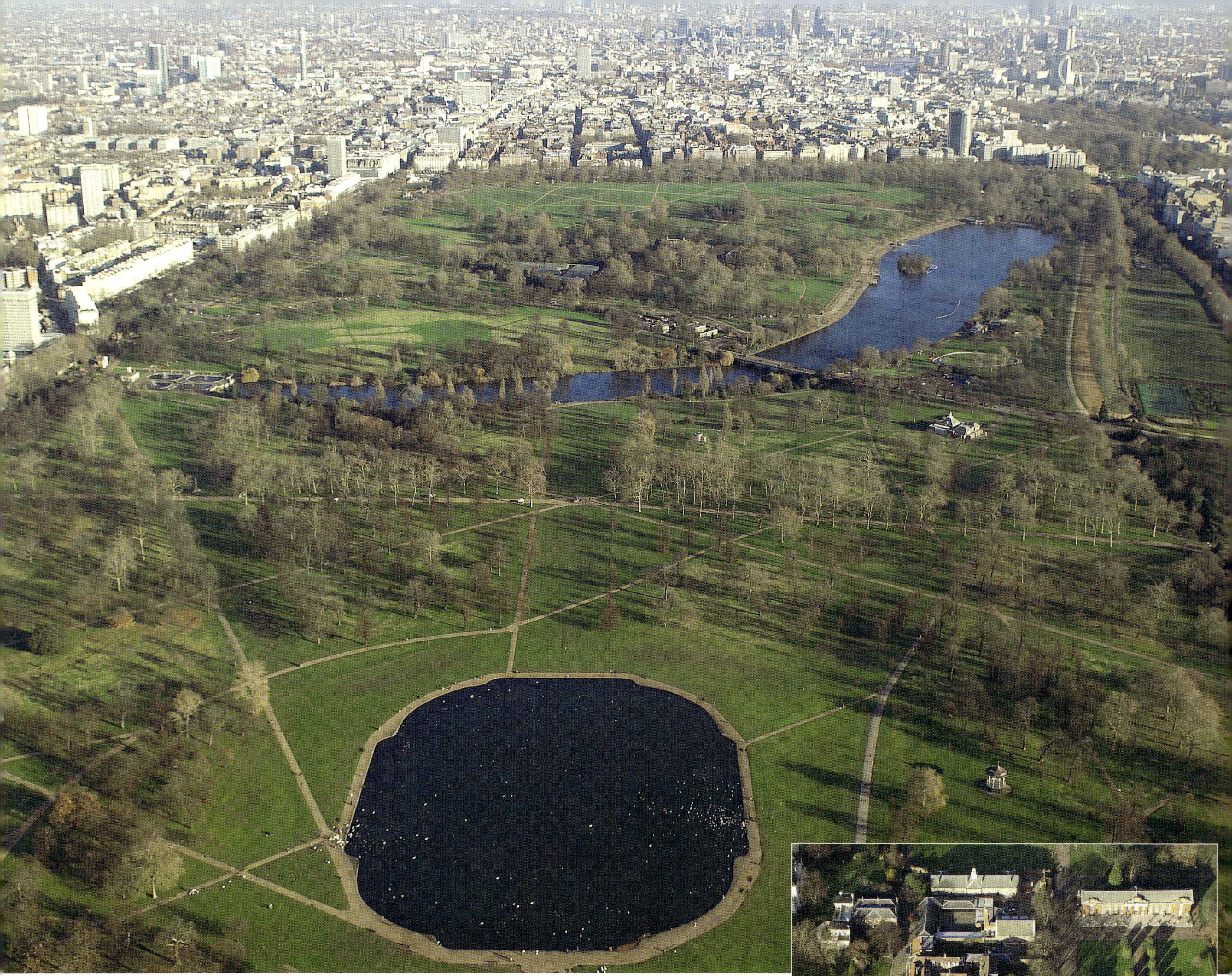

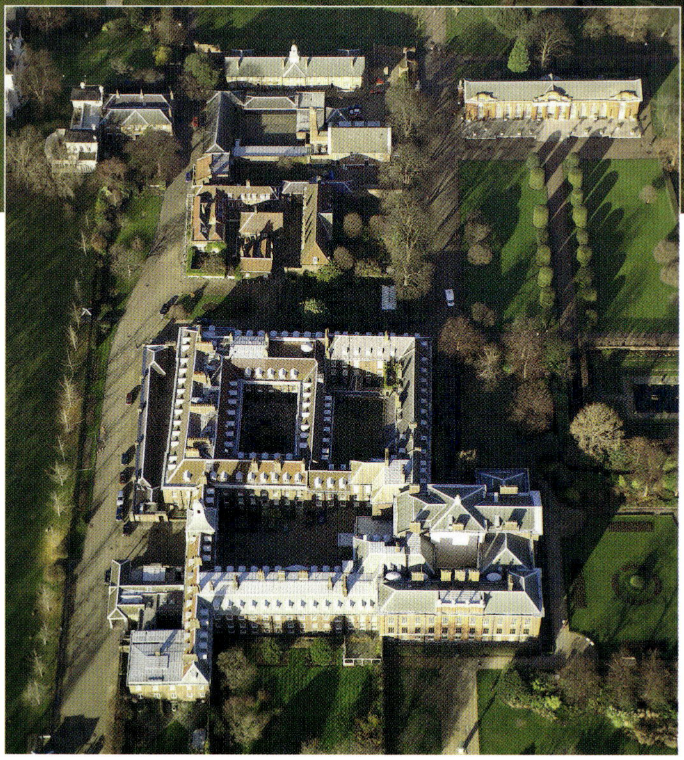

Hyde Park

London's first public park, Hyde Park was once Henry VIII's royal hunting ground and was gifted to the public in 1637. Today the park is popular for outdoor leisure activities such as open-air concerts, rollerskating and rowing on the Serpentine, a lake created in the 1730s by Caroline, George II's wife. A bridle path known as Rotten Row runs along the south side of the park. The name is thought to be a corruption of the French *Route de Roi* or King's Road as William III used this route to journey from Kensington Palace to St James'. Kensington Gardens, which lies alongside Hyde Park, contains the Round Pond on which children have sailed model boats for over two centuries. Also within Kensington Gardens is the royal residence, Kensington Palace (right), once home to Diana, the Princess of Wales.

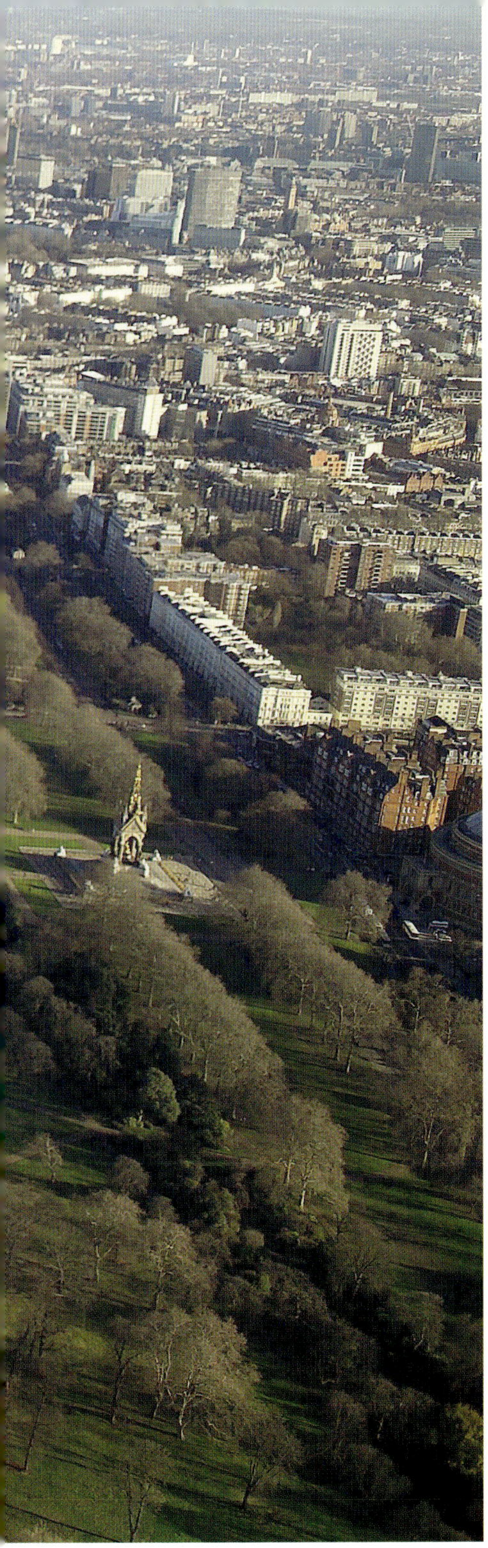

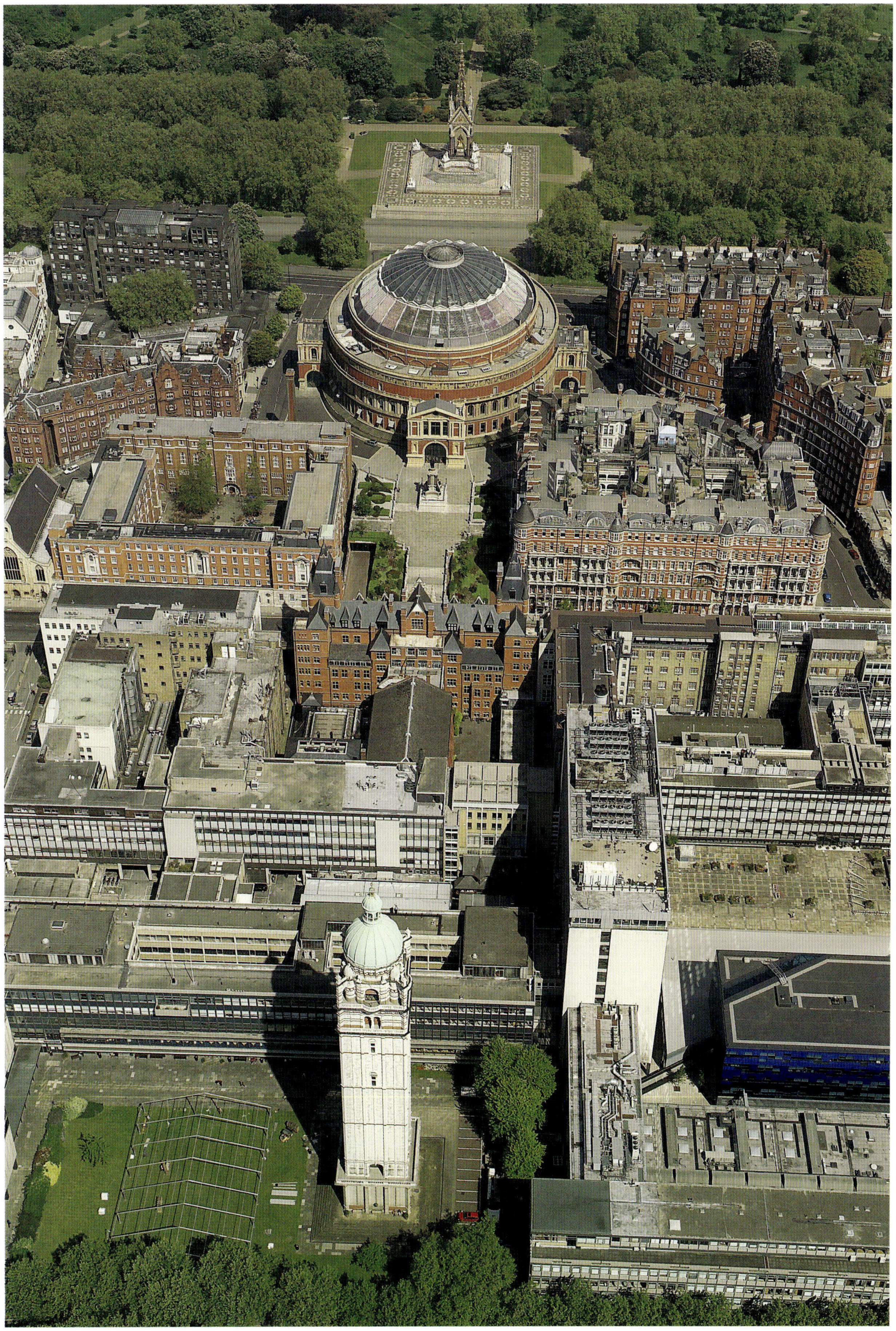

Albert Hall

Kensington Gore is home to the Royal Albert Hall of Arts and Sciences (right) as well as Queen Victoria's elaborate Albert Memorial. The Albert Hall was built in 1871 for just £200,000 from the proceeds of the 1851 Great Exhibition and hosts the Proms summer concerts and many other musical events. The Royal College of Music and Imperial College are close neighbours.

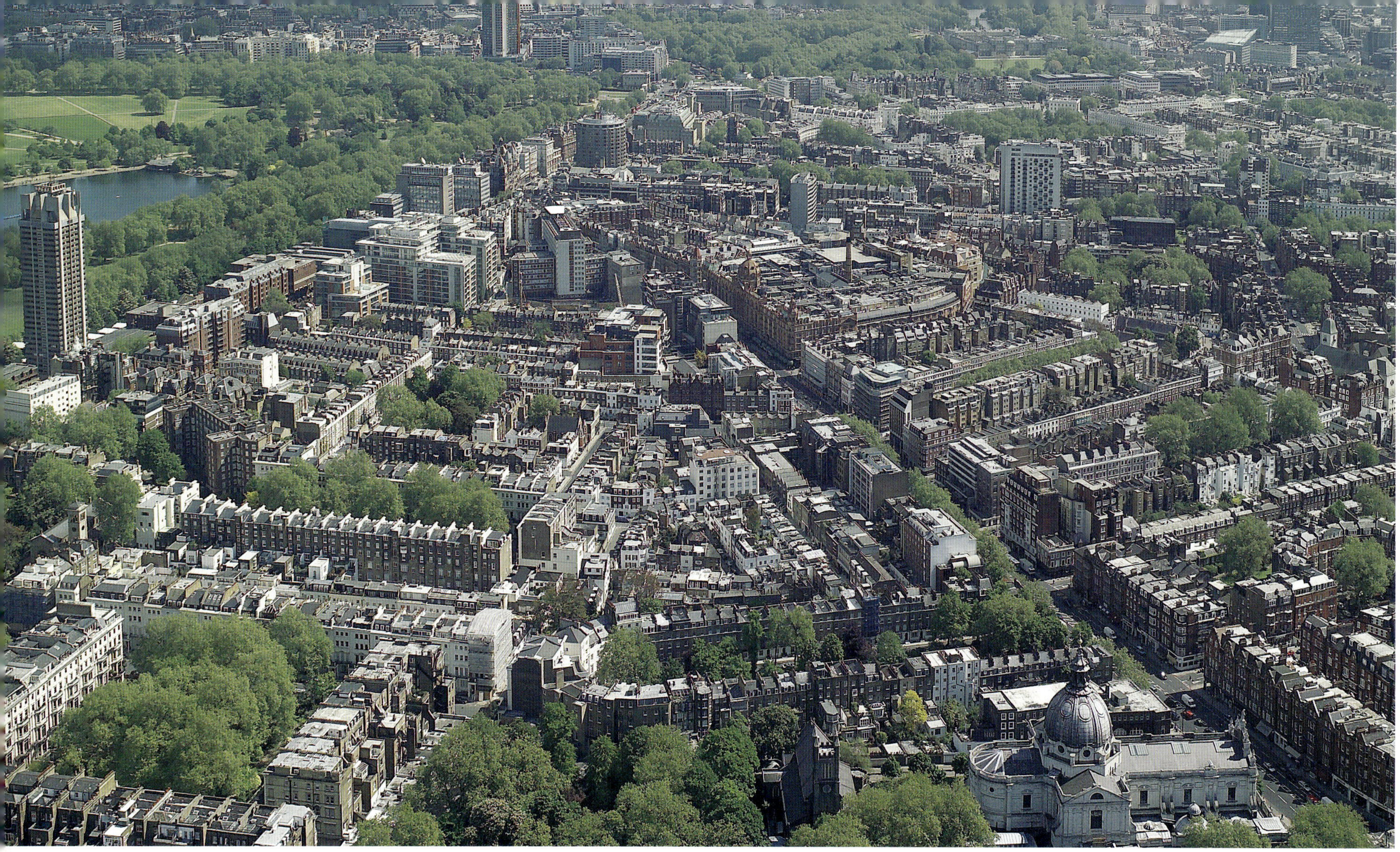

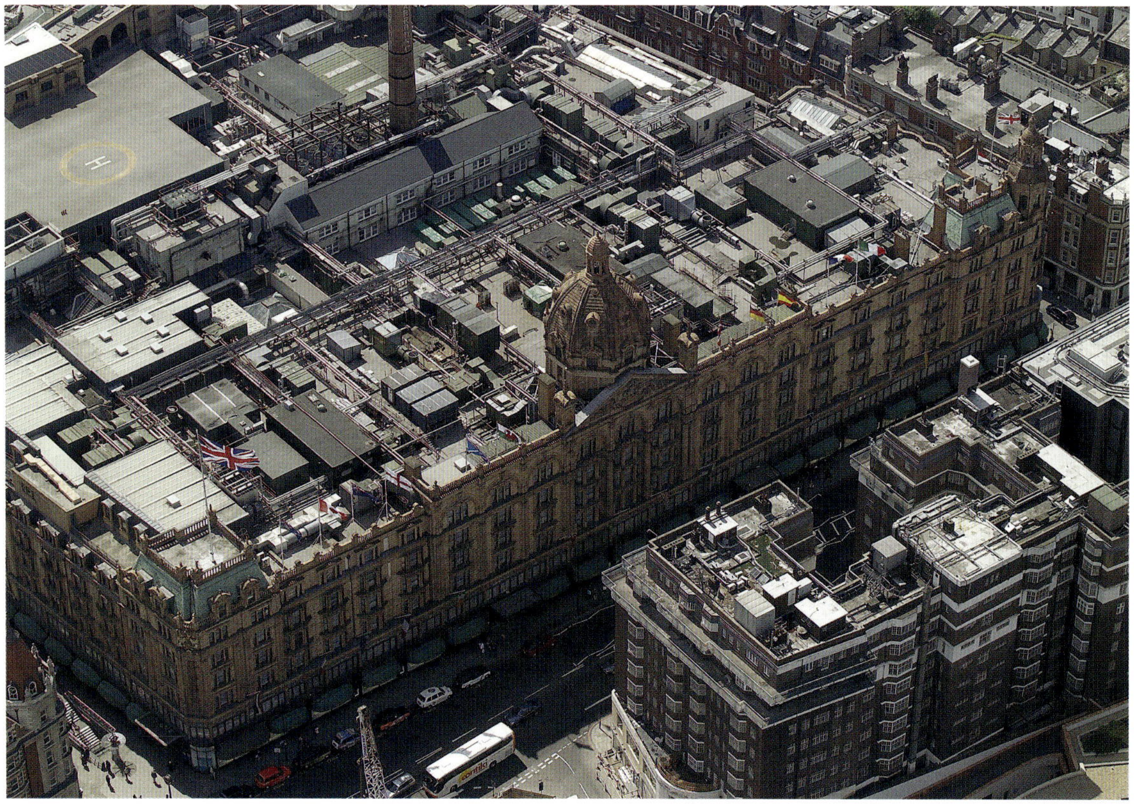

KENSINGTON

South of Hyde Park and Kensington Gardens, the affluent neighbourhood of Kensington contains some of London's most expensive streets and garden squares. Busy shopping centres include Kensington High Street and the upmarket boutiques and department stores of Knightsbridge. The world-famous luxury department store, Harrods (left), is located on Brompton Road. Based on a 4.5 acre site (18,000sq m), the store contains over one million square feet (90,000sq m) of retail space in 330 departments. Close by lies the Brompton Oratory, or Church of the Immaculate Heart of Mary, a 19th century design and the second largest Roman Catholic church in London after Westminster Cathedral. Italian Renaissance in style, its huge vaulted dome stands 200ft (61m tall). The church has strong ties with the nearby London Oratory school, and hosted the weddings of Sir Edward Elgar and Alfred Hitchcock.

Victoria and Albert Museum

Built on a huge 11 acre site (below), the Victoria and Albert Museum's art and design collection was founded as a legacy of Prince Albert's Great Exhibition of 1851, a celebration of Britain's achievements in industrial technology and design held in Hyde Park. The V&A's collection is wide-ranging and includes 5,000 years' worth of amazing artefacts from many of the world's richest cultures including ceramics, furniture, fashion, glass, jewellery, metalwork, photographs, sculpture, textiles and paintings. The V&A's photography collection is one of the world's most important, with more than half a million images dating from the advent of photography. The building itself is a mixture of Victorian and Edwardian styles and contains a recently redesigned formal central garden sometimes used for temporary exhibits of sculpture.

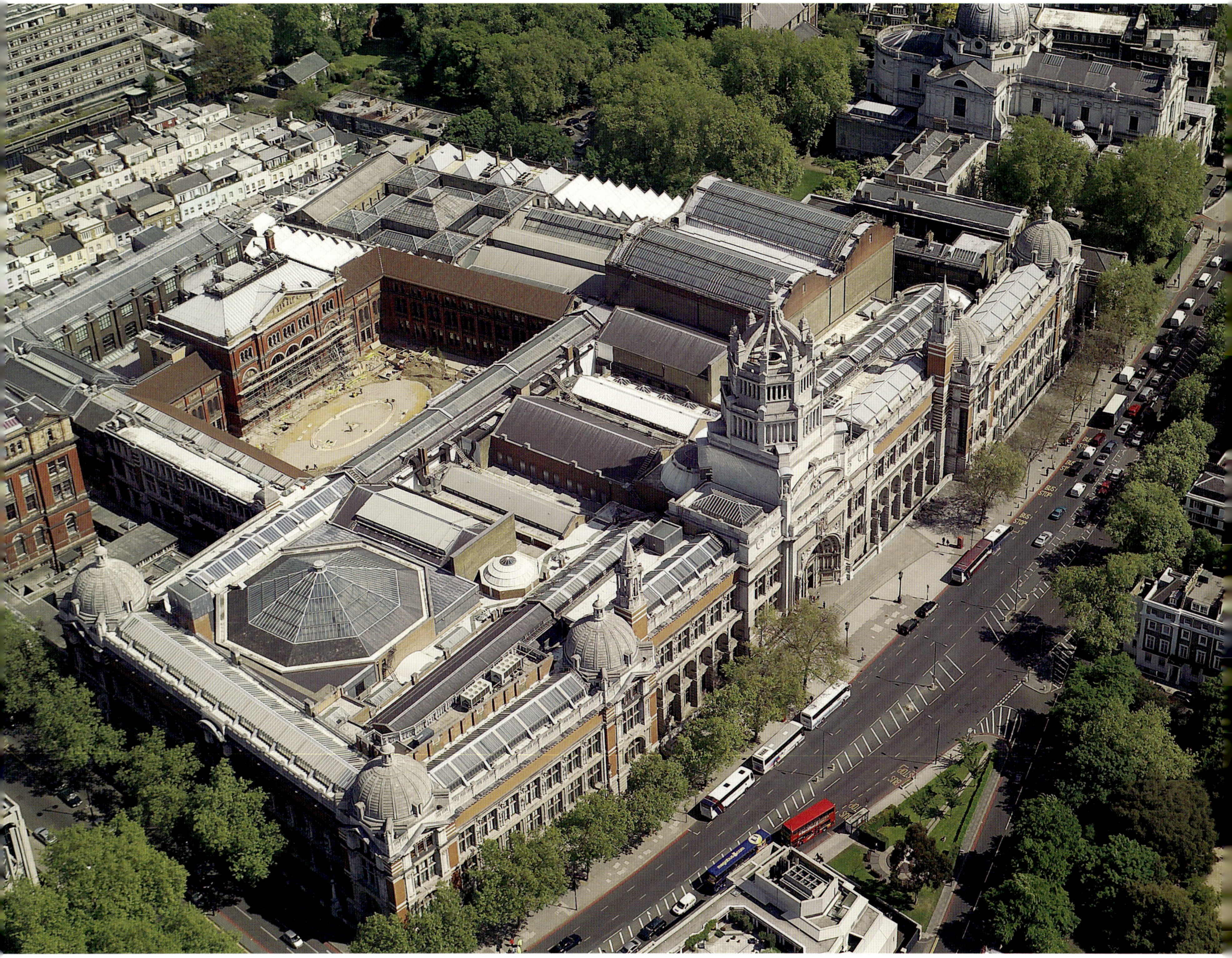

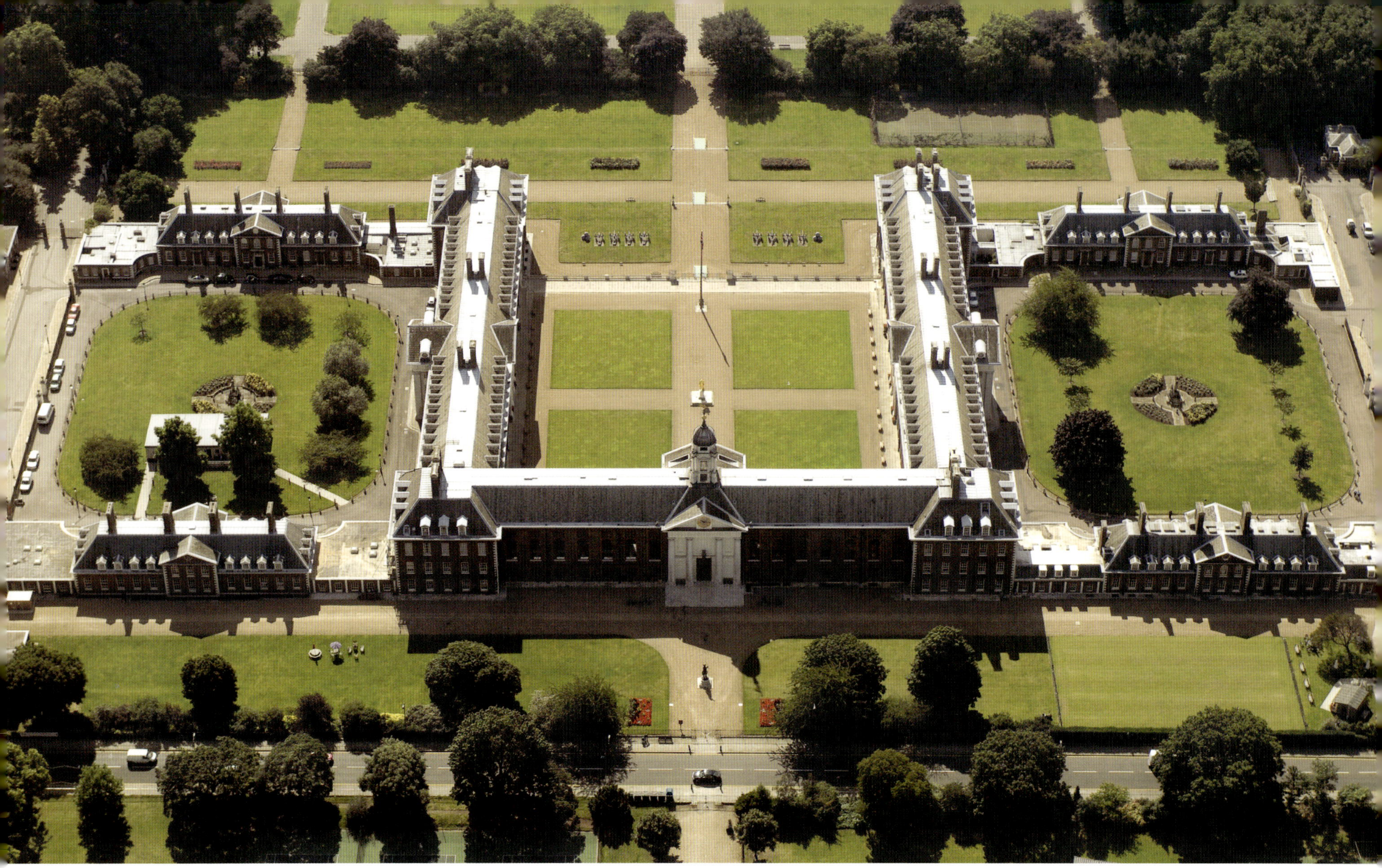

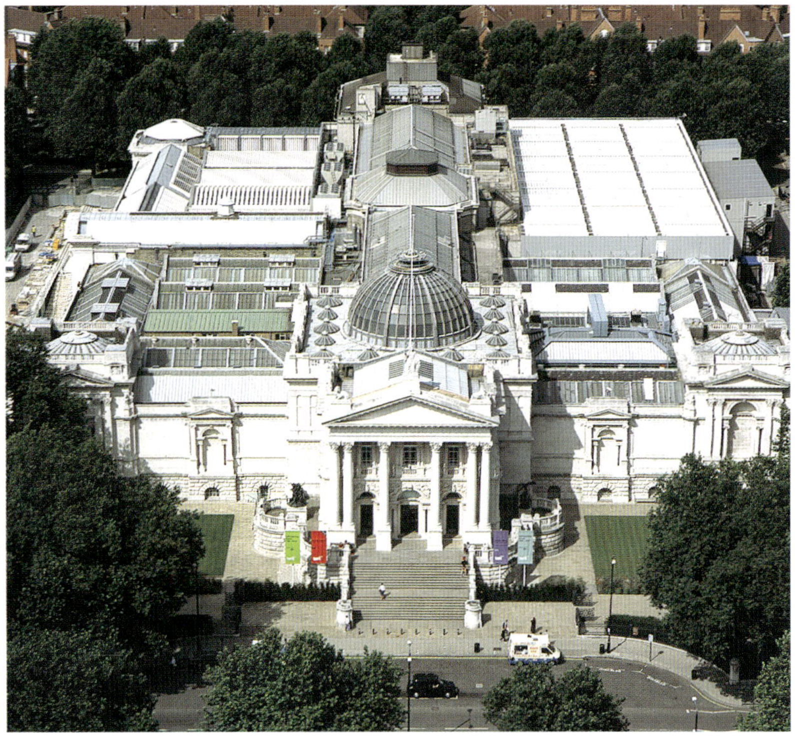

Royal Hospital

Founded in 1682 by King Charles II, the Royal Hospital Chelsea (above) has been the home of war veterans known as Chelsea Pensioners for over three centuries. Designed by Sir Christopher Wren, the distinctive redbrick building includes the Octagon Porch, above which rises the Royal Hospital's distinctive cupola and lantern, a figure court, a great hall where meals are served and living quarters for the pensioners – berths measuring six feet (1.8m) square – known as long wards. The Royal Horticultural Society's Chelsea Flower Show is held in the grounds every May.

Tate Britain

Sir Henry Tate, the grocer's apprentice turned sugar merchant who introduced the sugar lump to Britain, donated his art collection to the nation and paid for a gallery (left) to be built on Millbank to house it. Opened in 1897, its collection now focuses on British art from the 1500s including traditional artists such as Turner and Constable, as well as contemporary artists. Each year, the Tate Britain hosts the Turner Prize nominees' exhibits before the winner is announced.

ALBERT BRIDGE

Originally built in 1873 as a cable-stayed toll bridge, the design was modified in 1884 by Sir Joseph Bazalgette to incorporate suspension bridge elements. London's prettiest bridge (right) is painted in pastel colours and lit by bulbs at night and still retains the original tollbooths. It is overlooked by Albion Riverside, designed by the award-winning architects Foster and Partners. To the east lies Battersea Power Station (below right), the disused Art Deco power station depicted in the Beatles 1965 movie *Help!* and on the cover of Pink Floyd's 1977 album *Animals*.

MILLBANK TOWER

When built in 1963, Millbank Tower (known at the time as Vickers Tower) was the tallest building in London at 387ft (118m). This stainless steel and glass tower (below) has been home to government departments and, famously, the Labour Party, who occupied two floors from 1997 to 2001. It was during this time that the name Millbank became synonymous with political spin and tight party control of MPs.

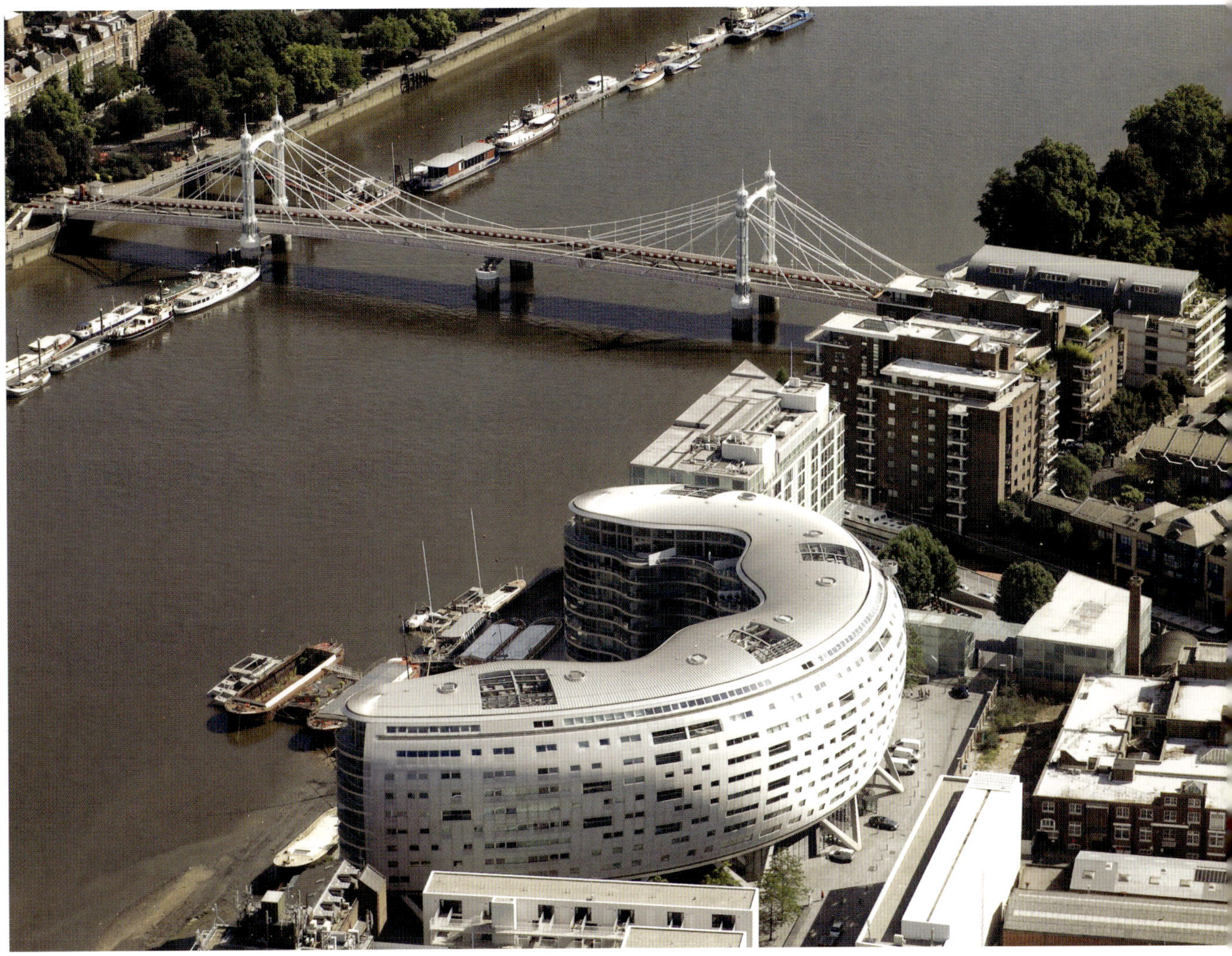

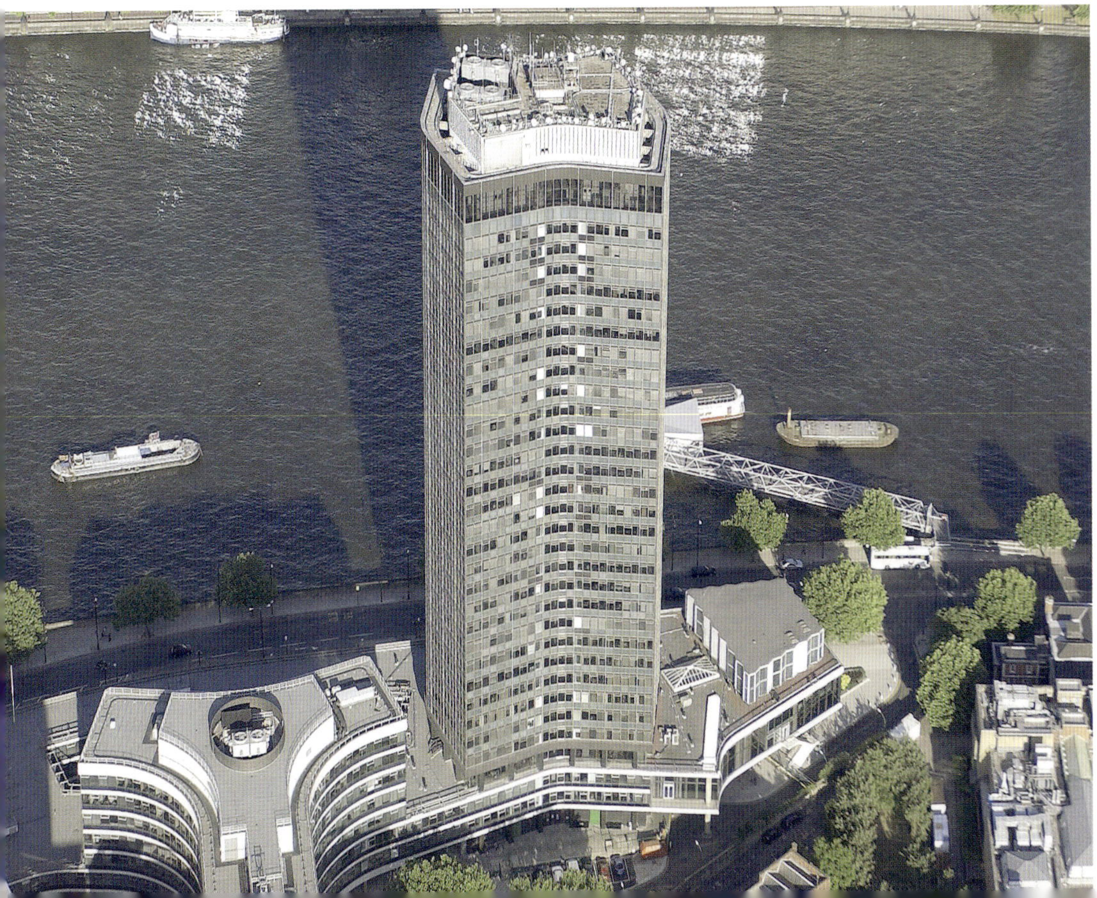

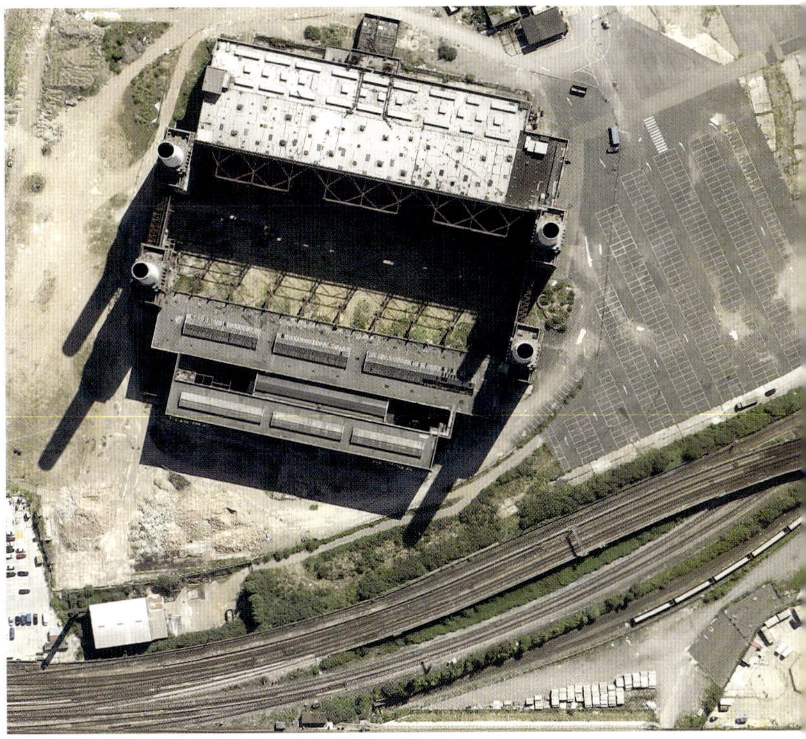

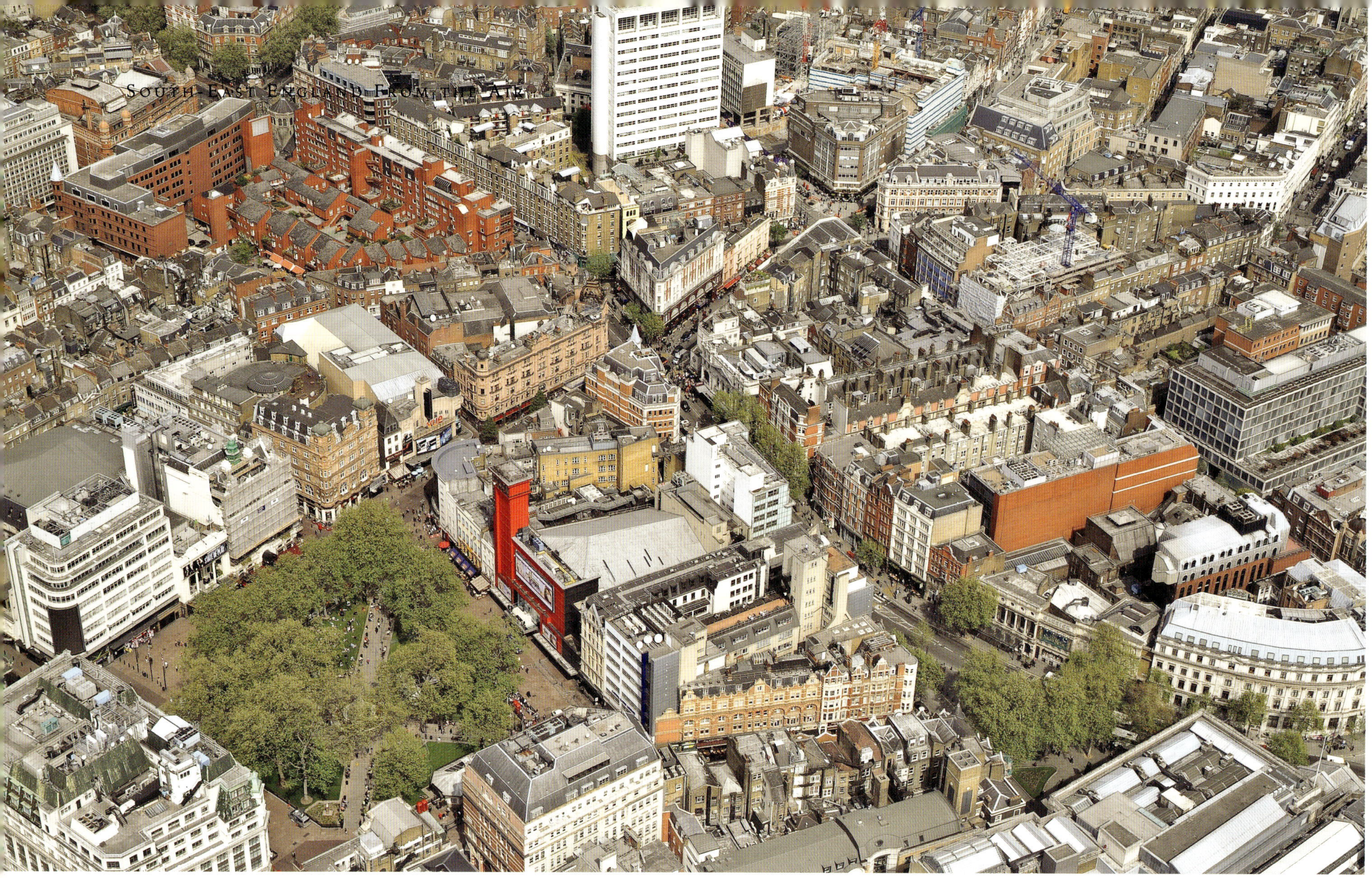

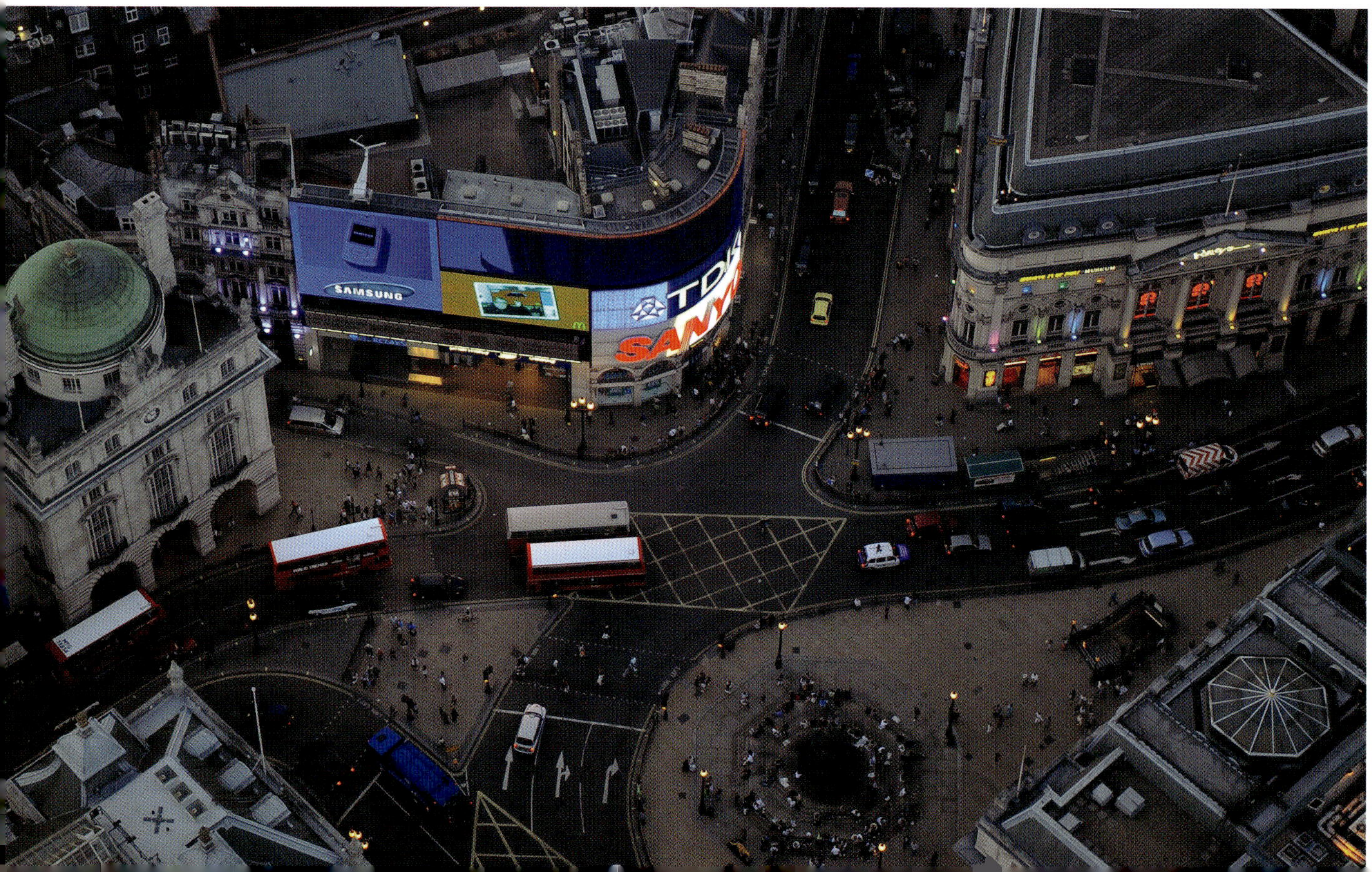

Leicester Square

Once a residential square, Leicester Square (above) is now the heart of the West End, with bustling pavement cafes, cinema multiplexes and bars. Famous residents over the years include Sir Isaac Newton, William Hogarth and society painter, Joshua Reynolds. Film premieres are a mainstay of the square.

Piccadilly Circus

Piccadilly Circus (left) is home to a statue of Eros – a popular meeting spot – and is the junction of five major roads including Piccadilly and Regent Street, as well as the theatres of Shaftesbury Avenue and Haymarket. Its famous neon signs glitter day and night.

Trafalgar Square

Designed by Sir John Nash in the 1820s, Trafalgar Square (below) has seen frequent rallies and demonstrations on political, religious and general issues. The 18ft high (5.5m) bronze of Admiral Horatio Nelson stands above the square atop Nelson's Column, a 151ft (46m) tall granite column built in 1843. Four large bronze lions by Landseer sit at the foot of the column and symbolic bronze reliefs show Nelson's four major victories, including the Battle of Trafalgar in 1805. The square's two central fountains were designed by Sir Edwin Lutyens in 1939. At the entrance to the Mall lies Admiralty Arch (right), designed by Sir Aston Webb and completed in 1911.

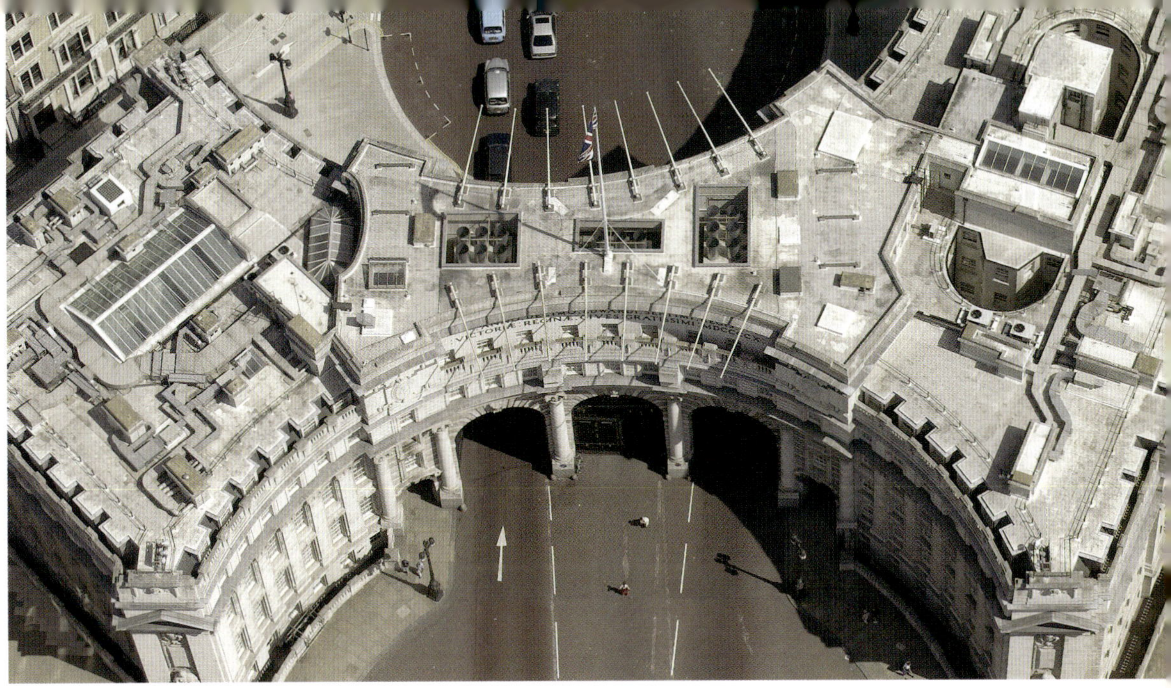

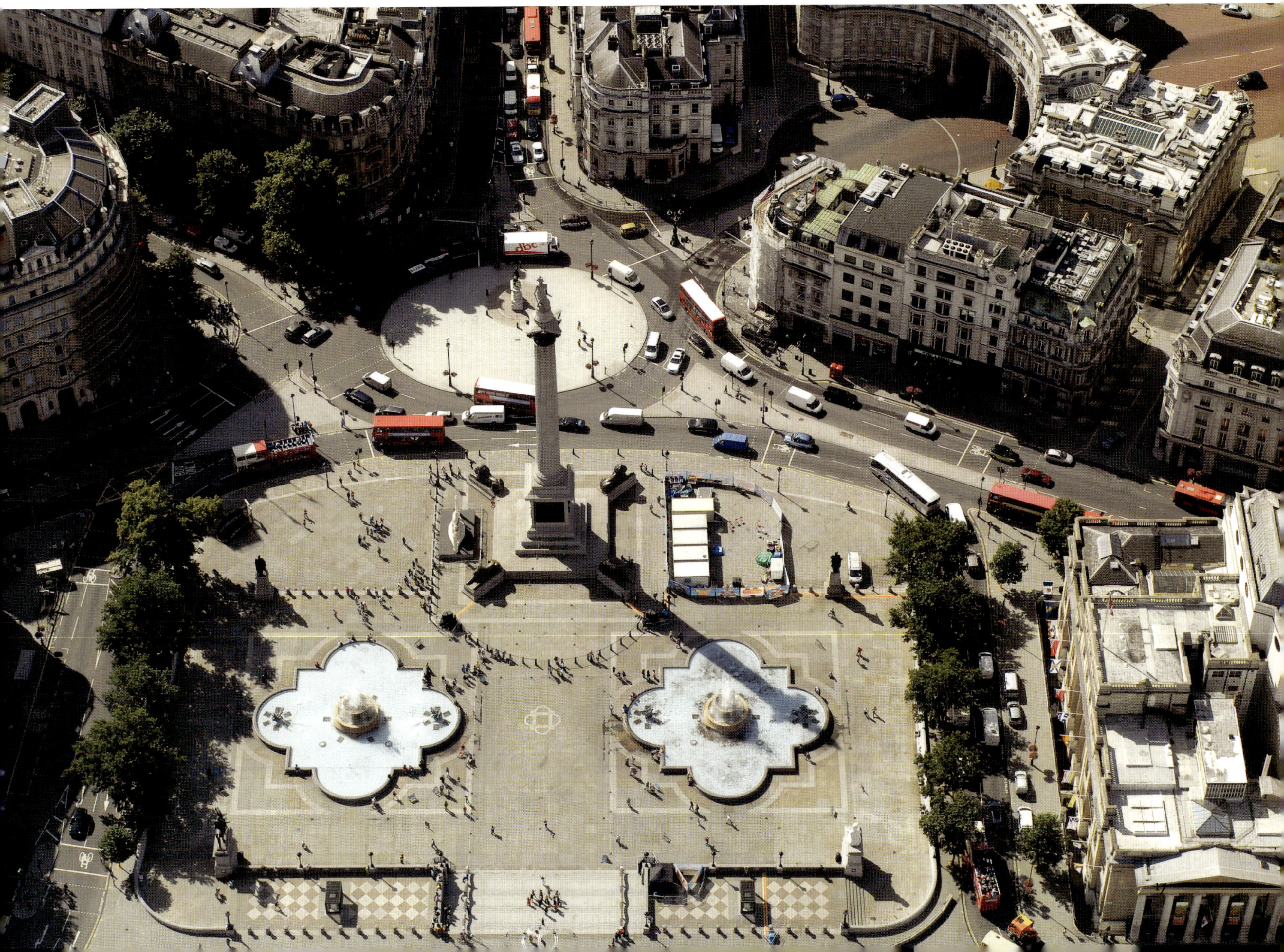

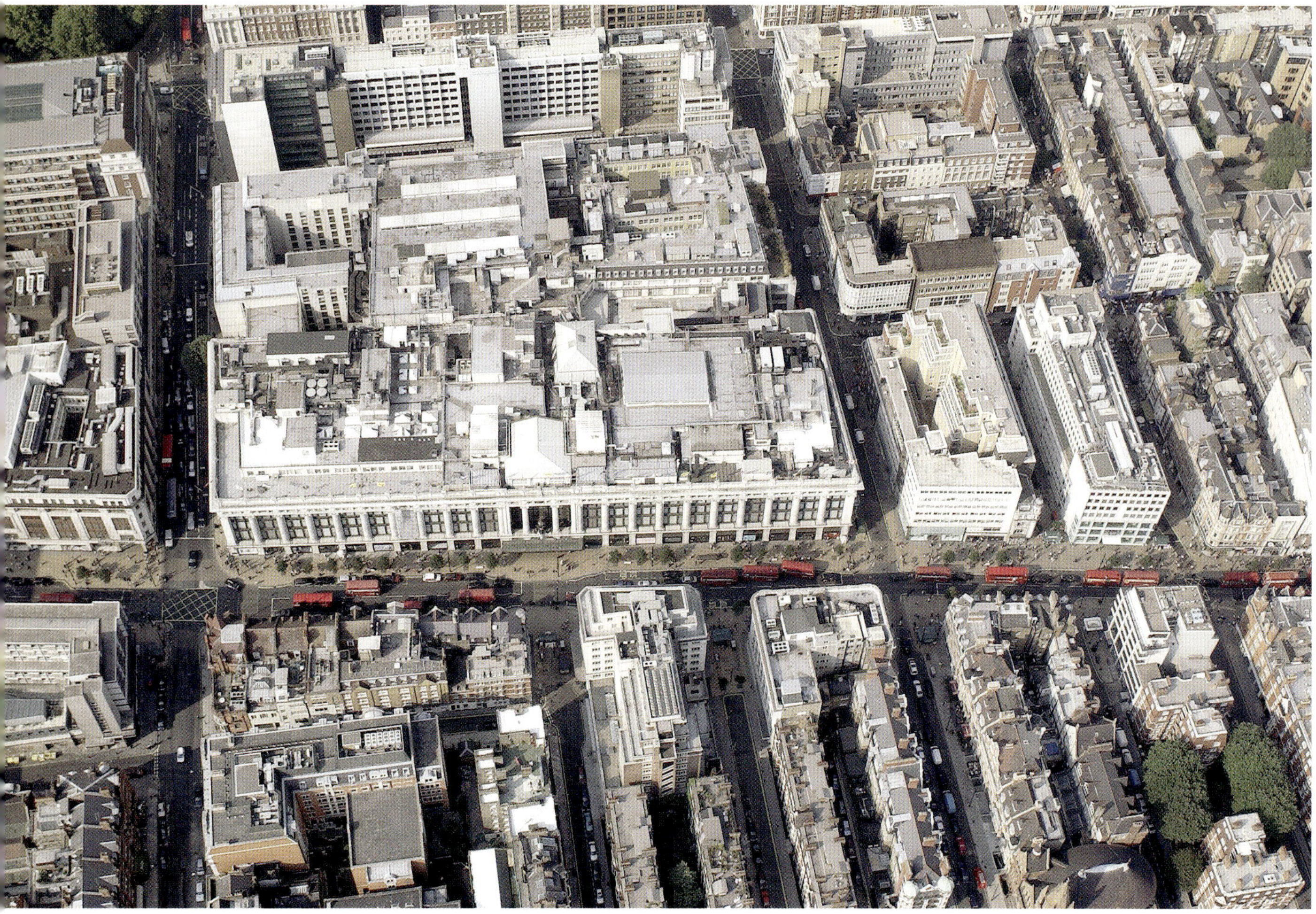

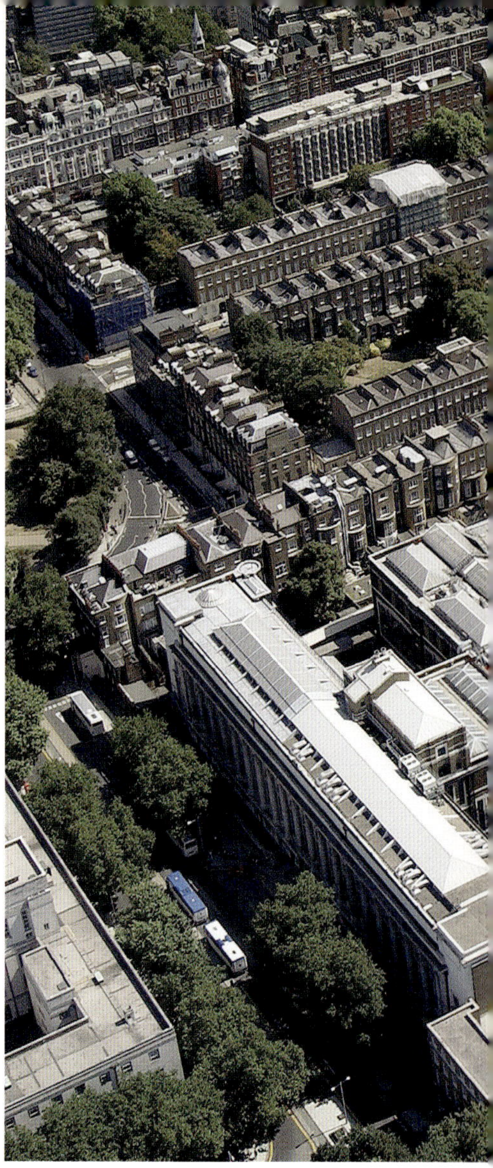

Oxford Street

One and a half miles long, Oxford Street (above) has one of the world's highest concentrations of large shops. The retail story began when Dan Harries Evans and John Lewis set up business on the former Roman road in the 1870s and were followed 40 years later by Harry Gordon Selfridge. With an annual turnover of £6bn, Oxford Street sees 200m shoppers a year and is Europe's busiest shopping street. It is served by four underground stations – Marble Arch, Bond Street, Oxford Circus and Tottenham Court Road – and 39 bus routes. Traffic moves slowly as 250 buses and 750 taxis make their way down Oxford Street each hour.

BT Tower

Built in 1965, the British Telecom Tower (right) was the first tower to be built specifically for the transmission of high-frequency radio waves. It was London's tallest building for 16 years and was known as the Post Office Tower before becoming more commonly known as the BT Tower. Now Grade II listed, transmissions are still made from the building. The top floors were designed as galleries and included a revolving restaurant, but a bomb explosion in 1971 led to the closure of the public areas.

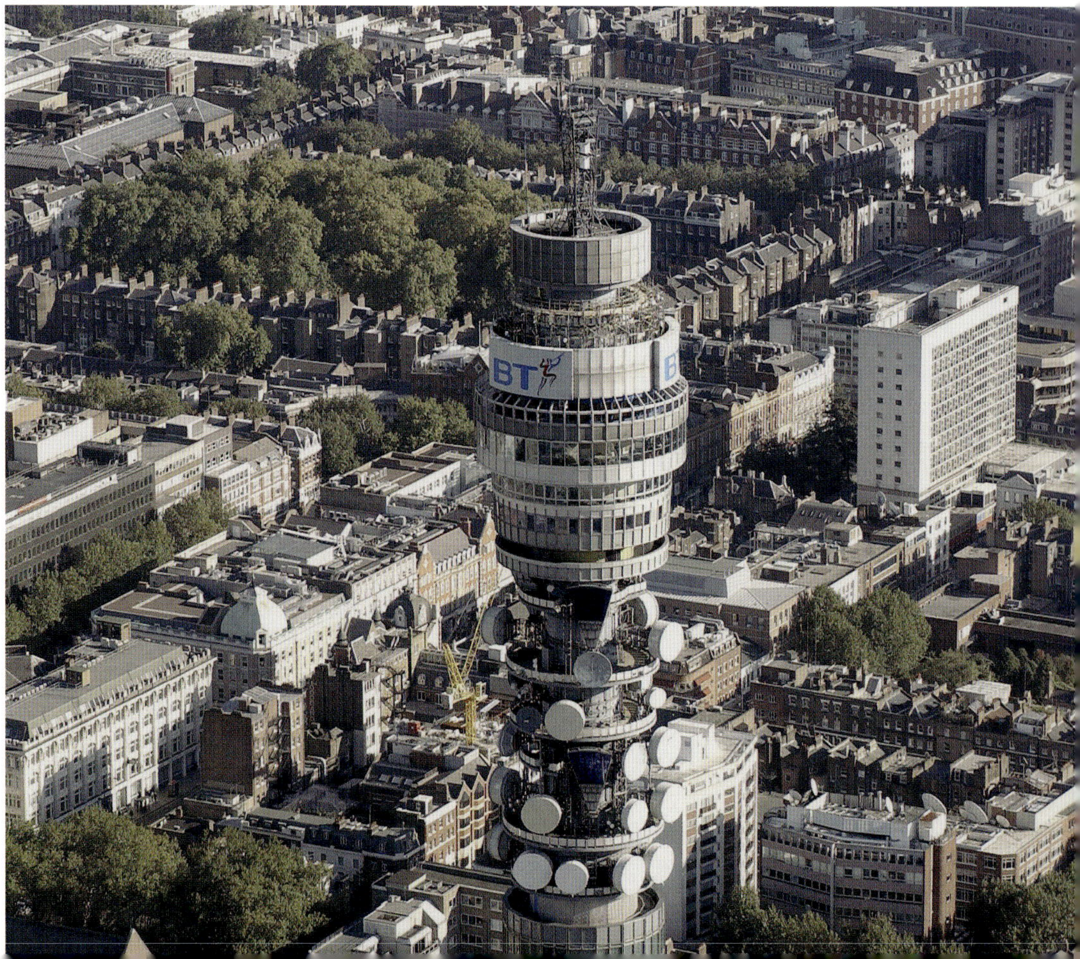

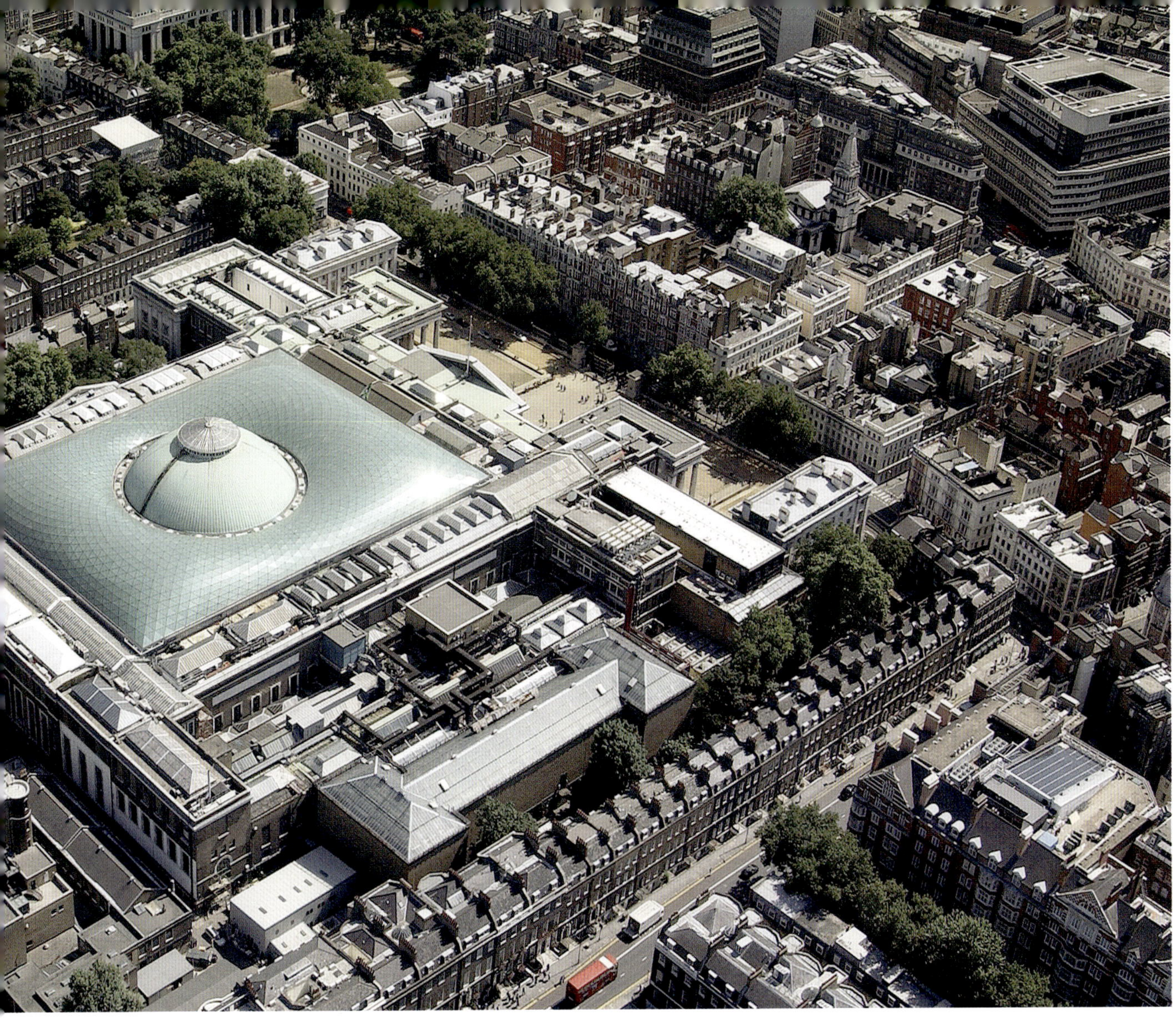

BRITISH MUSEUM

First opened in 1759, the British Museum (left) is today visited by 5m people each year. It houses a wide-ranging collection of art and artefacts from around the world. The collection began with the bequest of 71,000 objects by Sir Hans Sloane, a naturalist and physician, and grew rapidly leading to the construction of a reading room as well as the familiar quadrangular building we see today.

COVENT GARDEN

This area (below) was London's first attempt at town planning. The architect Inigo Jones was inspired by the classical architecture of Italy to design a 16th century piazza with arcaded houses on two sides. The piazza was home to a fruit and vegetable market, which moved to Vauxhall in 1973, and now houses boutique shops, craft stalls and cafes.

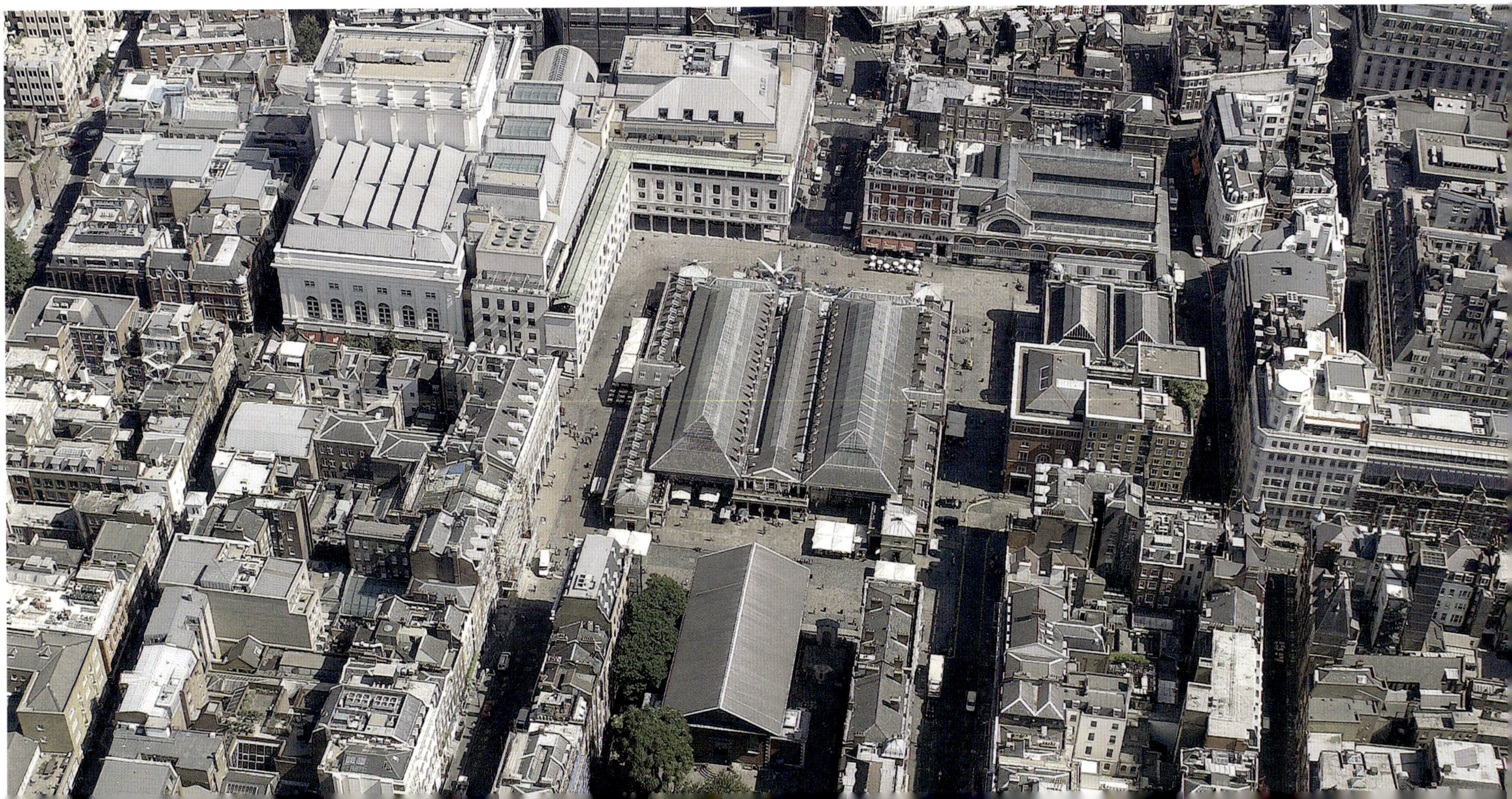

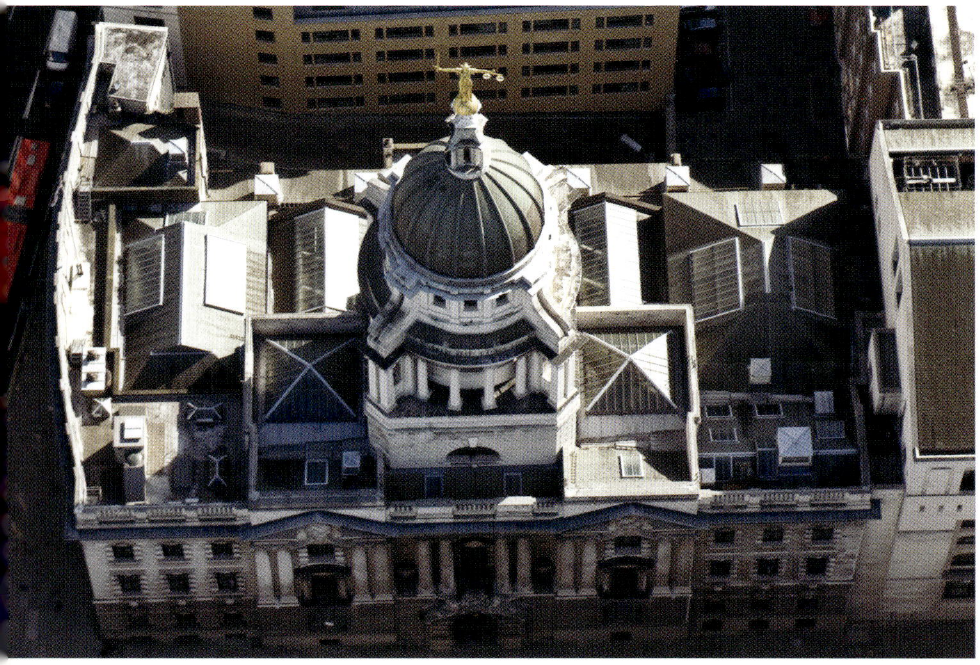

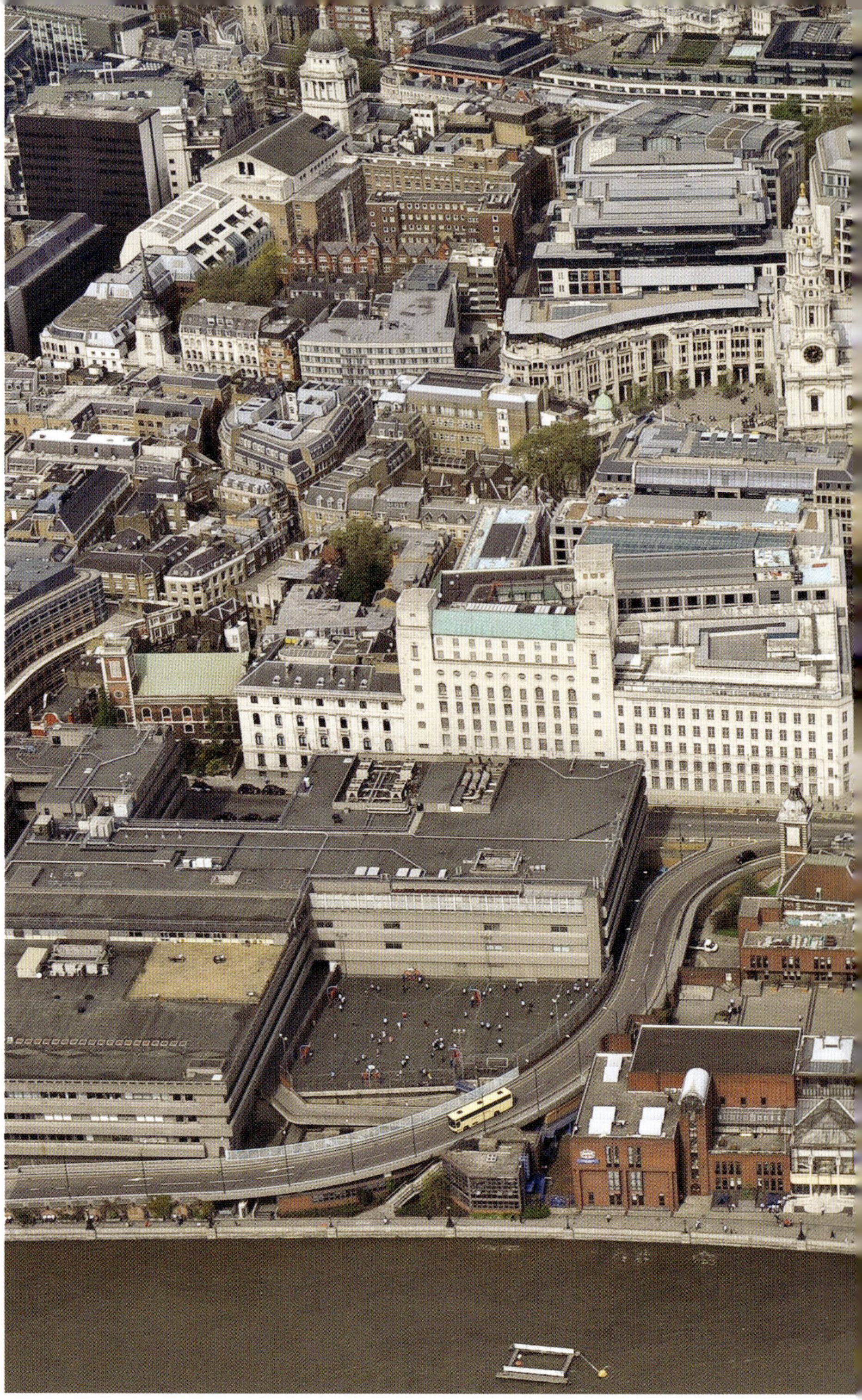

CITY SYMBOLS

Just over one square mile in size (2.6sq km), the City is the historic core of London. Also known as the Square Mile, its boundaries have stayed the same since medieval times when it was the full extent of London. The Central Criminal Court (above) is better known as the Old Bailey. A statue of Lady Justice stands on the roof with the scales of justice in her left hand and the sword of truth in her right. The Monument to the Great Fire of London (below) was designed by Sir Christopher Wren and is topped with flames. Built between 1671 and 1677 it commemorates the fire, which began in nearby Pudding Lane and destroyed the greater part of London, as well as the rebuilding of London. The Millennium Footbridge (below, right) was opened in the year 2000 to link the City at St Paul's to Bankside, the home of Tate Modern. Nicknamed the Wobbly Bridge, it was closed almost immediately after opening to eliminate sway, and reopened in 2002.

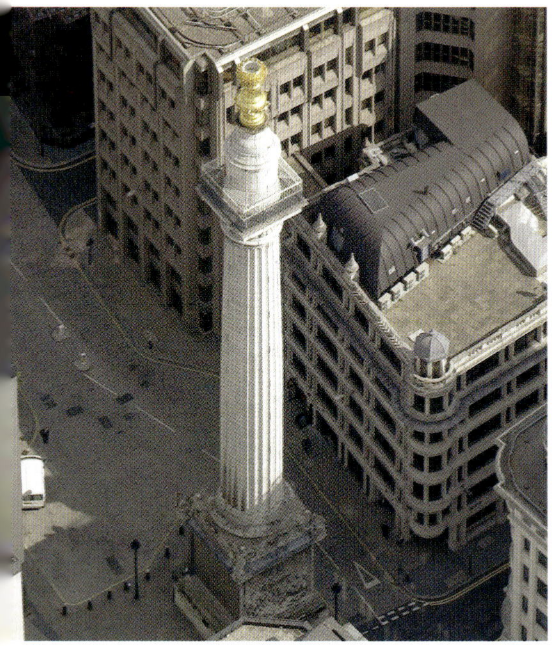

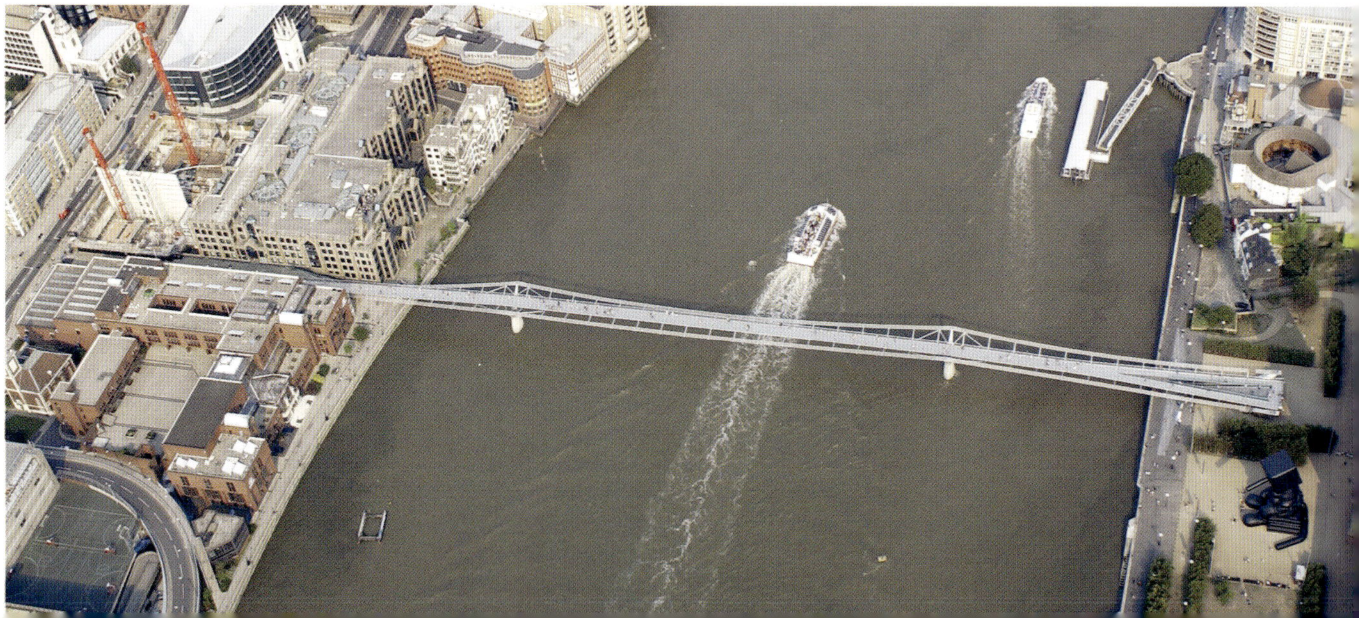

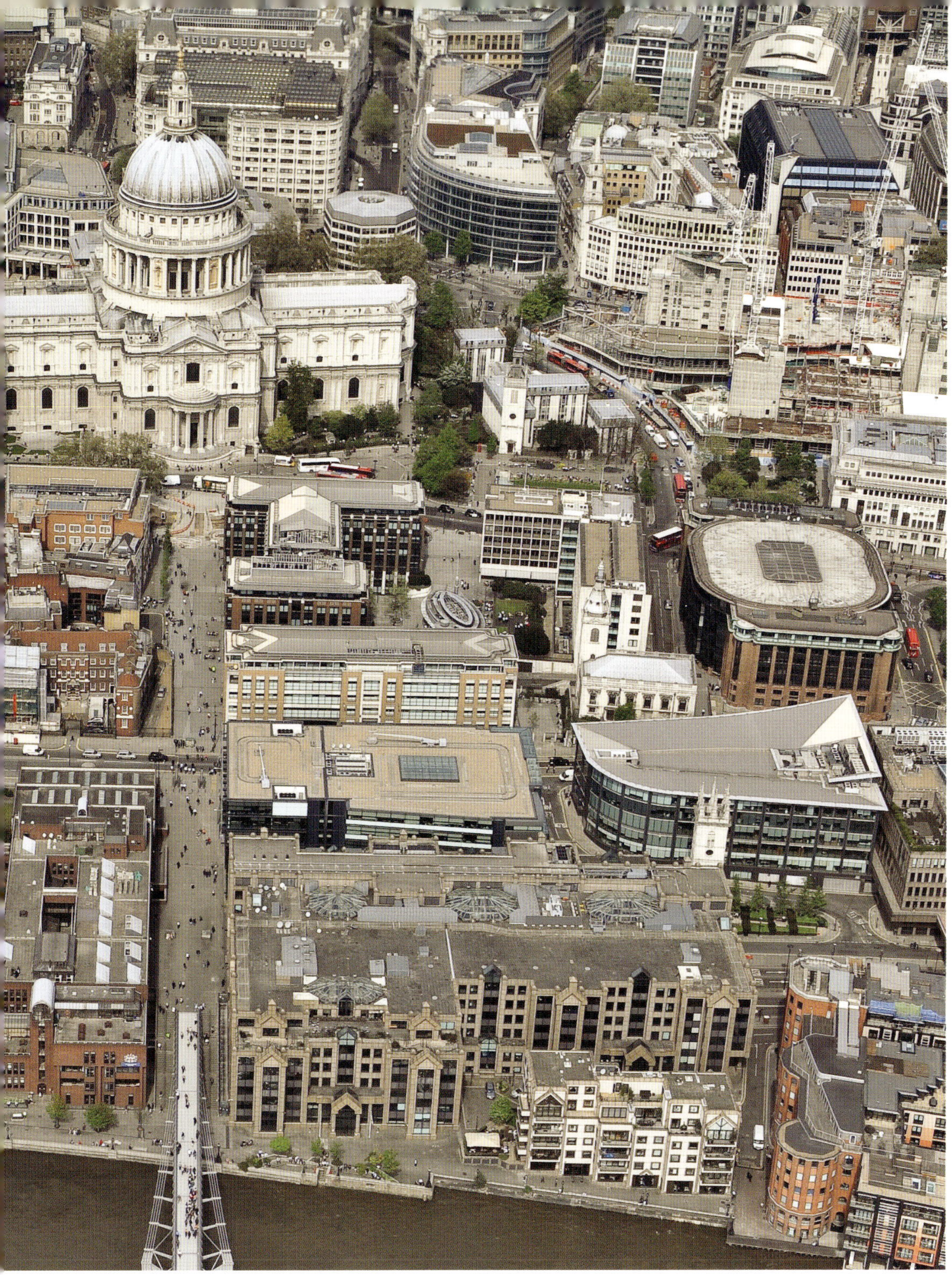

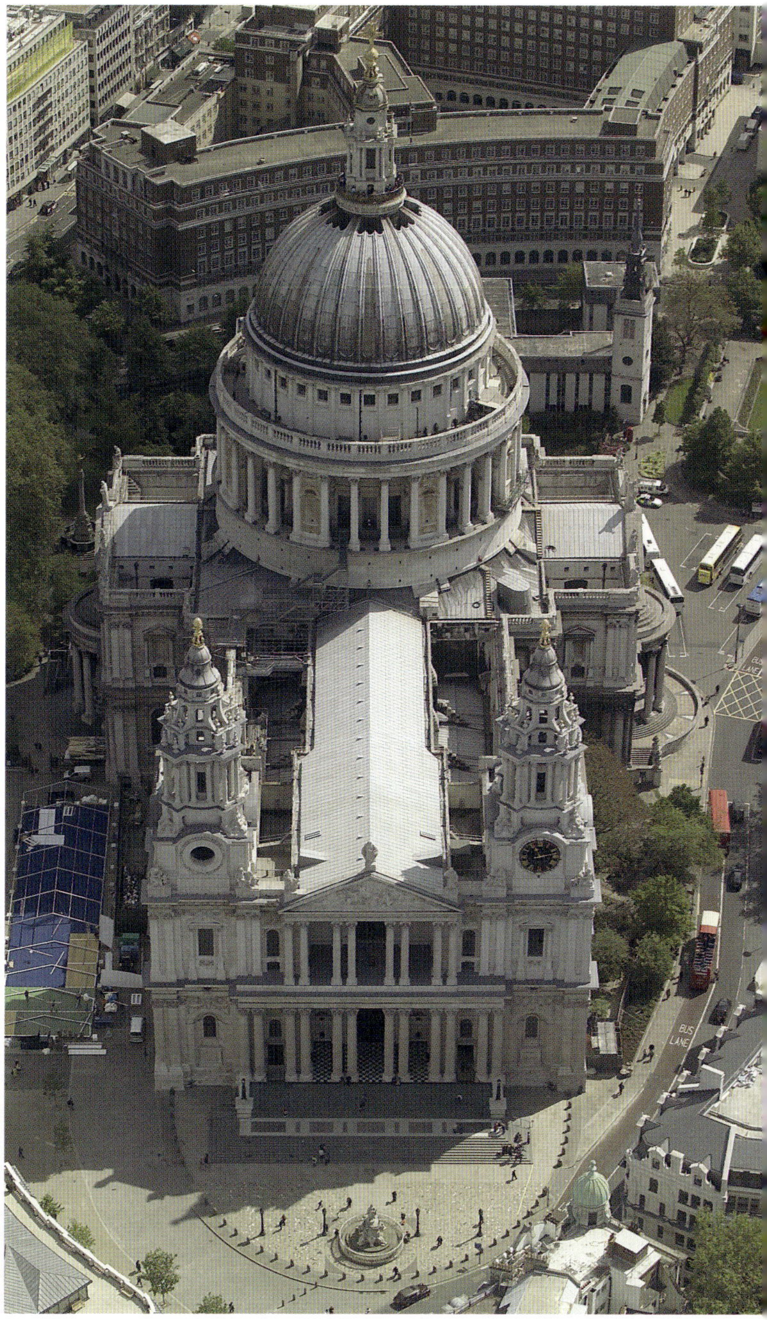

ST PAUL'S

Designed by Sir Christopher Wren, the current cathedral (above and above right) is thought to be the fourth cathedral to occupy this site on Ludgate Hill, the highest point in the City. The previous St Paul's, a Norman cathedral with a wooden roof, was destroyed by the Great Fire of London in 1666. Almost immediately, Wren started work on a new design and finally saw the cathedral completed 35 years later. He regarded the cathedral as his masterpiece, and visited each year to sit beneath the great dome until his death at the age of 90. He is buried in the crypt alongside other great men and women including Lord Nelson and the Duke of Wellington who was buried in 1852 in a granite sarcophagus. Wren was influenced by European building styles and based the shape of St Paul's on a traditional Latin cross. He designed the 360ft (110m) dome as a dramatic focus to be seen from afar and it is among the highest in the world. England's largest bell, the 17 tonne Great Paul, is housed in one of the twin Baroque towers and tolls at one o'clock each day. The American Memorial Chapel stands behind the High Altar in an area that was bomb-damaged during the Second World War – a gesture of gratitude to the American dead of the Second World War from the people of Britain. St Paul's has always been at the centre of British public life. The Jubilee celebrations for Queen Victoria were centred on the cathedral and peace services marking the end of the First and Second World Wars were held here. St Paul's launched the Festival of Britain; services held here include those marking the 80th and 100th birthdays of Queen Elizabeth, the Queen Mother and the wedding of Charles, Prince of Wales, to Lady Diana Spencer.

The City

Today the City of London is a global banking and business district, with 340,000 people working in mainly financial services. The resident population is only 8,000 and although the City of London Corporation is encouraging residential construction, the population is unlikely to reach much more than 10,000. Tower 42 (better known as the NatWest Tower and seen, centre) was the UK's first skyscraper in the 1970s, reaching 42 storeys and 600ft (183m). This part of the City saw another recent skyscraper built in 2003 at 30 St Mary Axe (right).

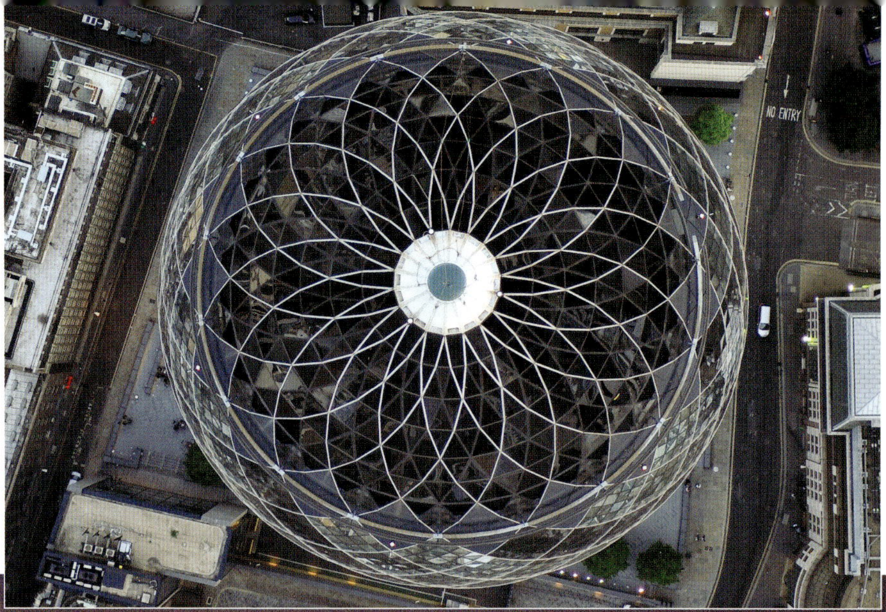

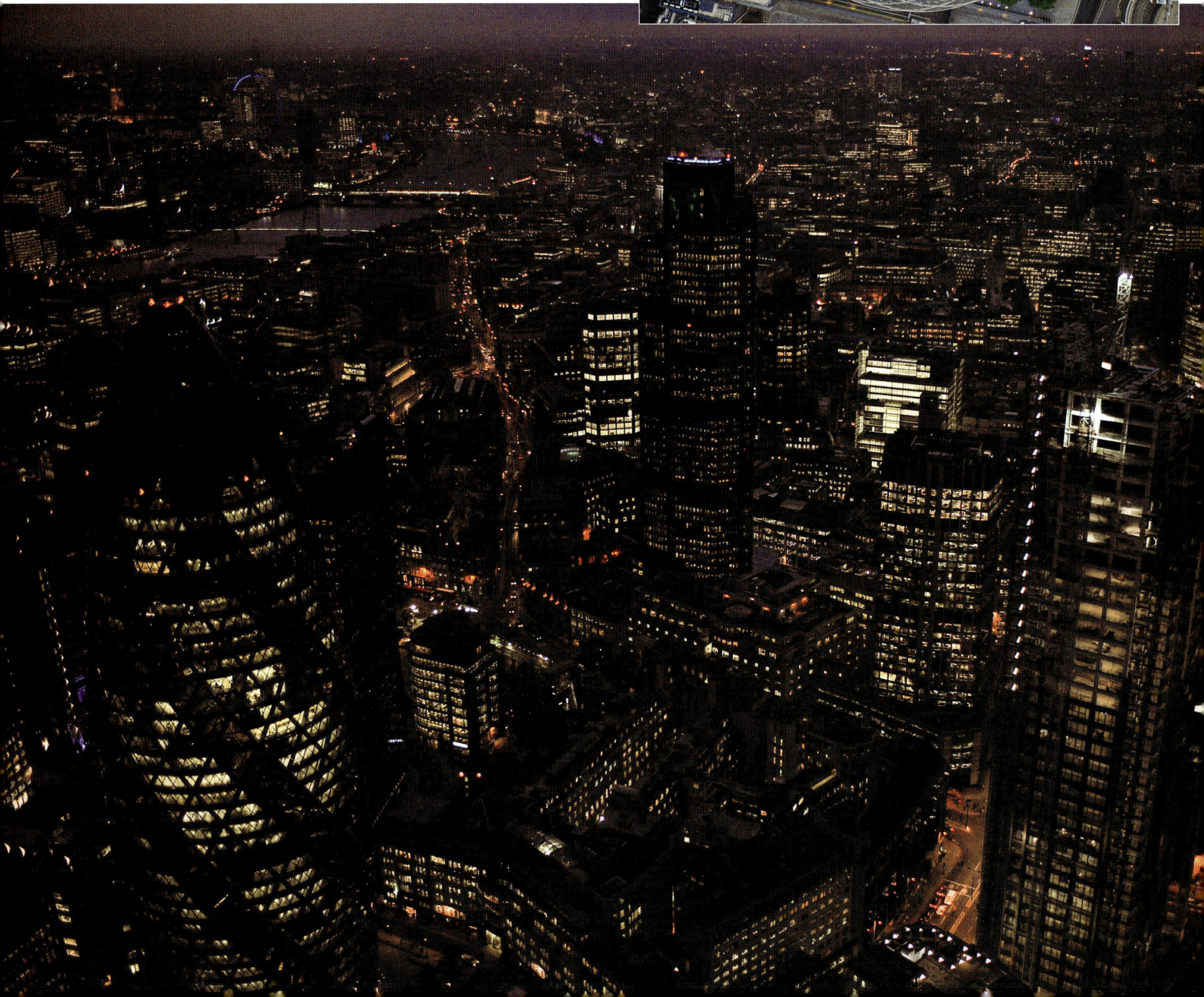

The Gherkin

Popularly known as "the Gherkin", the Swiss Re Building at Number 30 St Mary Axe was designed by Sir Norman Foster and Partners and rises to 590ft (180m). At 40 floors high, it replaced the Baltic Exchange, which was destroyed by an IRA bomb in 1992.

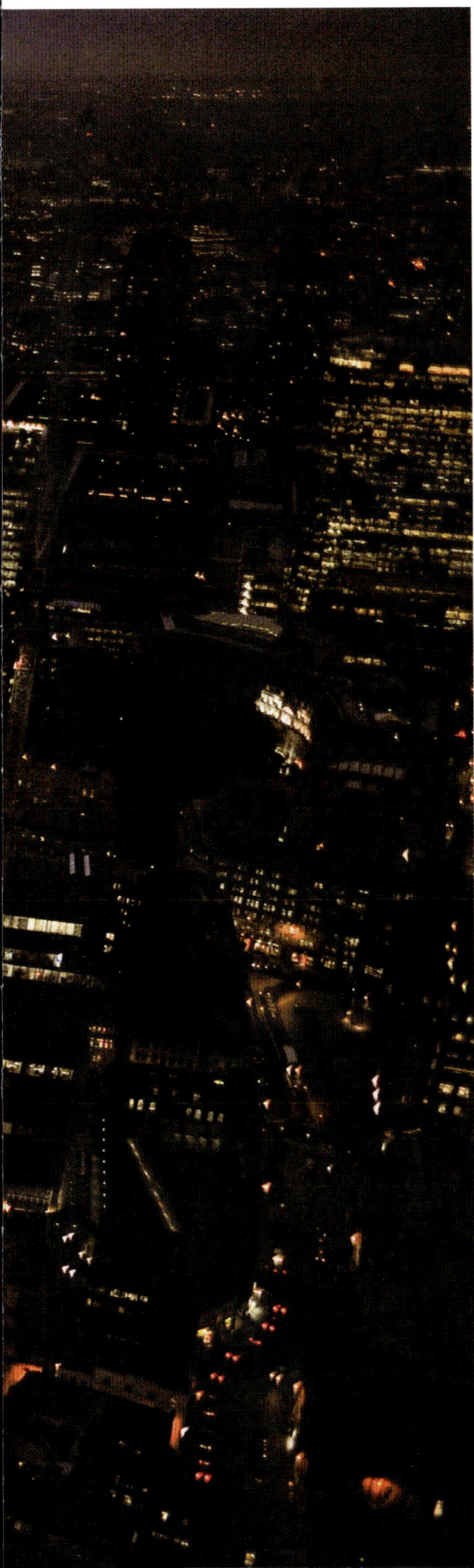

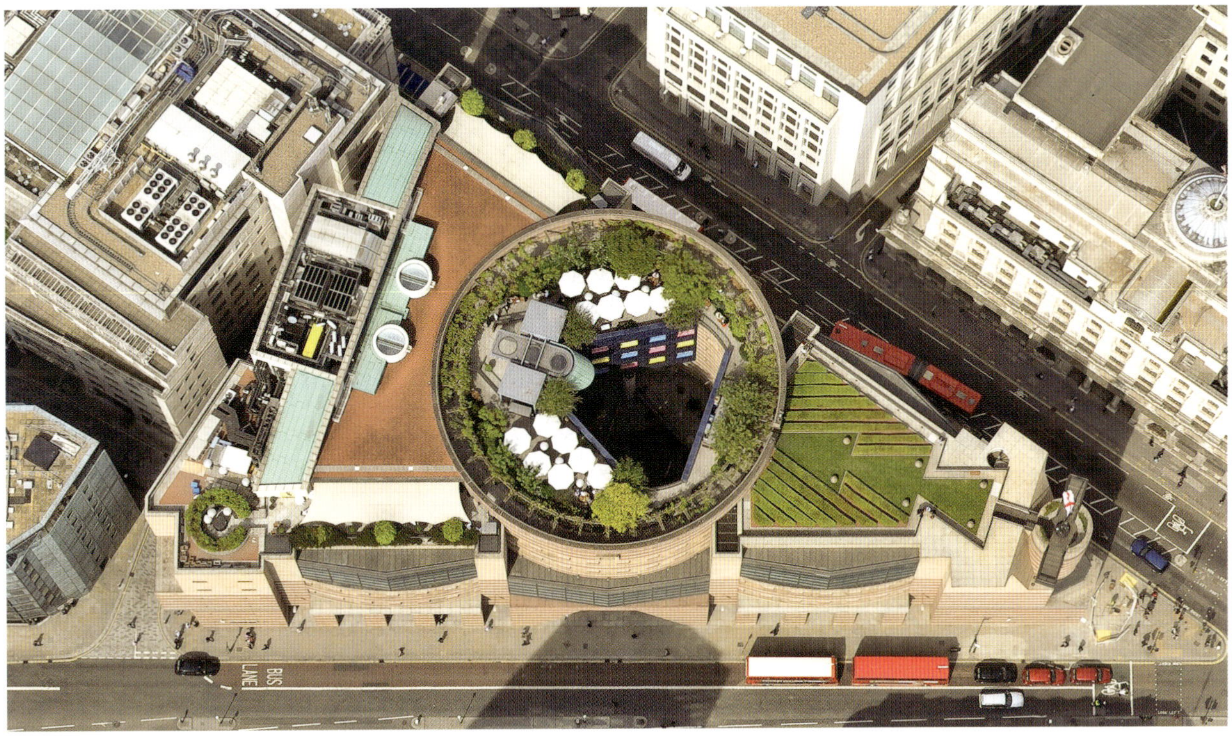

Number 1 Poultry and Lloyds

The post-modern Number 1 Poultry (above) was built in 1994 by Sir James Stirling with bold shapes and brick-work inspired by various structures including the previous Mappin and Webb building. It houses office space, shops, a tube station and restaurants including one on its remarkable manicured roof garden. Another architectural landmark in the City is the Lloyd's Building (below) at One Lime Street. Built between 1978 and 1986, its services such as staircases, electricity and and lifts were placed on the outside, in a design by Richard Rogers similar to the Centre Pompidou in Paris (by Renzo Piano and Rogers).

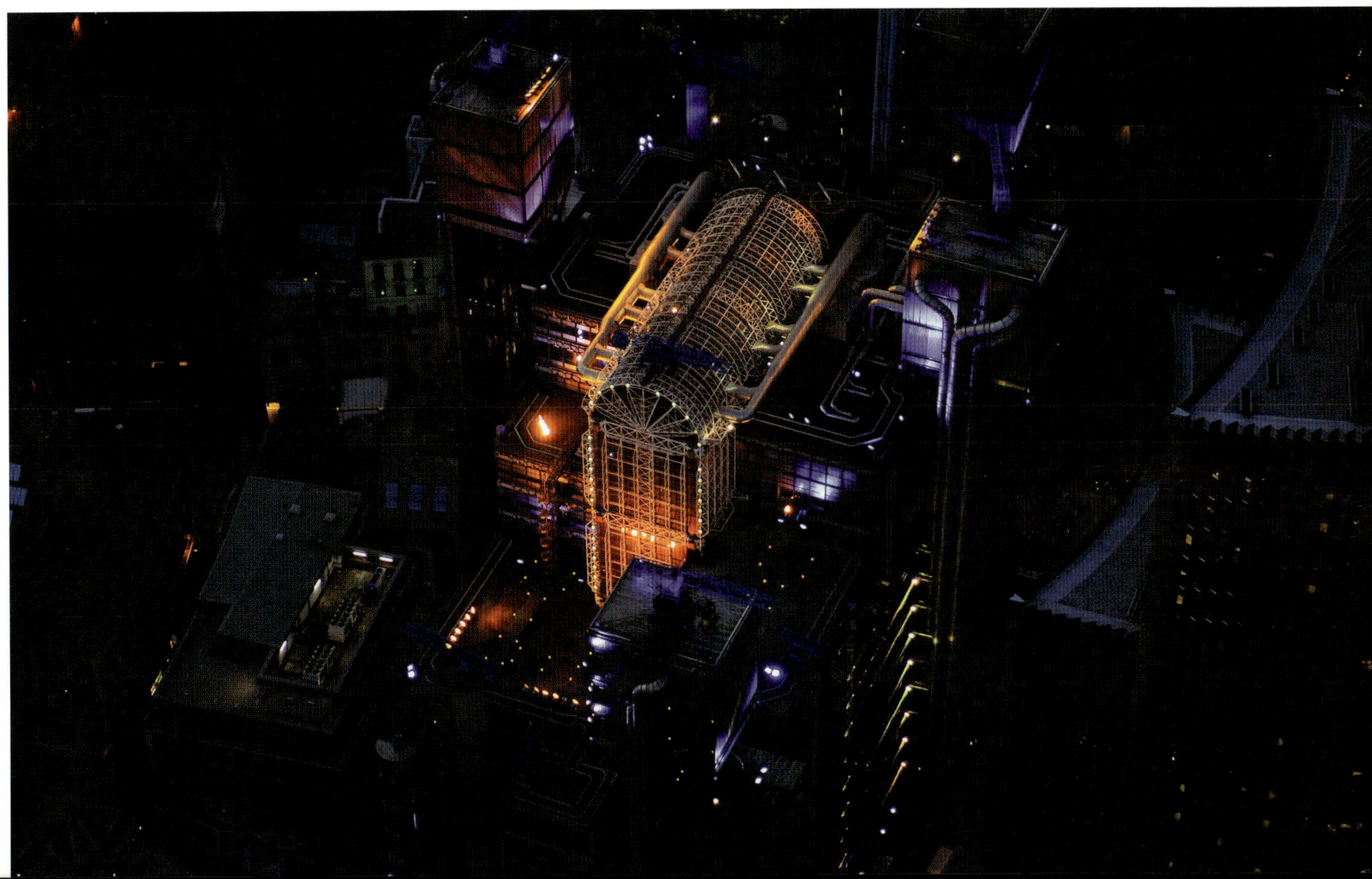

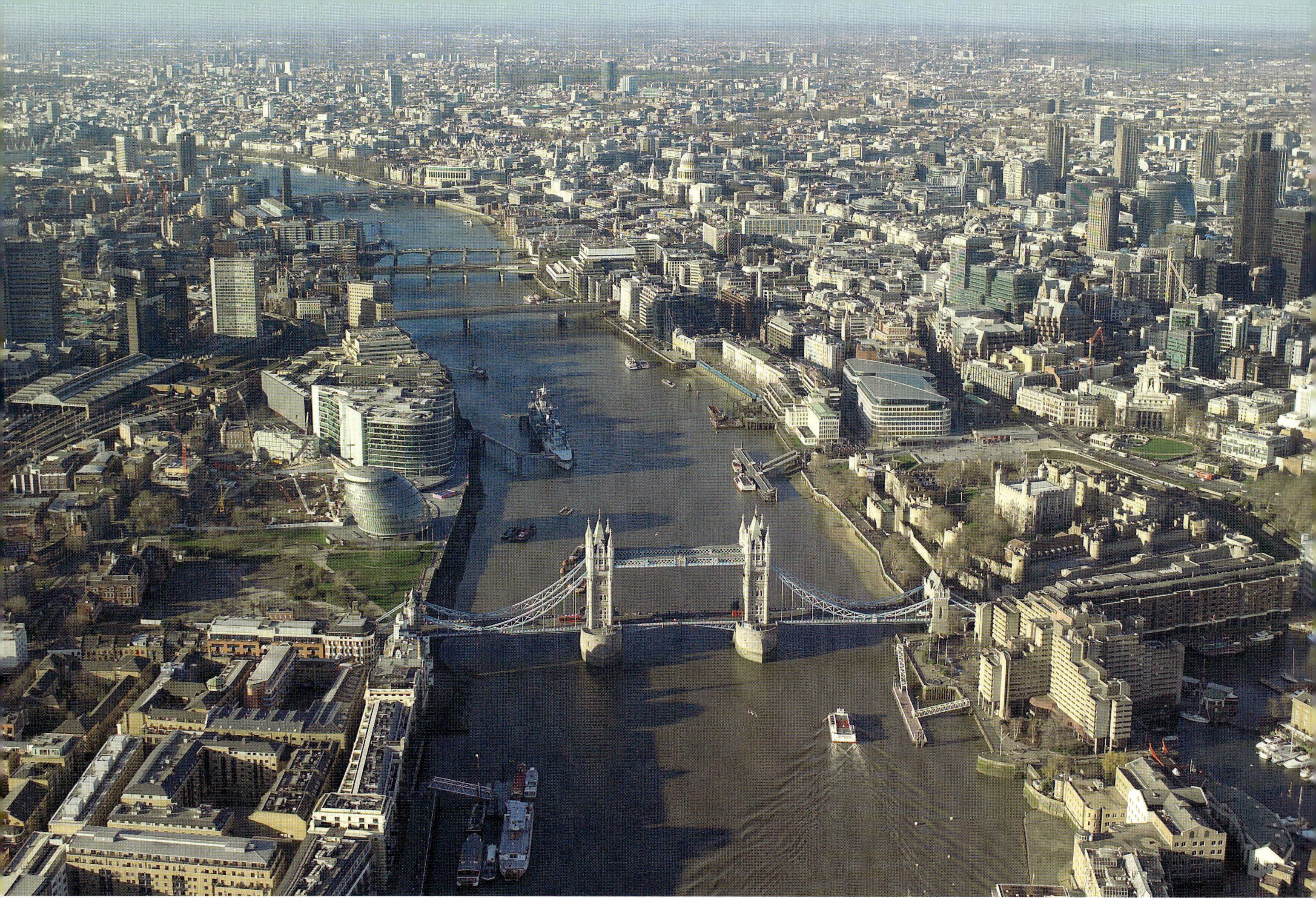

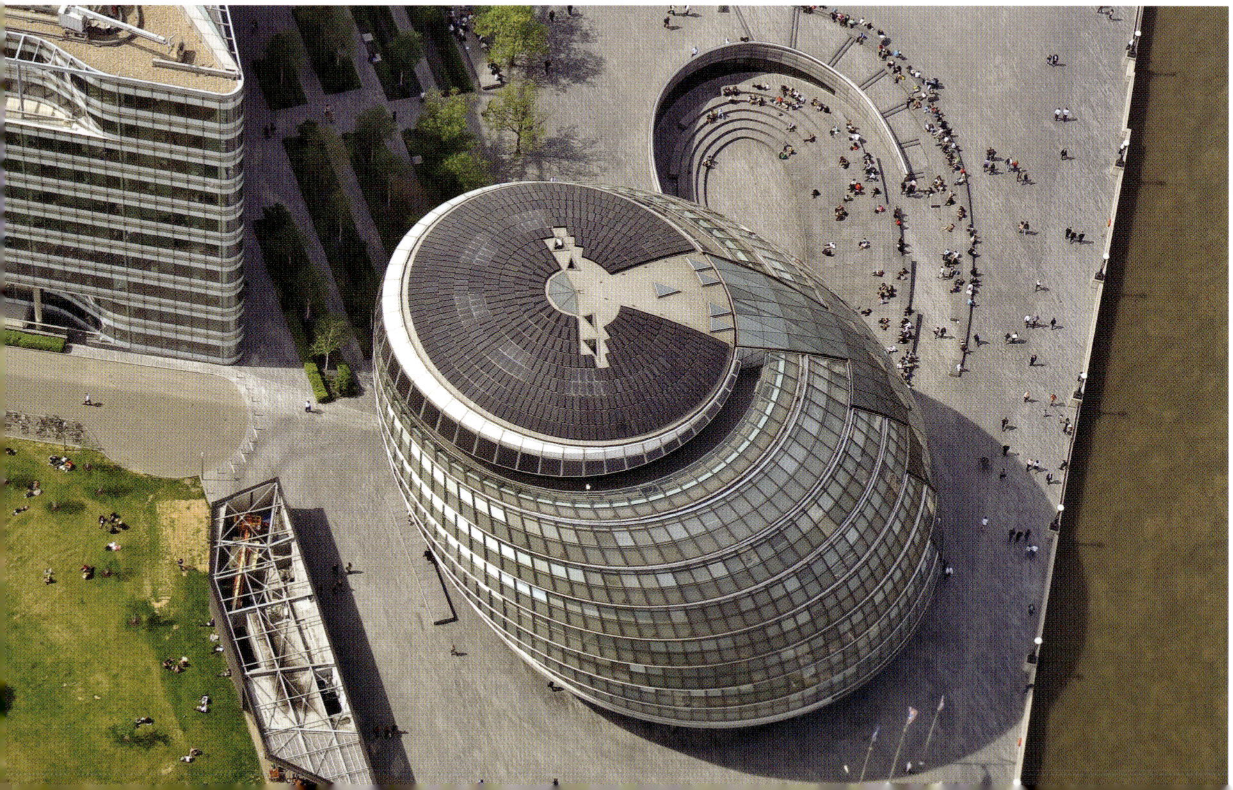

Tower Bridge

The Corporation of London commissioned Tower Bridge (above) in the late 1880s to act as a crossing point to link the City and east London to the south-eastern suburbs. The central section of Tower Bridge lifts to allow cruise ships, naval vessels and tall ships to pass between the upper and lower parts of the Pool of London. Originally, a steam-driven mechanism raised the central bascules, but now it is electrically-powered. At its peak, Tower Bridge was raised about 6,000 times a year, but today it opens only 600 times a year, with the bascules rising in less than two minutes. Overlooking the bridge is City Hall (left), home to the Mayor's office, the London Assembly and the Greater London Authority. The Globe Theatre (right), further west on Bankside, is a reconstruction of Shakespeare's Globe.

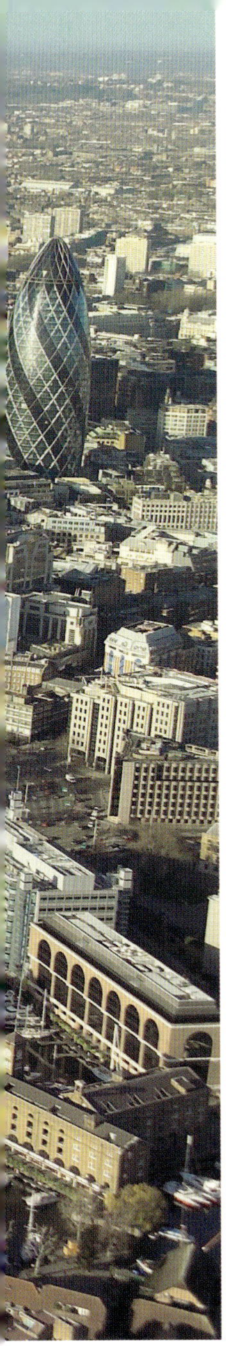

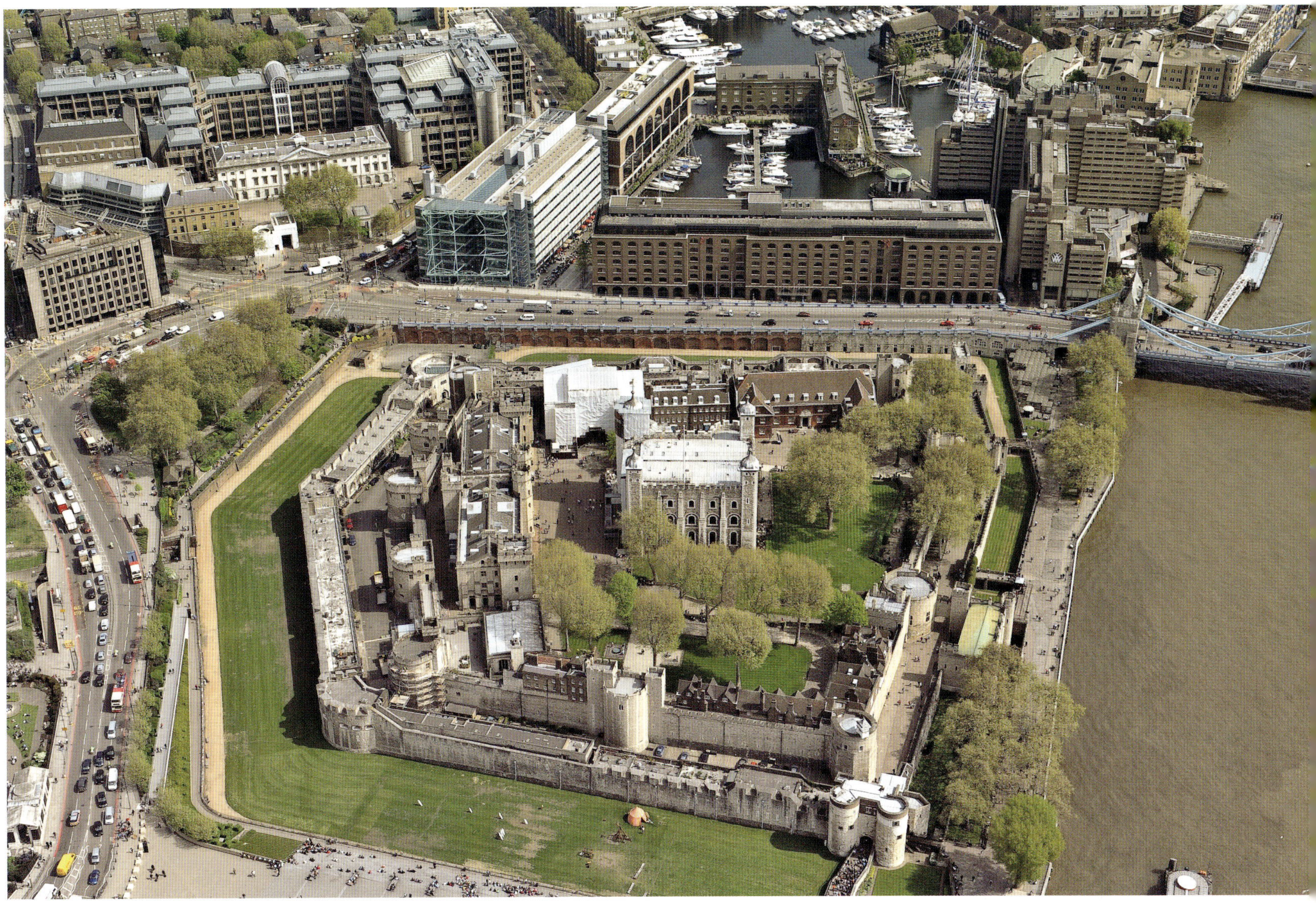

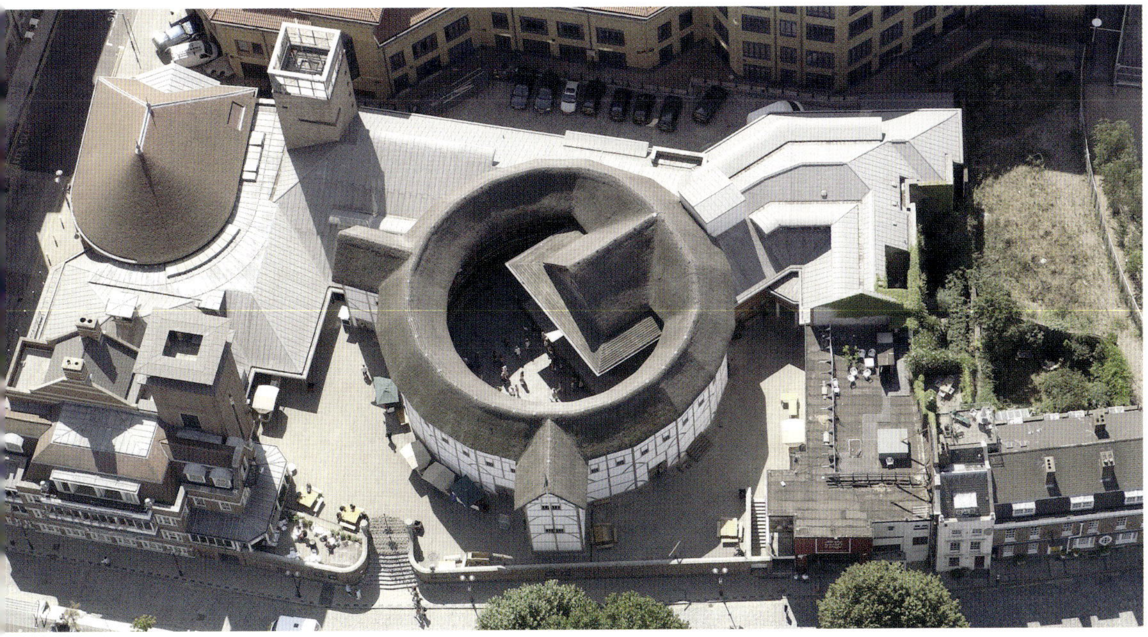

TOWER OF LONDON

Tower Hill (above), the site on which the Tower of London is located, was home to a Roman fortress built by the Emperor Claudius, as well as a stronghold belonging to William the Conqueror, before it became the site of the palace and fortress we see today. One of Britain's most popular tourist attractions, the Tower of London is home to a number of treasures including the Crown Jewels in Jewel House. Visitors can see the prison rooms in which the young Princes Edward and Richard were held, as well as Anne Boleyn, Sir Walter Raleigh and Guy Fawkes, and the green where executions took place. The Tower is surrounded by a deep moat, which was drained in Victorian times. Prisoners arrived by boat at the Traitor's Gate and many waited years before they were beheaded or hanged in public at nearby Tower Hill.

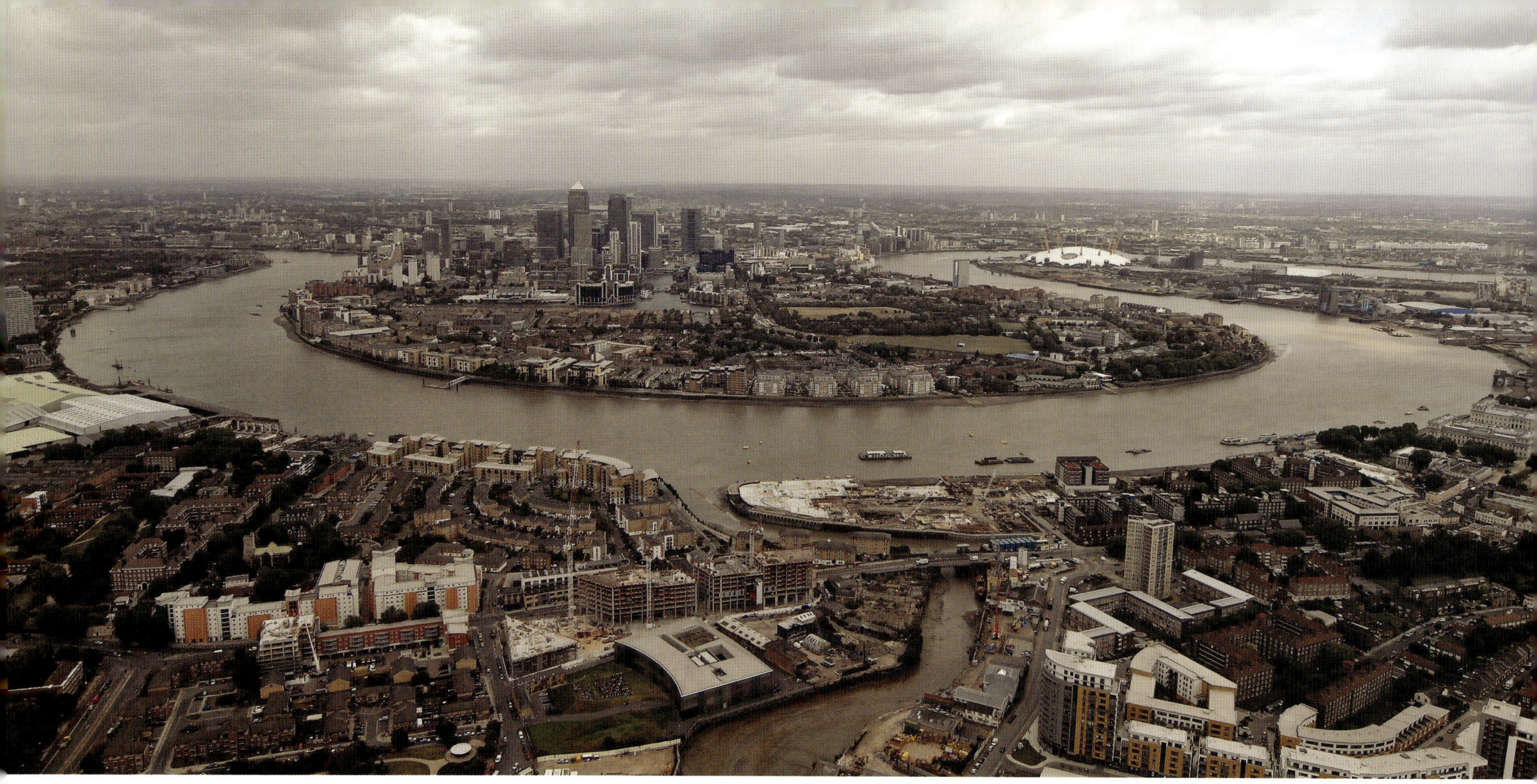

Isle of Dogs

The Thames loops around the Isle of Dogs between Limehouse Reach and North Greenwich. Once an island, the area was commercially successful from the early 1880s with imports and exports from the area's busy docks and shipyards. Dock-workers settled in the area, with the population growing to 21,000 by 1901. During the Second World War the Isle of Dogs sustained heavy bombing leading to much loss of life and the destruction of warehouses. Unexploded bombs continue to be found to this day. Regeneration in the 1980s and 1990s has brought about high rise and high-tech business accommodation and residential living concentrated around Canada Water and the Canary Wharf financial district. The peninsula is an area of social extremes with some of the most prosperous and deprived areas in the UK in close proximity.

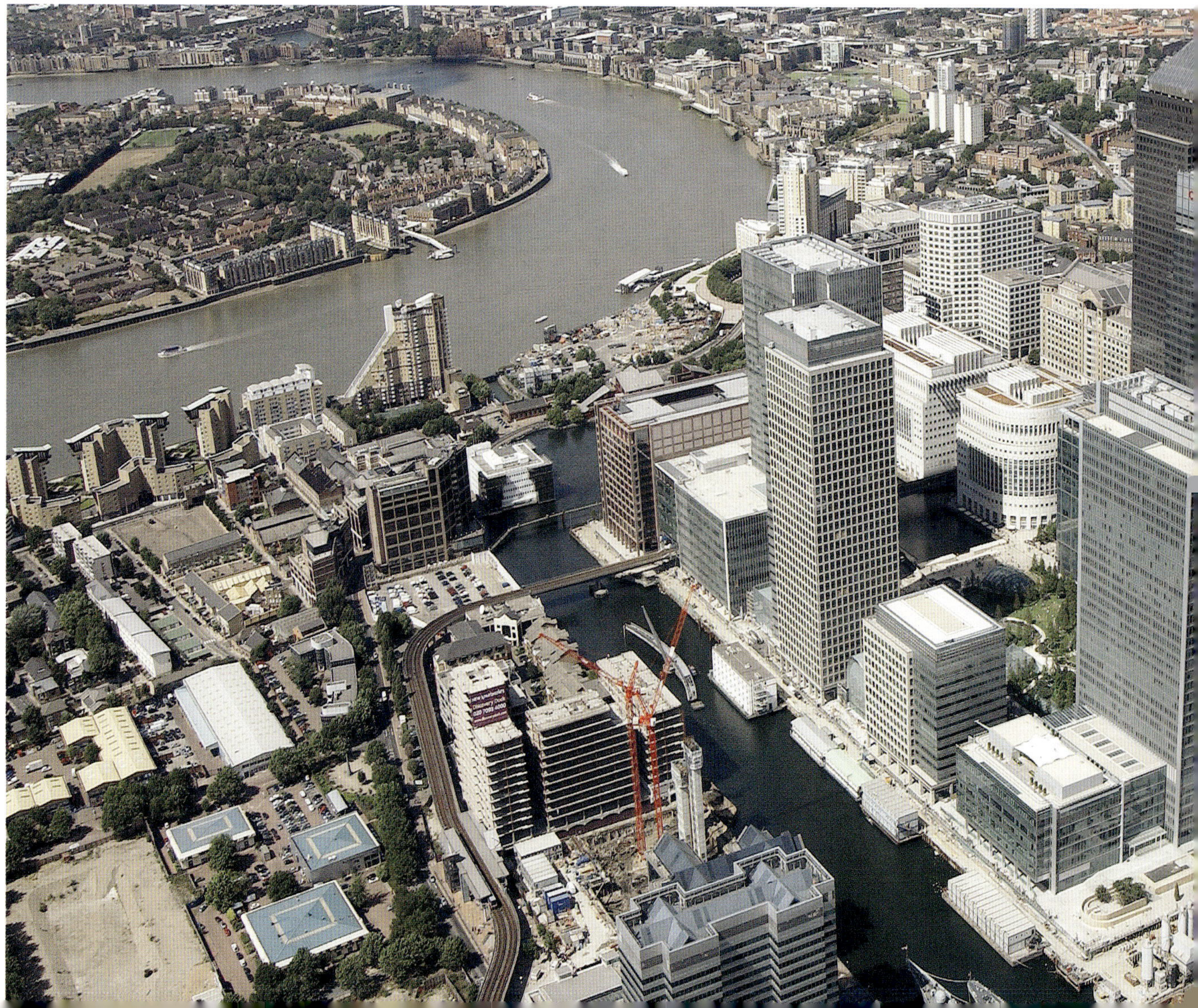

CANARY WHARF

London and the UK's current tallest building is formally known as 1 Canada Square (right), but is better known as Canary Wharf. It reaches 235m (770ft) in height and is topped by a pyramid structure. Designed by the architect Cesar Pelli, it was completed in 1991. Close neighbours are the Citigroup Centre and 8 Canada Square (also known as the HSBC Tower), the UK's joint second tallest buildings at 654ft (199m) high. Canary Wharf is served by the Docklands Light Railway and seen here is Canary Wharf DLR station, the centrepiece of the network.

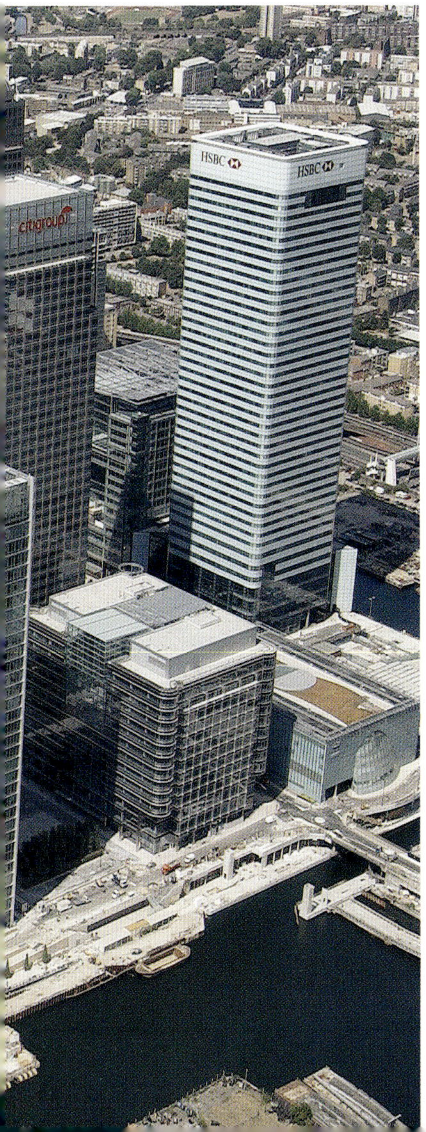

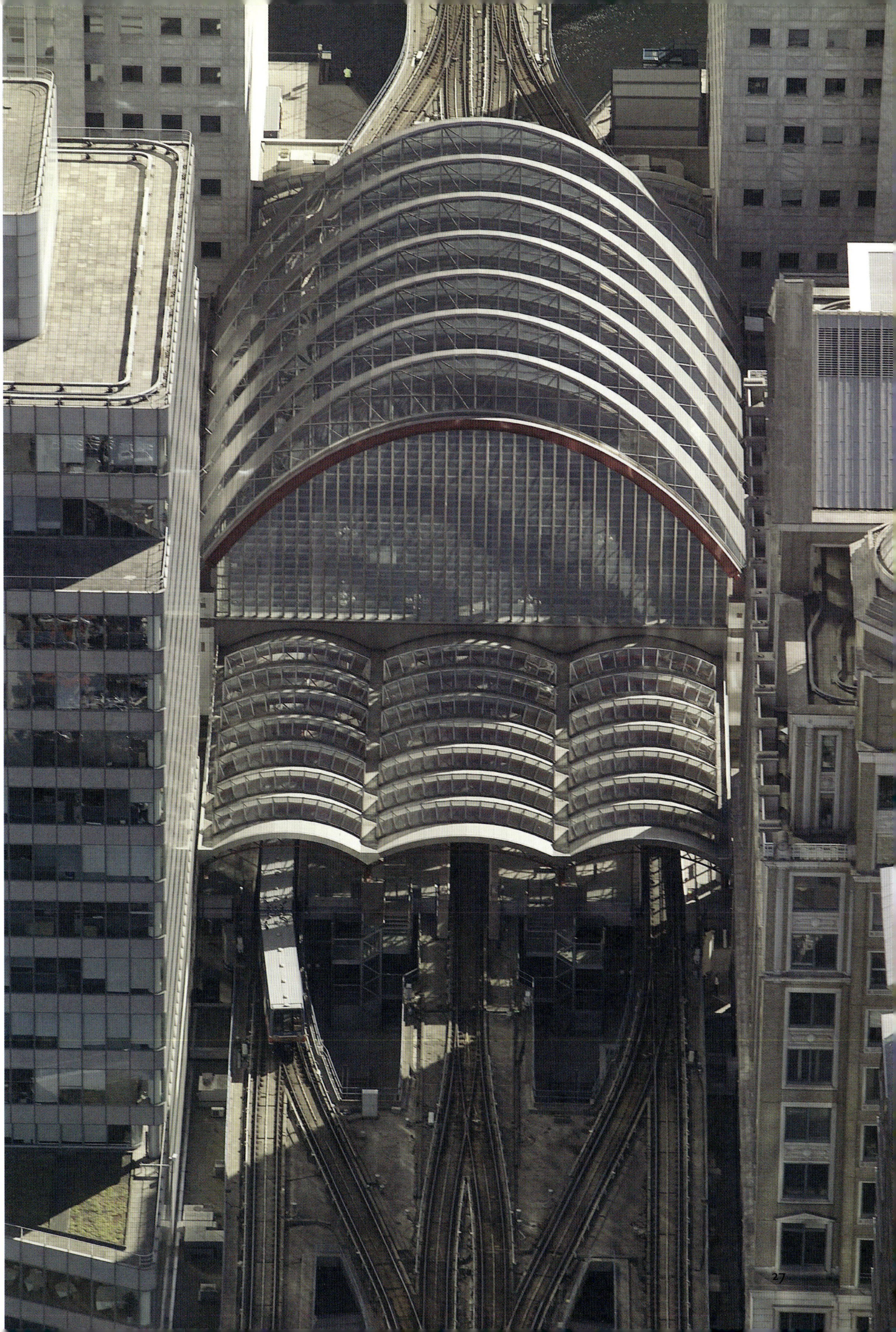

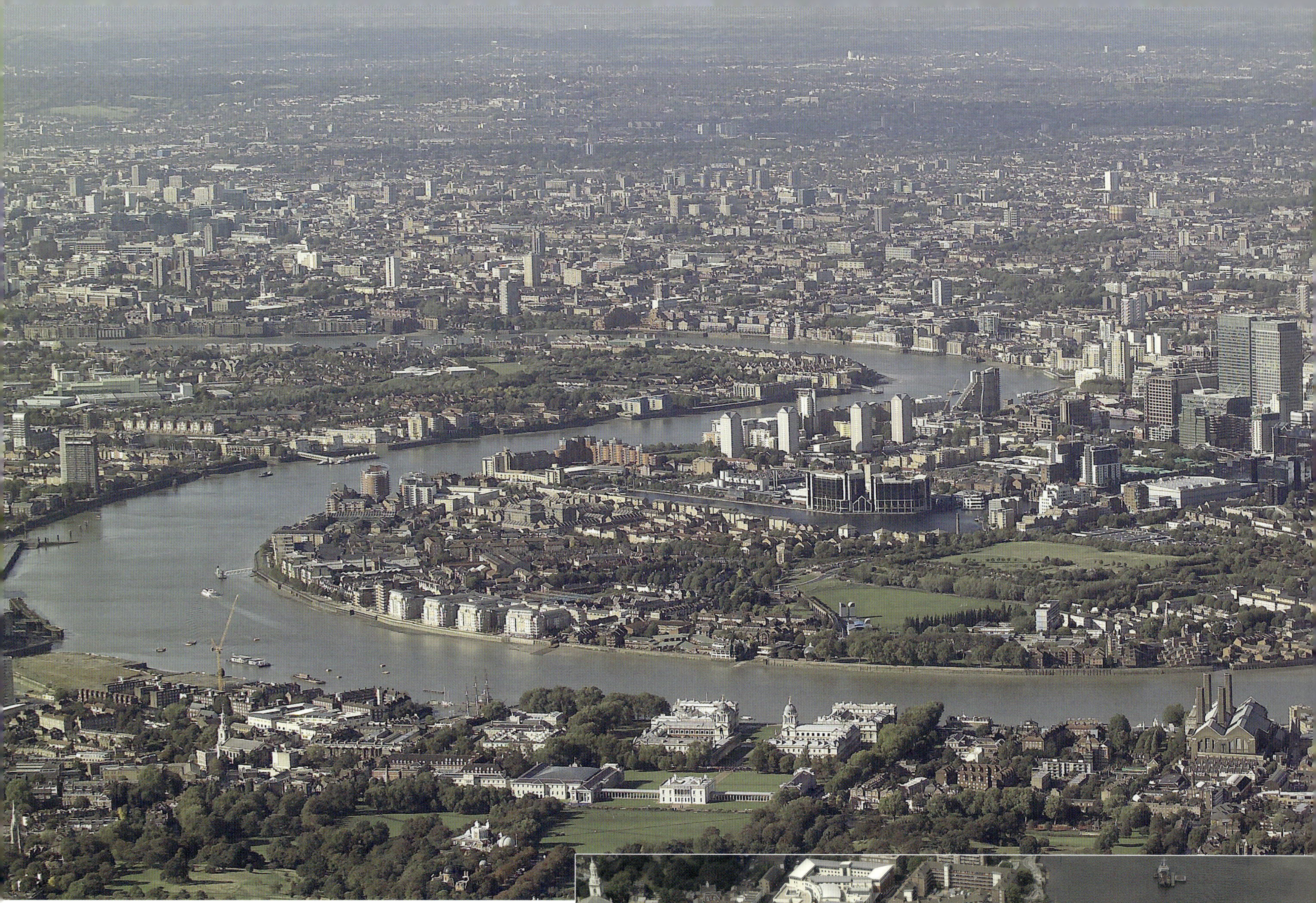

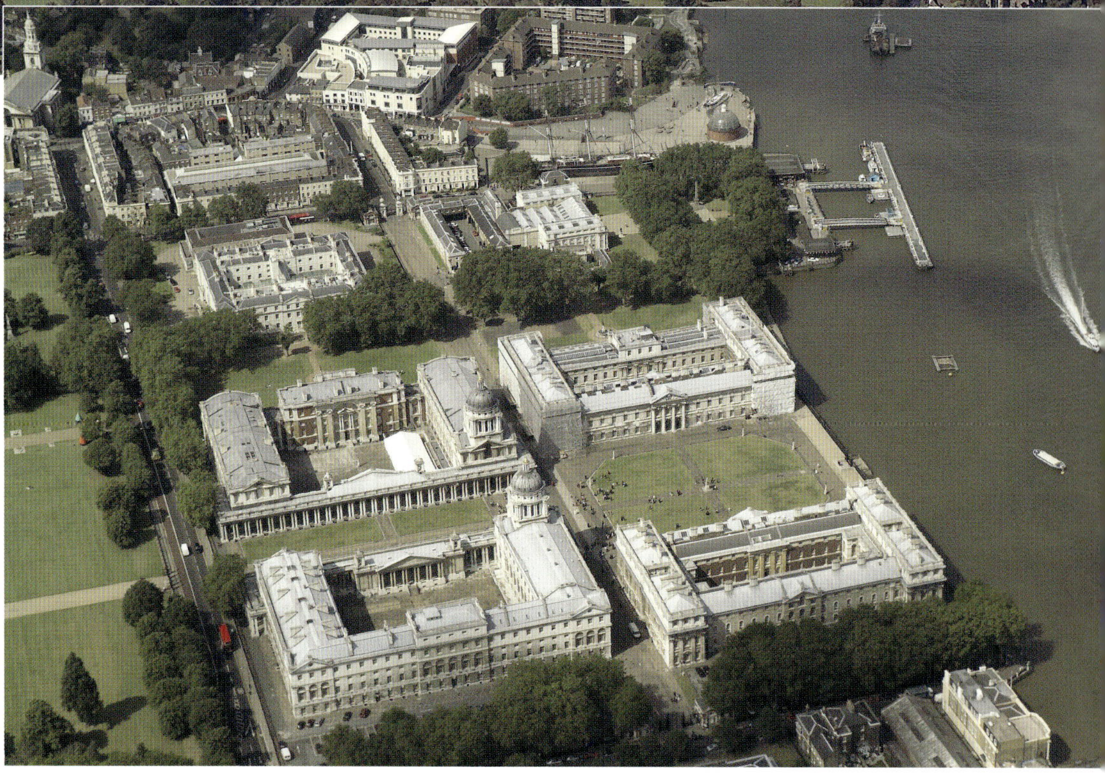

Docklands

Docklands today bears little resemblance to the area it was half a century ago. At their height, the docks were part of the Port of London, the world's largest port, but the rise of container shipping led to the closure of the docks and shipyards in 1969. The regeneration of Docklands in the 1980s led to the development of a commercial centre, with many banks and businesses moving to new buildings sited beside the original waterways. On the south bank of the river lies the Maritime Greenwich World Heritage Site including Sir Christopher Wren's Baroque masterpiece, the Old Royal Naval College (inset), the Royal Observatory, National Maritime Museum, Queen's House and Greenwich Park. Visitors can stand astride the Prime Meridian – Longitude 0° – at the Royal Observatory. To mark the Queen's Diamond Jubilee in 2012, the London Borough of Greenwich will become a Royal Borough.

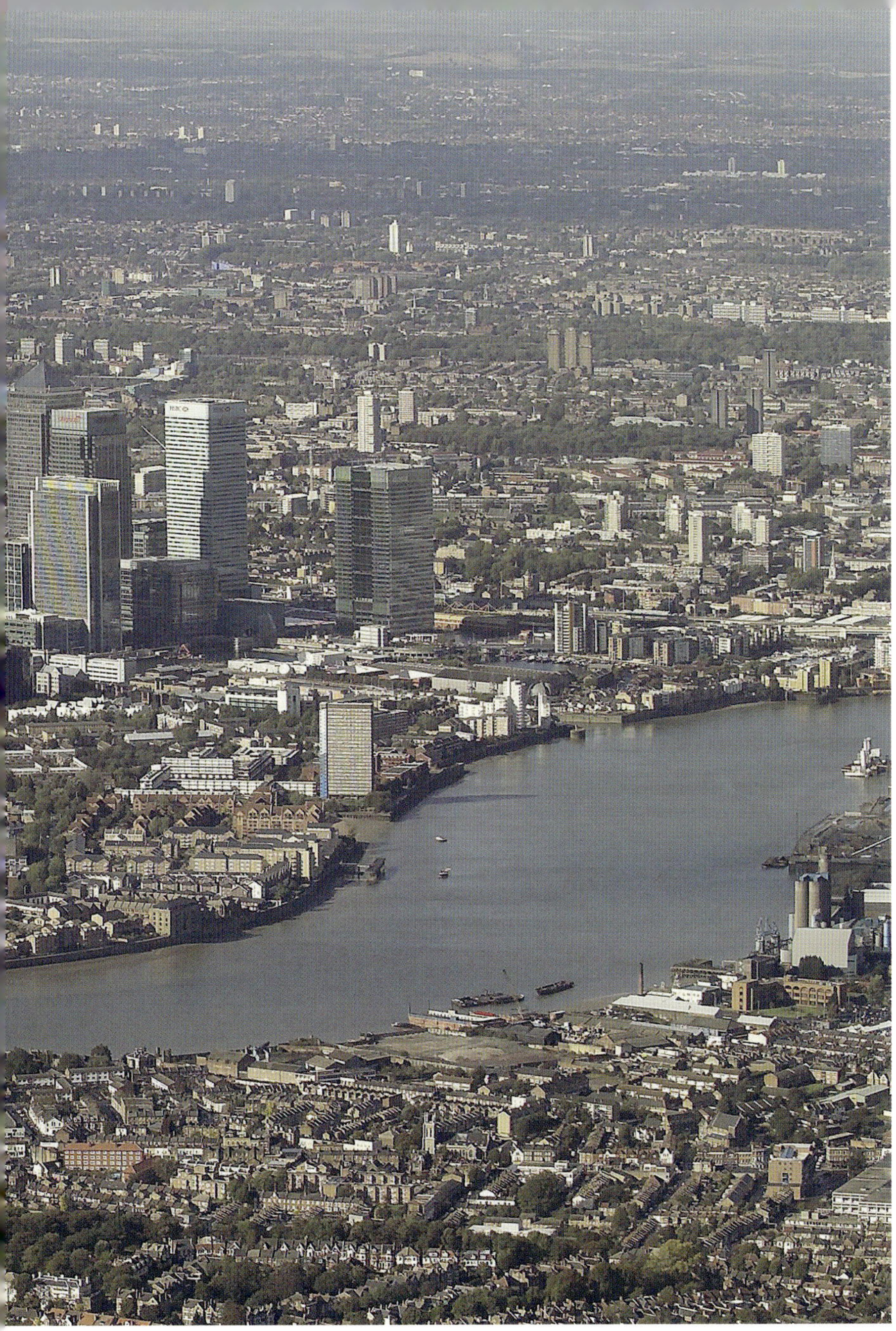

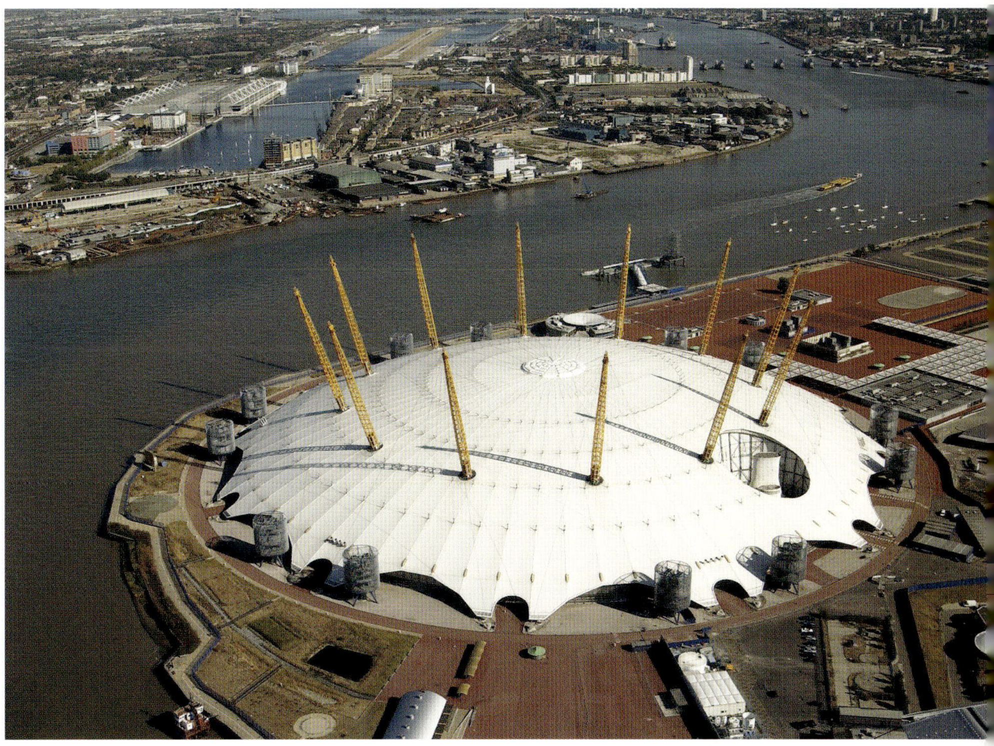

O2 ARENA

The once controversial Millennium Dome (above) has been re-branded as the O2 Arena and is a state of the art entertainment district on the Greenwich Peninsula. Designed by Sir Richard Rogers and intended to mark the millennium, visitors failed to arrive at the Dome in sufficient numbers and there was an outcry over the huge construction costs (£770m) paid for through public money. Now owned by British mobile phone company O2 and American-based Anschutz Entertainment Group, the building houses an 11-screen cinema, exhibition space, a 20,000 seat arena and almost 600 toilets.

THAMES BARRIER

Due to the tidal nature of the Thames in London, the capital is quite prone to flooding. An exceptionally high tide is a risk if there is a surge tide in the north Atlantic combined with north winds that force water upriver. The Thames Barrier (right) was completed in 1982 about a mile upstream from the Woolwich Ferry and was closed for the first time in 1983. Since 1990, the barriers have been closed on average four times a year.

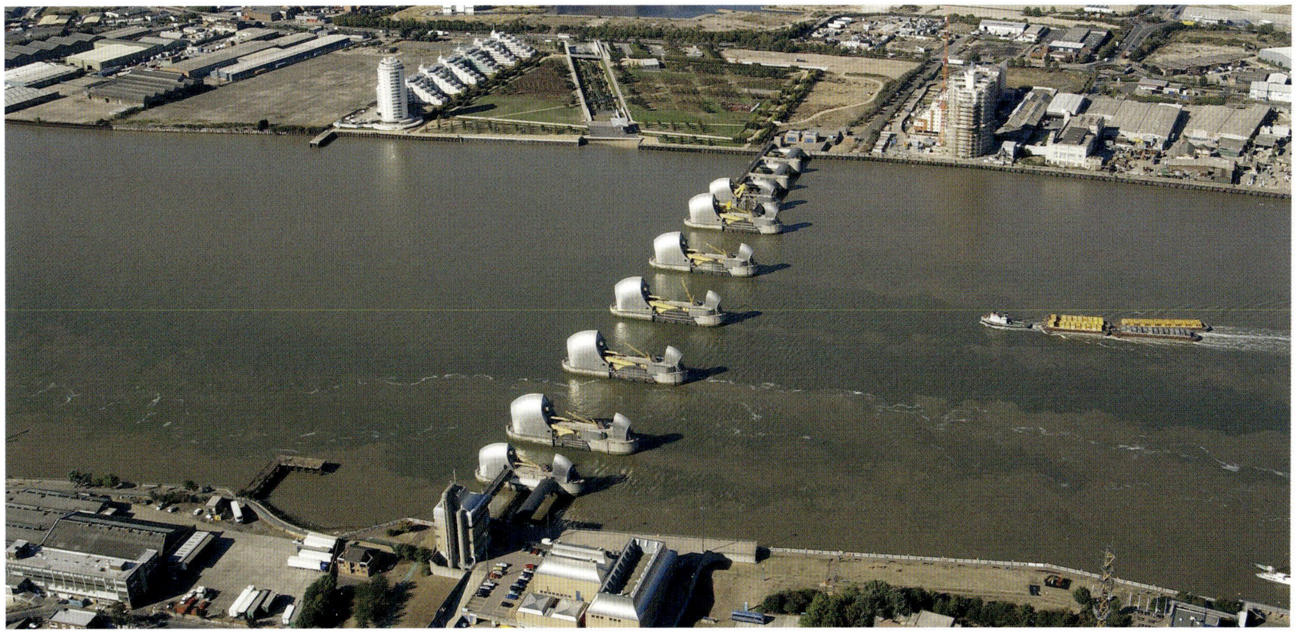

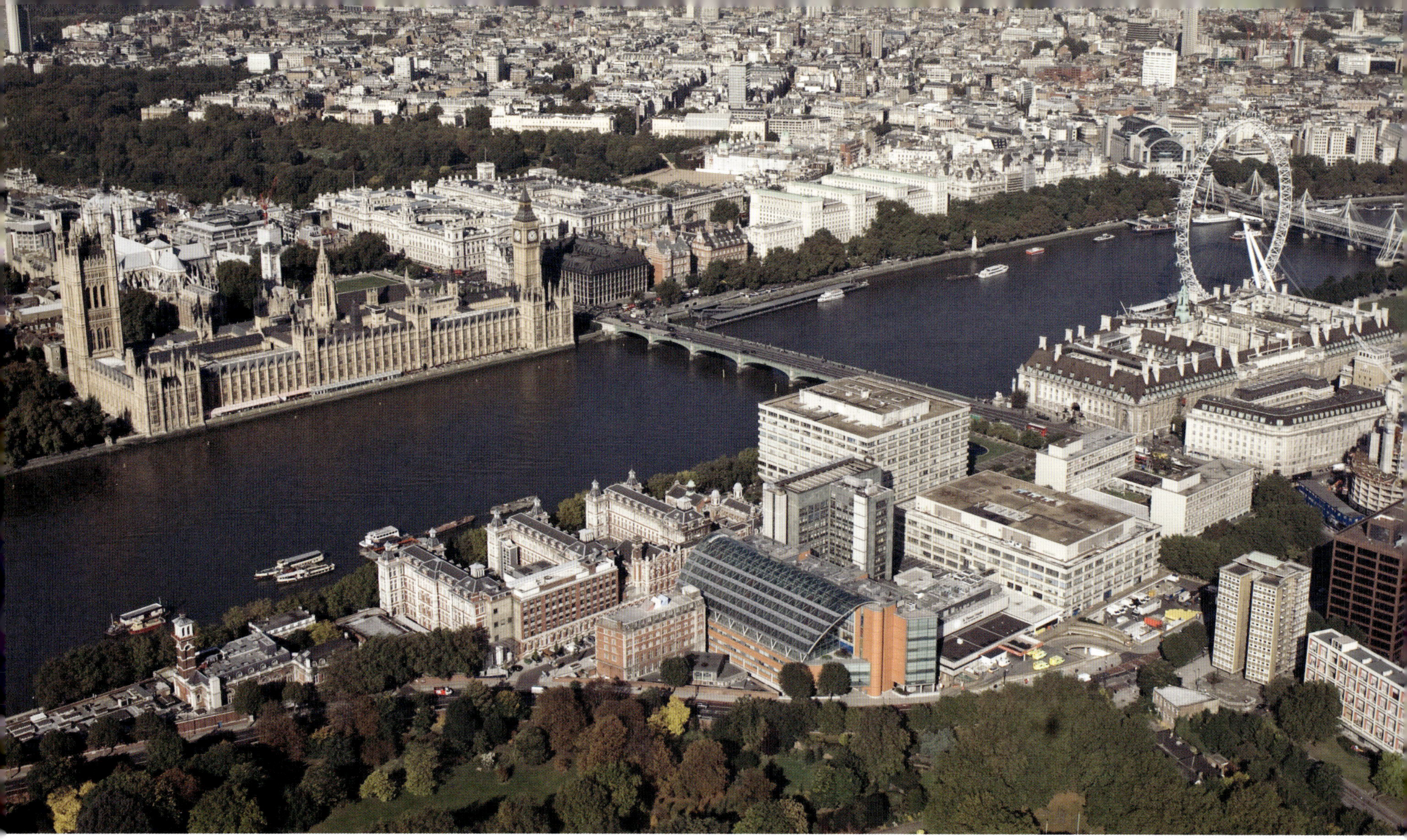

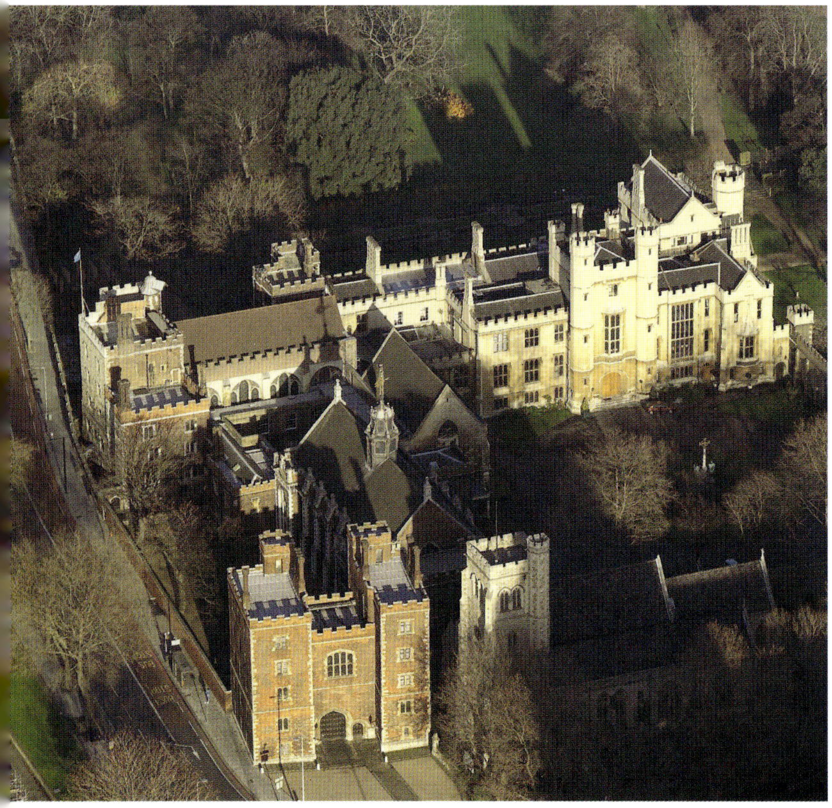

South Bank

Though the capital developed first north of the river, the cheap marshy land to the south (above) was developed from the 18th century onwards with factories, warehouses and low-cost housing. During the Second World War much of the area was bombed and this led to redevelopment of the riverside in the post-war era. Regeneration began with the 1951 Festival of Britain. The modernist Royal Festival Hall was built for the festival and over the next 25 years further buildings were completed including the National Theatre, the Hayward Gallery and the National Film Theatre. Recent additions include the London Eye and the two new footbridges completed in 2003 to replace Brunel's Hungerford Bridge. St Thomas' Hospital overlooks Parliament and, further west along the Thames, lies Lambeth Palace (left), the Archbishop of Canterbury's London residence. Clapham Junction (right), is situated to the south. One of Europe's busiest railway stations it caters for an average of 100 trains an hour.

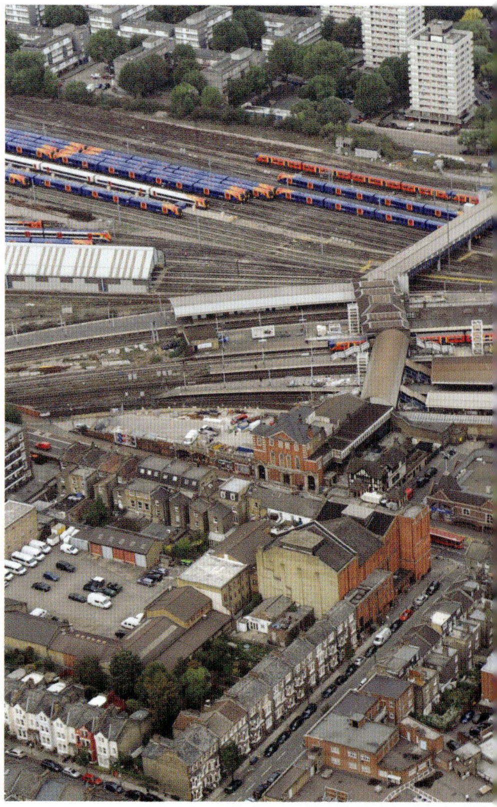

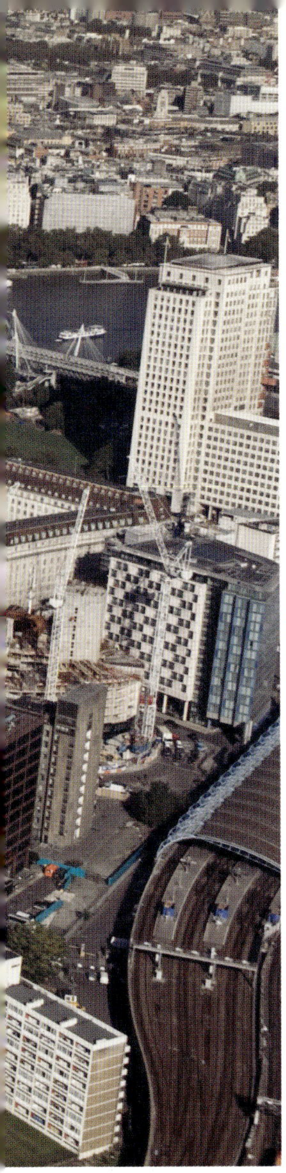

London Eye

The 32 capsules of the London Eye (right) each carry 25 passengers in a full revolution within half an hour. Travelling at 10 inches (26cm) a second, the largest observation wheel ever built gives viewers a fantastic panorama of London. On a clear day you can see 25 miles (40km) to beyond London from the peak. Opened in March 2000, the London Eye had a five-year license that has been extended for a further 24 years. Positioning the 1,700 tonne wheel took several days in October 1999. It was assembled from parts made by different suppliers, on a temporary river platform beside its current site in Jubilee Gardens.

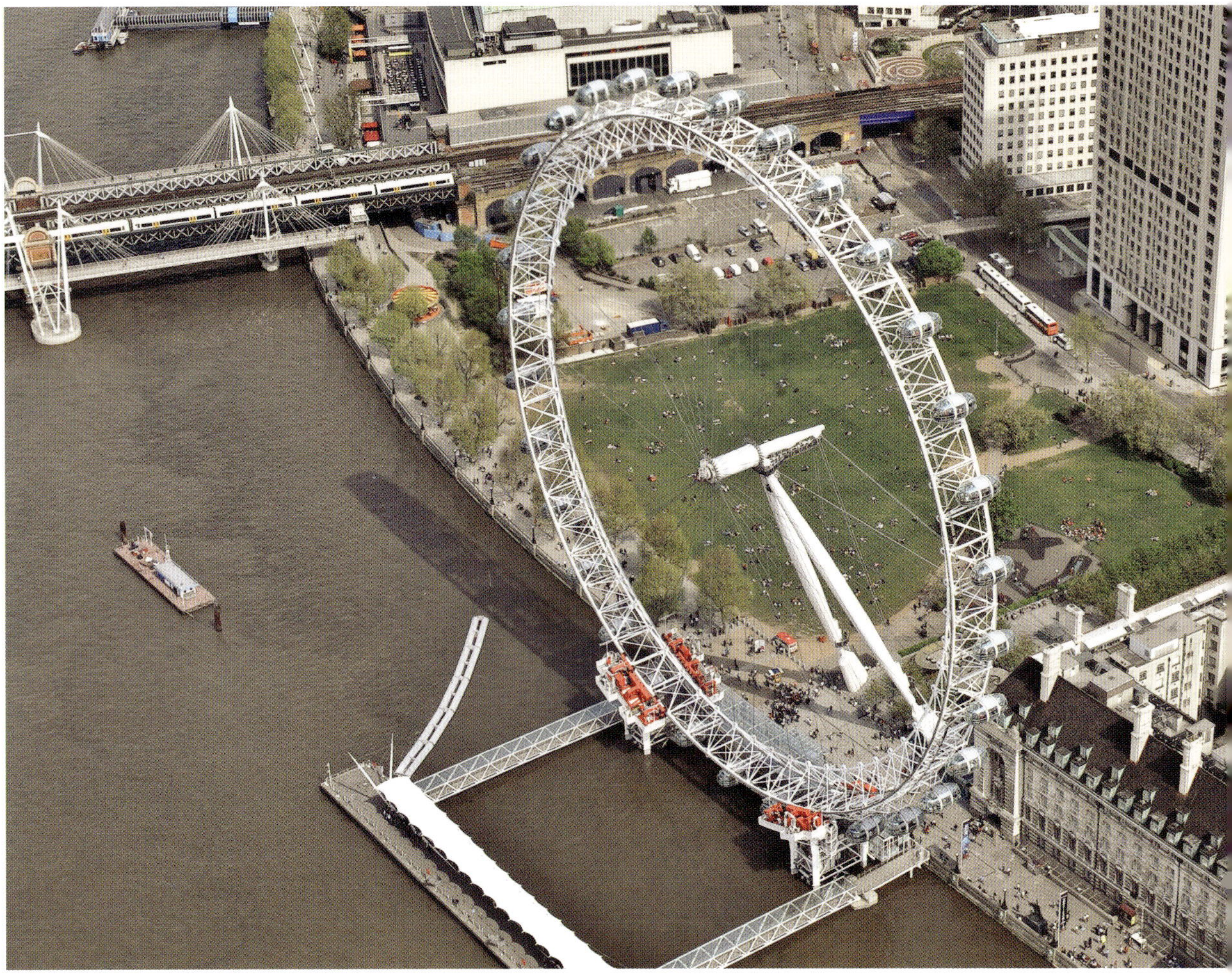

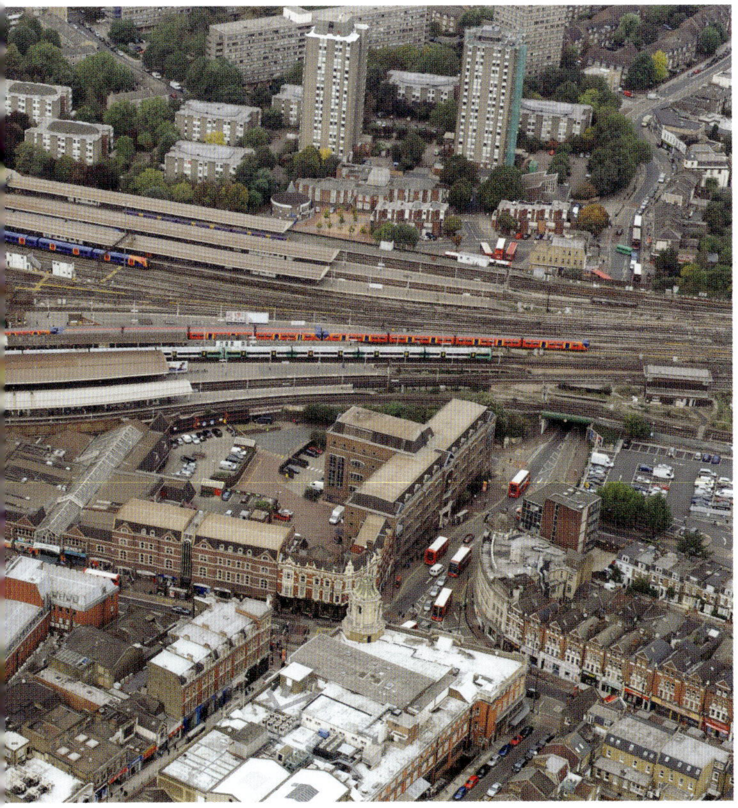

Imperial War Museum

The Imperial War Museum London (right) was founded during the First World War to collect and display material related to the war; it has since expanded its focus to include all modern warfare and its impact on society. It was originally housed in the Crystal Palace on Sydenham Hill, then moved to the Imperial Institute in South Kensington, before settling in its present home. Located in St George's Fields, Southwark, the IWM occupies the central section of the former Bethlem Royal Hospital, or Bedlam as it was known, a mental hospital designed by Sydney Smirke in the early 19th century.

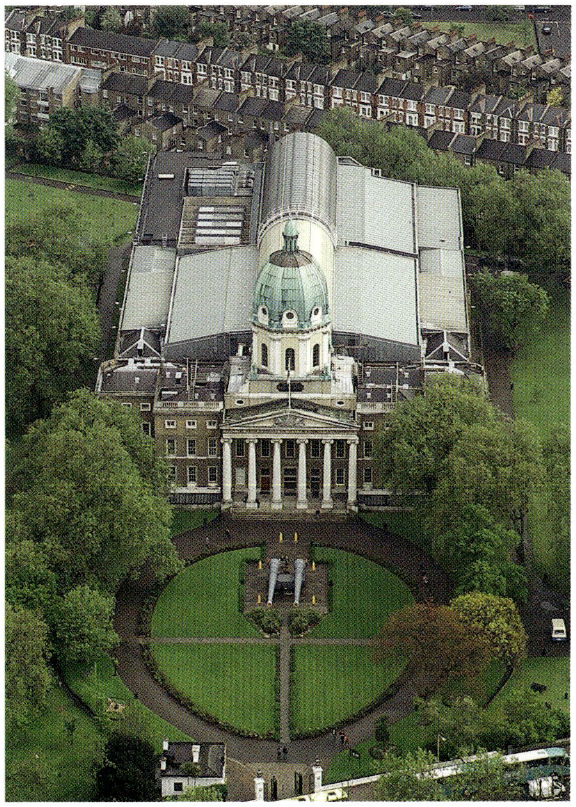

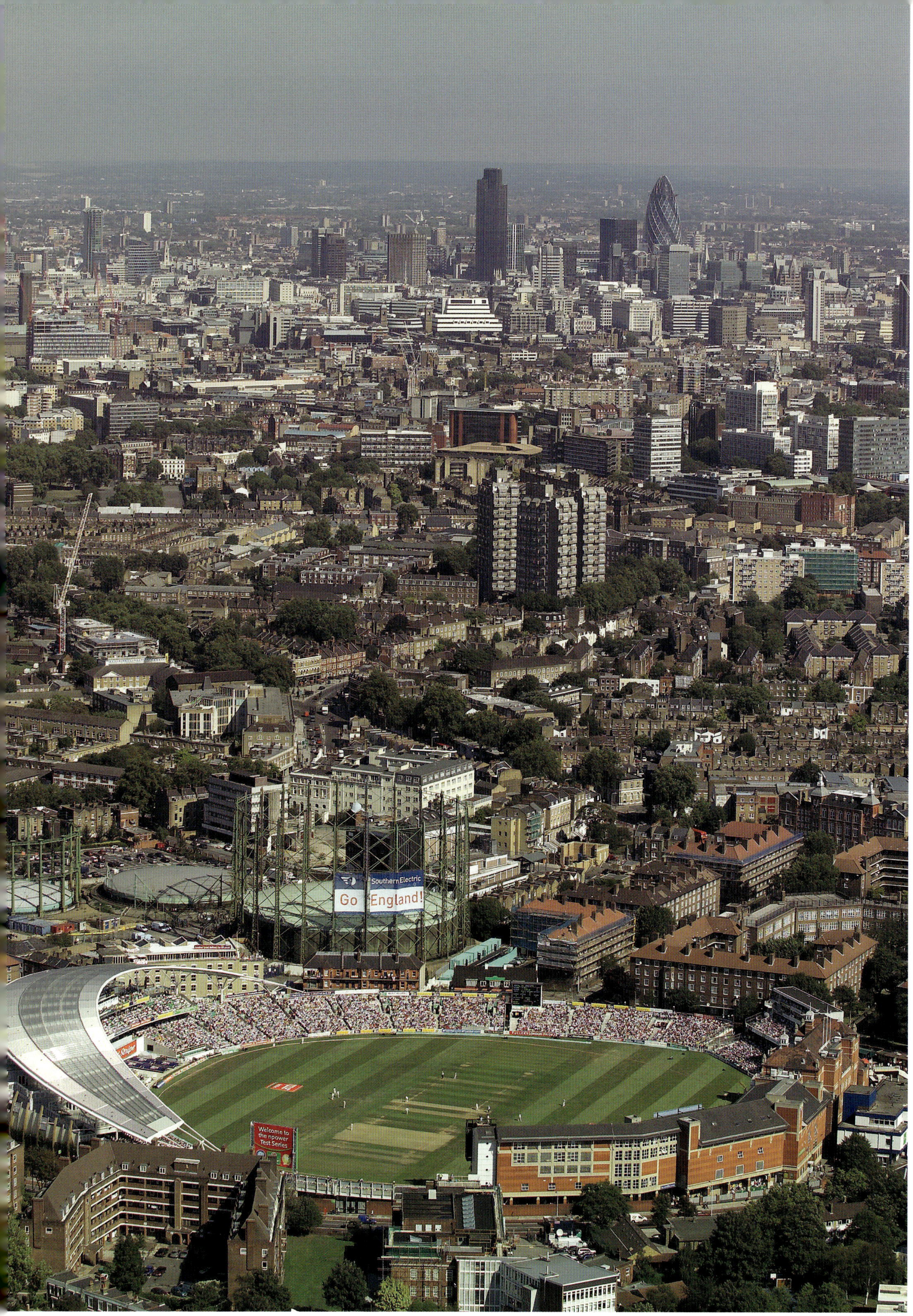

The Oval

The home of Surrey County Cricket Club, The Oval cricket ground (left) in Kennington, south London, is famous for hosting the last Test match of the season. Built on the site of a former market garden of oval shape, the land was leased from the Duchy of Cornwall in 1846 and turfed with grass from Tooting Common. In time the cricket club became the Surrey County Cricket Club. In the early days, The Oval hosted a number of football matches including the first FA Cup Final in 1872 and England's first international win, against Scotland, in 1873. Traditionally, The Oval hosts the final match of any Test series, so the ground has been the scene of many nail-biting matches, including the one photographed here – the dramatic fifth Test Match in the 2005 Ashes series which England won in a thrilling final. Construction of the new OCS stand at the Vauxhall End was given the go ahead despite local opposition and the stand opened in 2005.

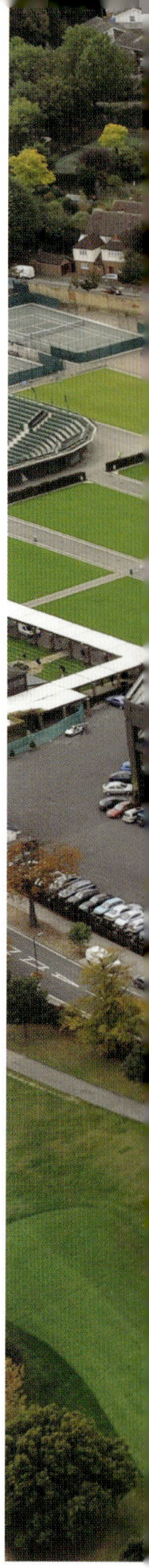

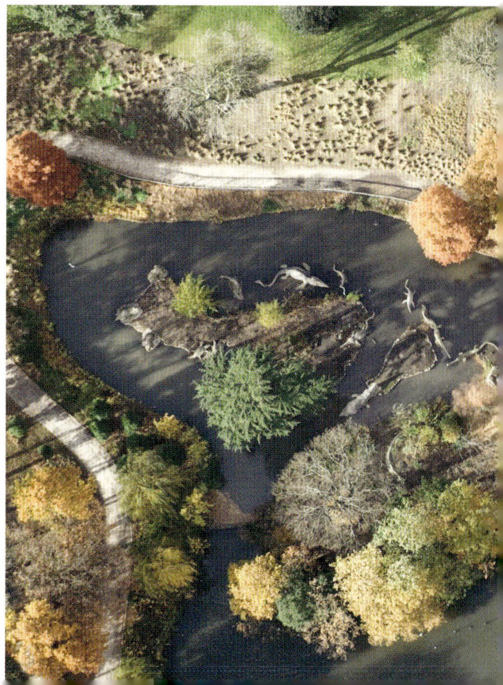

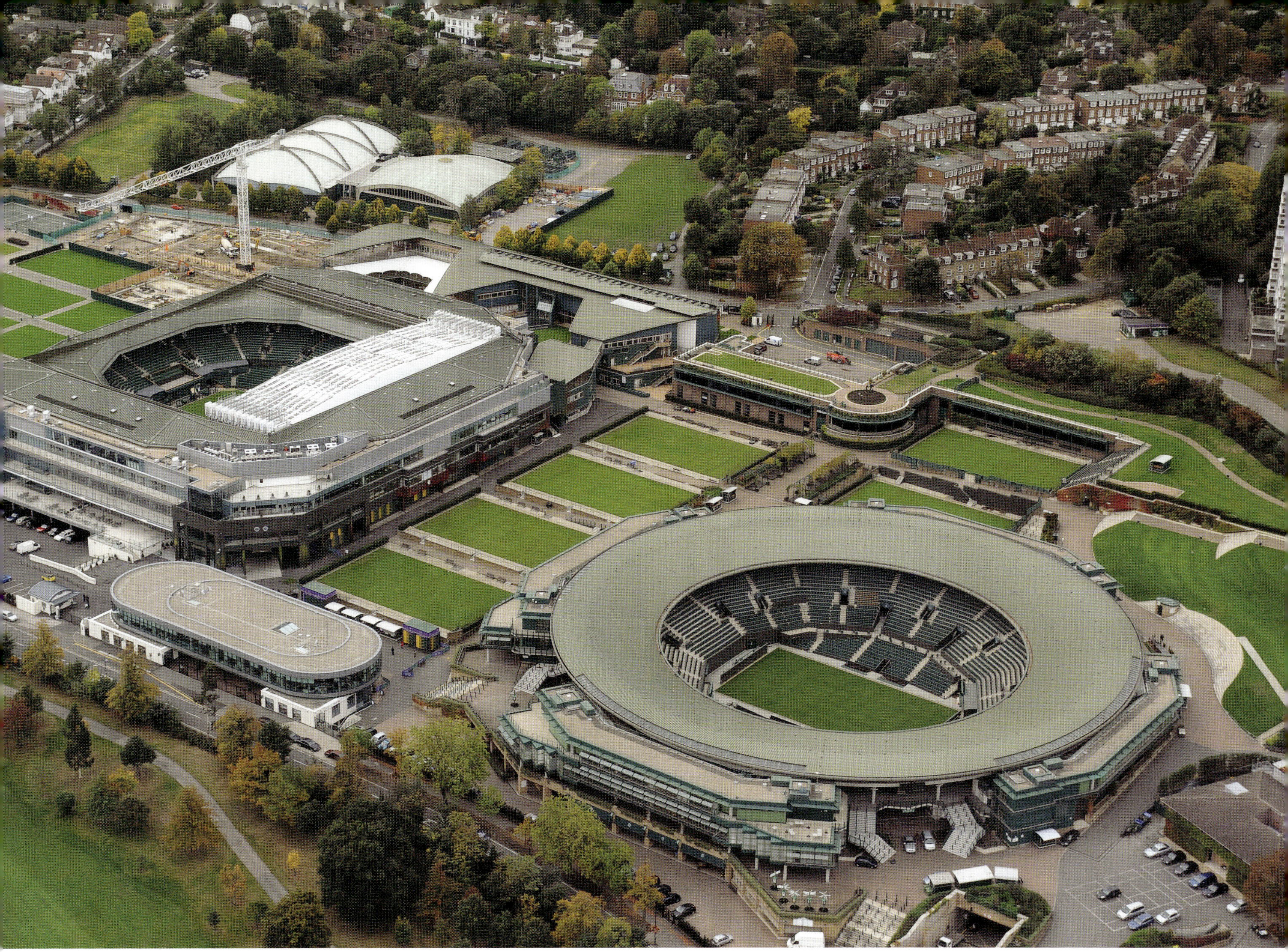

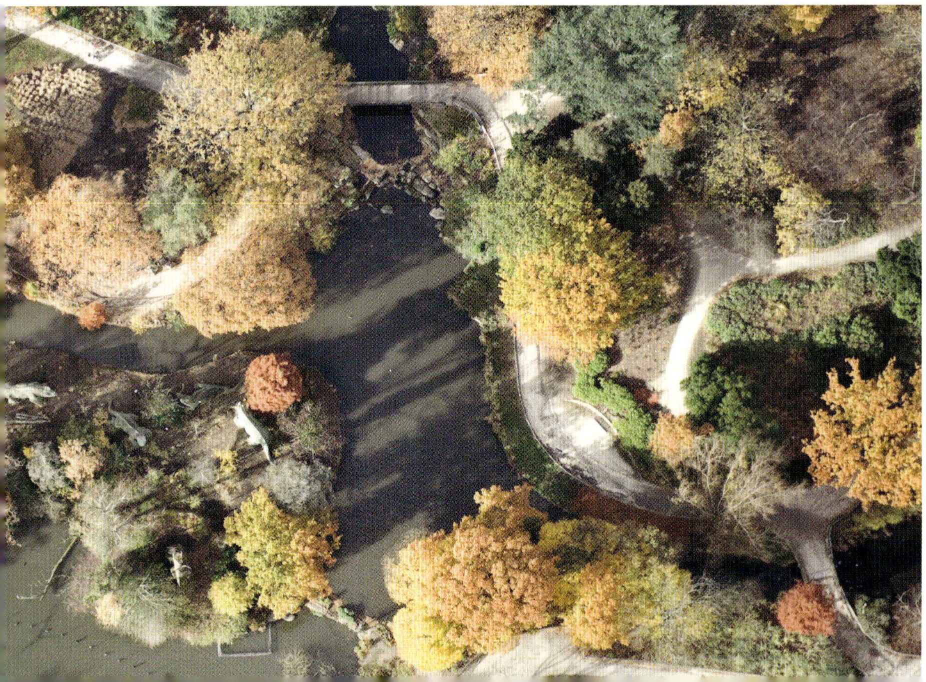

South London leisure

The All England Lawn Tennis and Croquet Club has its home in Wimbledon (above). Although it is a member's club open all year round, the club is most famous for the Wimbledon Championships each summer. The men's singles championship started in 1877, the women's in 1884 and, in 1905, an American woman was the first overseas player to win here. Today Wimbledon is the only Grand Slam tournament still played on grass. Centre Court has a capacity of 15,000 and a new retractable roof to enable all-weather play.

The park at Crystal Palace (left) was created as a home for the great cast iron and glass structure that started its life in Hyde Park as the centrepiece of the 1851 Great Exhibition before being moved to Sydenham Hill. Surrounded by fountains and temples, the palace was destroyed by a disastrous fire in 1936 and little remains. The park today is home to the National Sports Centre and a boating lake surrounded by the world's first model dinosaurs commissioned in 1852.

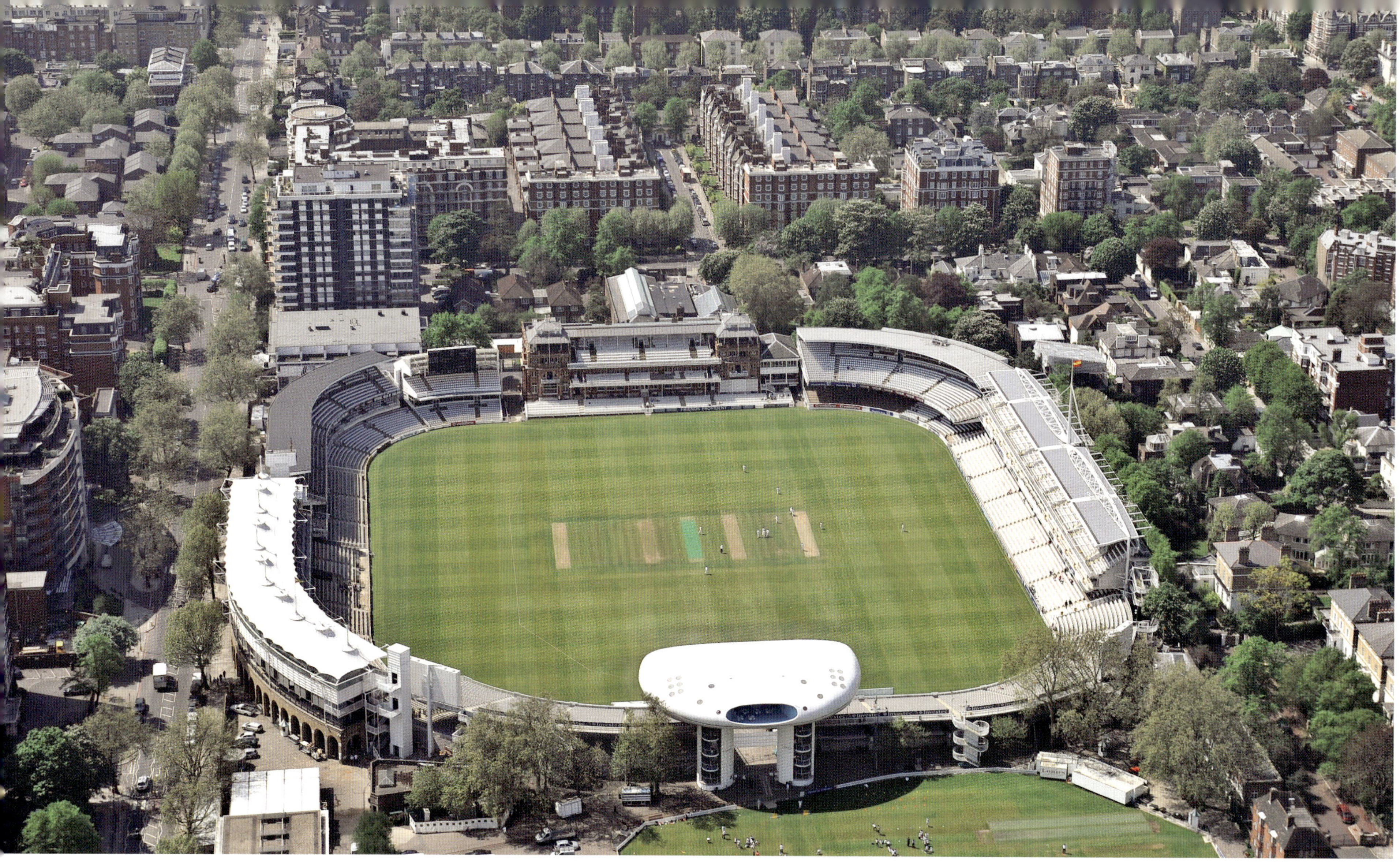

NORTH LONDON
LEISURE

Surrounded by the wealthy houses and apartments of St John's Wood, Lords Cricket Ground (above) has occupied this site for almost a century after moving from the original site of Dorset Square and a ground 250 yards away. Founded by Thomas Lord in 1787, it is owned by Marylebone Cricket Club (MCC) and thought of as the home of cricket. The ground holds up to 32,000 spectators and the futuristic Media Centre overlooking the Nursery End won the Royal Institute of British Architects Stirling Prize in 1999.

For over 130 years "Ally-Pally" (right), with its indoor ice rink and landscaped gardens, has been a popular attraction for north Londoners. Famous as the birthplace of the BBC's television services, the building was the main TV transmitting centre from 1936-1956, with regular concerts and live shows.

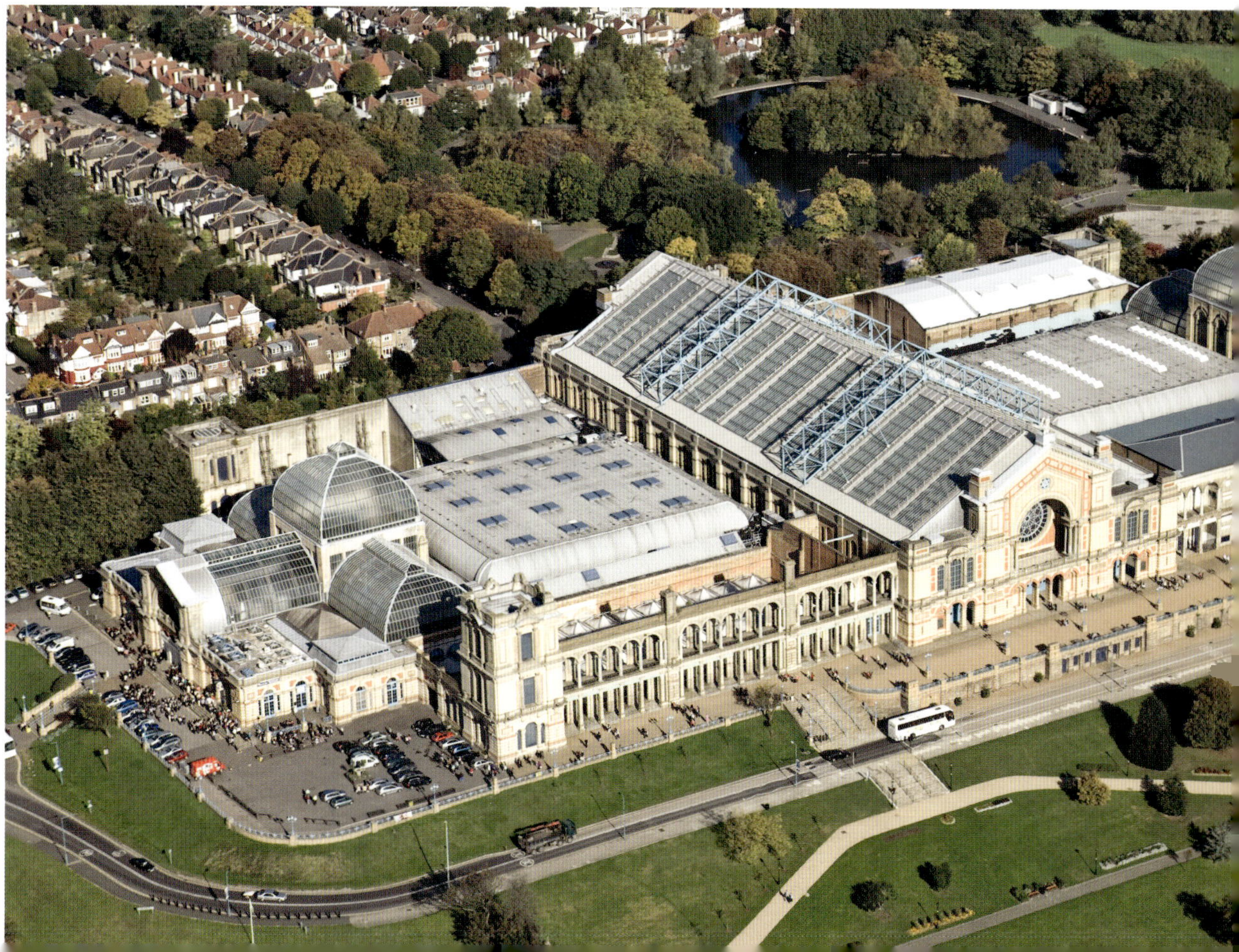

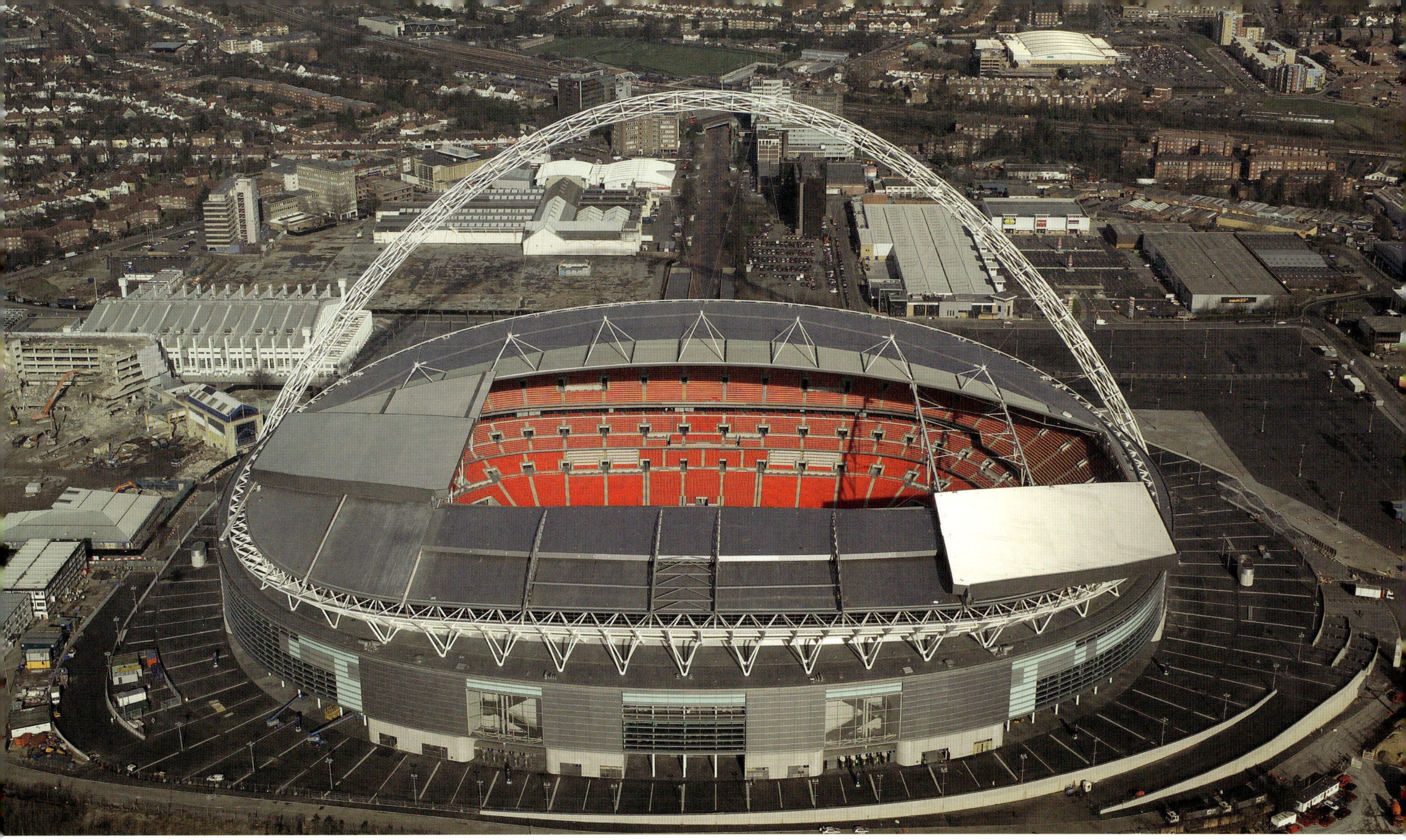

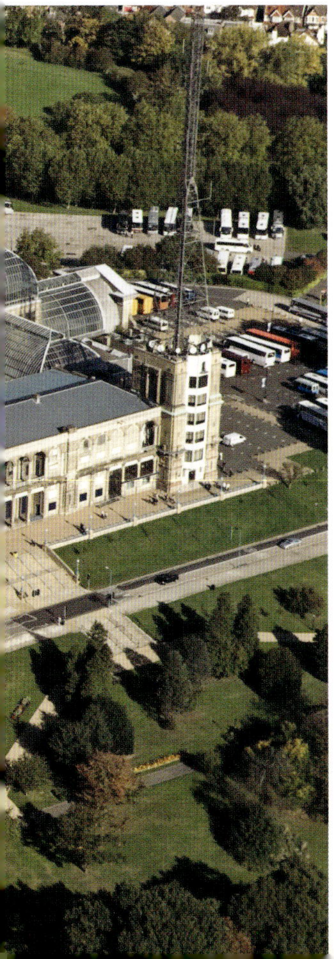

Wembley and Arsenal

Two of London's most modern stadia, Wembley (above) and Arsenal's new football ground, the Emirates Stadium (right), incorporate state-of-the-art facilities. The giant arch of Wembley Stadium can be seen across London and is intended to be as iconic as the twin towers of the old Wembley, which was famous for hosting a number of sporting triumphs including England's win in the 1966 World Cup. The 436ft (133m) tall arch serves to support the retractable roof in a design that ensures no pillars obscure the view from 90,000 seats. Wembley is the national football stadium but also hosts concerts and other sporting events including athletics. Arsenal's Emirates Stadium opened in July 2006 with a capacity of over 60,000 close to the original stadium in Highbury. Completed within three years, the stadium cost £390m to construct and provided 2,000 new homes on the site. High demand for tickets, and the relative wealth of Arsenal fans, has meant that revenue from premium seating and corporate boxes is expected to be nearly as high as revenue from the old stadium.

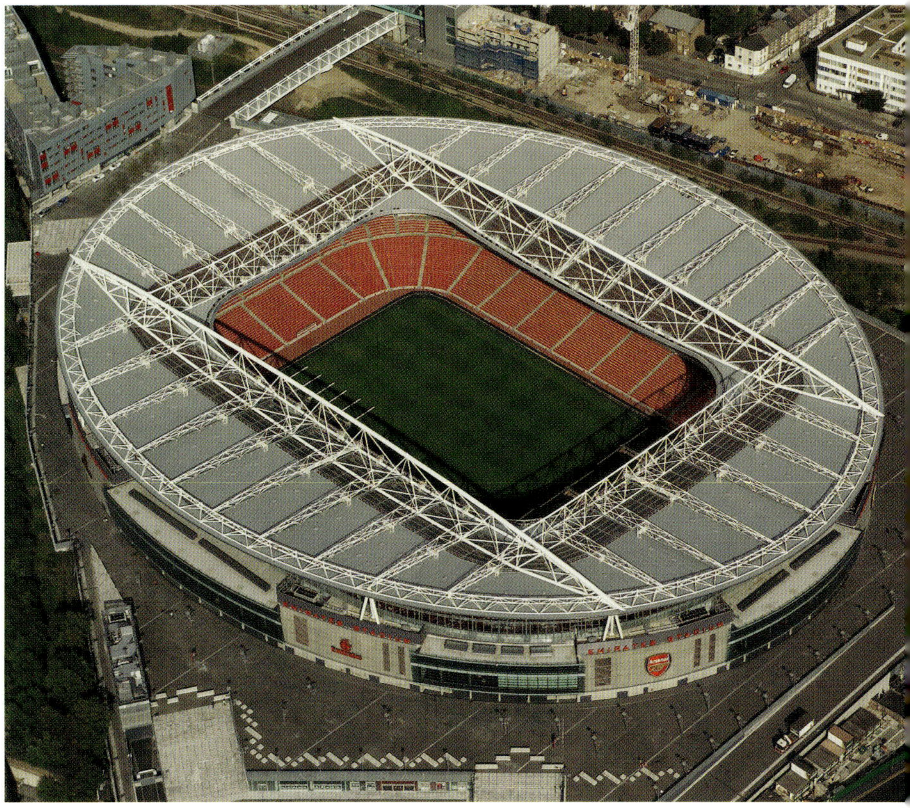

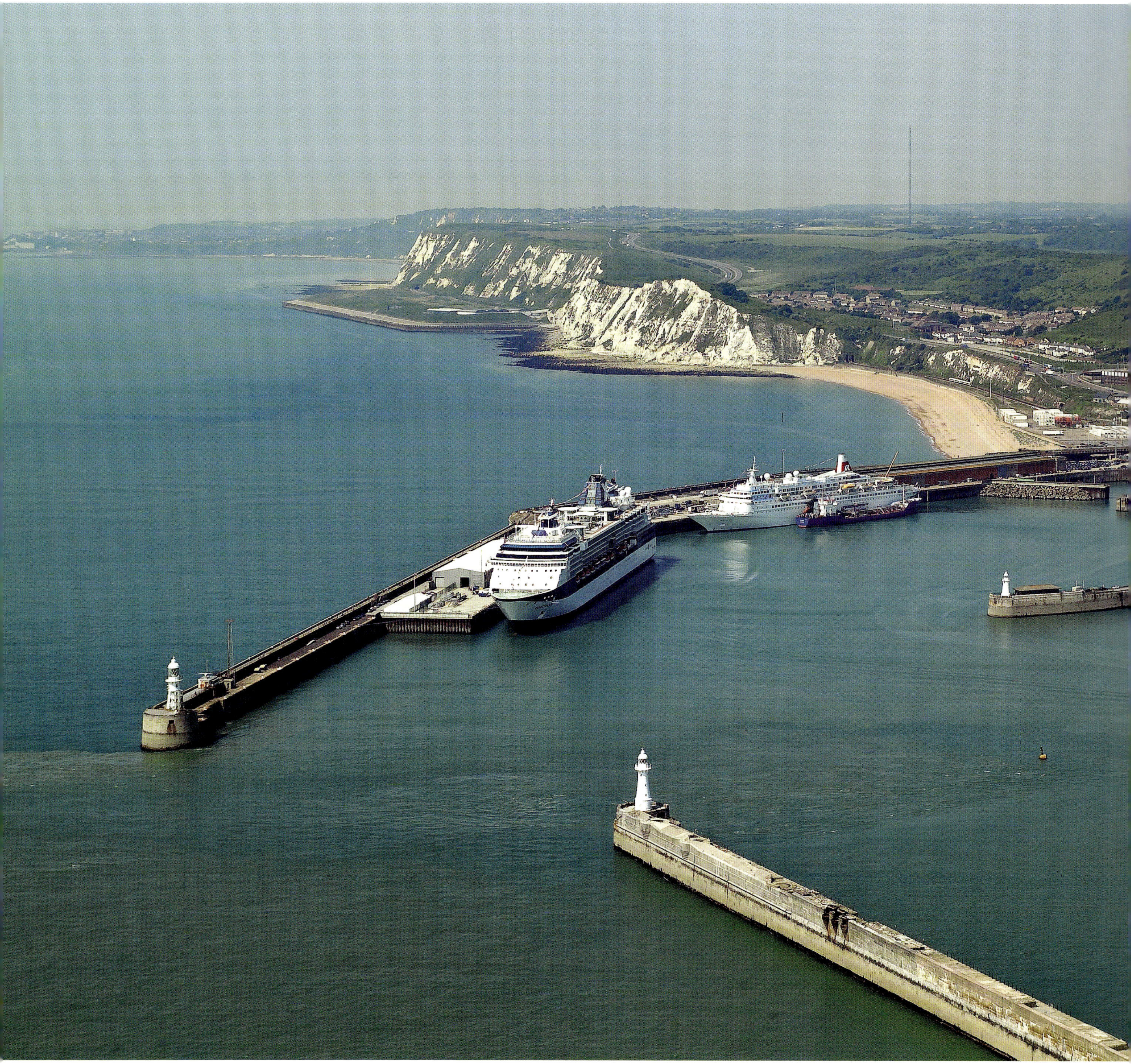

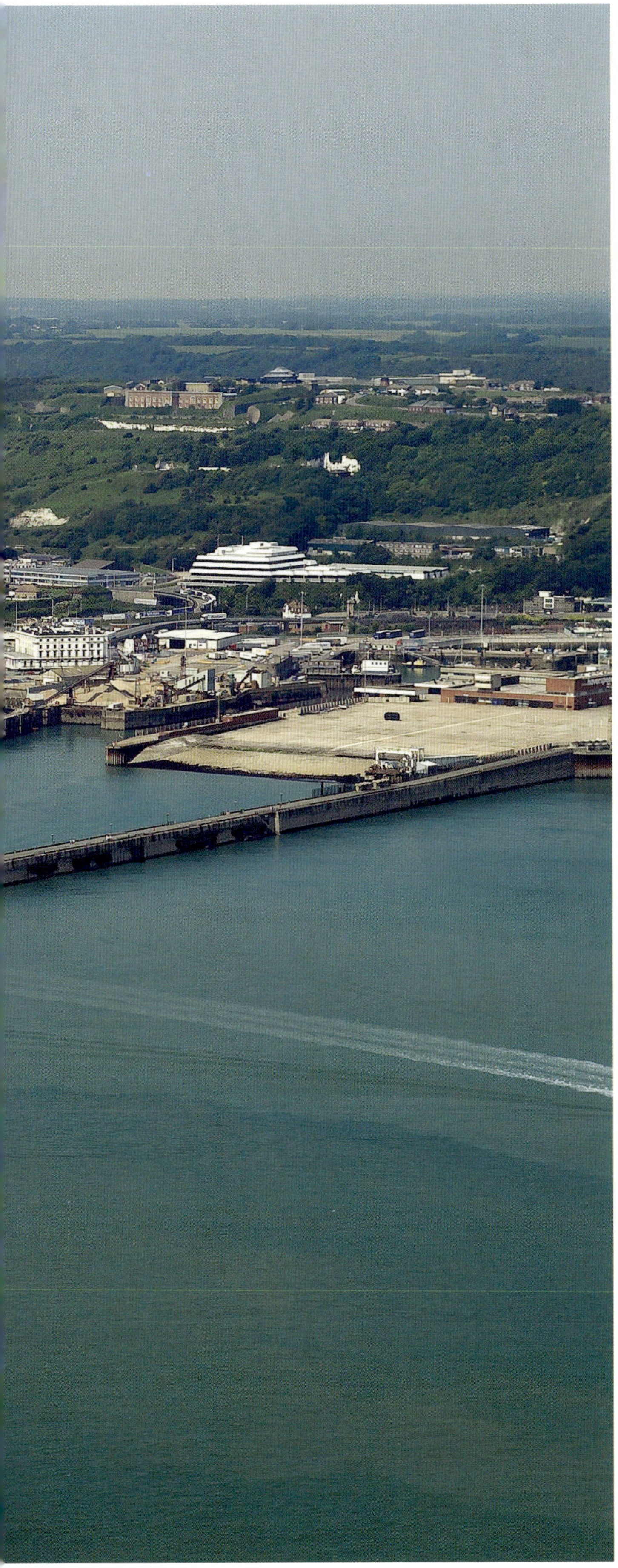

KENT

Known as the Garden of England due to its abundance of orchards and hop farms, Kent is blessed with idyllic countryside, historic towns and coastal resorts. The closest county to the continent, Kent has developed in recent years as a transport hub including the Dover Ferry Port and the Channel Tunnel terminal at Ashford. The county has a long tradition of naval excellence and is home to the royal dockyards at Chatham as well as four of Edward I's Confederation of Cinque Ports, originally formed to maintain ships ready for the Crown. To the north, Gravesend guards the entrance to the river Thames. Iconic landmarks include the chalk cliffs at Dover, Leeds Castle and Canterbury Cathedral. One of the country's finest Christian monuments, the 11th century cathedral was built on the site of St Augustine's missionary base, making the town a centre of early Christianity.

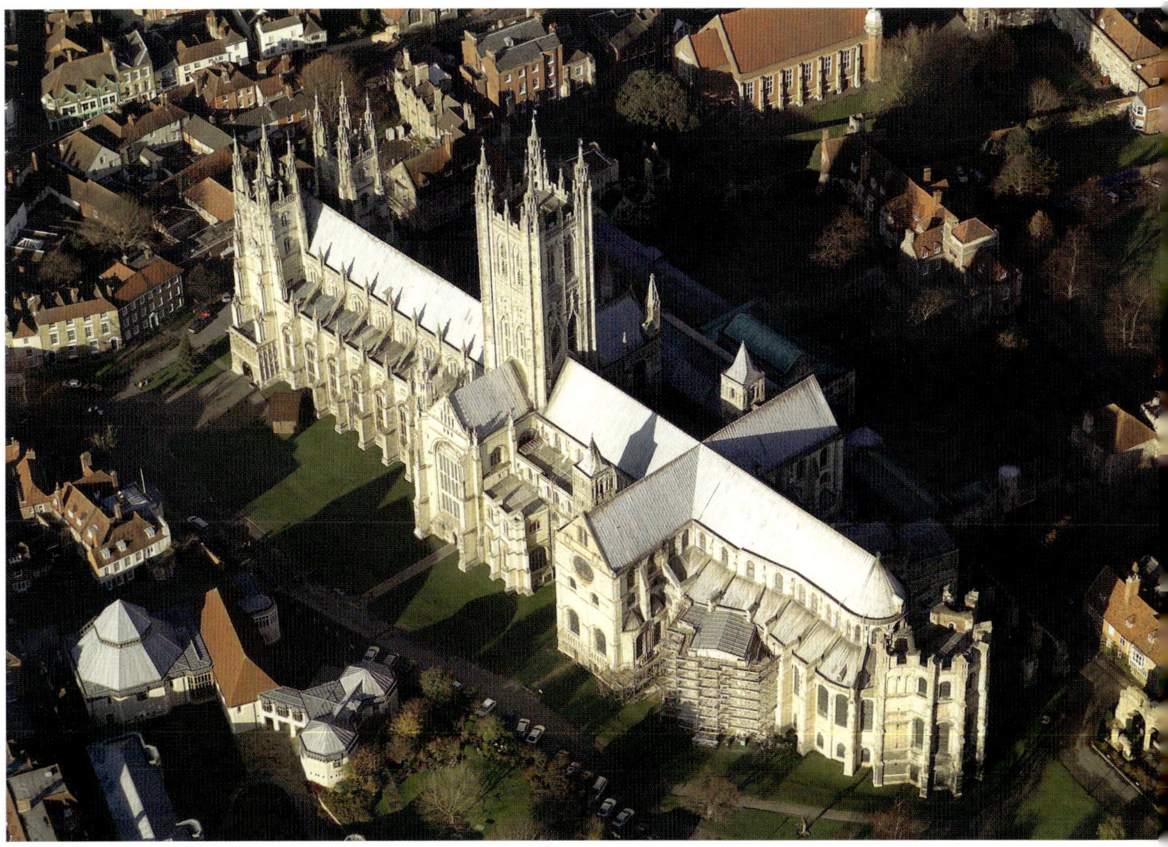

ANCIENT AND MODERN-DAY PILGRIMAGE

During the Middle Ages, Canterbury Cathedral was the journey's end for thousands of pilgrims who travelled to visit the shrine of the saint and martyr Thomas à Becket (above). Kent is also a gateway for journeys to and from Europe, with Dover (left) the nearest English port to France.

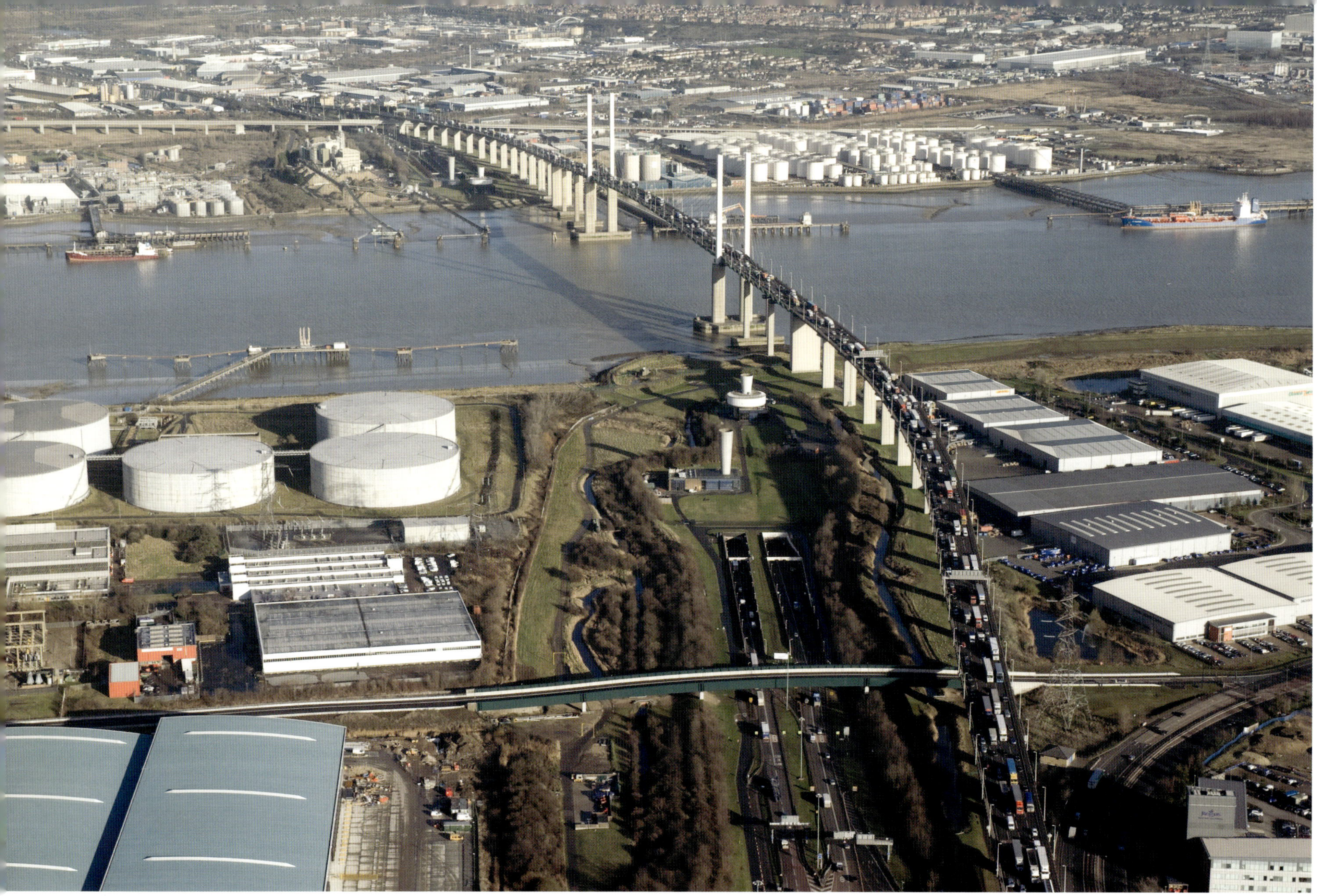

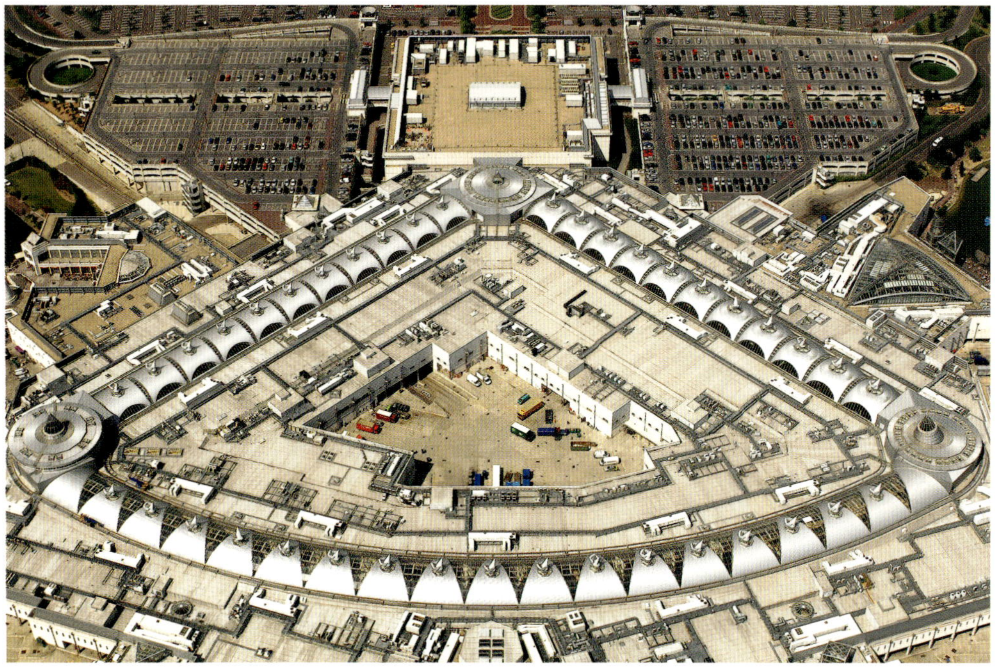

Dartford Crossing & Bluewater

The Dartford to Thurrock river crossing (above) forms a vital link in the M25 motorway, and takes Britain's most important orbital road across the river Thames. Traffic moving in an anticlockwise direction travels through two dual-lane tunnels, while traffic moving in a clockwise direction travels over the four-lane Queen Elizabeth II bridge opened in 1991. Close by lies Bluewater (left and right) a giant retail park which opened for business in March 1999. Built on the site of a former chalk quarry, it is Europe's third largest shopping centre and leisure complex and is the size of 100 football pitches. In the first 10 years over a quarter of a billion people visited Bluewater's 330 retail outlets and entertainment facilities, including a 13-screen cinema, gyms and family areas. The triangular shape allows for a department store at each corner and the building is topped with glass-sided domes enabling natural light to stream in. The site includes parking for 13,000 cars and over 50 acres of parkland containing over a million trees and shrubs.

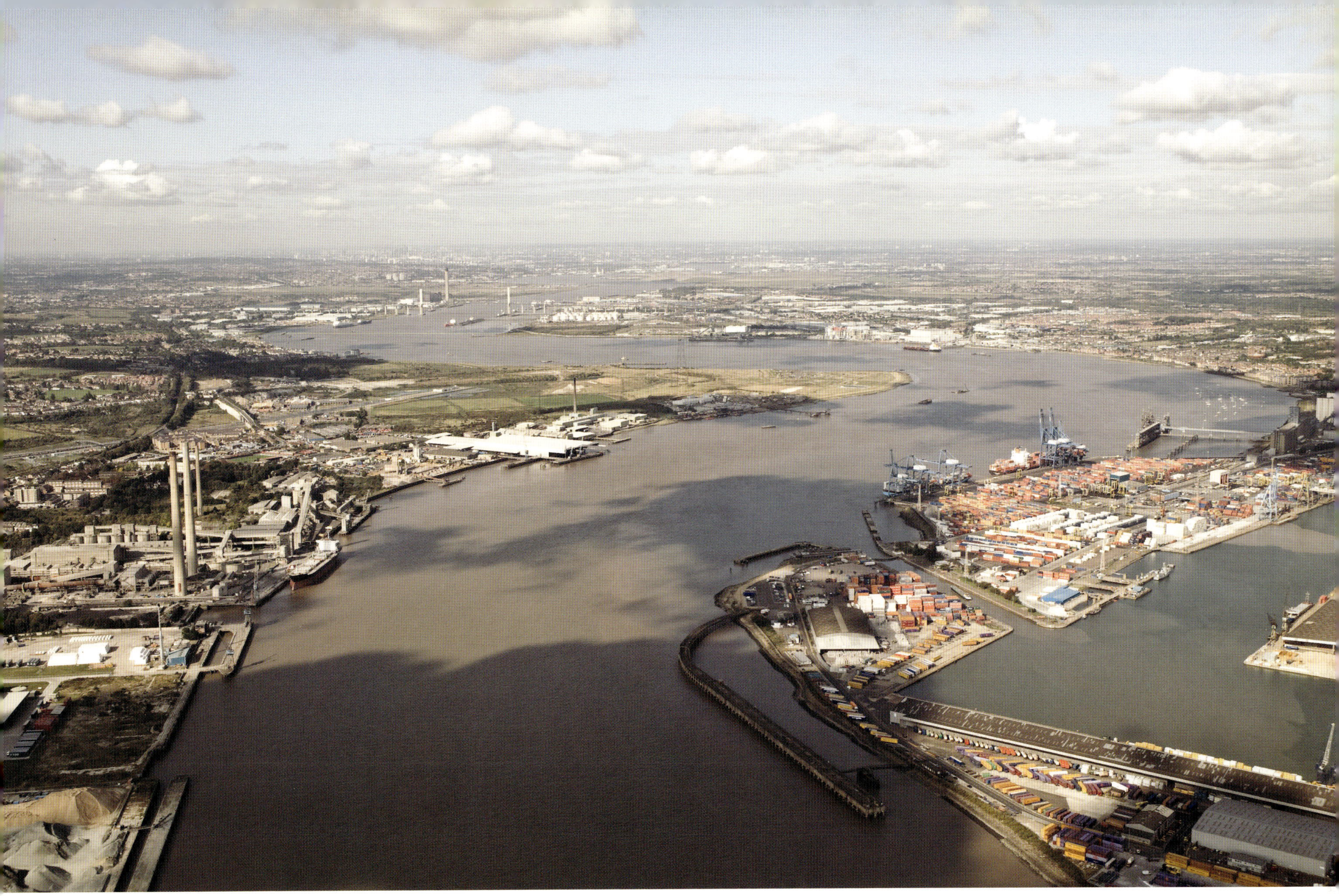

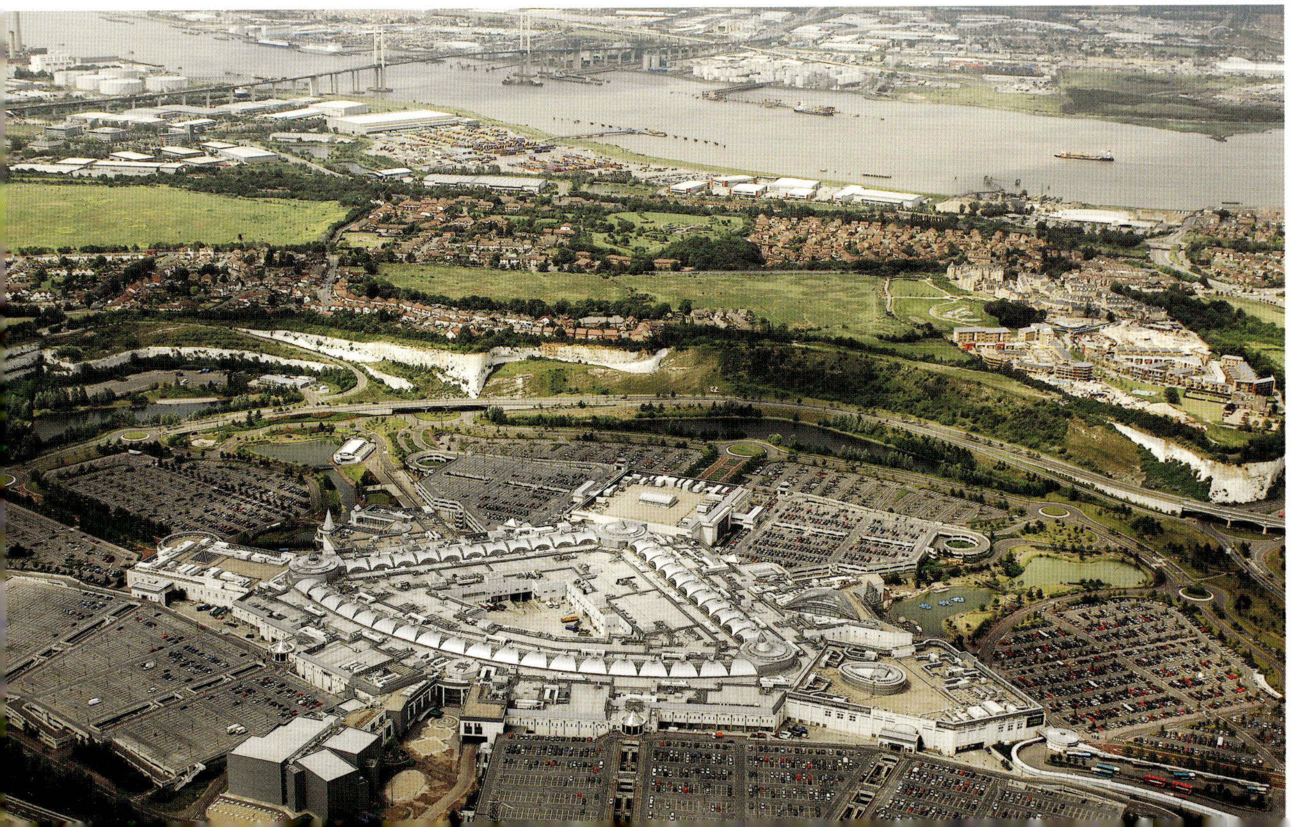

Gravesend

Gravesend (above) lies downstream from the Dartford Crossing on the south bank of the Thames at a meander more than 25 miles (40 km) below London Bridge. Though the settlement at Gravesend grew around a point where high land reaches the river bank, much of the area was once marshland made habitable through embanking the river and enclosing areas of marsh. Until the building of Tilbury Docks on the other side of the river, Gravesend was the first port of call for foreign ships on their way to London. Since 1959 the town has been the headquarters of the Port of London Authority Thames Navigation Service – the central control point for all shipping movements on the Thames.

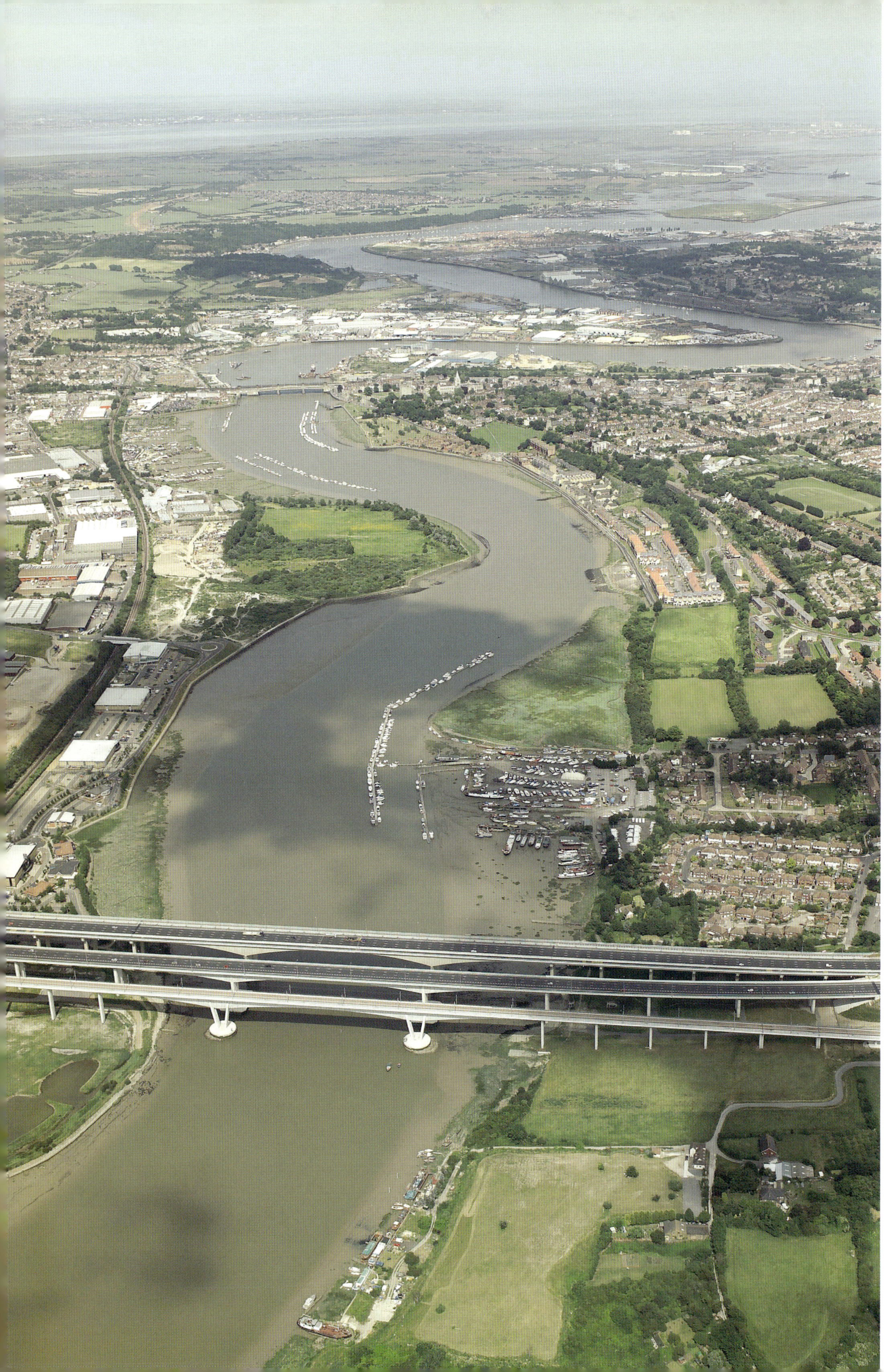

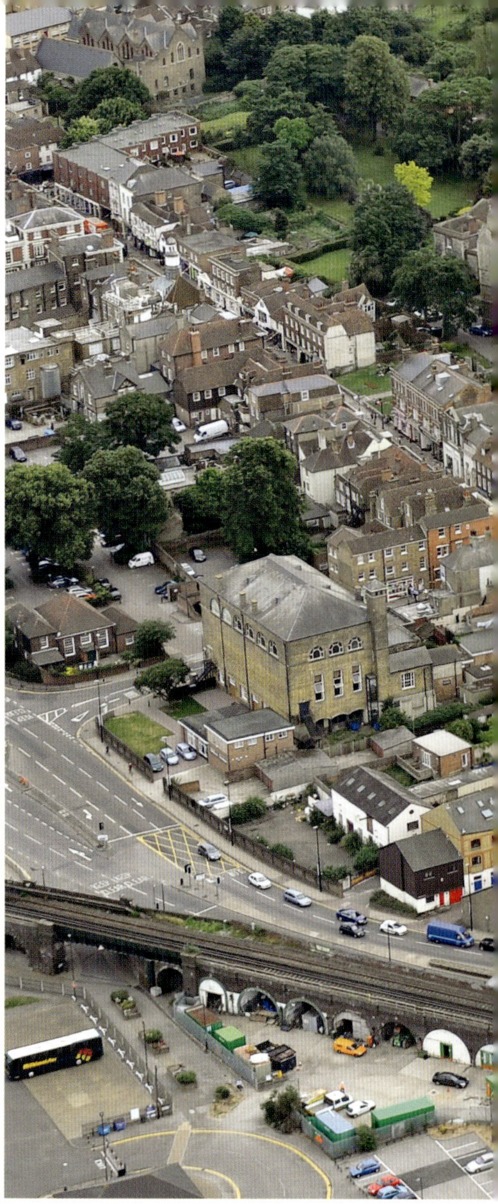

Rochester

Along with Chatham and Gillingham, Rochester forms part of an urban area known as the Medway Towns, which lie along the river Medway close to the confluence with the river Thames. Charles Dickens lived nearby and described Rochester in *The Pickwick Papers* and *Great Expectations*; in his memory, two Dickens festivals are held in the town each year. Rochester has a cathedral and a Norman castle (above) with a four-turreted keep built to guard the river crossing. The historic town centre boasts a clutch of beautiful buildings including the Guildhall and Eastgate House. The river is crossed by the M2 motorway Medway bypass (left) and the high-speed railway line running from the capital to the Channel Tunnel.

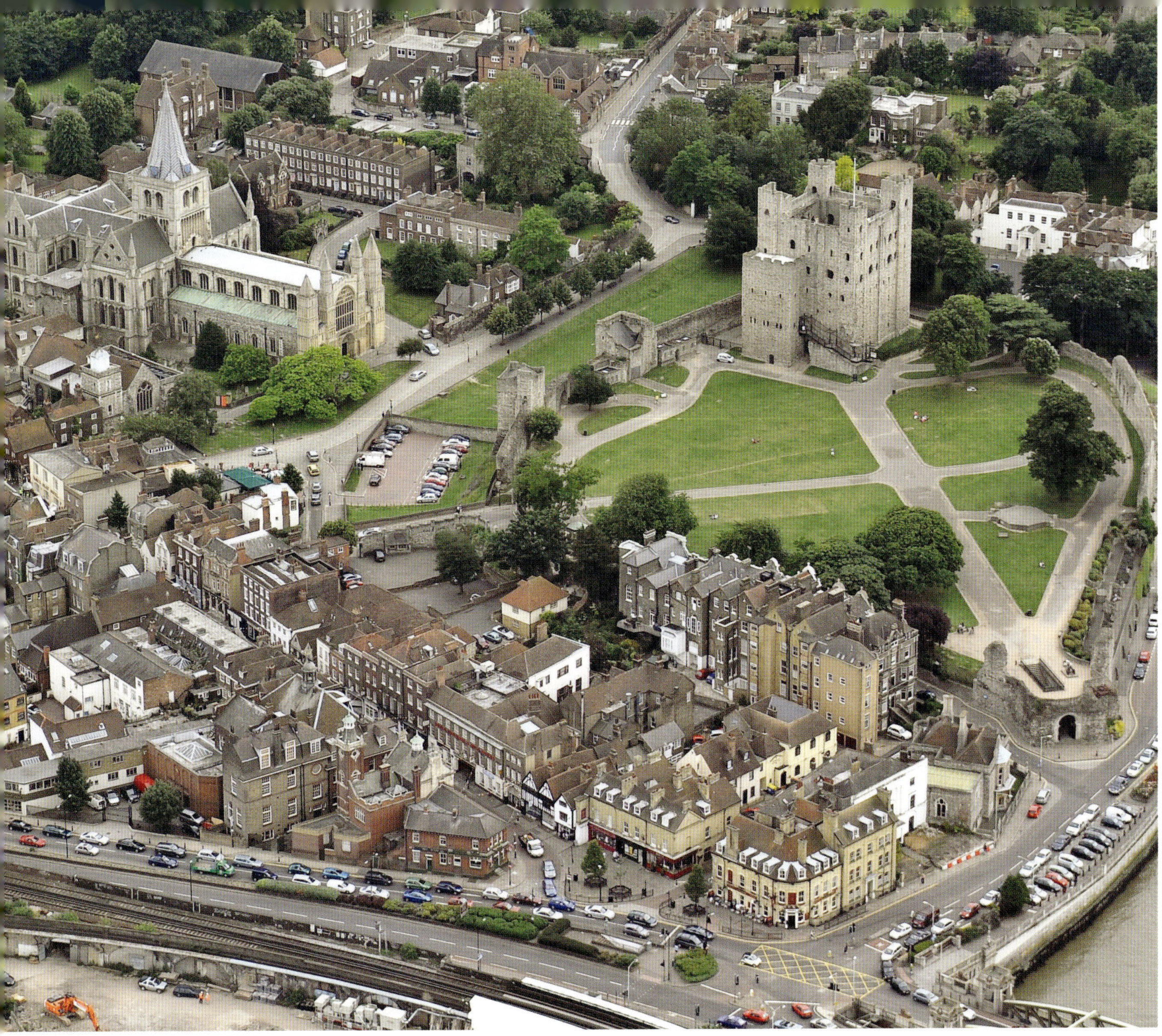

CHATHAM

Opposite Rochester, on the southern bank of the river Medway, lies Chatham and its historic dockyard (below). Commissioned by Henry VIII, the royal docks were the birthplace of the British Navy: numerous warships were built at Chatham and, by the outbreak of the Second World War, over 13,000 people worked there.

The closure of the docks was announced in 1981 but the site, with its fine collection of Georgian buildings, is now a superb visitor attraction charting the history of British shipbuilding. Three historic warships are docked – the HMS *Cavalier*, HMS *Ocelot* and HMS *Gannet* – and there is a collection of historic lifeboats. Also located within the dockyard is a museum charting the history of the Royal Naval Auxiliary Service (RNXS) and the *Kingswear Castle*, Britain's last coal-fired paddle steamer on which visitors can cruise the Medway in the summer months.

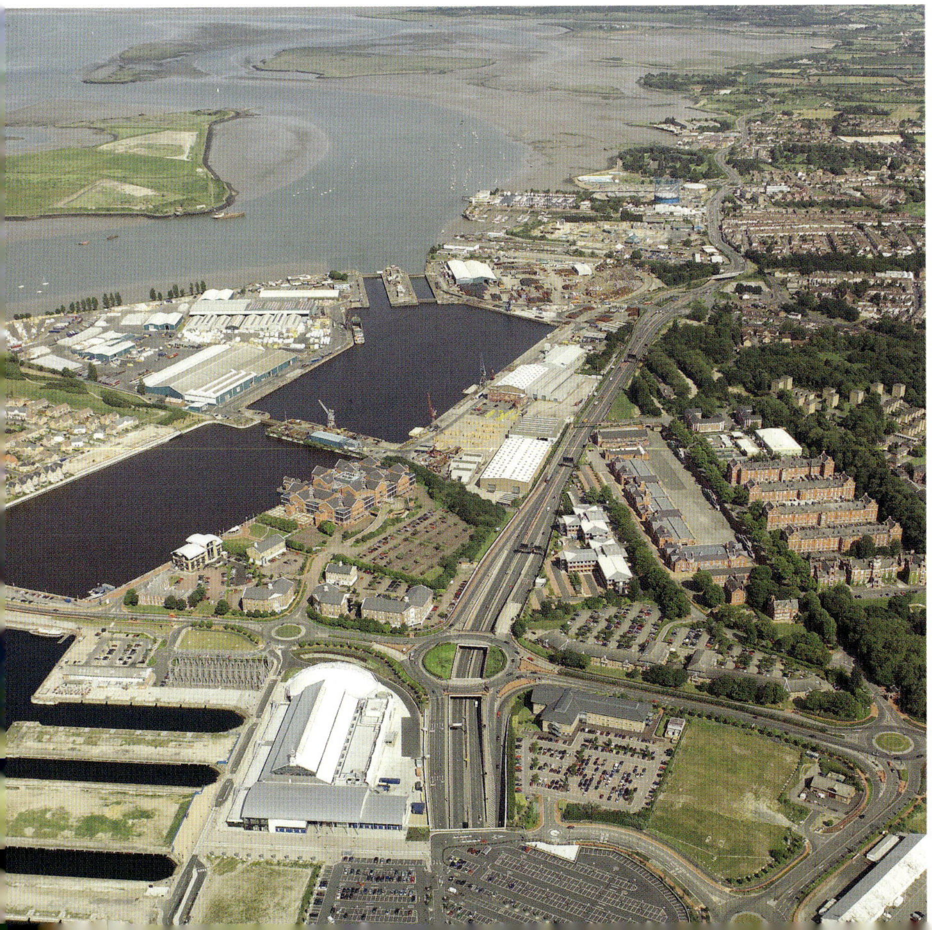

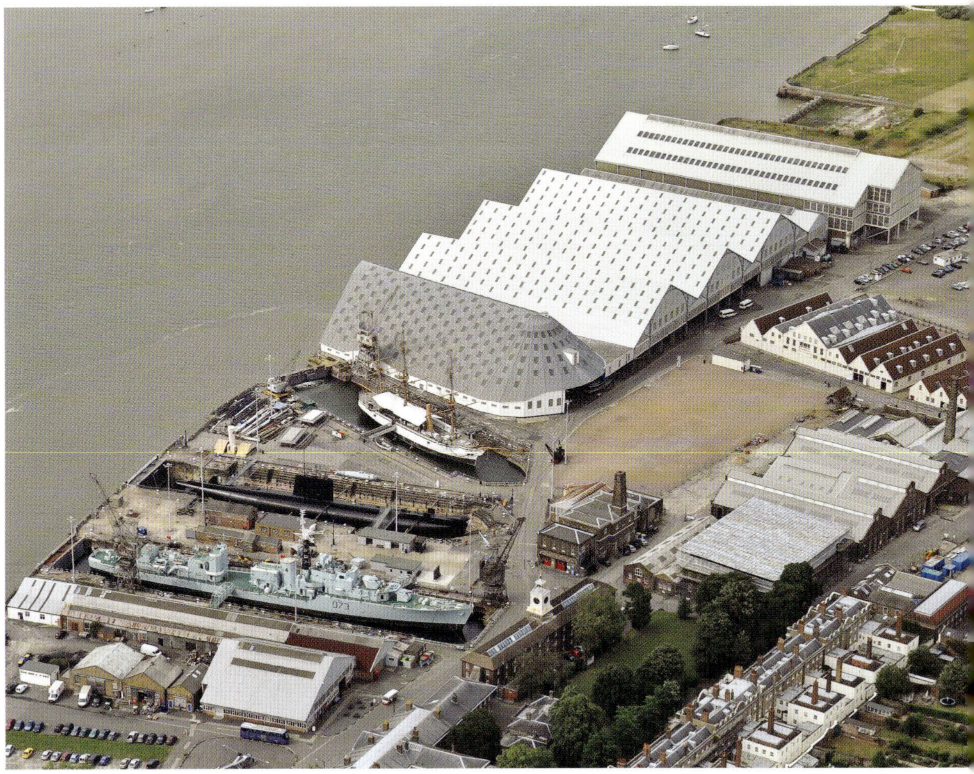

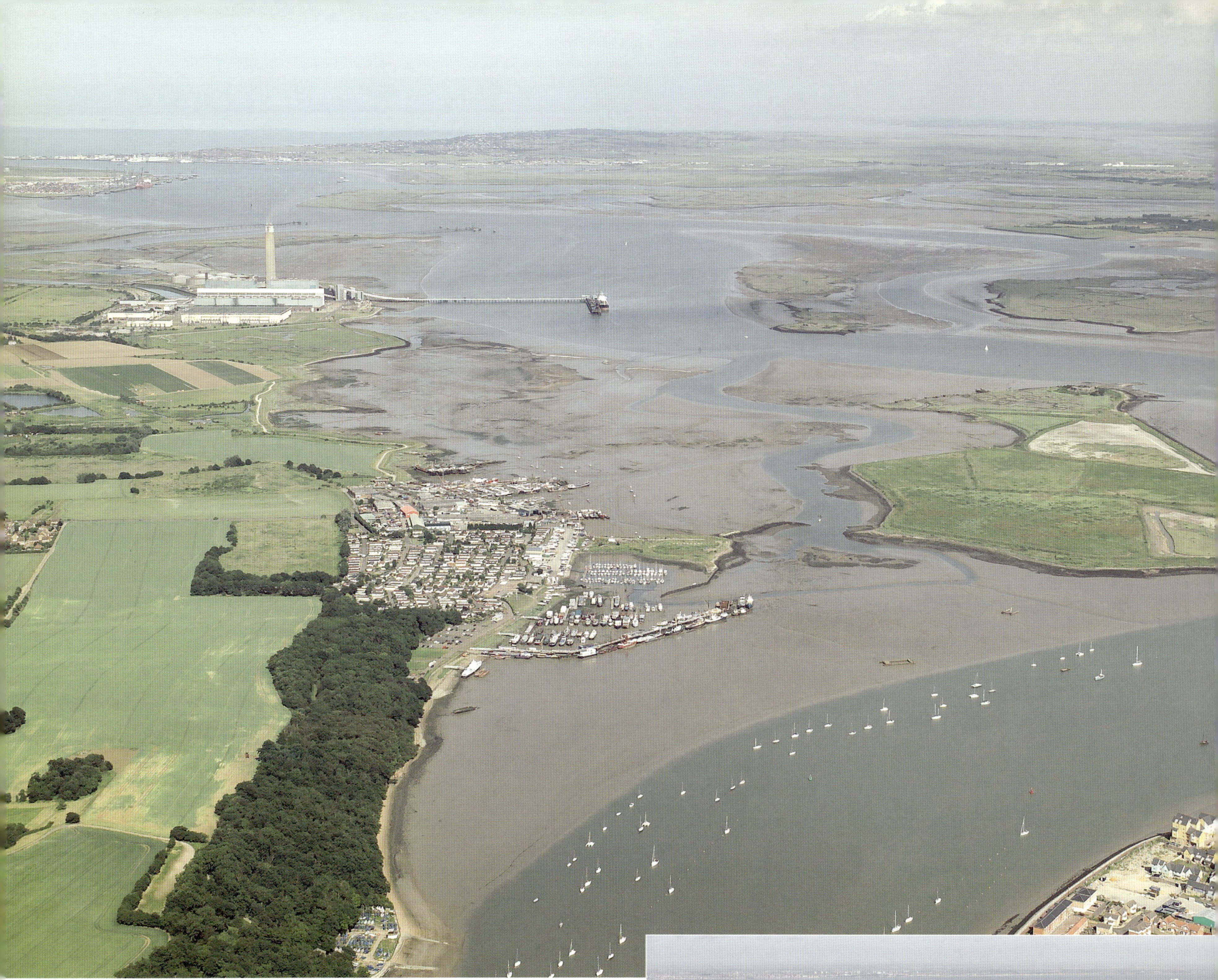

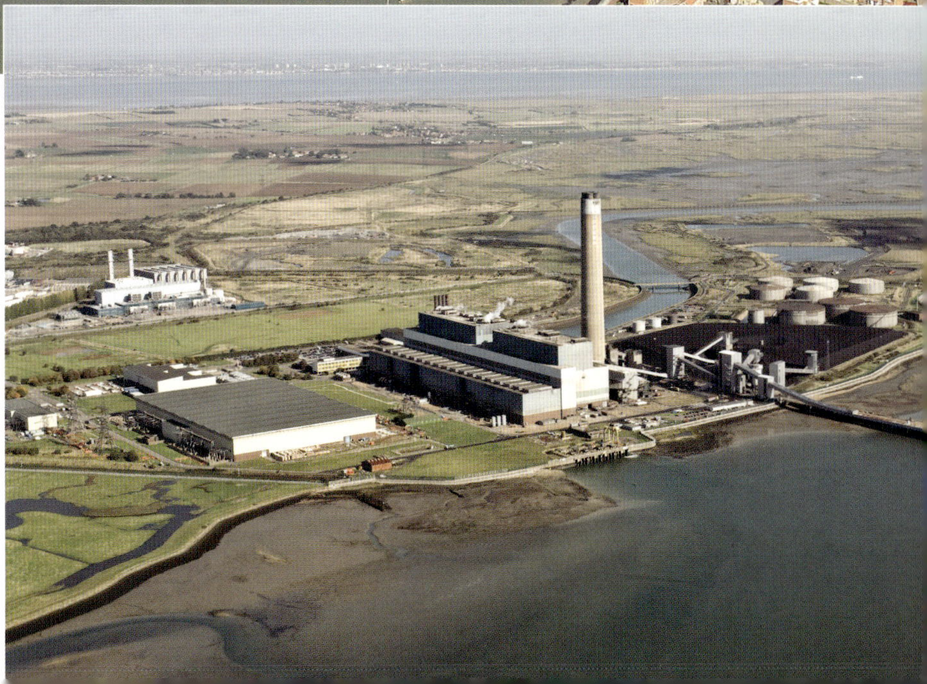

MEDWAY

The Hoo Peninsula lies to the north of the Medway and separates the Thames and Medway estuaries. Hoo is an Old English word meaning spur of land and the land forms part of the North Kent Marshes including several Sites of Special Scientific Interest (SSSIs). Hoo St Werburgh and Kingsnorth Power Station (right) lie on the southern edge of the peninsula. Opened in 1967, the power station was built on ground 4ft (1.2m) below the highest tide and water levels have since risen. Controversial plans to build a new coal-fired power station here have been shelved after protests from environmental campaigners concerned about CO_2 emissions.

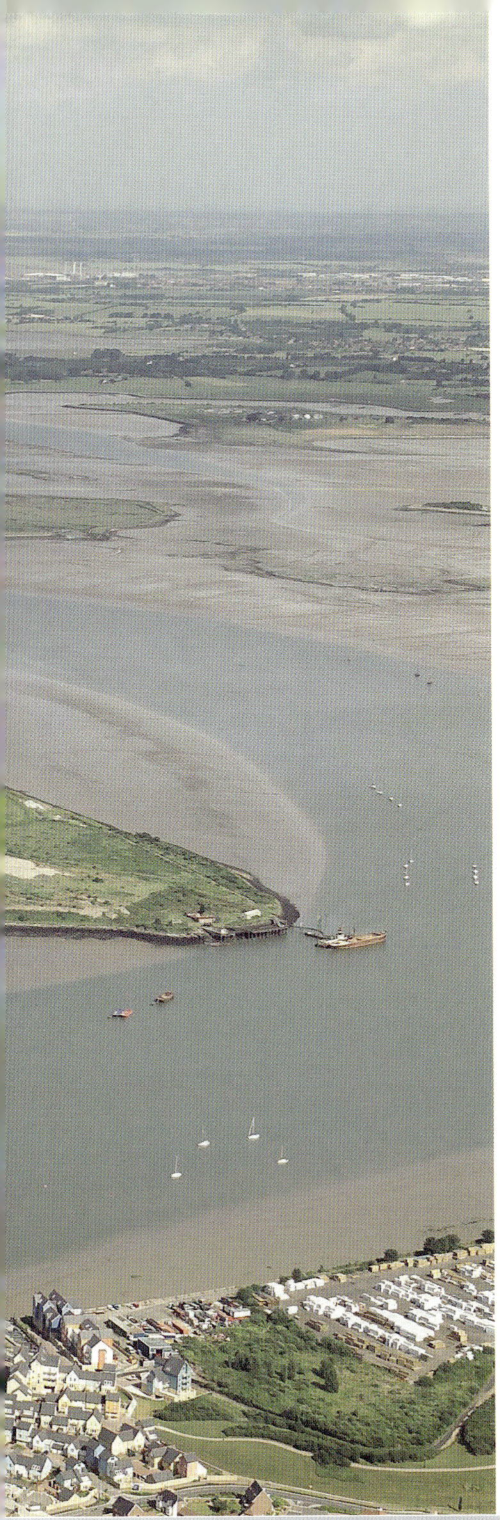

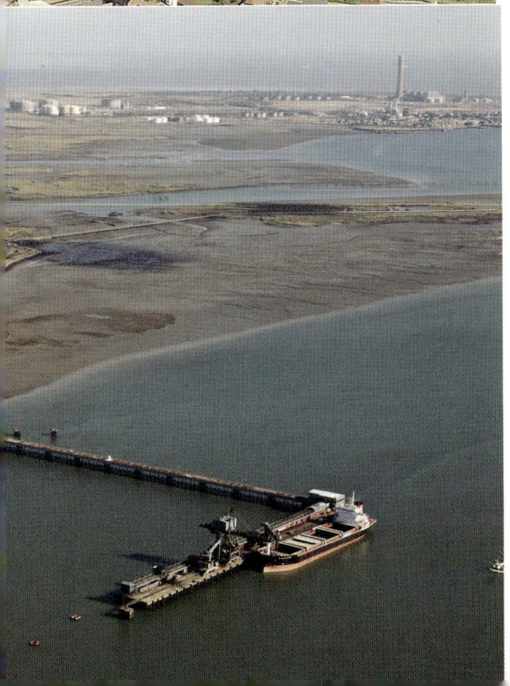

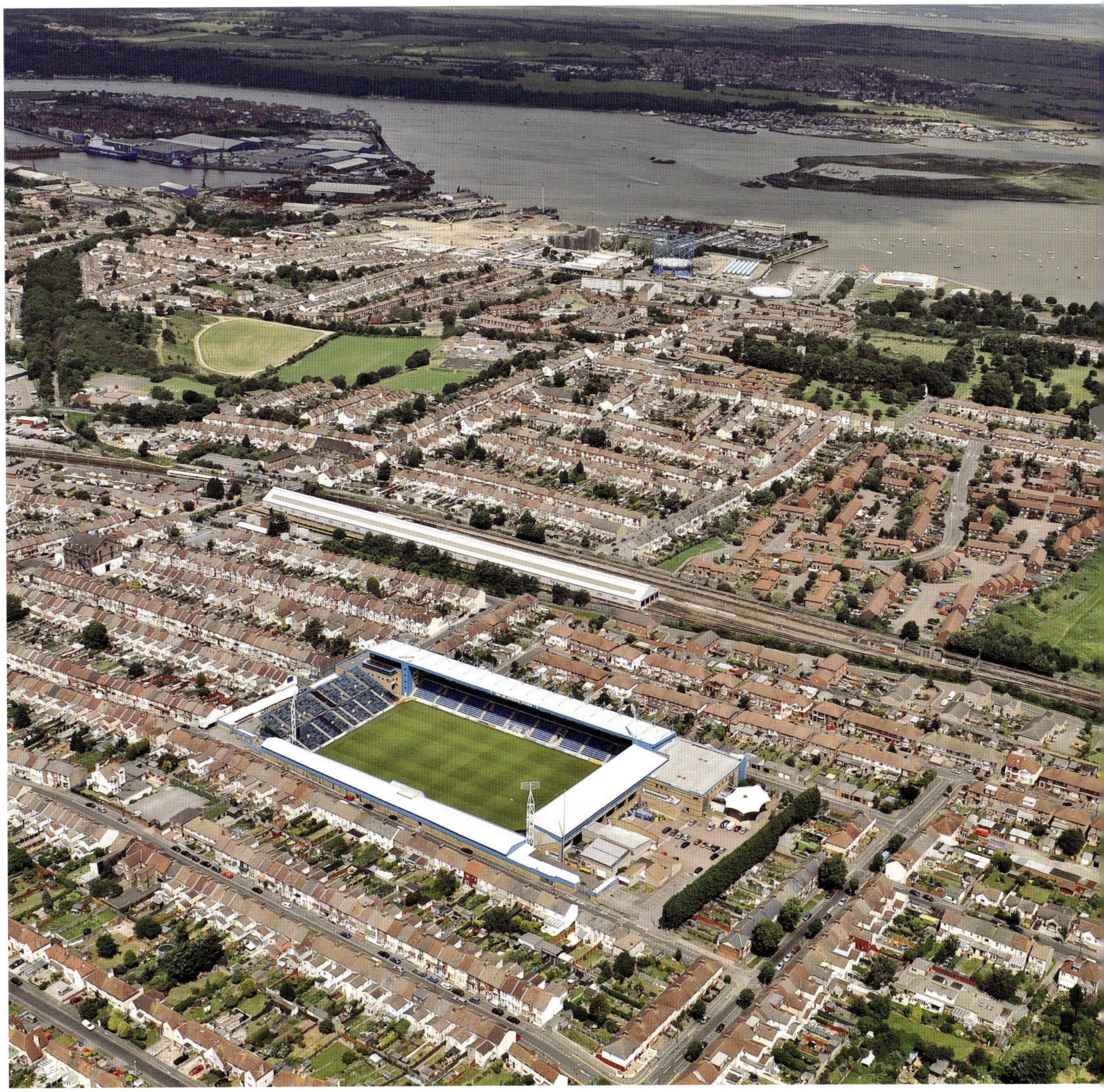

GILLINGHAM

Gillingham is probably best known for its football club (above), founded in 1893 and the only football club in the county of Kent to maintain a place in the Football League. Gillingham FC reached the first division in the year 2000 and notable players have included Steve Bruce and Glenn Roeder. The club's home is Priestfield Stadium, known simply as Priestfield. Gillingham is also the birthplace of the navigator Will Adams, who travelled to Japan in the 17th century and is believed to be the first westerner to have visited that country. James Clavell based the character of John Blackthorne on Adams in his bestselling book, *Shogun*. Most of the historic dockyard at Chatham is actually located in Gillingham as well as the Royal School of Military Engineering. The A289 disappears into the Medway Tunnel at Gillingham, one of only two immersed tube tunnels in Britain, the other being at Conwy. Across the water from Gillingham lies Hoo Island, a dredging deposition centre since the 1900s that handles over 500,000 tonnes of material a year in order to maintain water navigation.

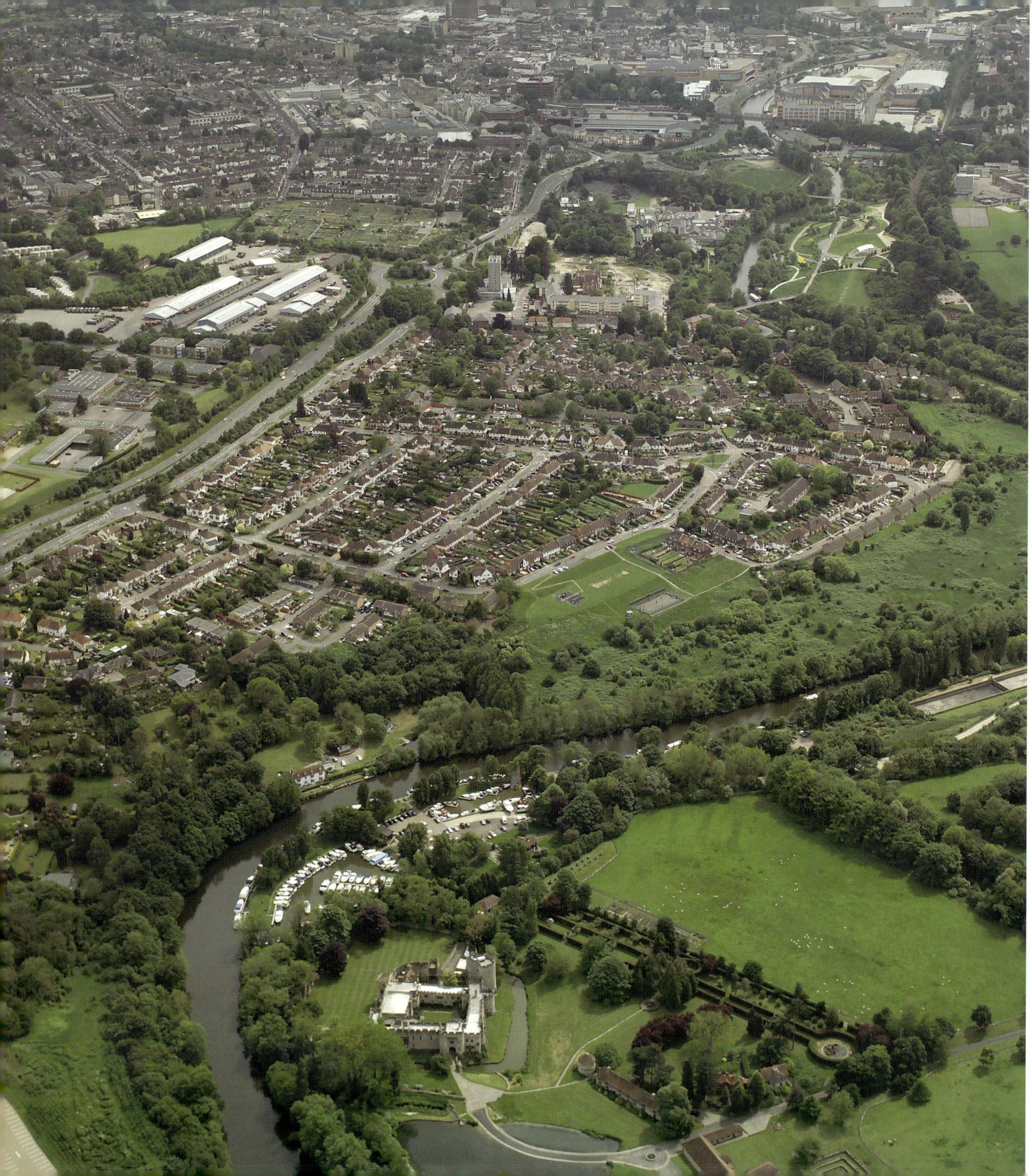

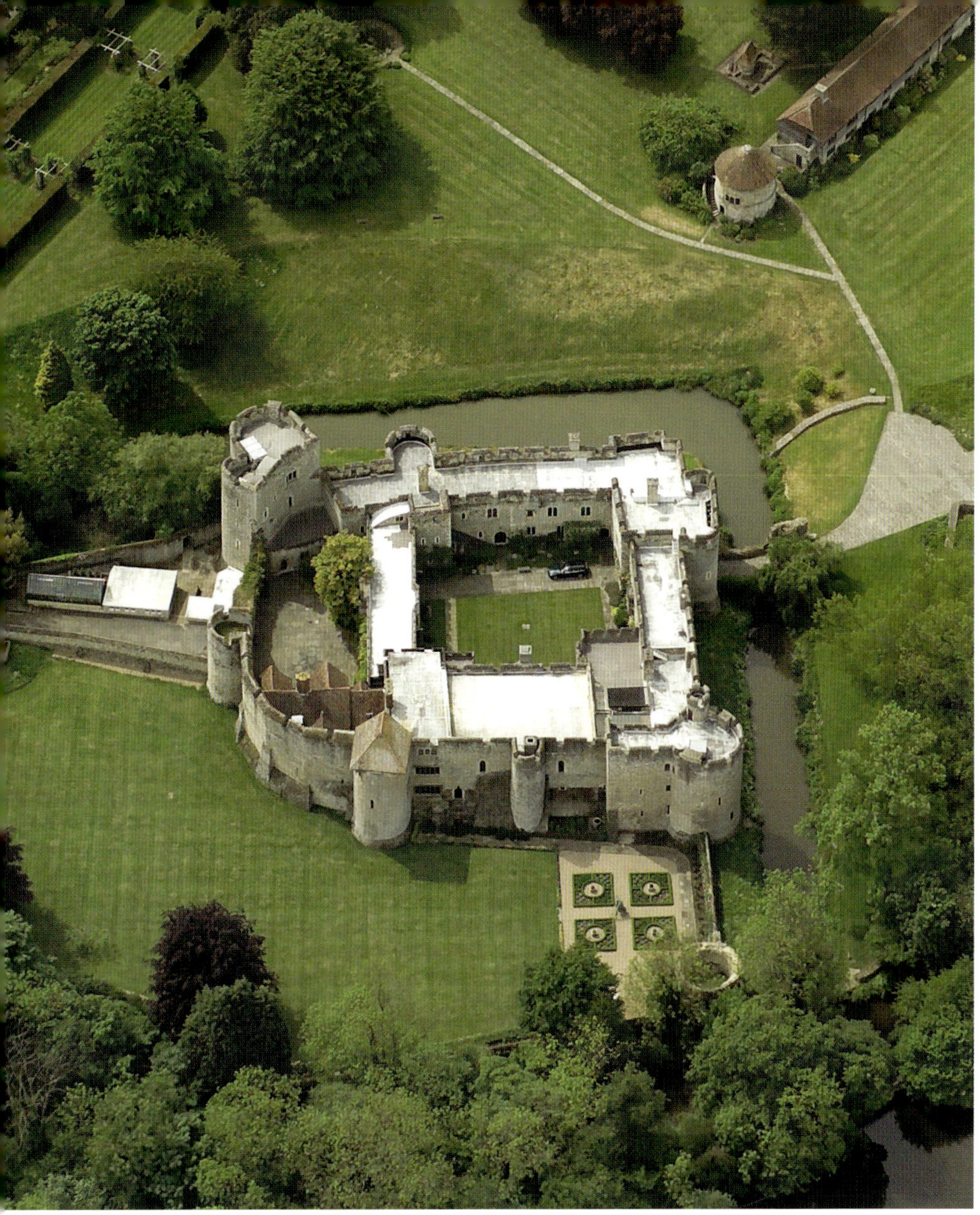

MAIDSTONE

Alongside the river Medway, in the heart of the "Garden of England", lies Maidstone (below), the county town of Kent. Maidstone was once a centre for brewing and papermaking and the Fremlin Walk shopping centre is built on the site of a former brewery. Today the area is still a base for the paper and packaging industry with Europe's largest newspaper recycling plant at Aylesford on the north-west side of Maidstone. HM Prison Maidstone is found at the north edge of town. Built to the most advanced design of its time, the prison was completed in 1819 from local Kentish ragstone. Its exterior was shown in the title sequence of the 1970s BBC series, *Porridge*. Also north of Maidstone lies Allington Castle (left and far left), a stone-built moated castle now a private home. Originally a manor house, it was turned into a fortified castle by Stephen de Penchester in 1281 and restored in 1905.

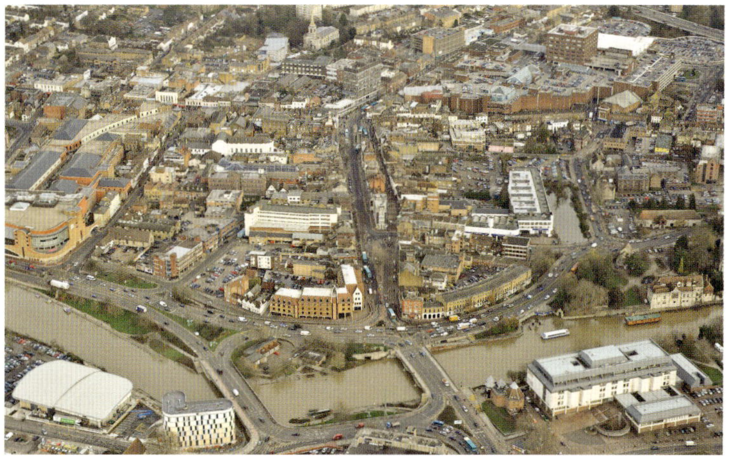

LEEDS CASTLE

Situated on two islands on the river Len, romantic Leeds Castle (right) has, for centuries, been a home for royalty, lords and ladies. The present building dates from 1119, but there has been a castle on the site since 857. Edward I rebuilt and extended the castle, adding a barbican and D-shaped tower, known as the "gloriette", on the smaller of the two islands. Henry VIII further modernised it in 1517. Parts of the present banqueting hall date from that period and further restoration work took place in the 19th century.

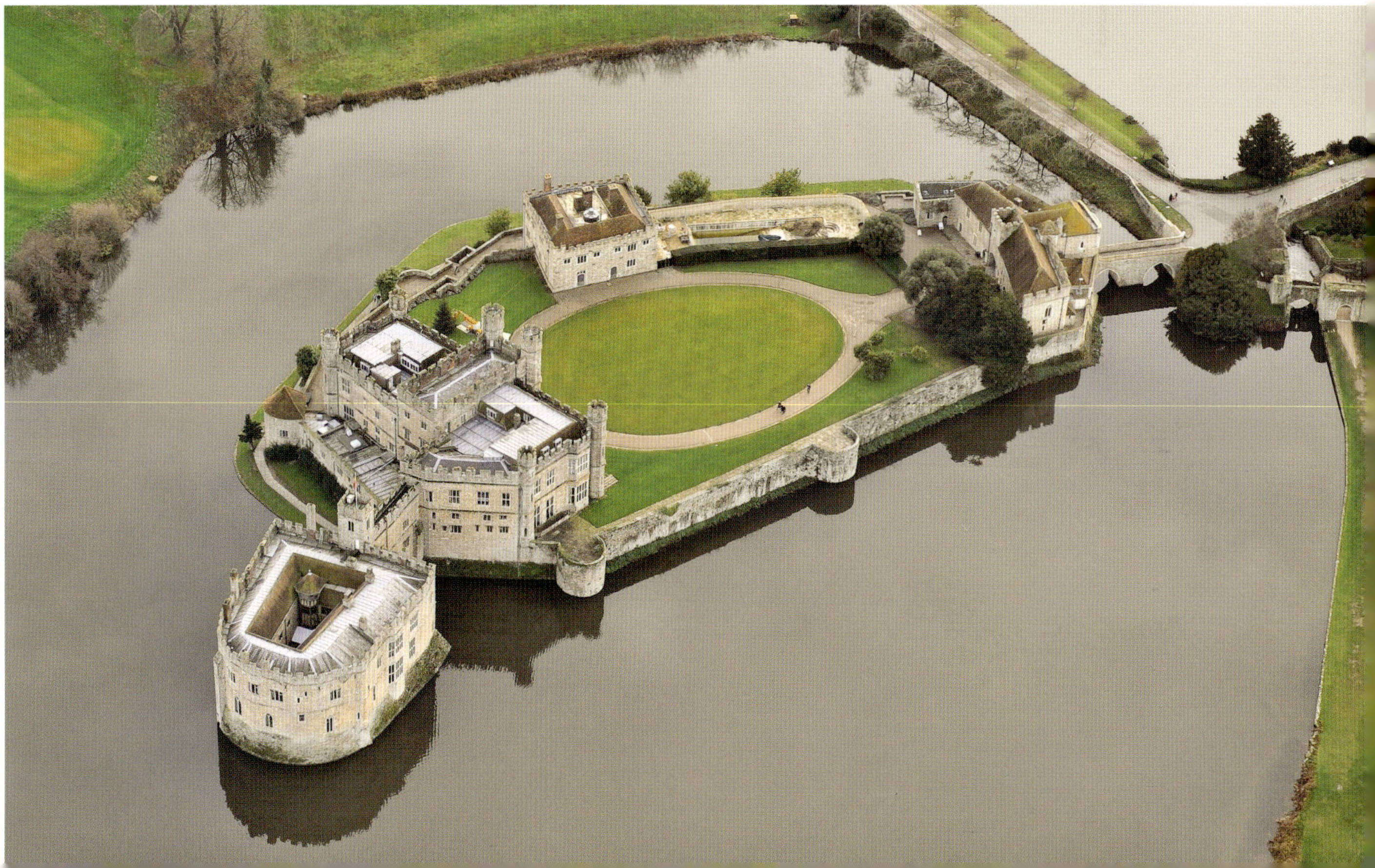

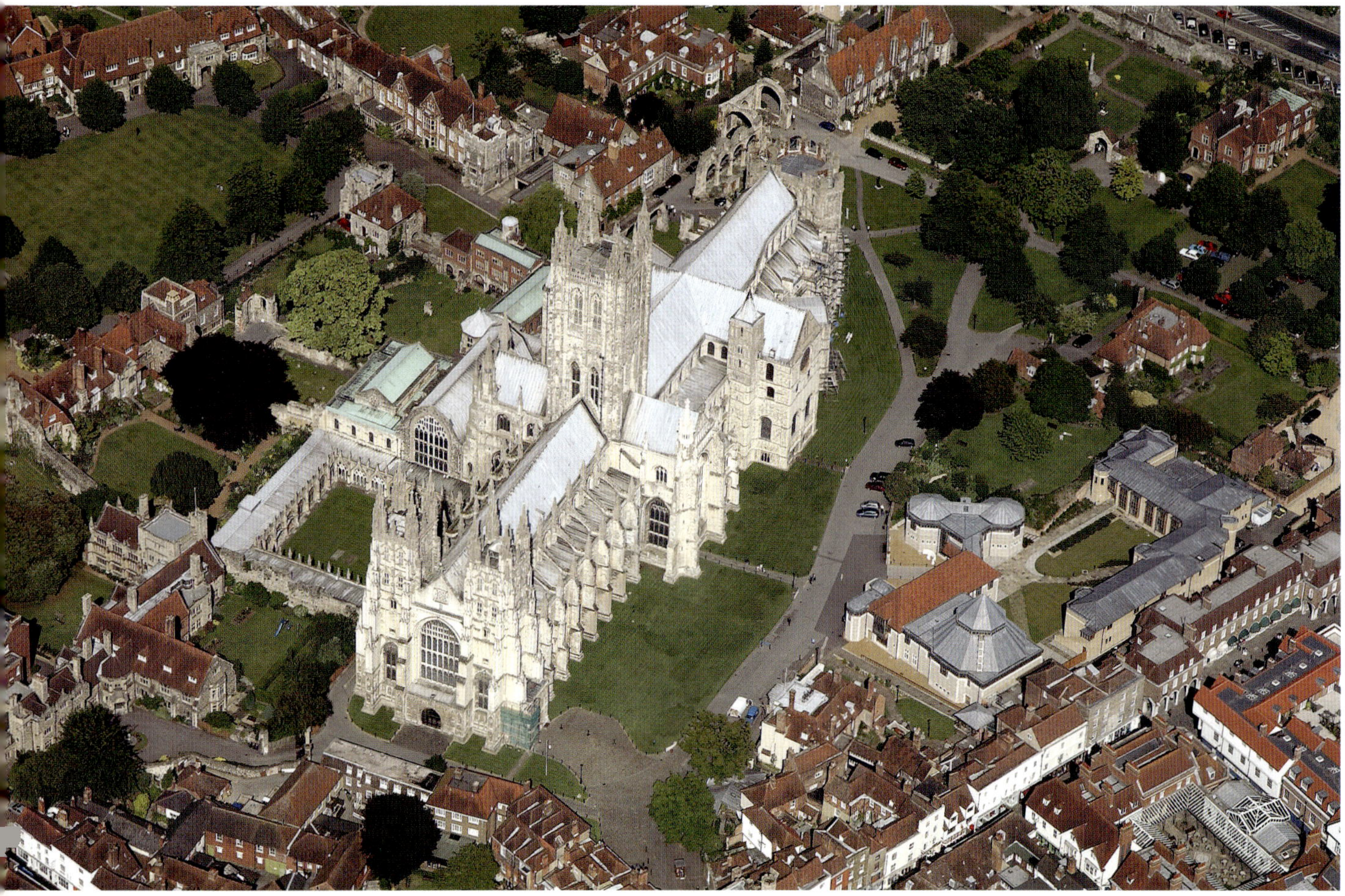

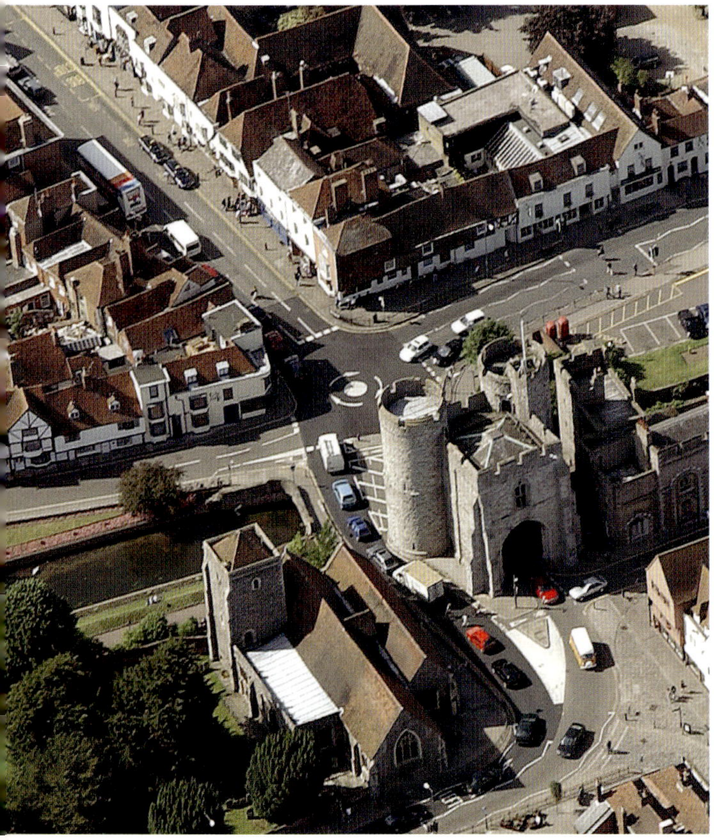

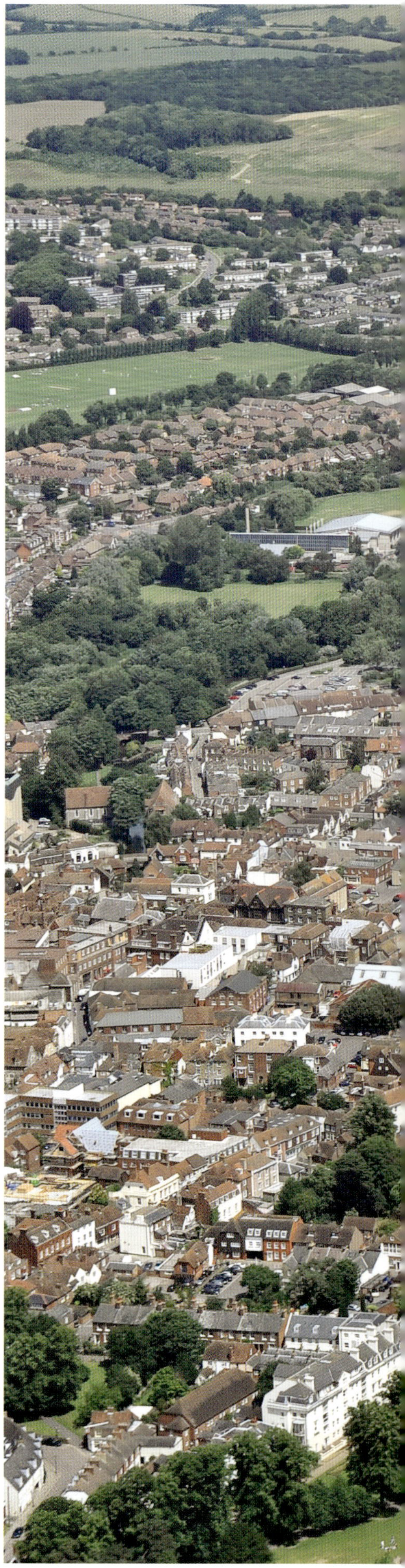

CANTERBURY

St Augustine of Rome made Canterbury his missionary base in 597, making it one of the earliest centres of Christianity in Britain. The city takes its name from *Cantwareburh*, old English for "fortress of the men of Kent". The dramatic cathedral, which dominates the town, combines a mixture of Gothic and Perpendicular styles and was built in the 11th century. King Henry II appointed his friend Thomas à Becket as Archbishop of Canterbury in 1162 but when Becket vigorously defended the church against royal intervention, Henry called the Archbishop a "meddlesome priest" and on December 20, 1170 he was murdered at the altar by four knights who thought they were carrying out Henry's wishes. Becket was declared a martyr and saint and Canterbury became one of the most popular destinations for pilgrimage in the Middle Ages. Chaucer's *Canterbury Tales* recounts the stories of a group of pilgrims on their journey from London to the cathedral. Canterbury's cathedral, St Martin's (England's oldest church) and the ruins of St Augustine's abbey are now a World Heritage Site. The current Archbishop of Canterbury, Dr Rowan Williams, is head of the Anglican Communion which has 70m followers worldwide. The Westgate Tower (left), once the city jail, is the only tower left in the city wall and is now a museum.

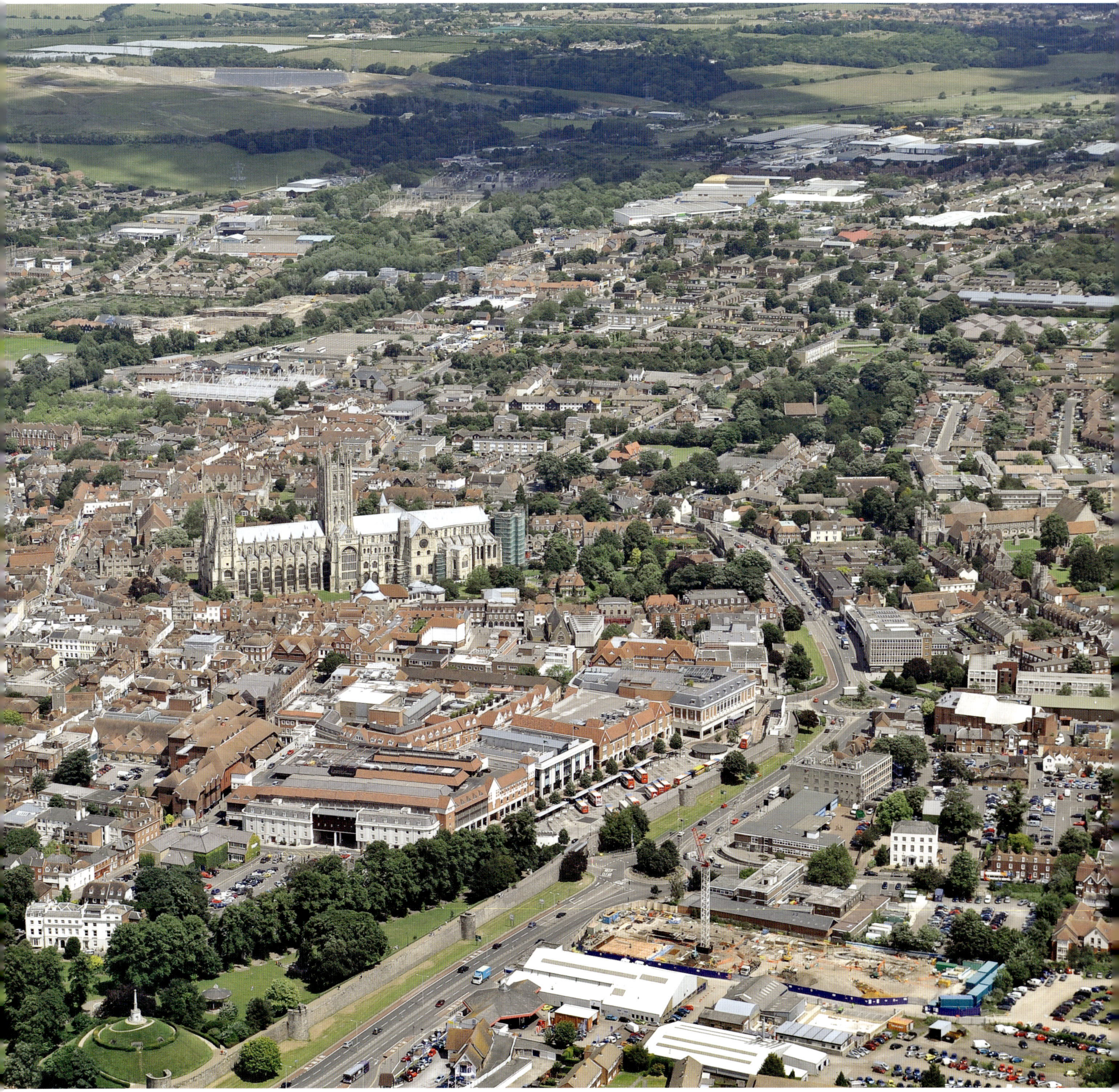

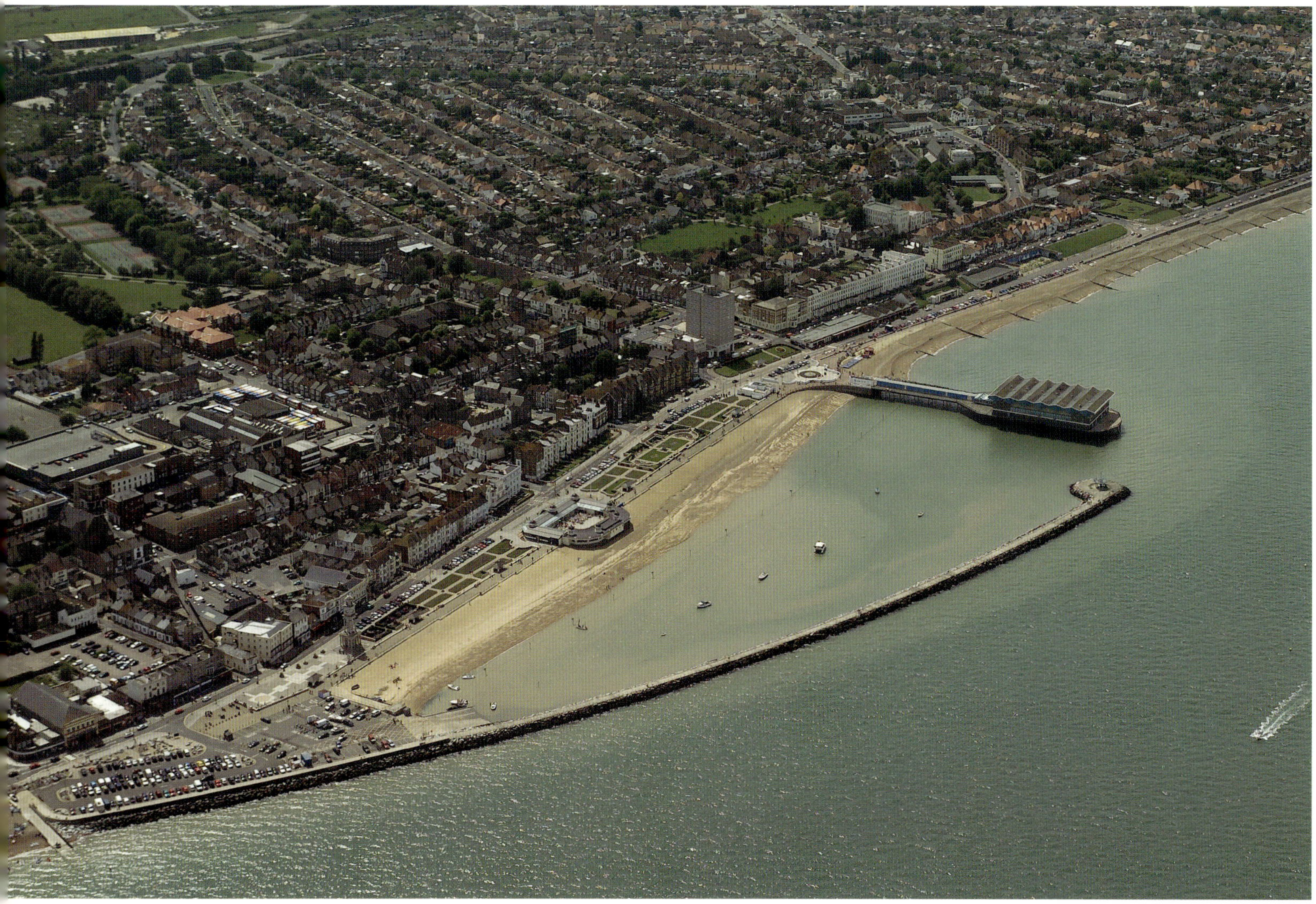

HERNE BAY

The pleasure pier and Central Parade at Herne Bay (above) were critical to the town's growth as a seaside resort in the early 19th century. Built by London investors, the town grew rapidly during this time nearly doubling in size between 1881 and 1901. During stormy weather the sea levels can rise by up to 6.5ft (2m) and flooding has prevented the redevelopment of the town centre. Coastal defences have been added including sea walls, groynes, a shingle beach and an offshore breakwater known as Neptune's Arm, which has allowed seafront regeneration. Currently under construction, the Thanet Wind Farm (left) lies off the coast from Margate and is part of the planned London Array, set to be the world's largest offshore wind farm covering 90 square miles (230sq km). The Thanet project is expected to have a total capacity of up to 300 MW, sufficient to supply approximately 240,000 homes.

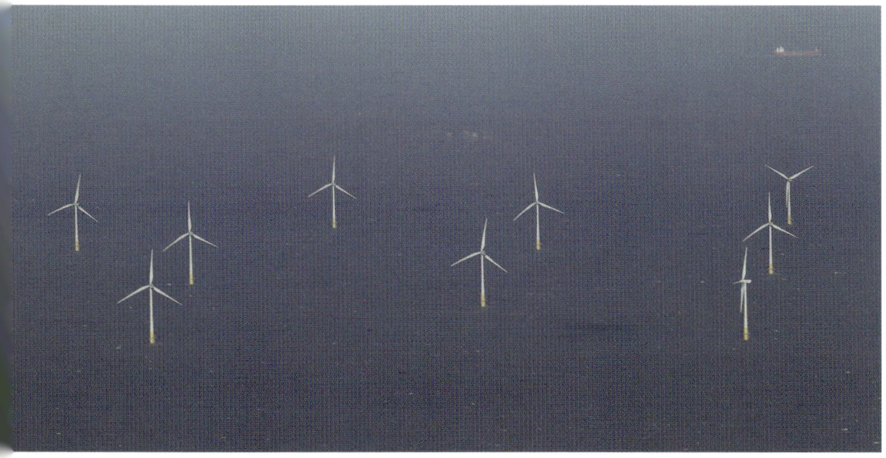

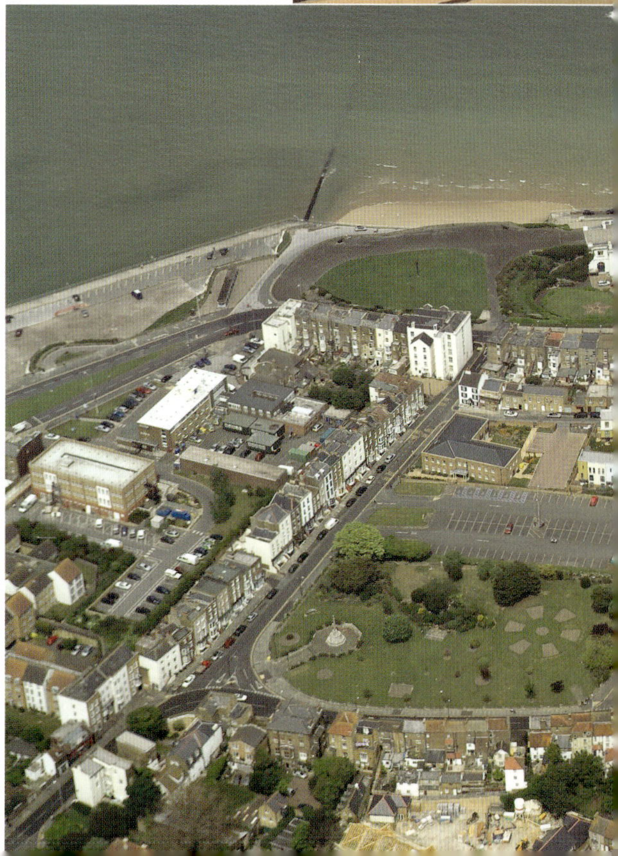

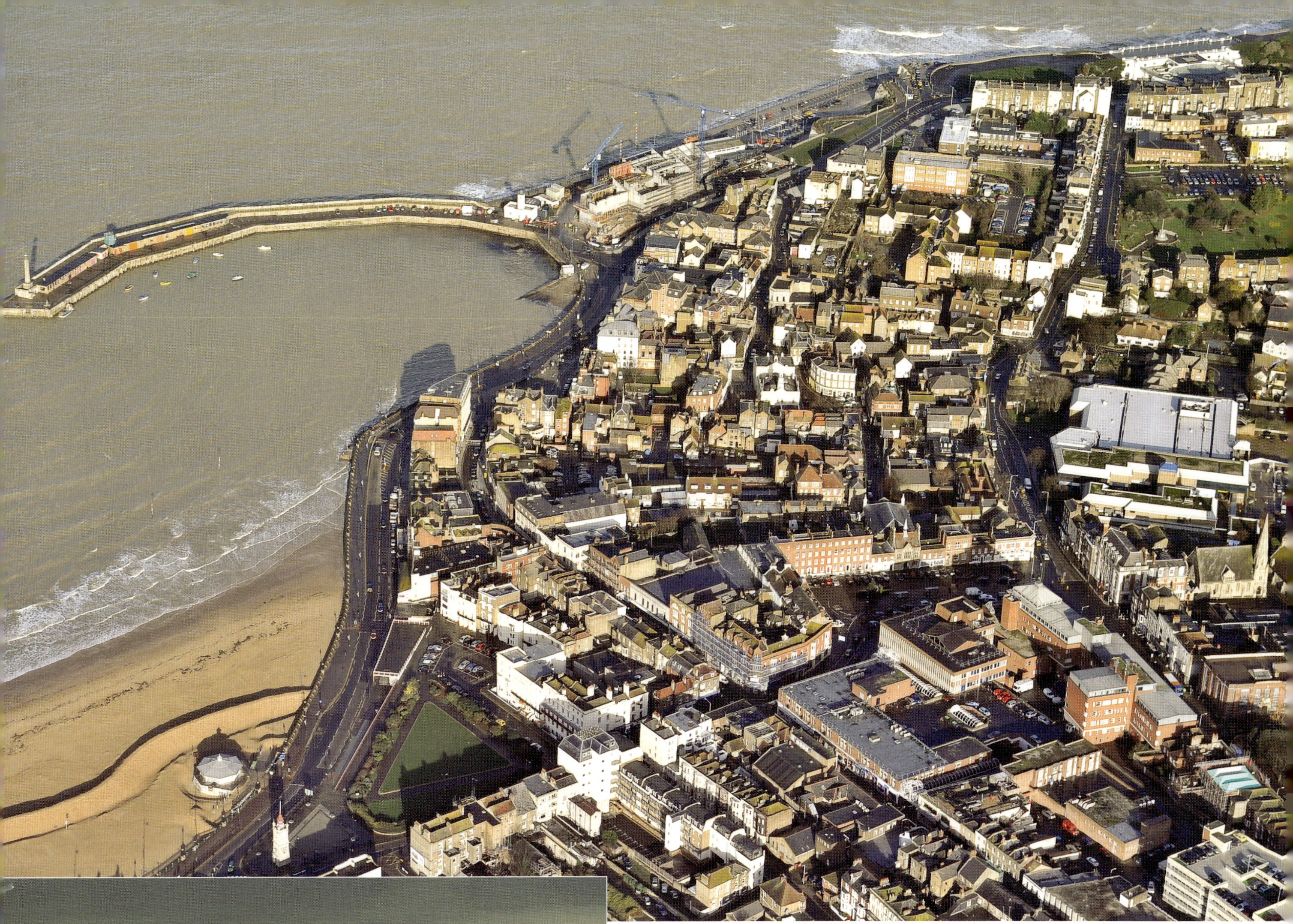

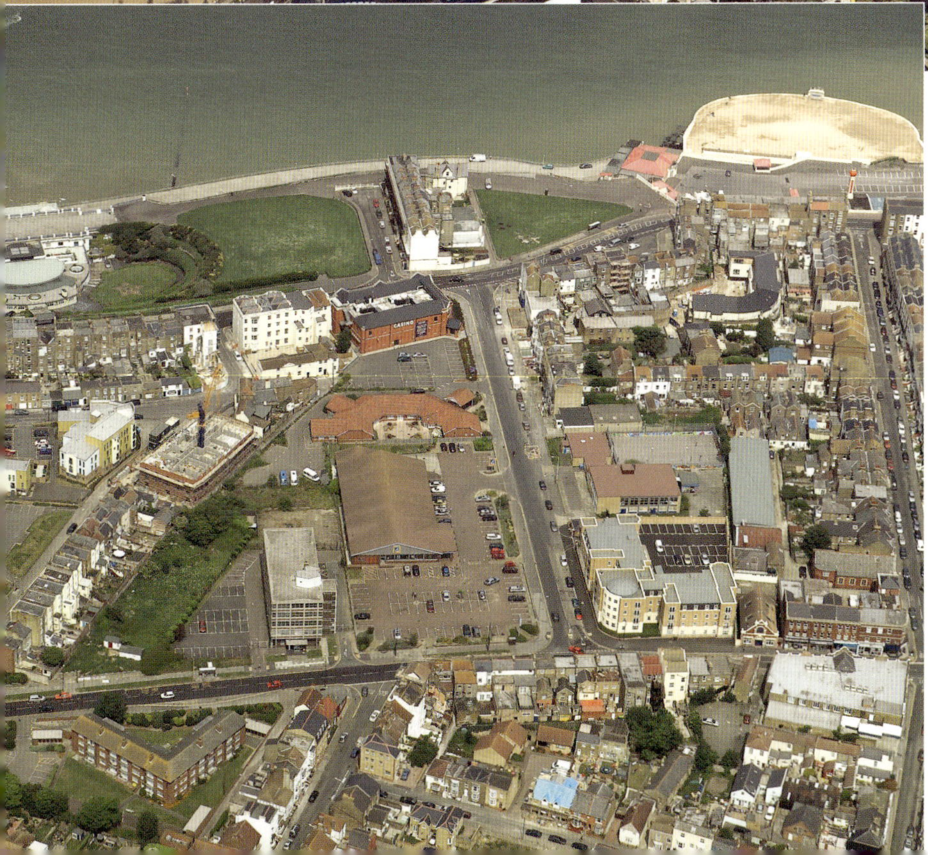

Margate

Close to Kent's most easterly point on the Isle of Thanet lies Margate (above and left), a town with a proud maritime tradition. A leading seaside resort for over 250 years, the beaches at Margate Sands have long attracted Londoners looking for sea, sun and sand. Entertainment included theatre productions at the Winter Gardens, opened in 1911. But the rise of package holidays and the ravages of the North Sea have led more recently to a decline in Margate's fortunes and some key features from its Victorian heyday are in disrepair. The Victorian pier was destroyed by a storm in 1978 and the cliff railway to Cliftonville Lido, a sea bathing pool, was closed in the 1970s. But recent investment is likely to see significant changes in the town. The Dreamland Amusement Park, which contains a wooden rollercoaster, the second oldest scenic railway surviving in the world, is threatened with closure but a Trust has been established to campaign for the park's restoration. One of the south-east's largest art galleries outside London, the Turner Contemporary, is due to open in 2011.

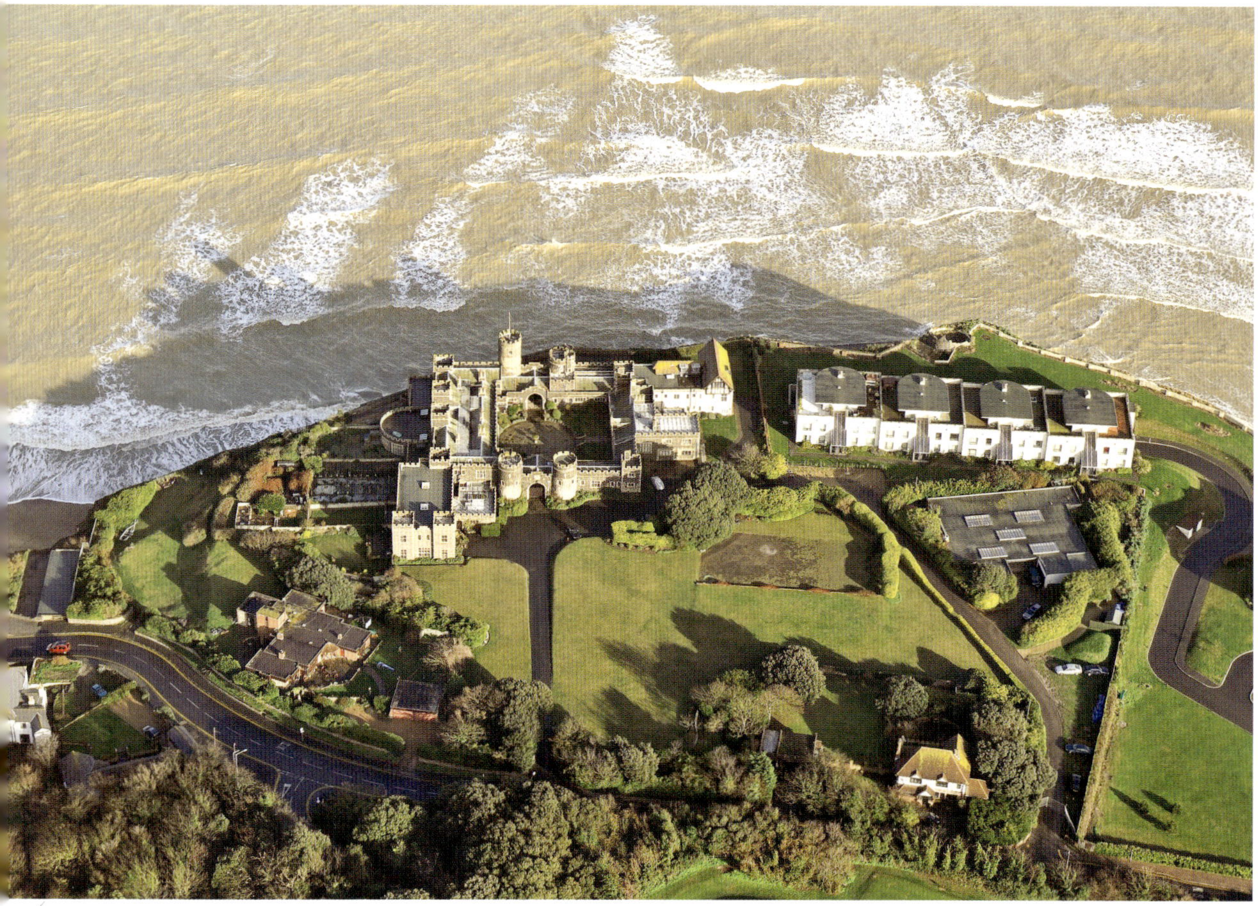

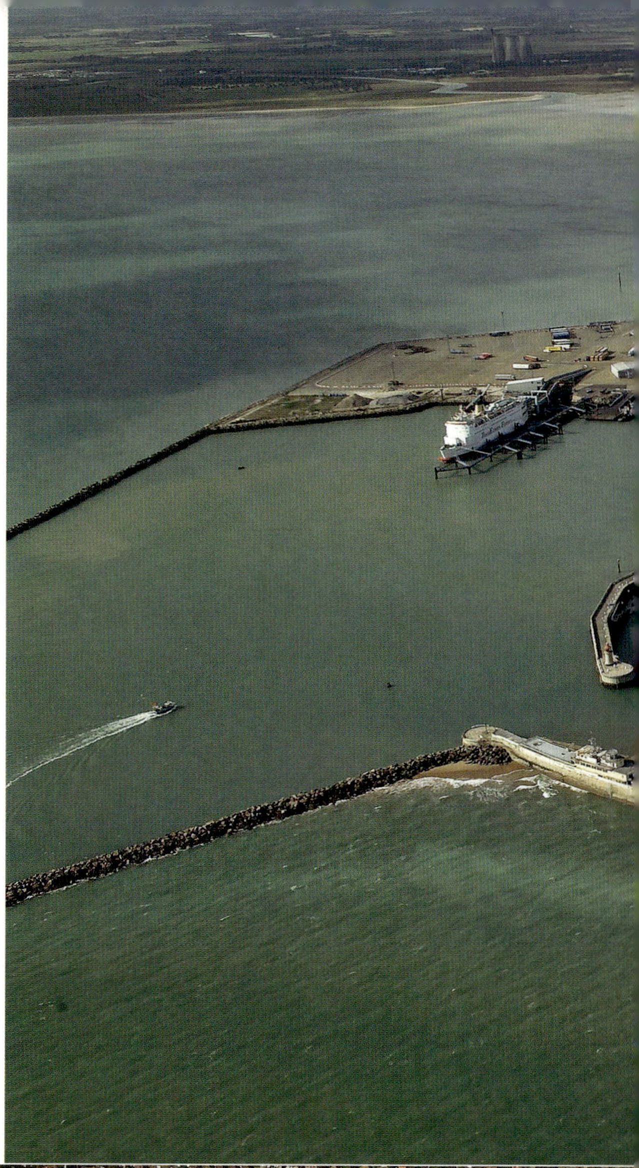

Broadstairs

Like Margate, Broadstairs (right) was a traditional holiday destination during the Victorian era. Described as "The Jewel in Thanet's Crown", it was named after a flight of broad stairs carved into the white chalk leading from the sands to a 12th century shrine on the cliffs above. With seven bays of golden sand, Broadstairs continues to attract holidaymakers. Brightly coloured beach huts line the shore of Viking Bay, which is overlooked by the Victoria Gardens and bandstand. Close to the pier stands Bleak House, Dickens' holiday retreat, whose name inspired the novel. Kingsgate Castle (above), overlooking Kingsgate Bay, was once the home of Lord Holland and has now been converted into private residences.

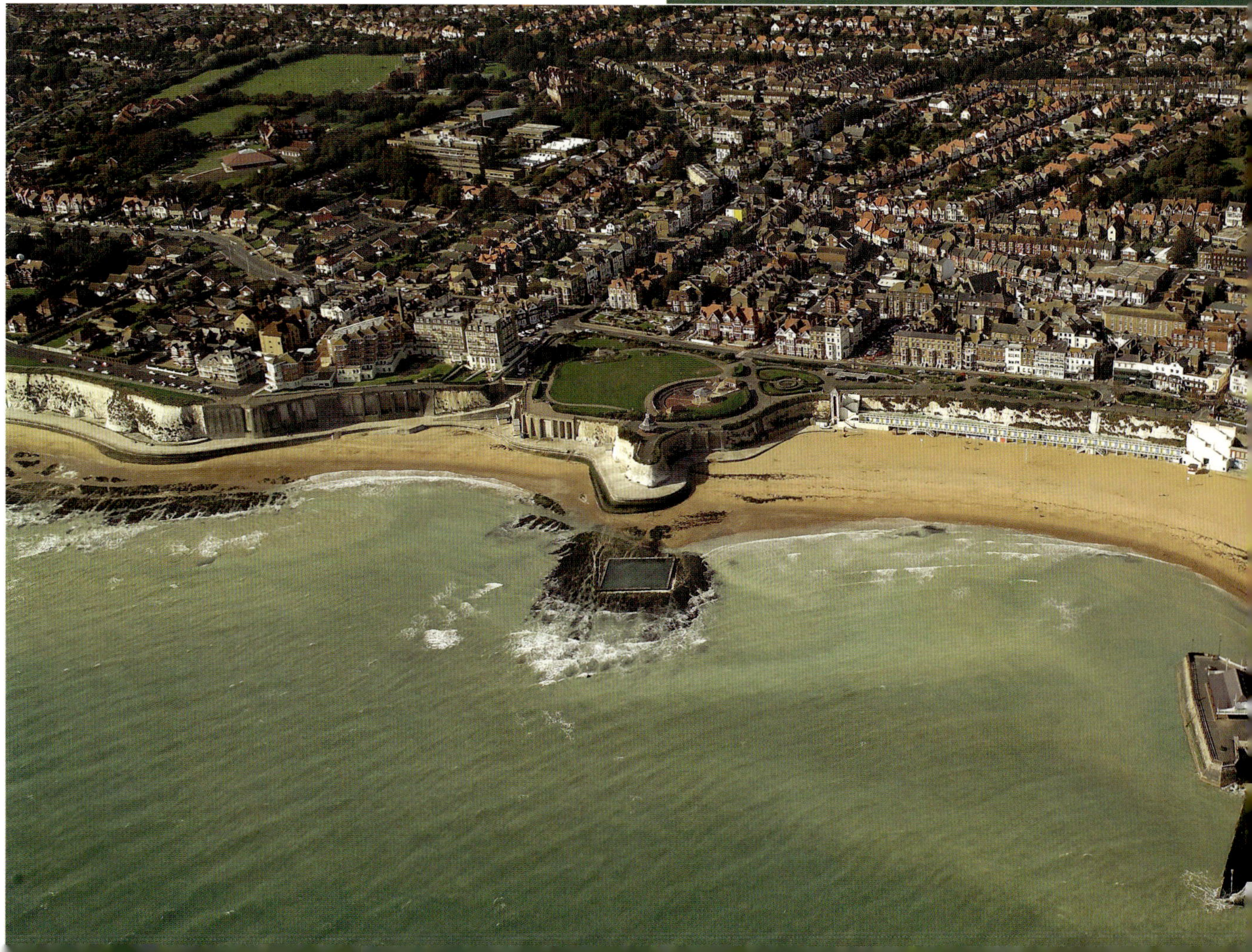

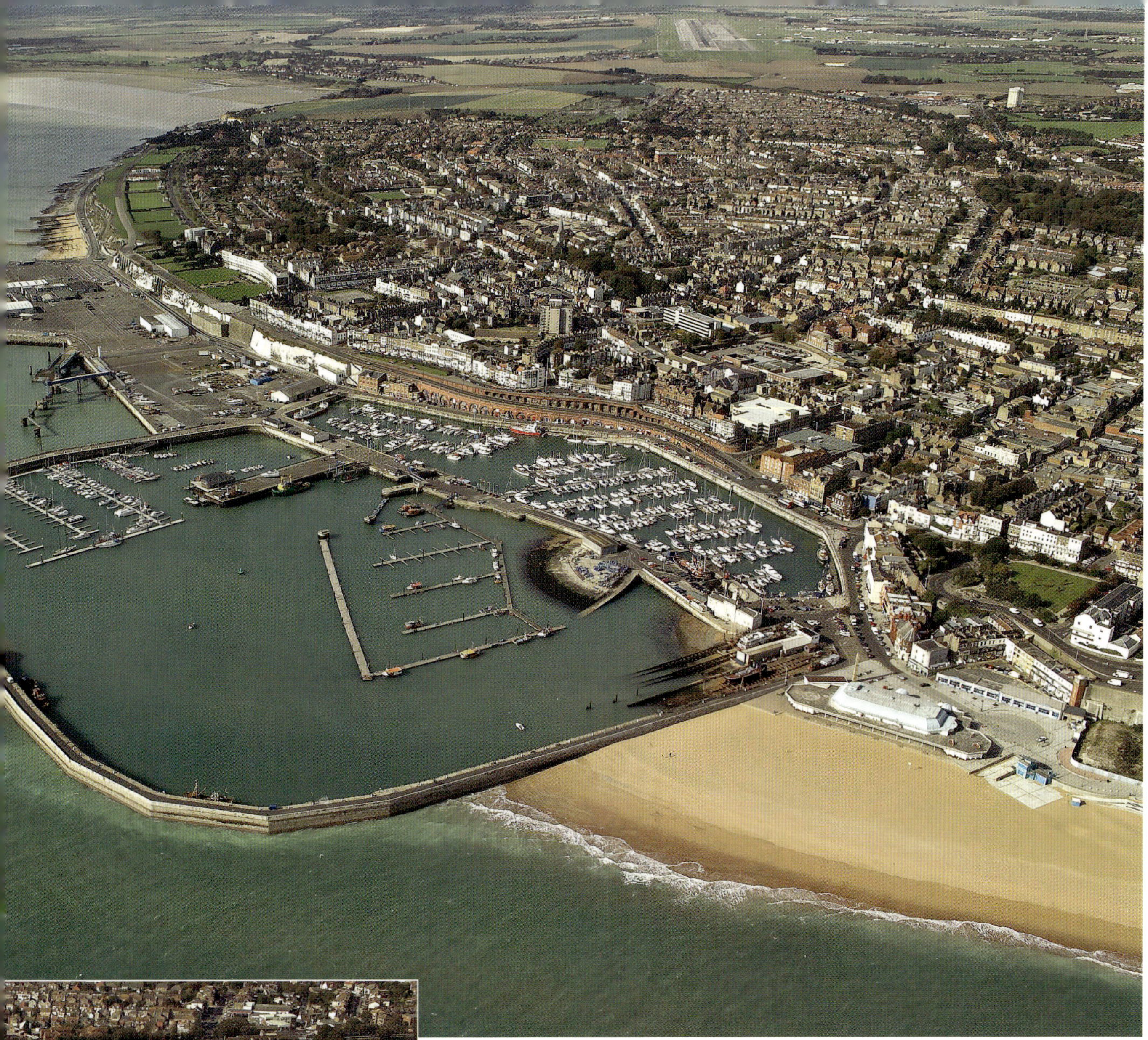

RAMSGATE

A popular 19th century seaside town and fishing community, Ramsgate (left) is a member of the ancient Confederation of Cinque Ports. The Port today provides the only passenger ferry service between England and Belgium, with up to eight sailings a day between Ramsgate and Ostend. Five ships currently undertake up to 20 crossings a day of car and freight services. The Royal Harbour, with its graceful Victorian arches, sees many yachts visiting from the Netherlands as it is the shortest crossing point. Built between 1749 and 1850 it is the only royal harbour in the UK and was used in the Napoleonic wars and during the evacuation of Dunkirk in the Second World War. Ramsgate Main Sands, a Blue Flag beach, is overlooked by the Promenade at East Cliff (below).

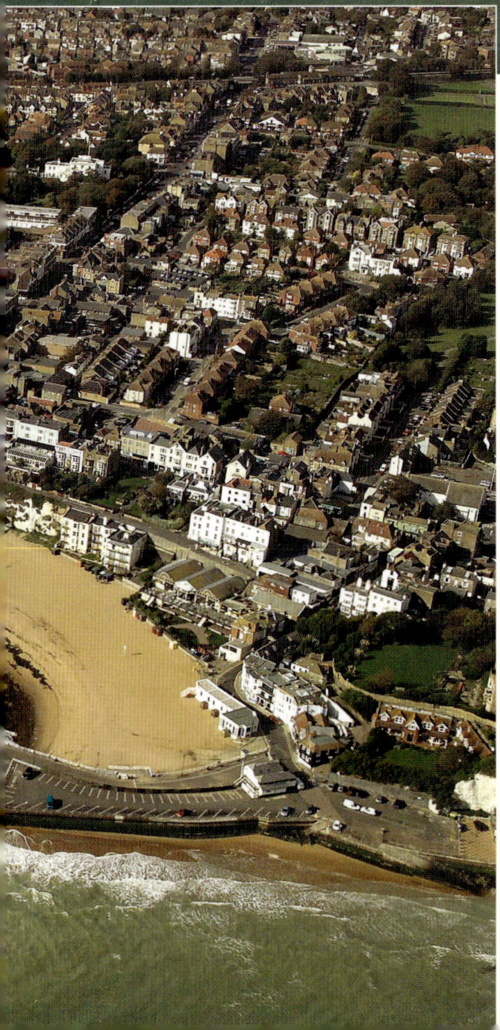

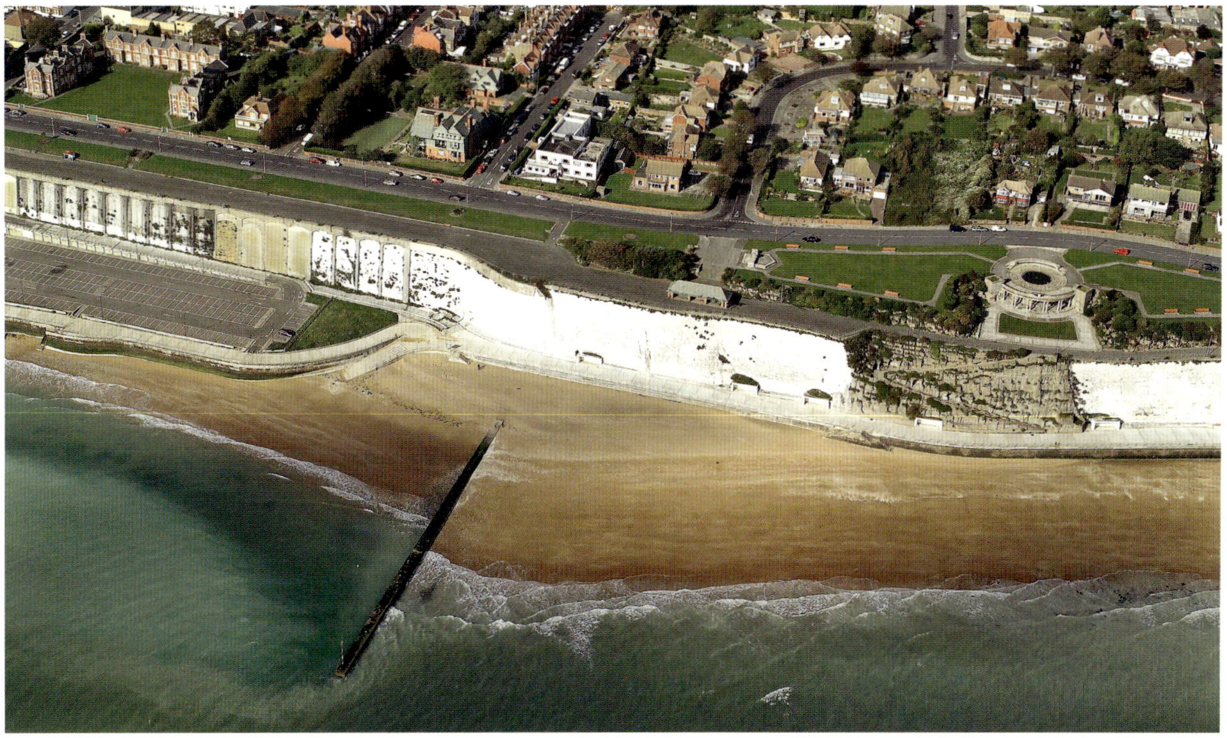

Dover

Known by the Romans as *Portus Dubris*, and one of the Cinque Ports, Dover is located at the English Channel's narrowest point, just 21 miles from Calais. Famous for its ferry terminal backed by dramatic white chalk cliffs, the port is overlooked by Dover Castle. It is the country's leading cross-channel ferry port and the busiest in northern Europe with over 2m freight vehicles, roughly 3m cars and 14m passengers using the terminal each year. There have been castles at Dover since the Iron Age, but the present building dates mostly from the time of Henry II. Beneath the castle there is a vast network of underground tunnels built during the Middle Ages but greatly extended during the Napoleonic Wars and used as recently as the Second World War. Between Dover and Folkestone at Capel-le-Ferne is the National Battle of Britain memorial (inset) designed in the shape of a propellor.

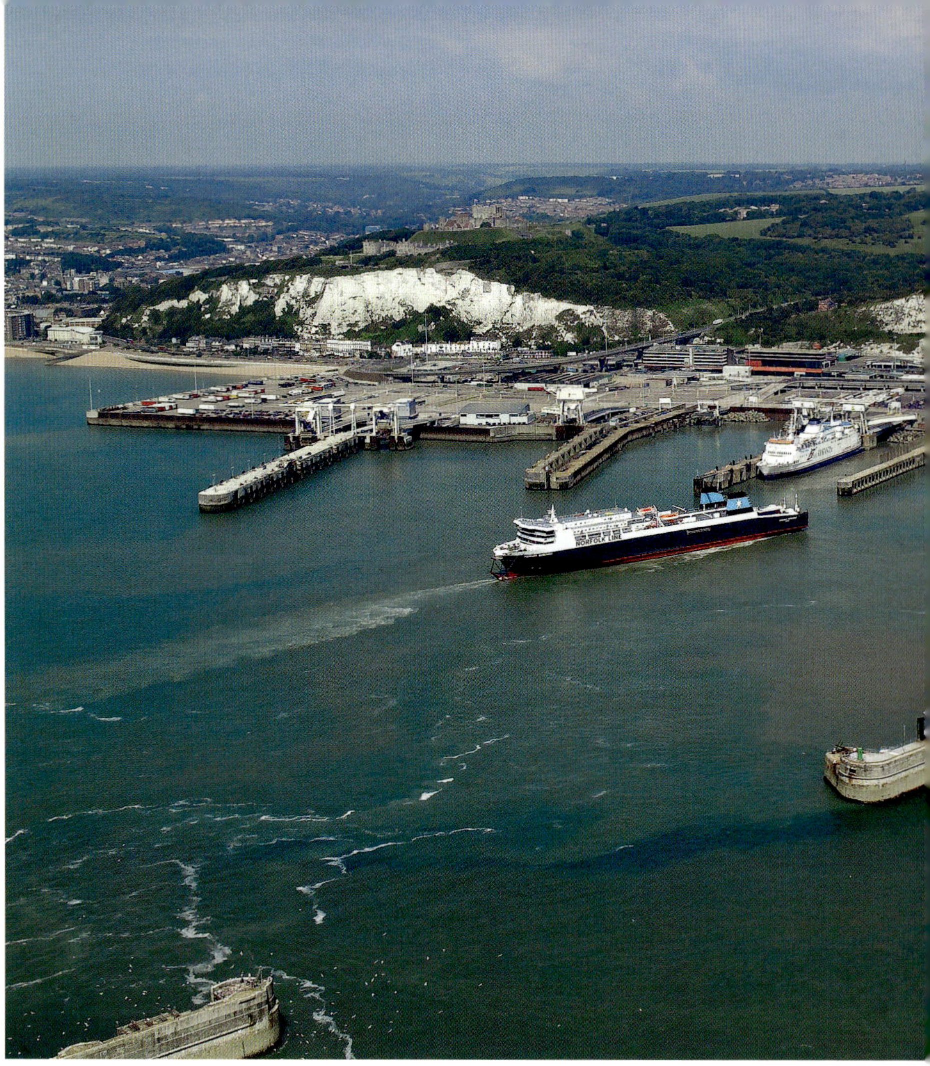

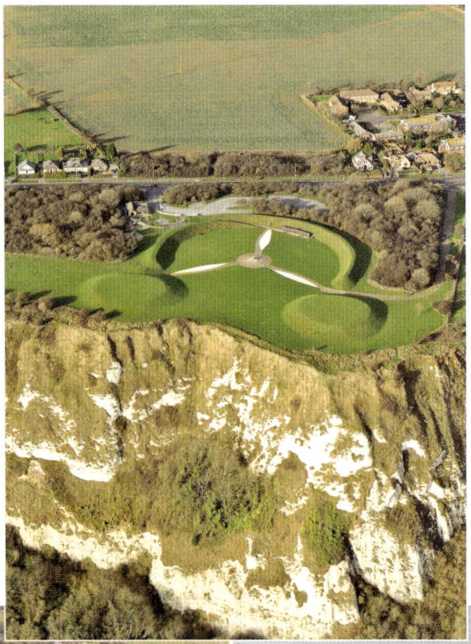

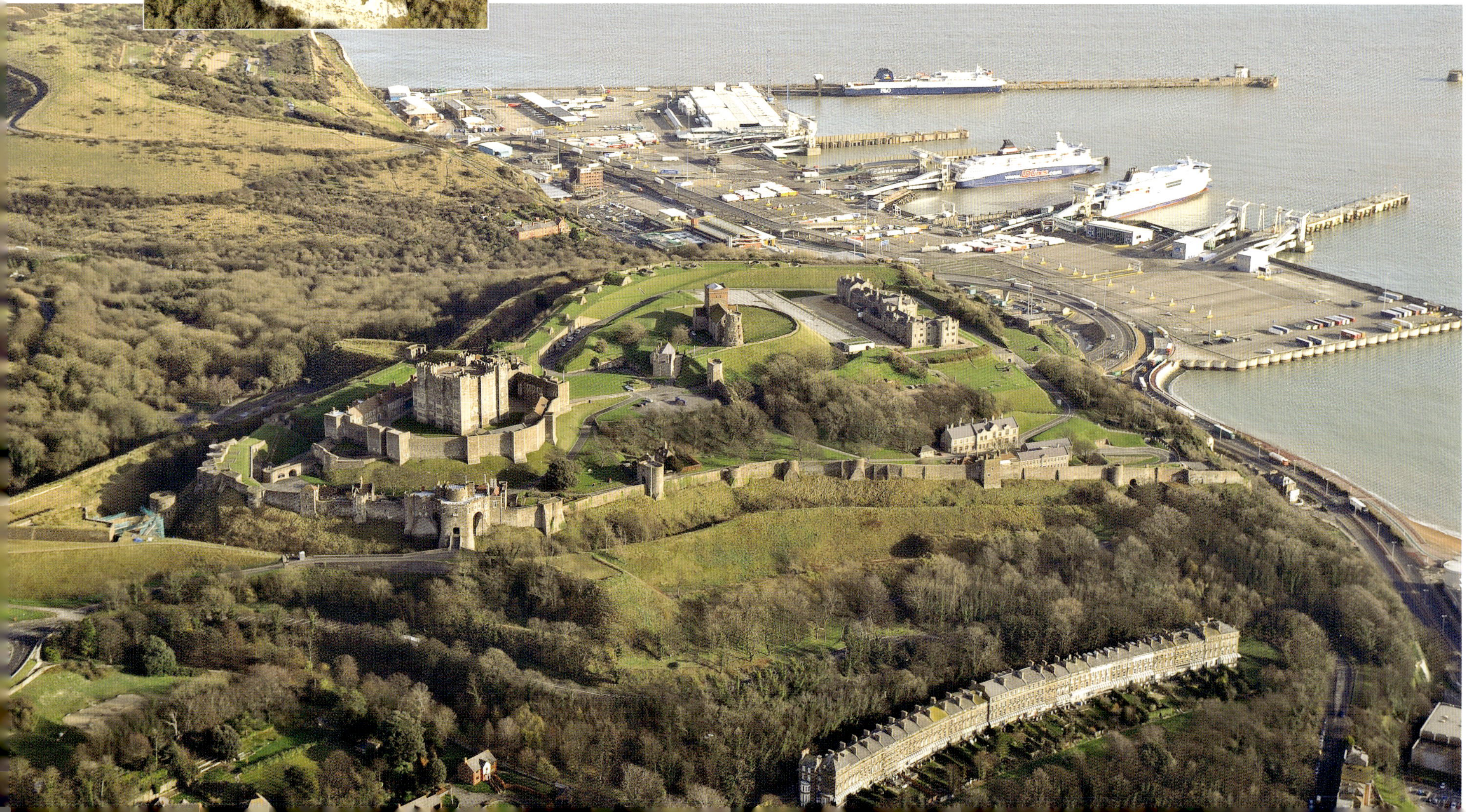

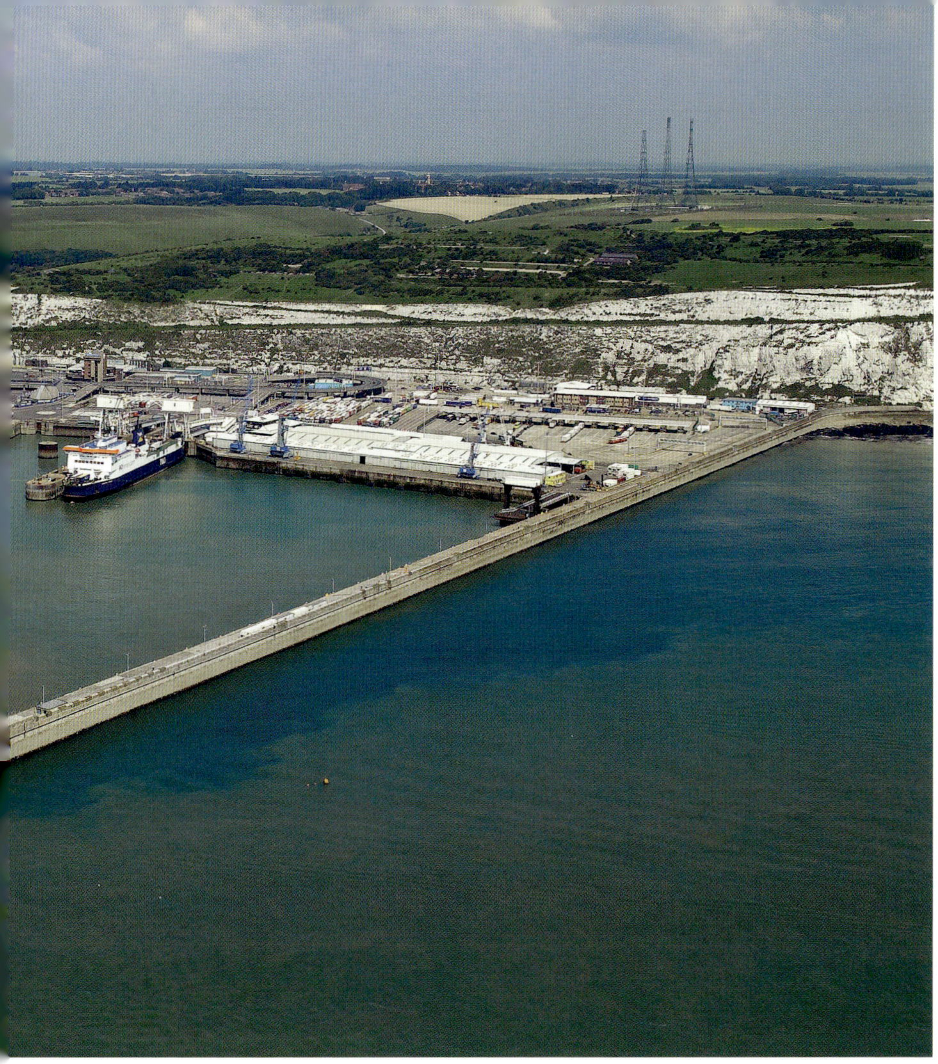

FOLKESTONE

The fishing village of Folkestone (bottom) grew up around the Anglo-Saxon church and castle, becoming a famous centre for smuggling in the 18th century. A new harbour was built in the 19th century and, with the arrival of the railways, Folkestone became a popular seaside resort. The Leas clifftop promenade was a popular walk and the Leas Cliff Hall concert venue still provides entertainment. The Lower Leas Coastal Park, between the clifftop and the Marine Parade, still contains some original stairways, paths and Mediterranean trees and plants as well as new facilities including a cycle route and playground. The Channel Tunnel's UK entrance is close to Folkestone (below). Officially opened by the Queen and the French President in May 1994, the tunnel is 31 miles (50.5km) long, of which 24 miles (39km) run under the English Channel, making it the world's longest undersea tunnel.

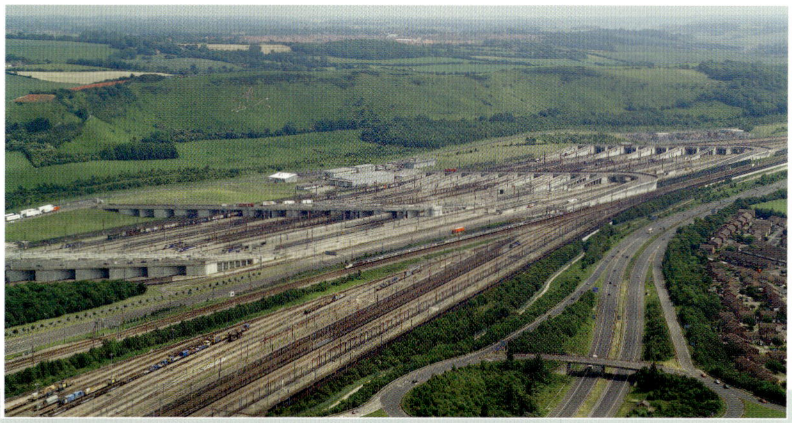

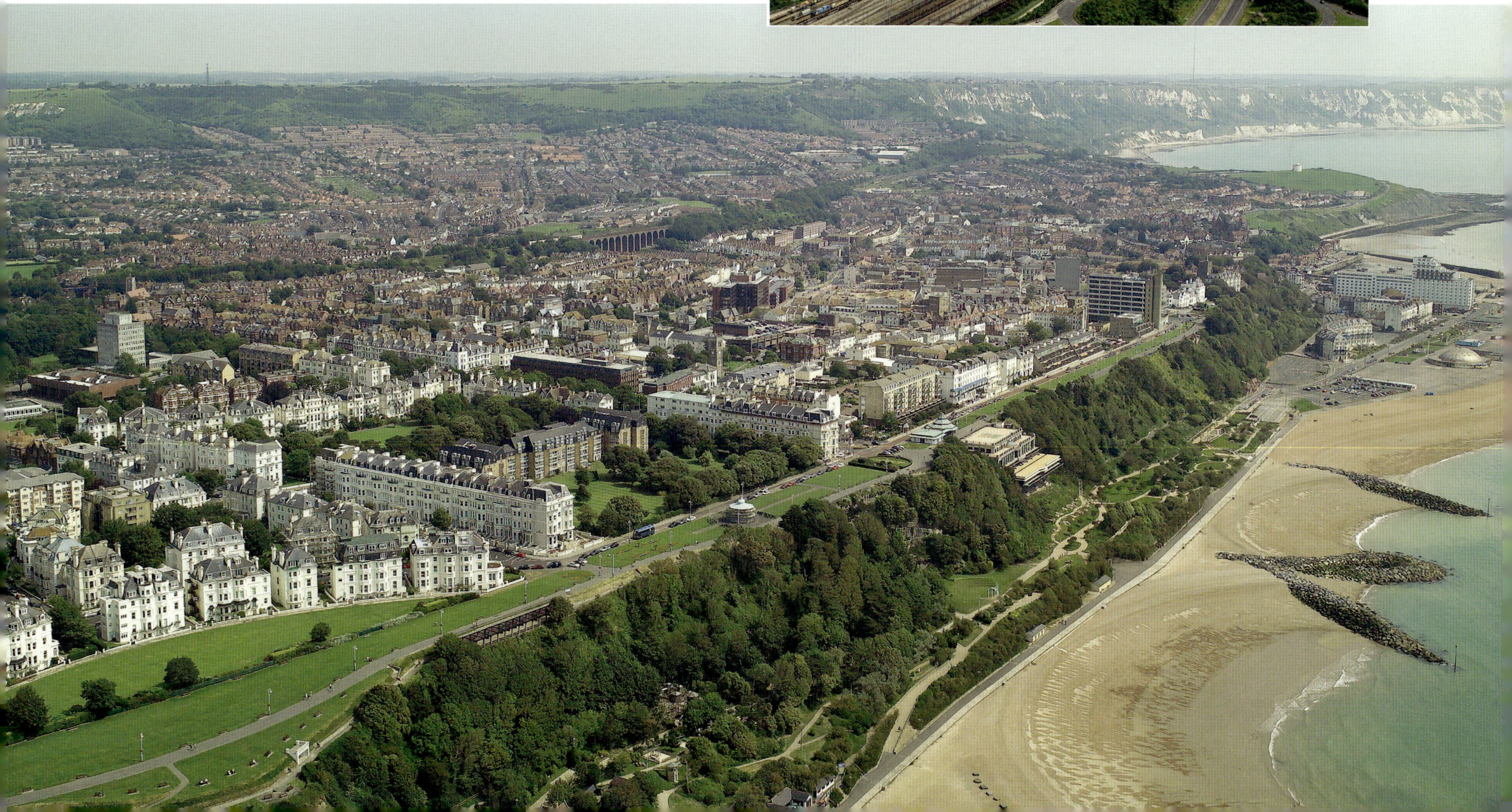

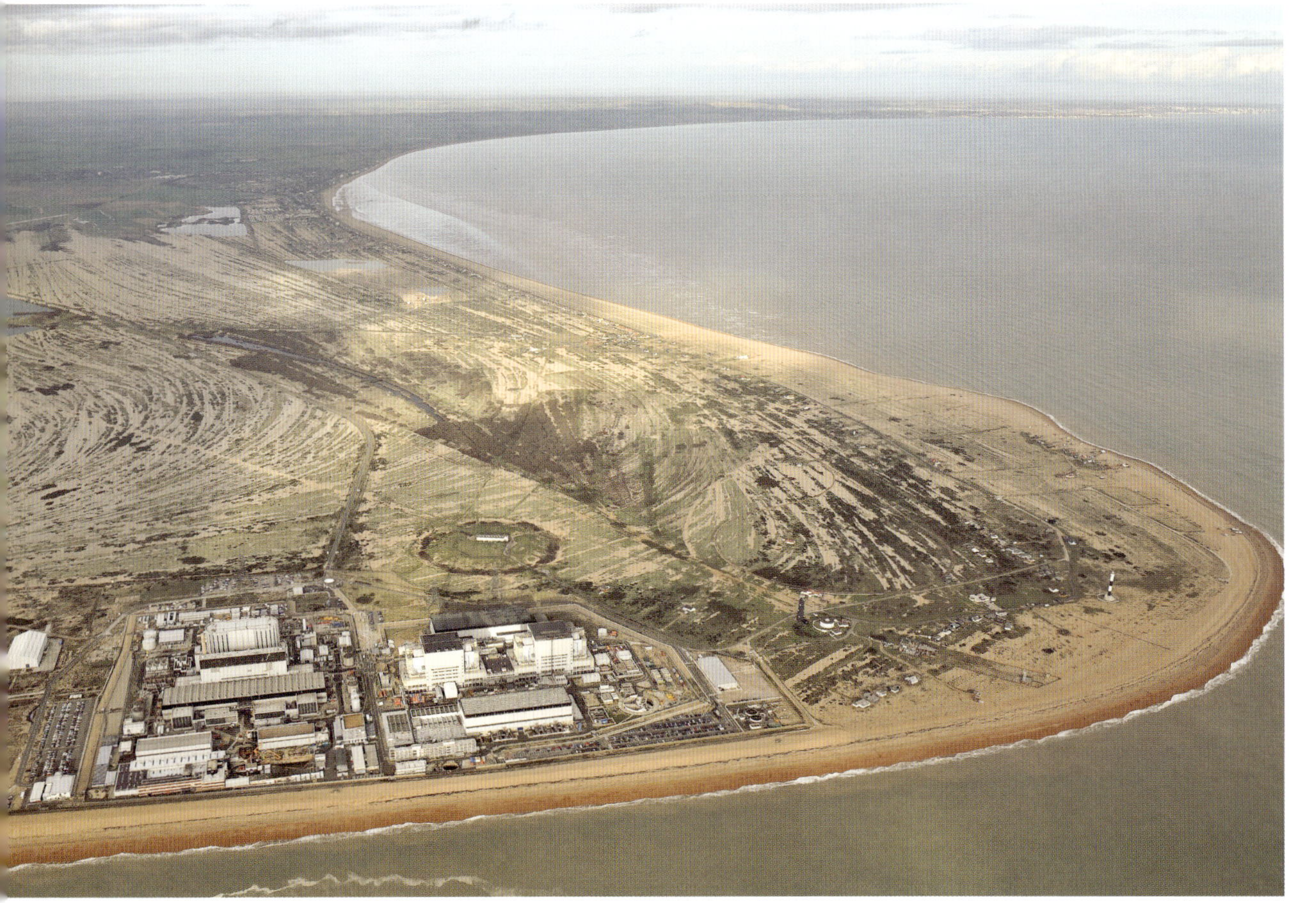

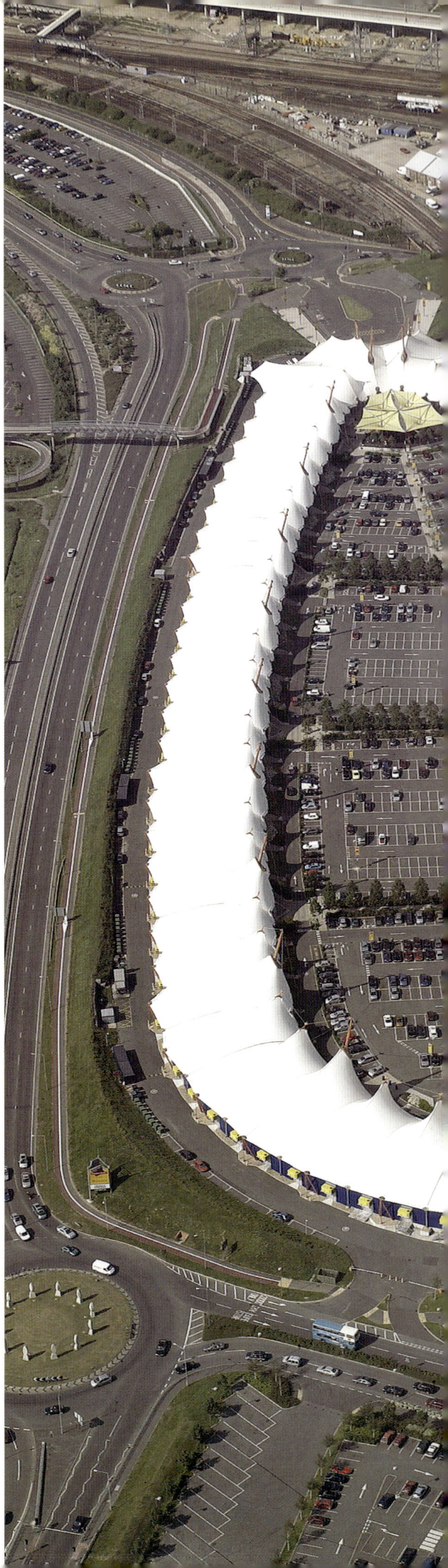

Dungeness

The bleak and windswept headland at Dungeness is a unique landscape containing two nuclear power stations, an area of quiet fisherman's huts by the shore, and a remarkable ecology. As one of the largest expanses of shingle in the world, Dungeness is home to over 600 varieties of plants, a third of the plant varieties in Britain, and a wide variety of insects. The village includes the attractive house and garden of the artist and film director, Derek Jarman (1942-1994). Flooded gravelpits (below) provide an important refuge for coastal and migratory birds, making Dungeness a popular site for birdwatching.

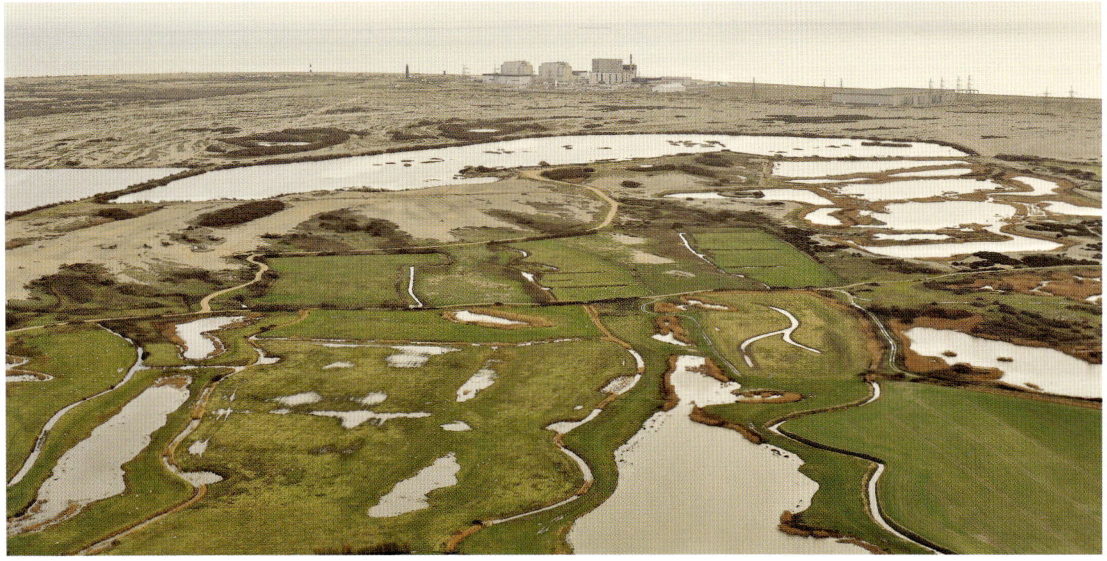

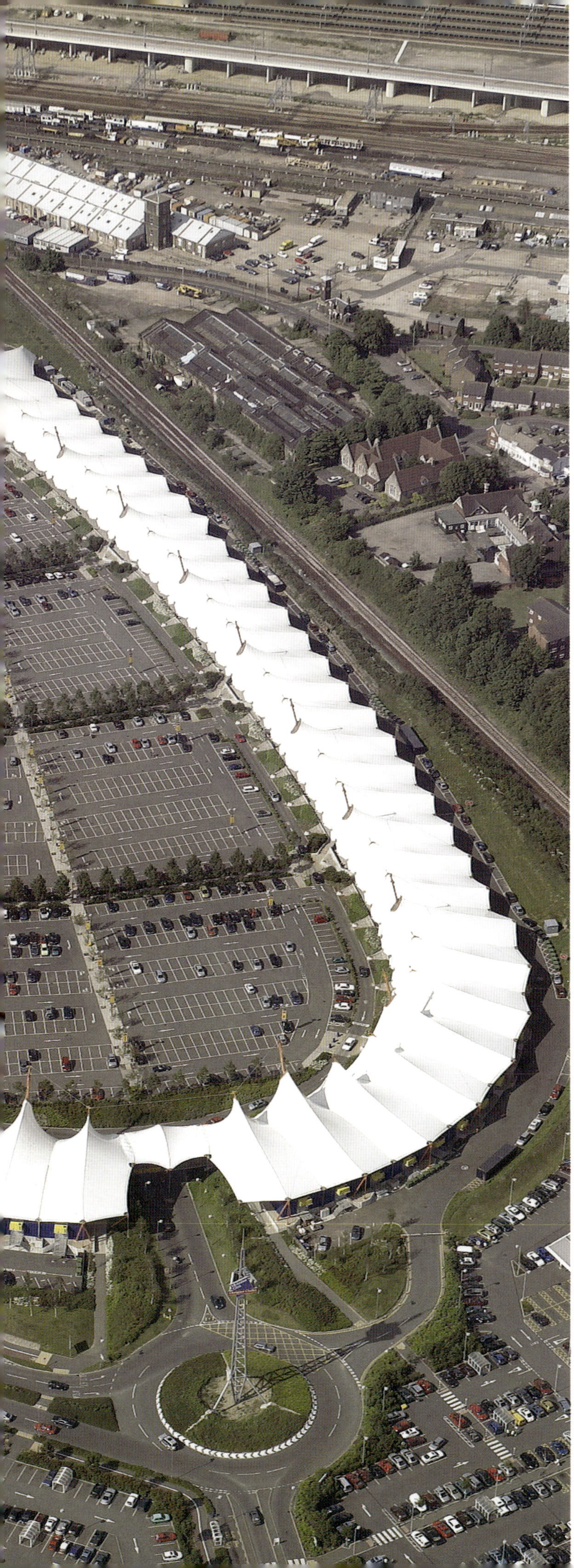

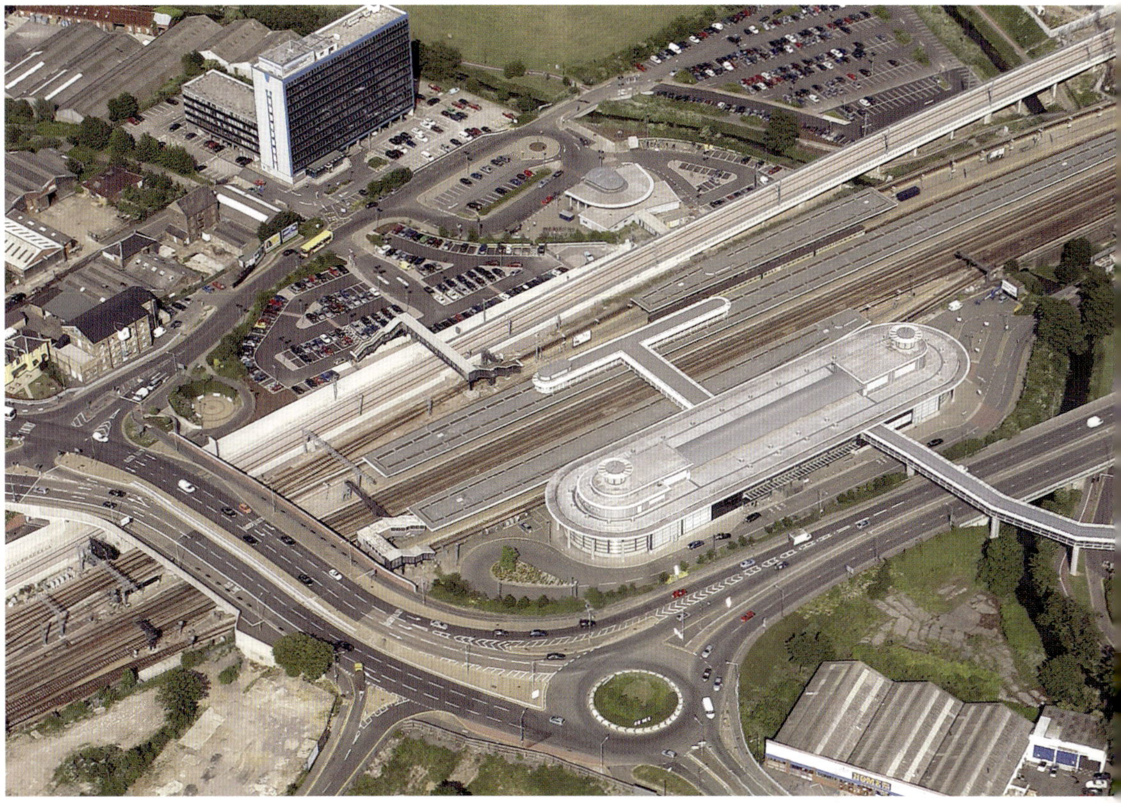

ASHFORD

For centuries a busy agricultural and market town, Ashford is now an important European communications centre following the opening of the Ashford International Passenger Station. Three modern shopping centres are located in the town including the Ashford Designer Outlet (McArthur Glen). Built on the site of a former railway works, this unusual shopping centre (left) was designed by Sir Richard Rogers. Intended to evoke a medieval encampment, it was described by the architect as "a Bedouin tent in an English meadow". More than 80 shops are found within the ovoid loop, all covered by the world's largest continuous membrane structure, which extends over half a mile (1km). Parking is provided for 1450 cars within the central area. Ashford station (above) was rebuilt as Ashford International during the 1990s, with the first international services in 1996. Now high-speed trains from Ashford travel to Paris, Brussels and Disneyland Paris.

WILLESBOROUGH WINDMILL

New Mill in Willesborough (right) was built in 1869 and is a former smock mill, once common in Kent, and now a museum open to the public. Restored in 1991 by Ashford Borough Council, with replacement sails added in 2007, the mill is fully operational and grinds its own wholemeal bread flour.

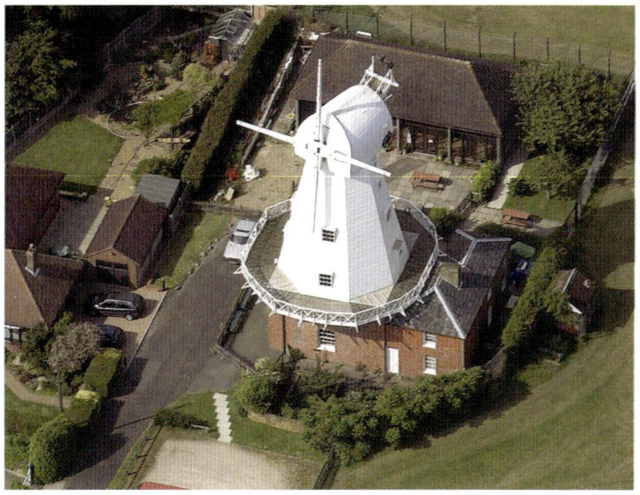

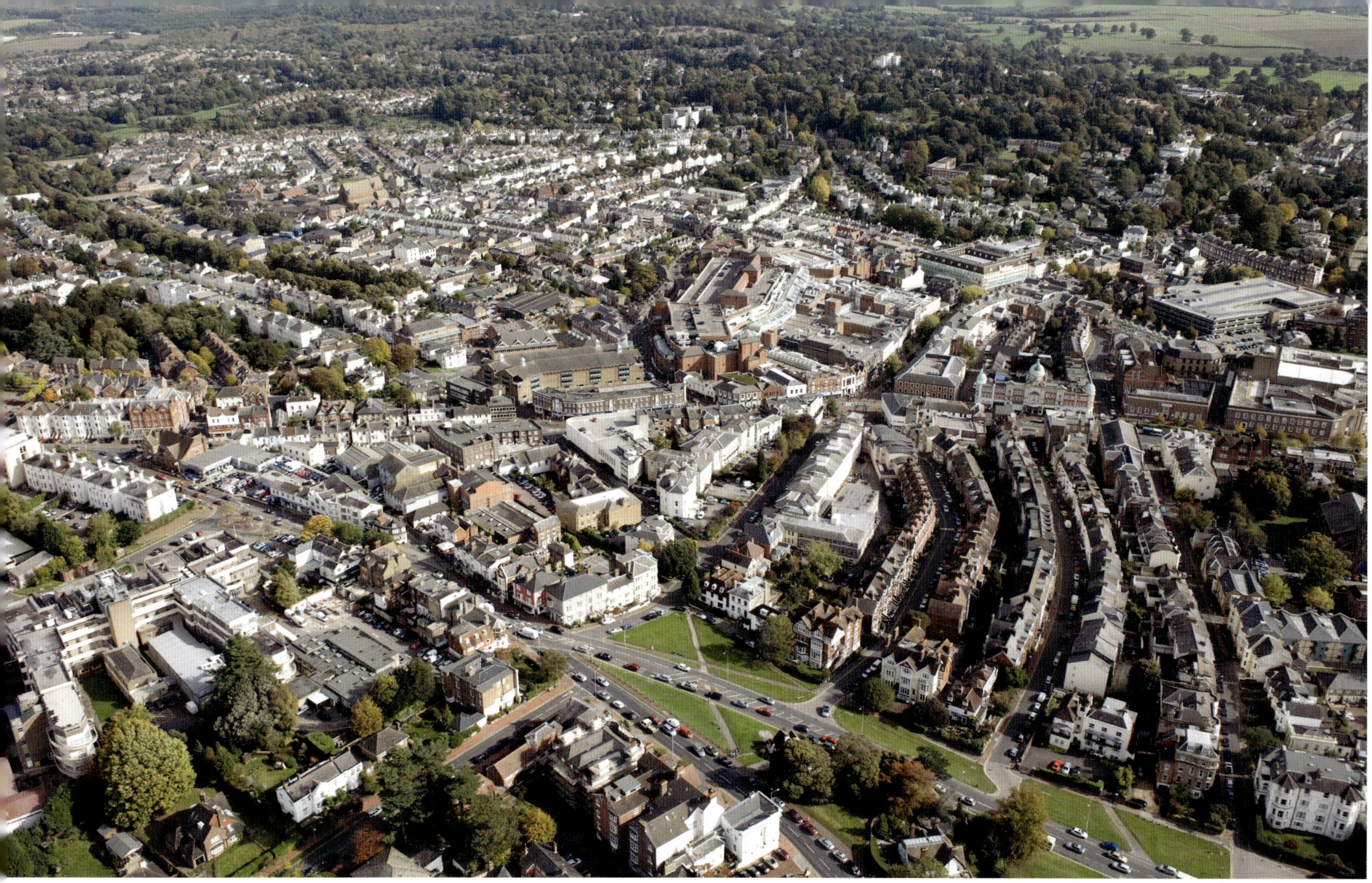

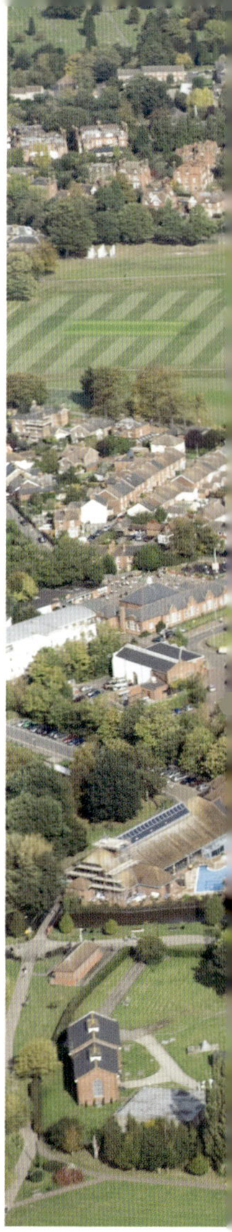

Royal Tunbridge Wells

Prior to the advent of sea bathing, Tunbridge Wells (above) was a popular tourist destination for Londoners wishing to improve their health in its spa waters. Discovered in 1606, the chalybeate spring considered to have healing powers is still open today. The town's heyday was during the Georgian era and Regency buildings sprung up around the spring including a colonnaded walkway, the Pantiles. Royalty and aristocracy continued to visit during the Victorian era and the town was awarded its royal status in 1909. Now a public house, the 1902 Opera House (right) with its three green domes has hosted many famous performers over the years.

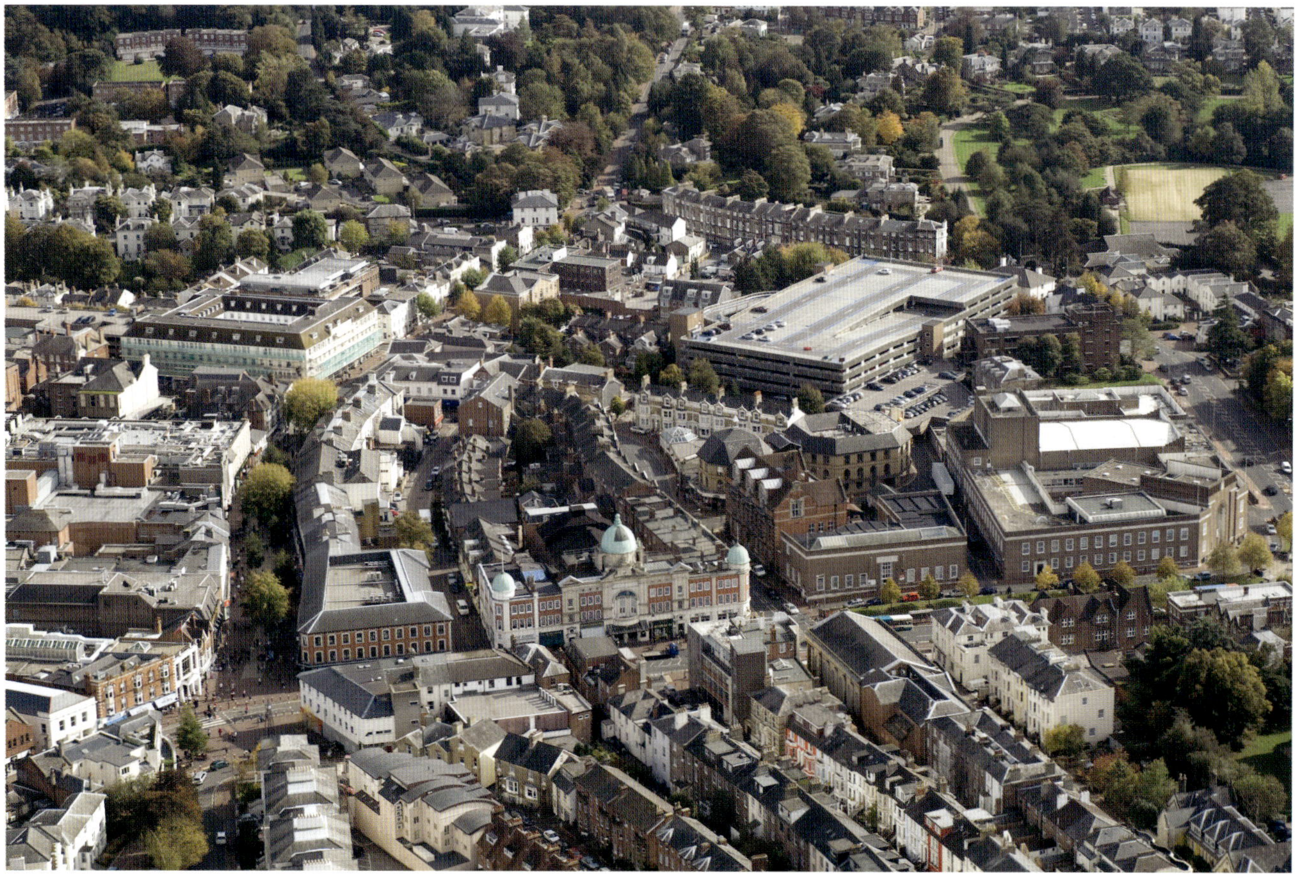

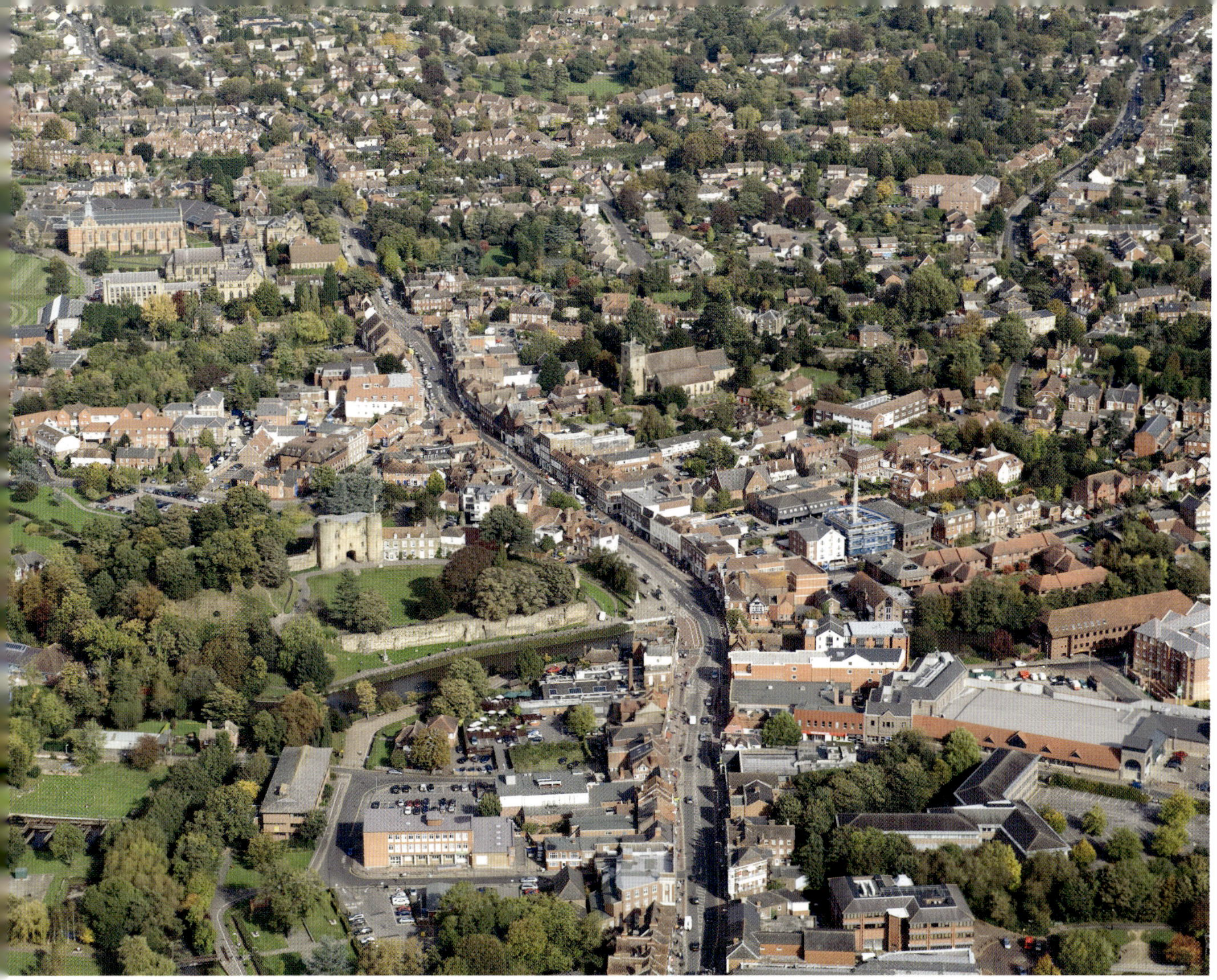

TONBRIDGE

Situated on a spur of higher ground by the river Medway, Tonbridge (left, below and below left) has been a centre for trade and transport since Anglo-Saxon times. The town is home to an 11th-century motte and bailey castle, rebuilt in the 13th century and once an official residence of Edward II. Tonbridge contains a number of well-preserved Elizabethan timber-framed buildings and fine 18th-century weatherboarded and tiled houses. Tonbridge School, founded in 1553, can be seen at the top of the town and is one of Britain's most expensive public schools for boys. Famous ex-Tonbridge pupils include EM Forster, Vikram Seth and Frederick Forsyth.

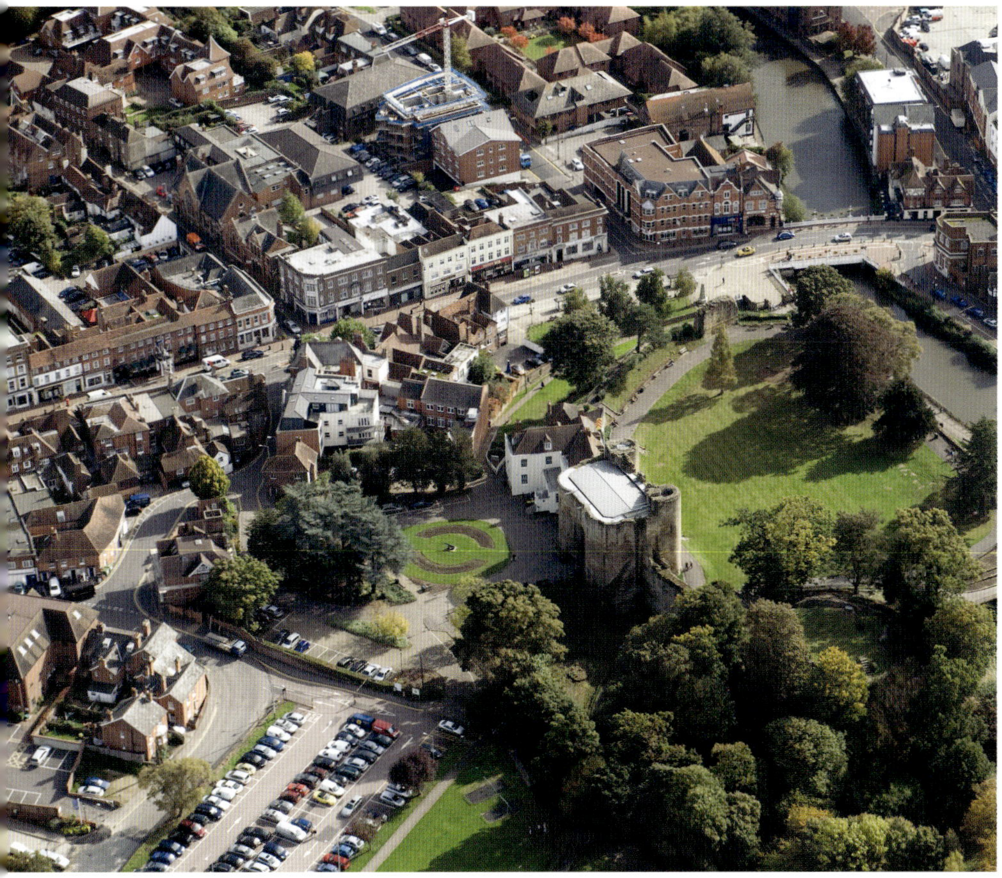

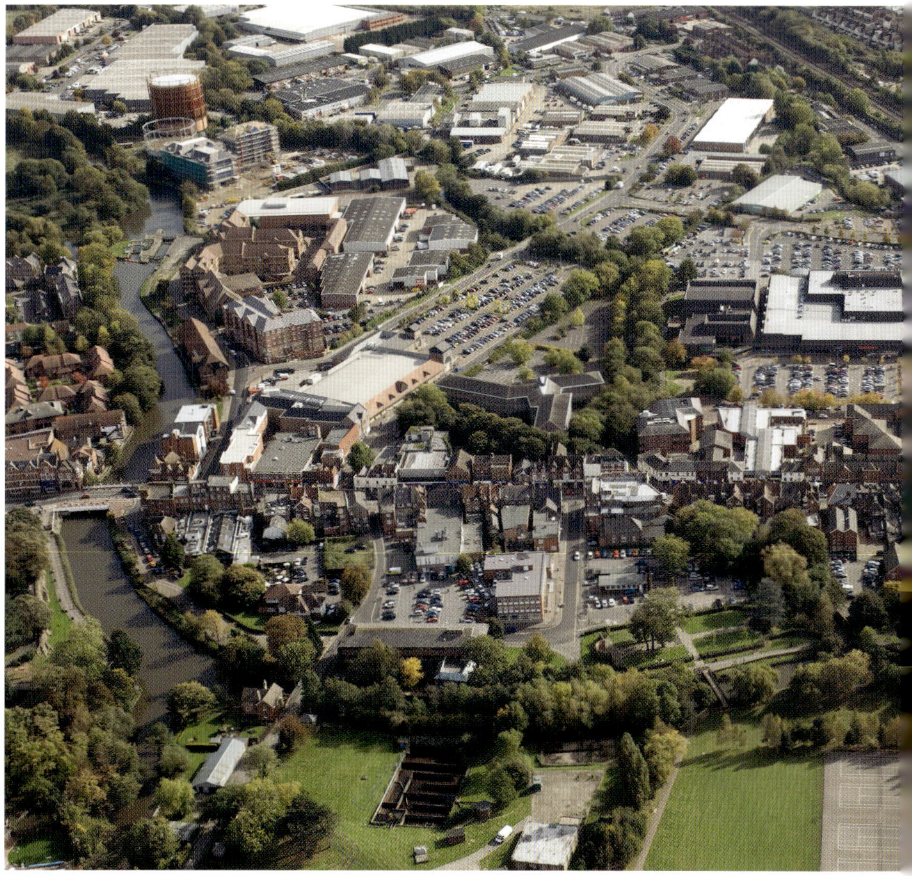

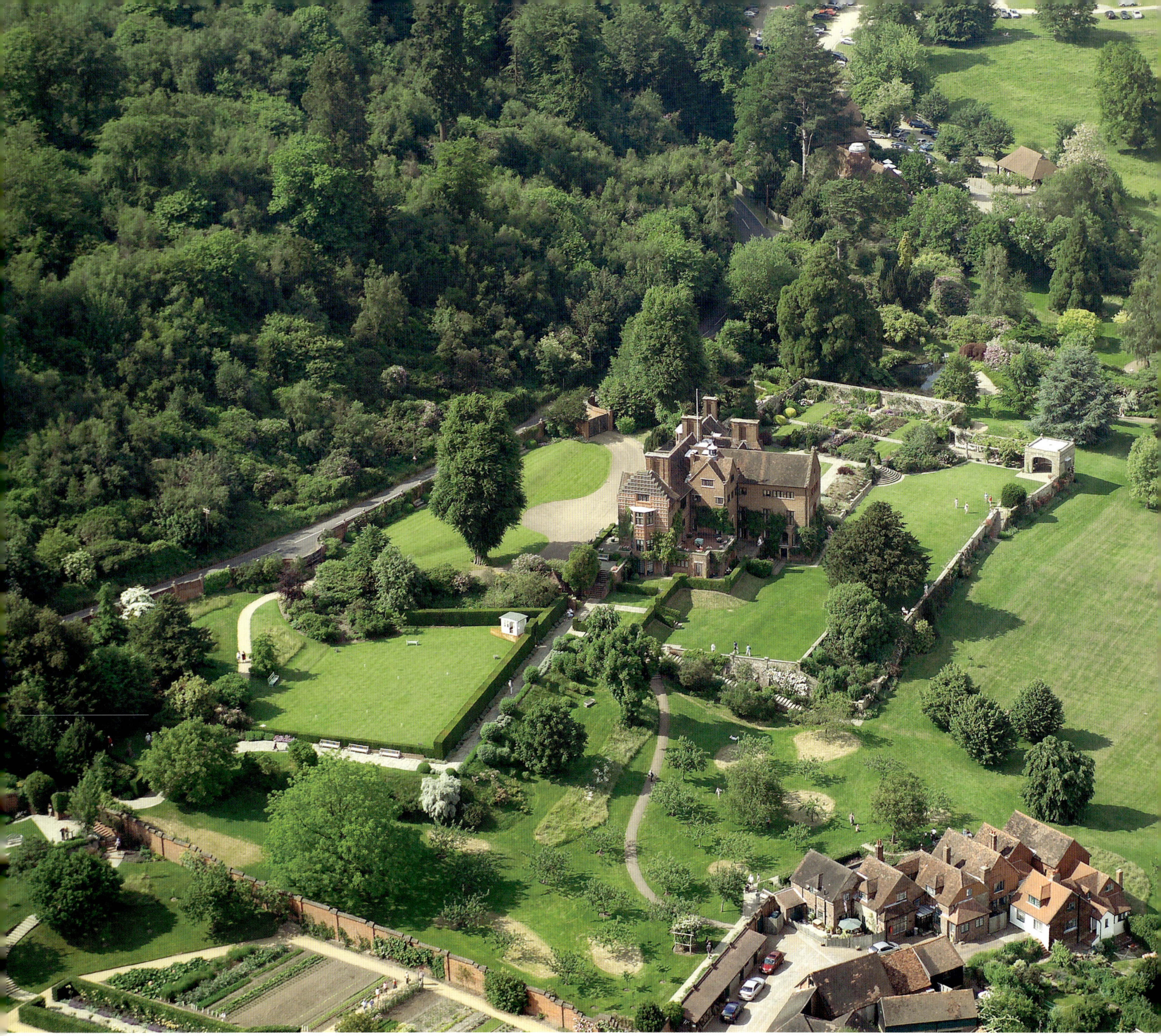

Chartwell

Formerly an Elizabethan manor house, Chartwell (above) was the much-loved home of Sir Winston Churchill from 1922 until his death in 1965. Considered by many to be Britain's greatest politician, Churchill served for two periods as prime minister: from 1940-1945 and 1951-55. The house takes its name from the Chart Well on the western edge of the estate and now belongs to the National Trust. Visitors can see Churchill's paintings and drawings, visit the garden studio and explore the beautiful rose and water gardens. The rooms and gardens remain much as they were when Churchill lived at Chartwell, giving visitors a sense of the great statesman's career and wide-ranging interests.

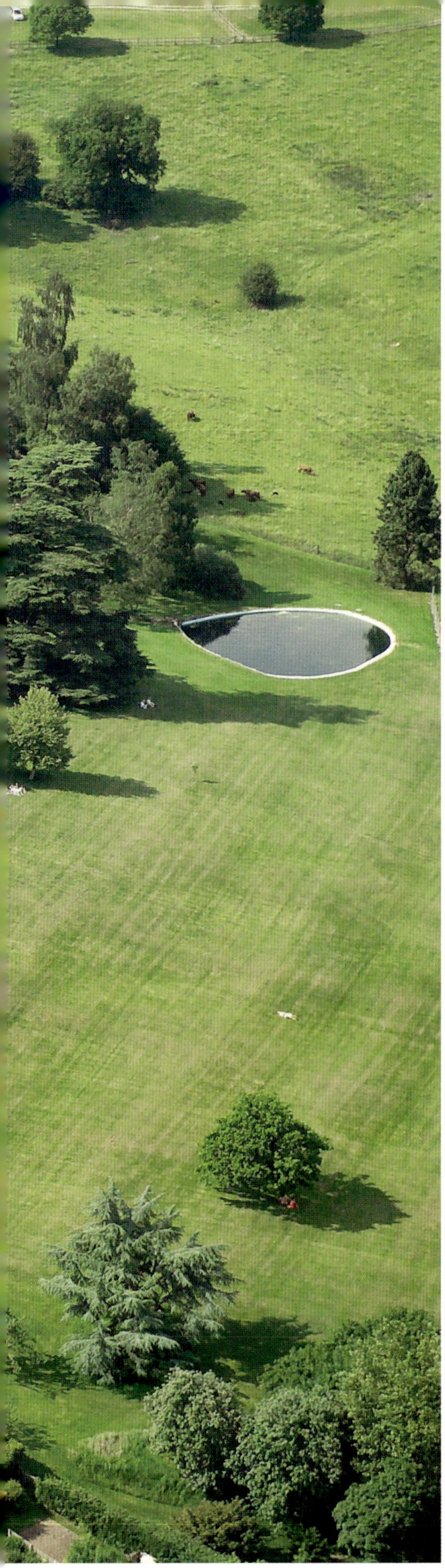

Biggin Hill

A few miles from Chartwell is London Biggin Hill Airport (right and below), an RAF station which played an important role during the Second World War. The German Air Force's massive air campaign against the Royal Air Force in the summer and autumn of 1940 was named after a famous speech by Churchill in which he referred to the coming Battle of Britain. Biggin Hill was one of the principal fighter bases protecting London and the south-east from enemy bombing and was home to Spitfires and Hurricanes from a variety of squadrons. The failure of Germany to destroy Britain's air defences has been seen as a crucial turning point in the war. A chapel of remembrance with gardens and replica aircraft commemorates the aircrew who died during the battle. Now a commercial regional airport, the location has been popular with film producers ever since Battle of Britain films were produced in the 1950s. More recently, the airport was used as a location in the film *The Da Vinci Code*.

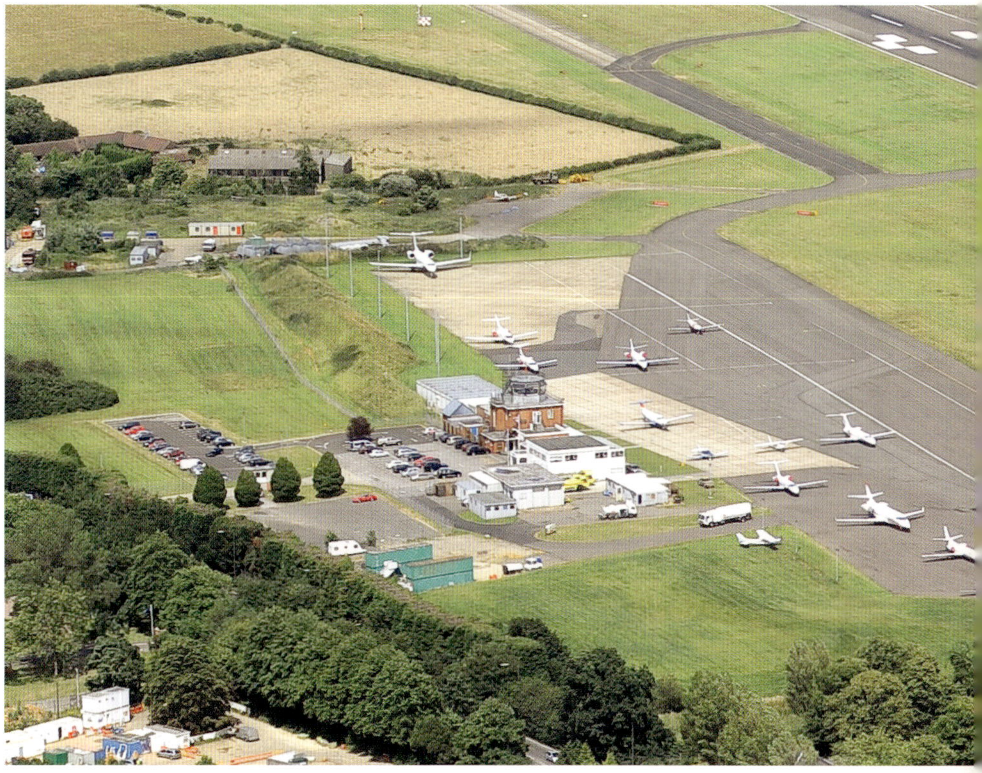

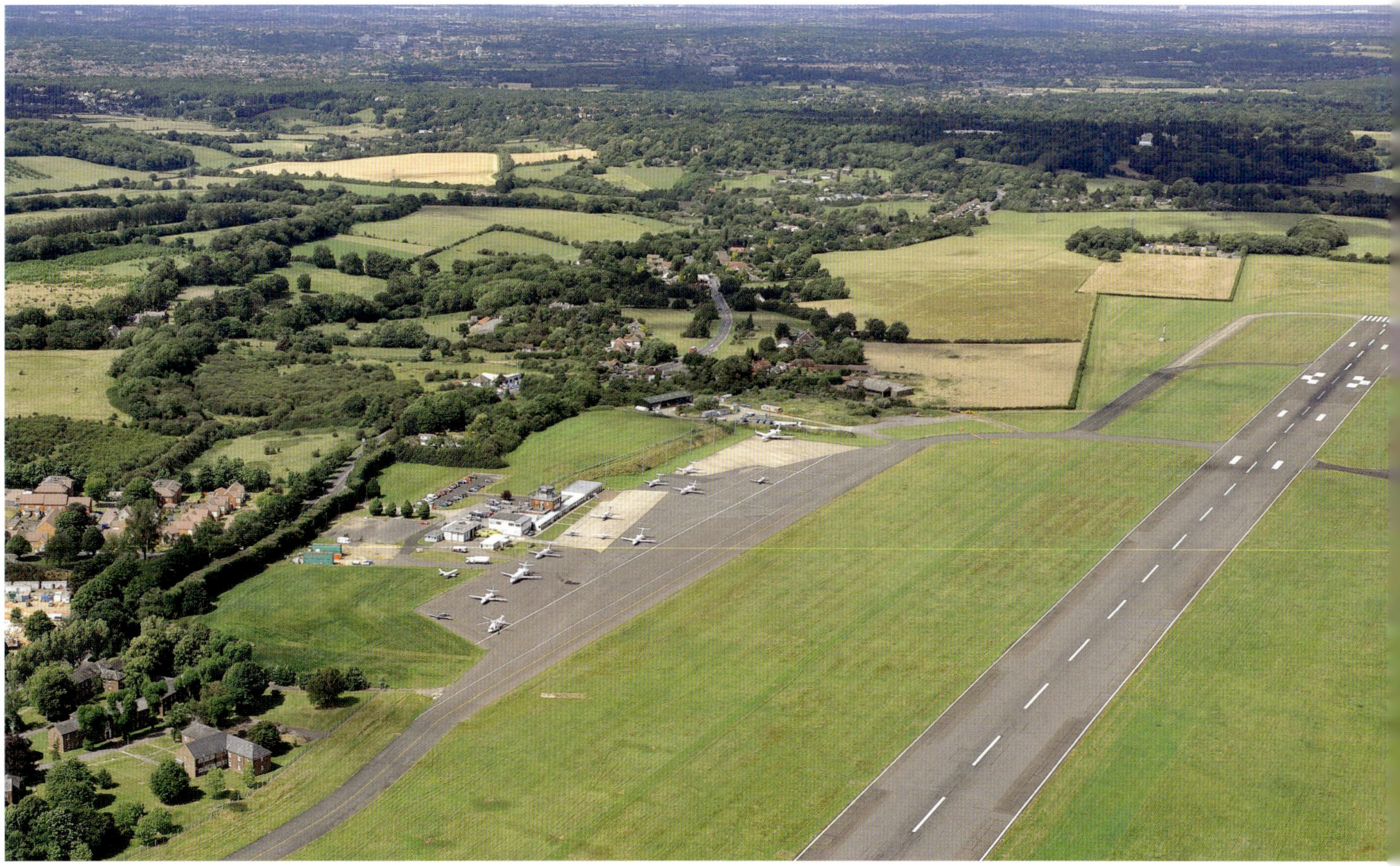

Surrey

Often referred to as London's "Stockbroker Belt", Surrey has the highest proportion of millionaires in Britain, living in some of the county's historic towns and centuries-old villages. Surrey stretches from the outskirts of London, including Richmond and Kingston-upon-Thames, to the borders of Berkshire, Hampshire, Sussex and Kent, and contains beautiful woodland as well as conurbations. Major urban centres such as Woking, Camberley and Leatherhead are within easy reach of London and this has certainly contributed to Surrey being the most densely populated county outside the capital. Much of Surrey is in the London Green Belt, with the Surrey Hills an area of outstanding natural beauty. This includes Leith Hill, the highest point in south-east England, reaching 1,000ft (300m) at the 18th century Gothic tower on its peak, and the North Downs chalk escarpment beauty spot at Box Hill.

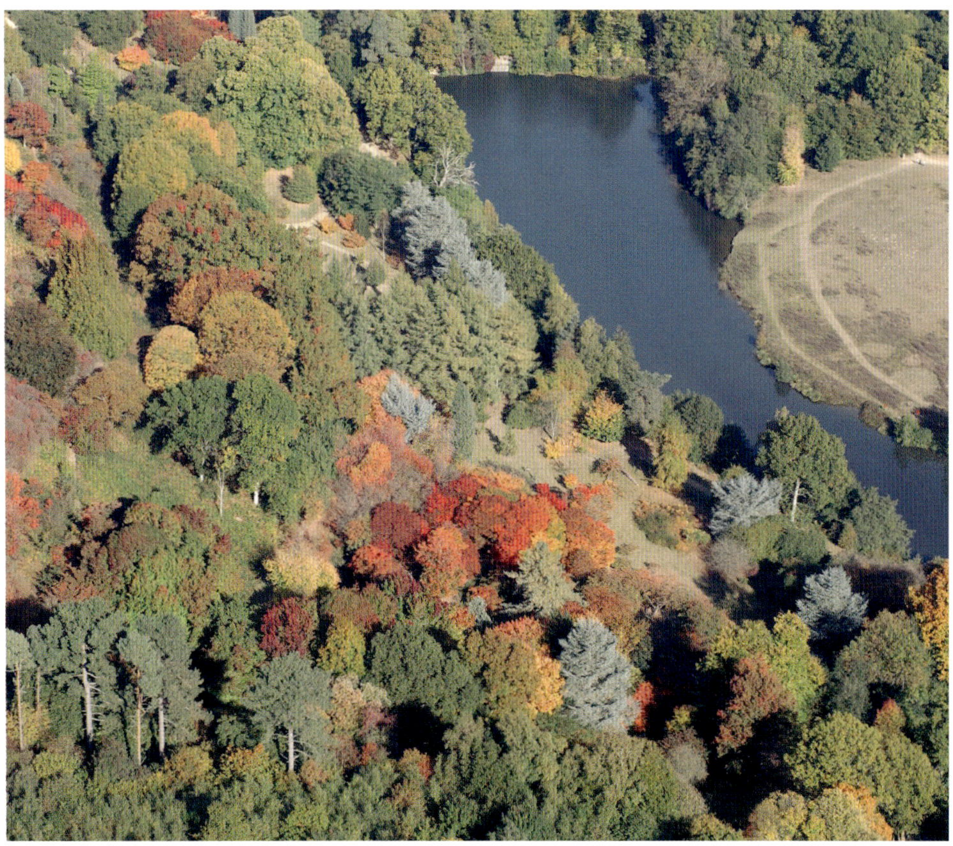

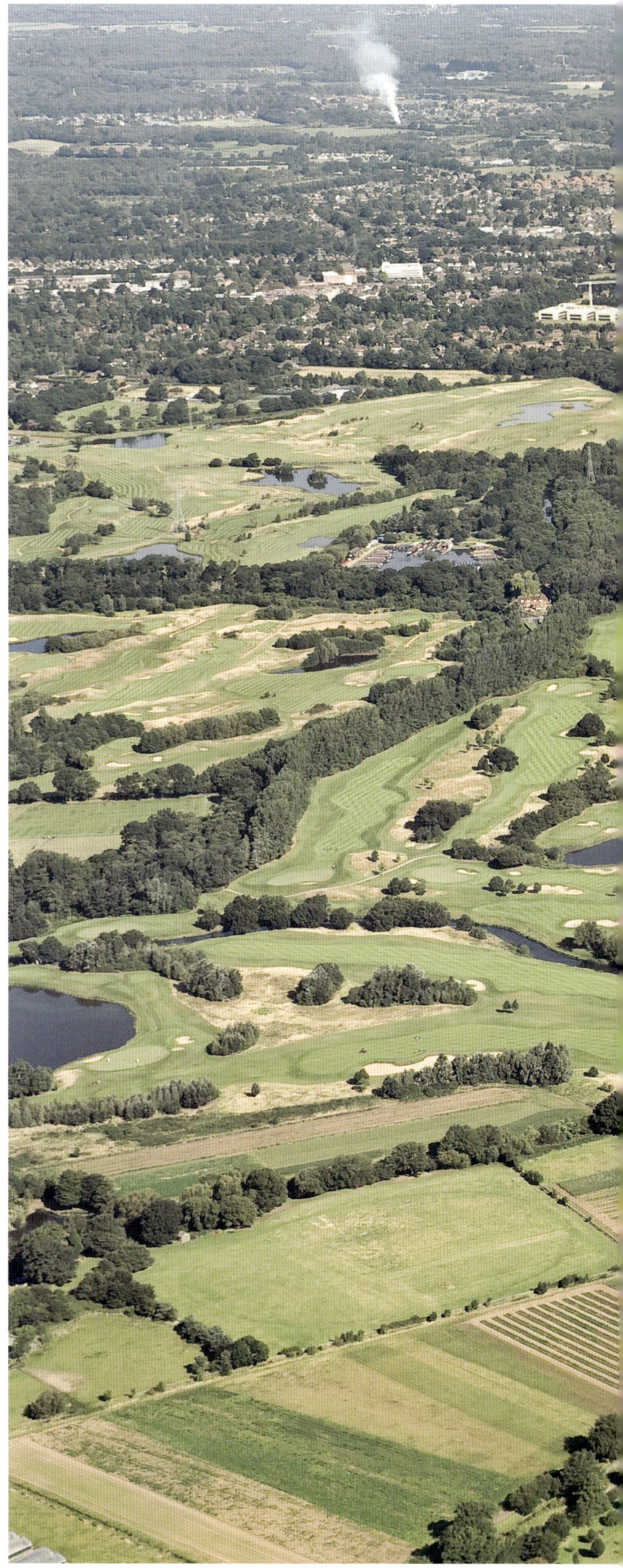

Gardens and golf courses

Renowned for gardening, Surrey is home to Winkworth Arboretum (above) and RHS Wisley (right) as well as the famous Wentworth and Walton Heath golf courses used by its affluent residents. Close to Wisley lies Brooklands, the famous motor racing circuit.

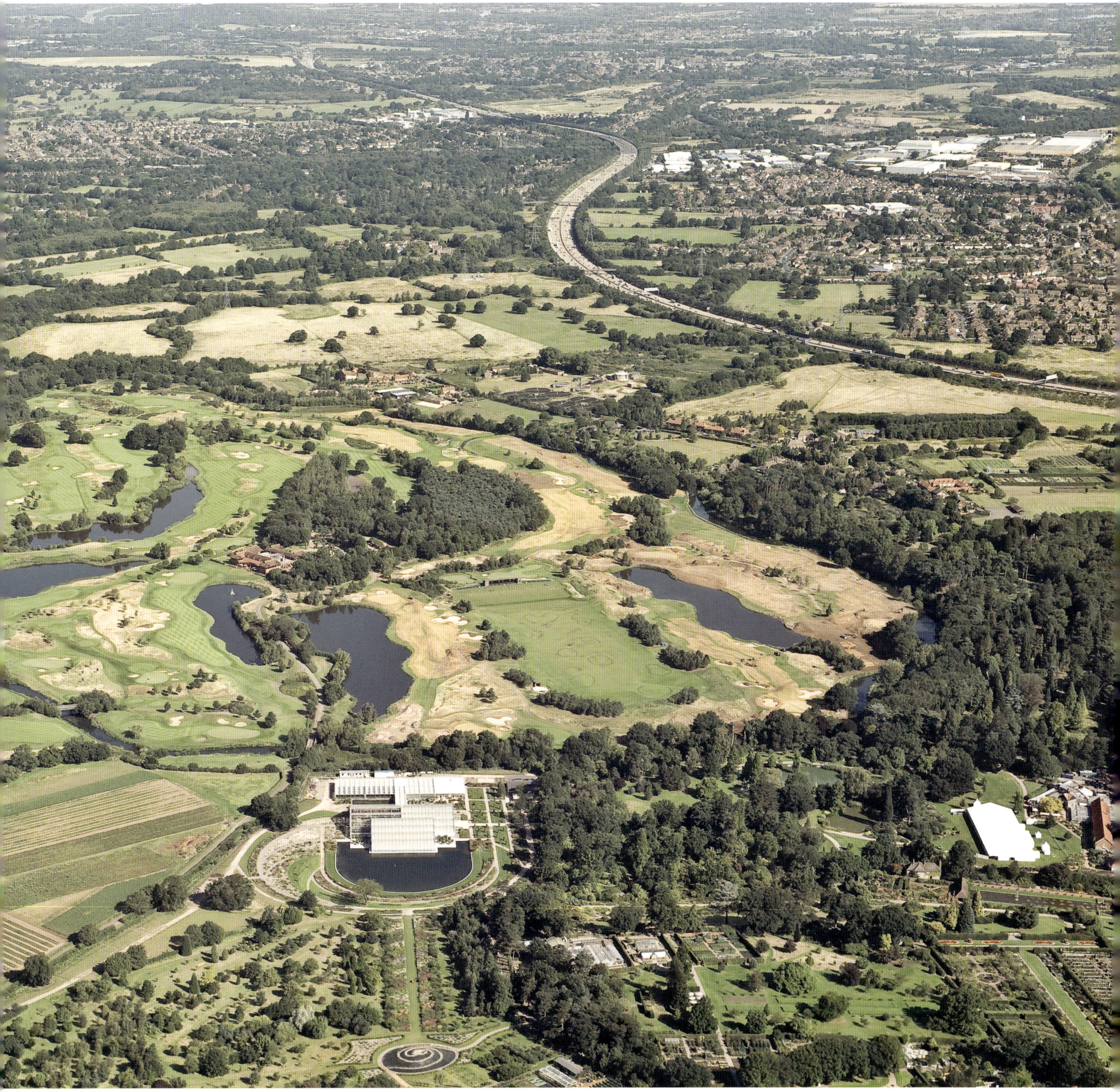

Thames at Richmond

The river Thames takes on a rural feel at Richmond (below), with parks and meadows interspersed with historic houses dating from the days when the area was a popular royal retreat. Richmond Hill overlooks a large bend of the river and provides superb views of Surrey. The Petersham Hotel sits halfway up the hill and, near the top, by the entrance to Richmond Park, is the neo-Classical redbrick Royal Star and Garter, a home for disabled ex-servicemen and women. On the opposite side of the river lies Marble Hill House set within Marble Hill Park, the suburbs of Twickenham and St Margaret's beyond, and Twickenham Rugby Stadium, the home of English rugby.

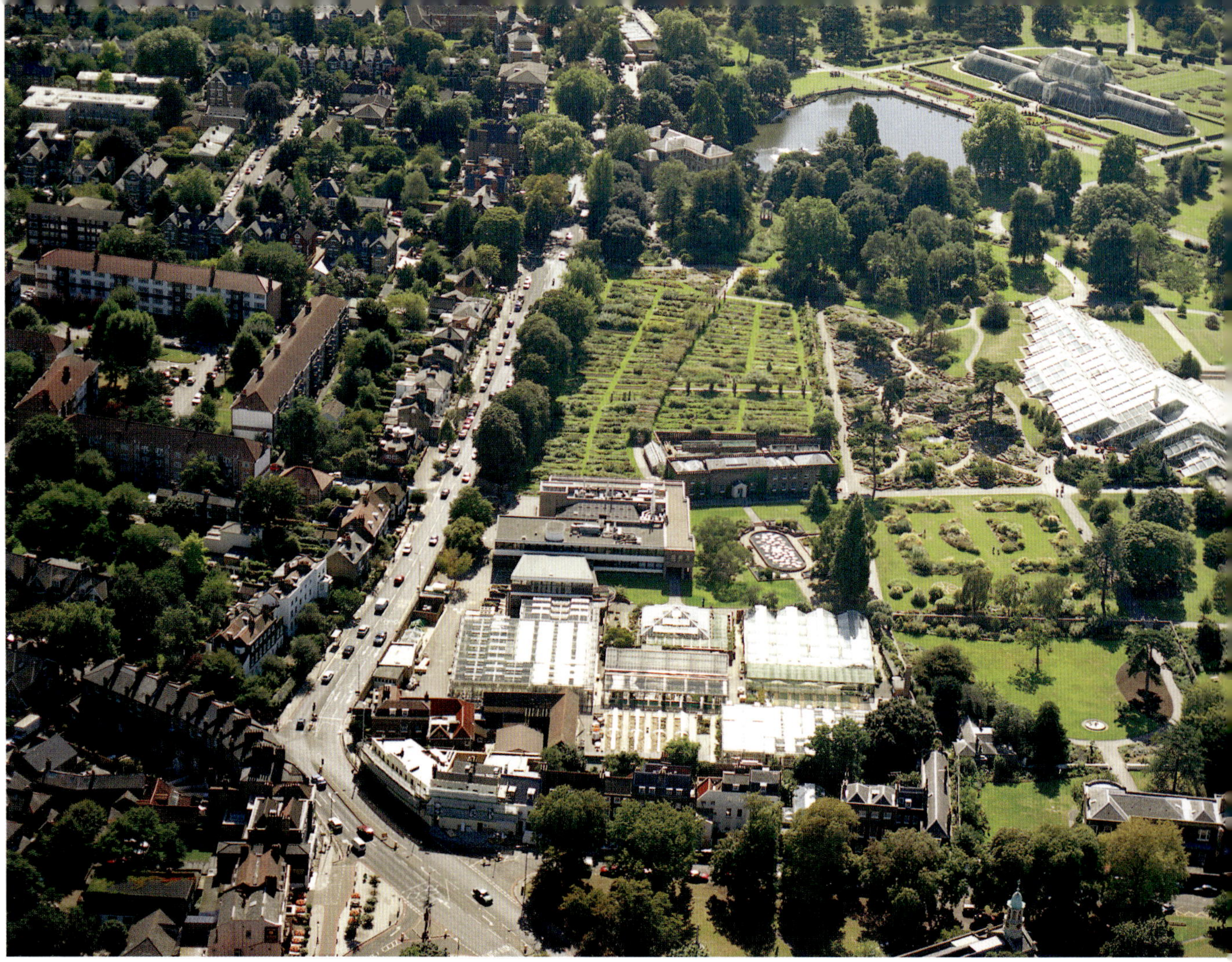

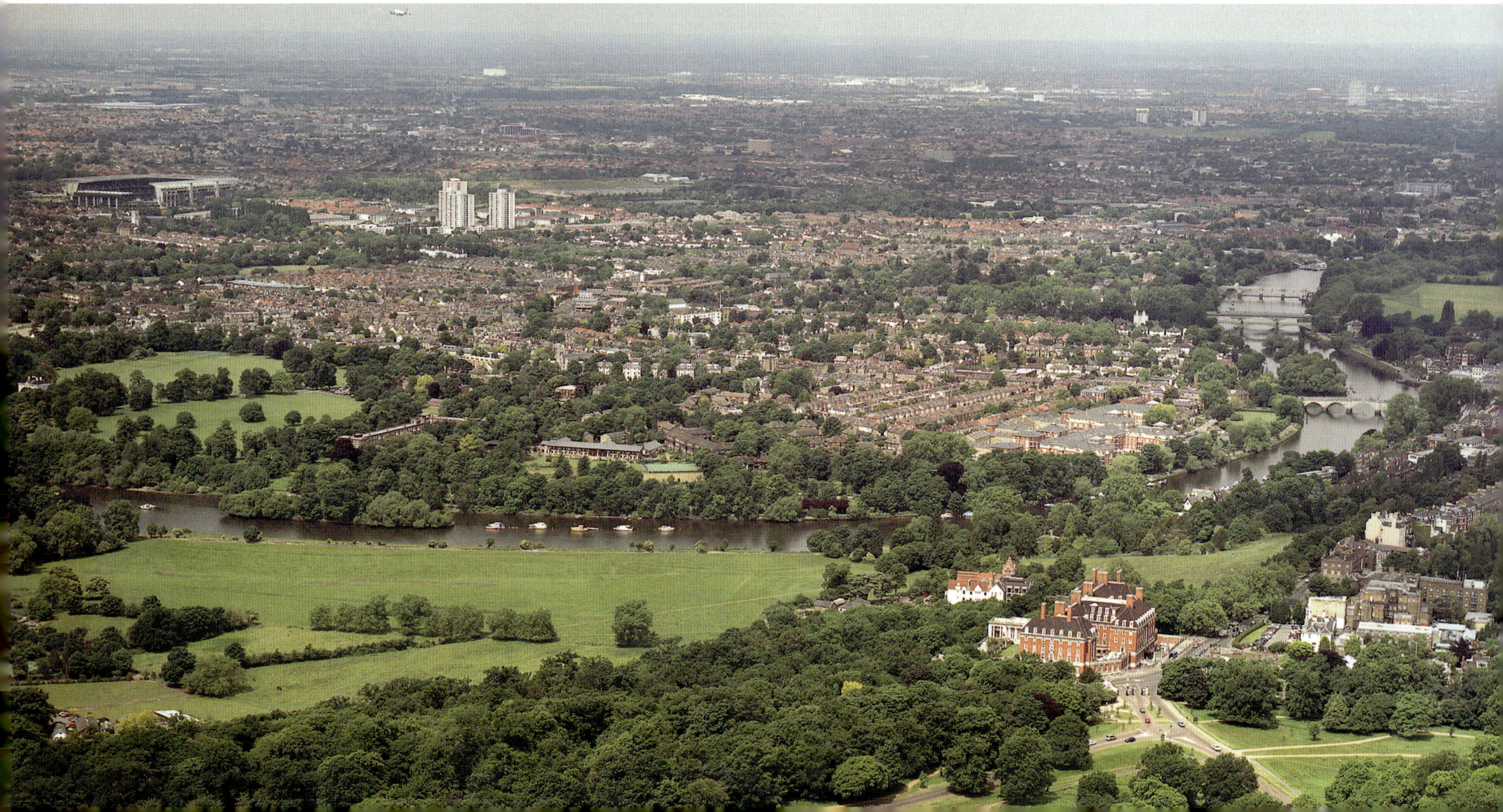

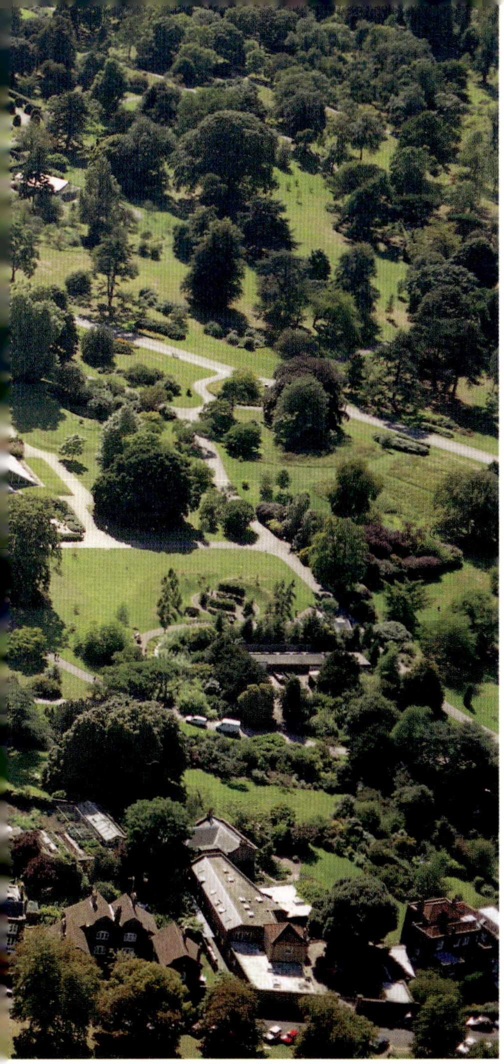

Hampton Court

Cardinal Wolsey acquired Hampton Manor (below) in 1514 and set about creating a lavish Tudor palace that rivalled King Henry VIII's royal palaces at the time. After Wolsey's fall from favour, he lost the palace to the King who spent the equivalent of £18m on additions including a hunting park, Great Hall and extensive Tudor kitchens. In the 17th century, William III made significant Baroque additions to create a palace that rivalled Versailles, with Sir Christopher Wren redesigning the king's and queen's main apartments to transform the south and east facades and landscaping 60 acres of gardens with features such as a canal known as the Long Water. The grounds also include a famous maze and a Great Vine, planted in 1768 by the celebrated gardener, Lancelot "Capability" Brown. Opened to the public in 1838 by Queen Victoria, Hampton Court is a major tourist attraction today.

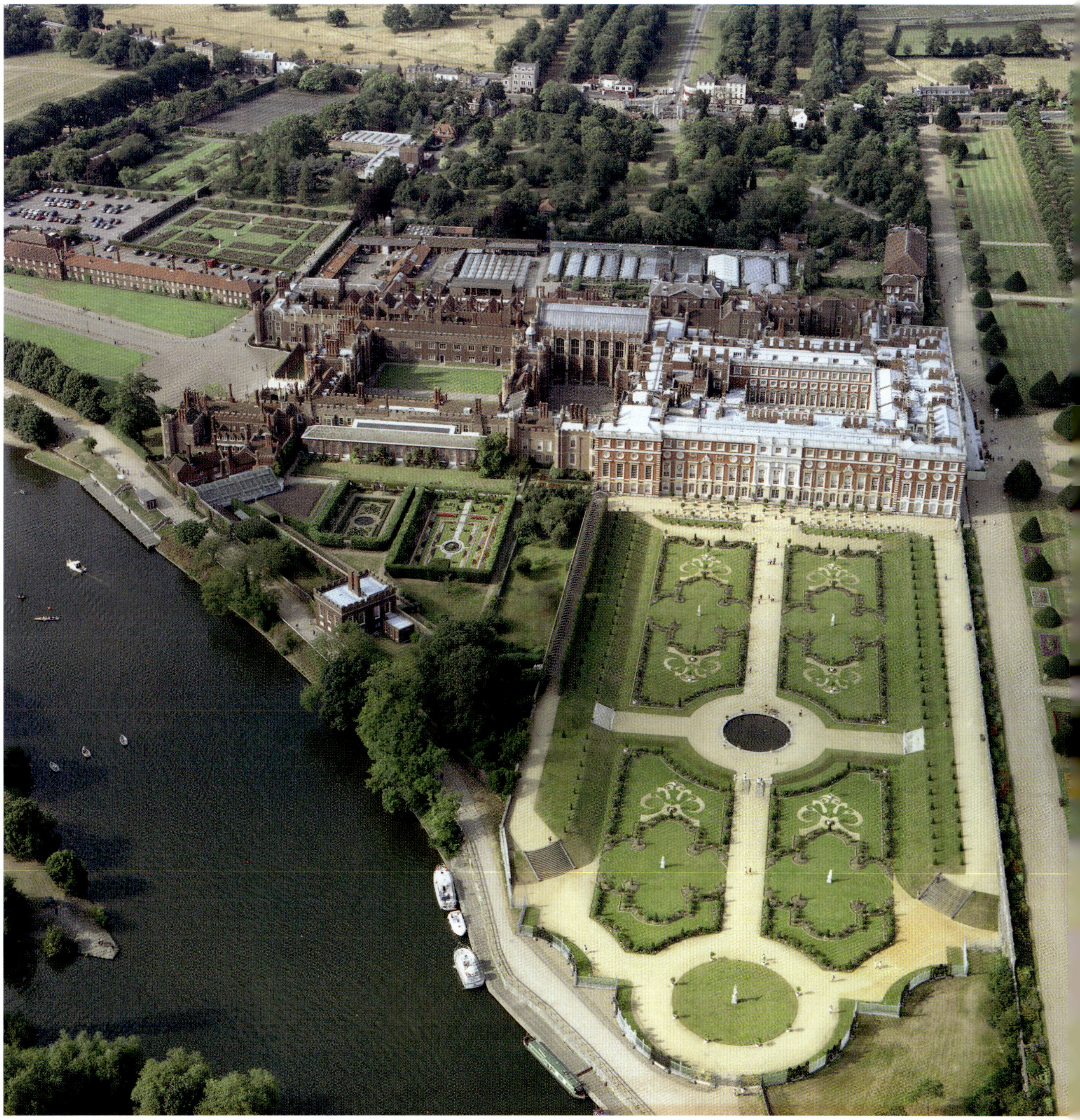

Kew Gardens

The Royal Botanic Gardens at Kew (above) is a World Heritage Site containing 300 acres of gardens, listed buildings and glasshouses located alongside a bend in the river Thames. Created in 1759, the exotic garden at Kew Park was originally formed by Lord Capel of Tewkesbury. It was enlarged, extended and enriched over the years and became a national botanic garden in 1840. Nowadays, it is a major attraction with almost two million visitors a year, as well as a botanical research and education institution, with the world's largest collection of living plants shared between Kew and Wakehurst Place, Sussex.

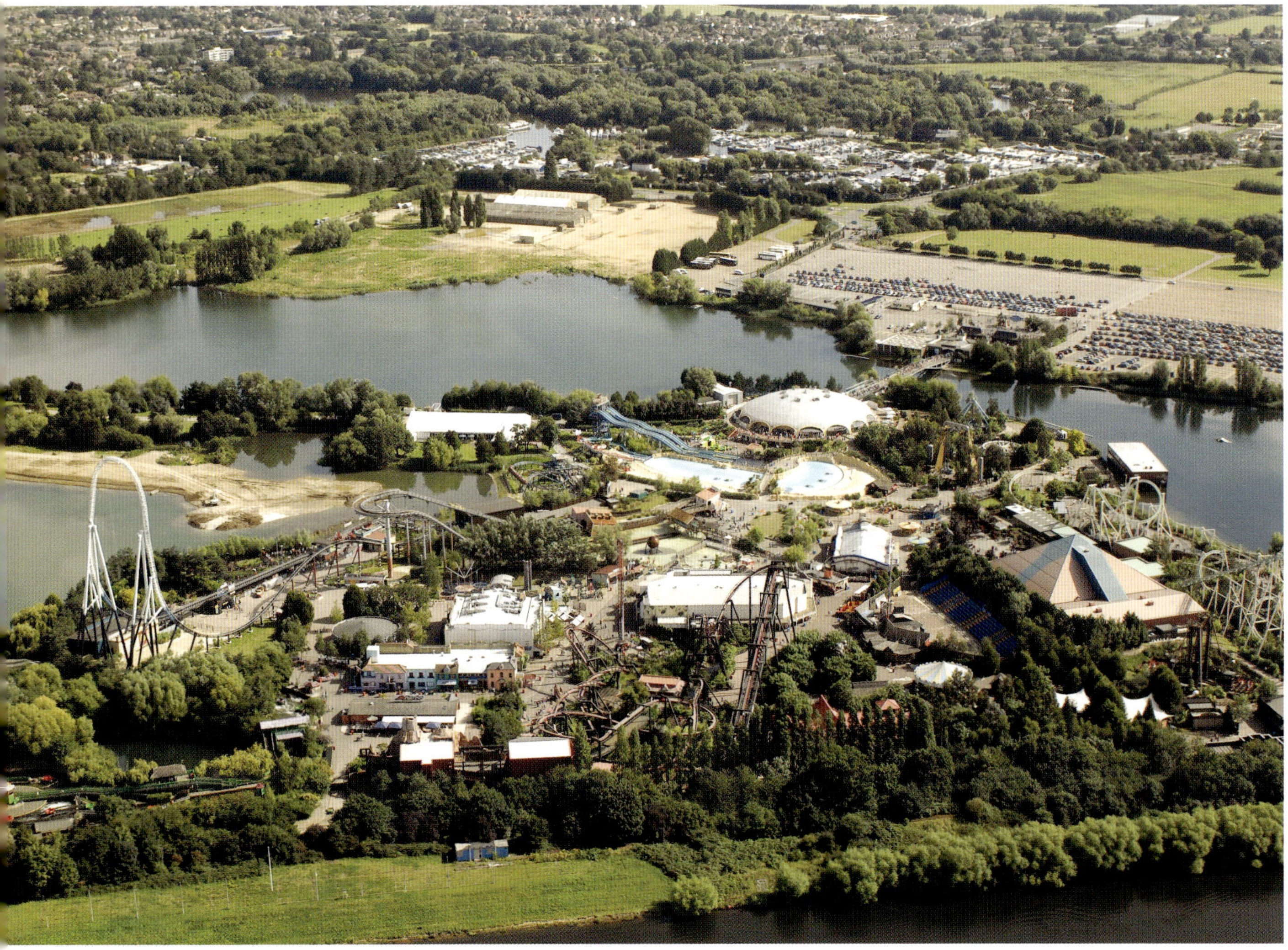

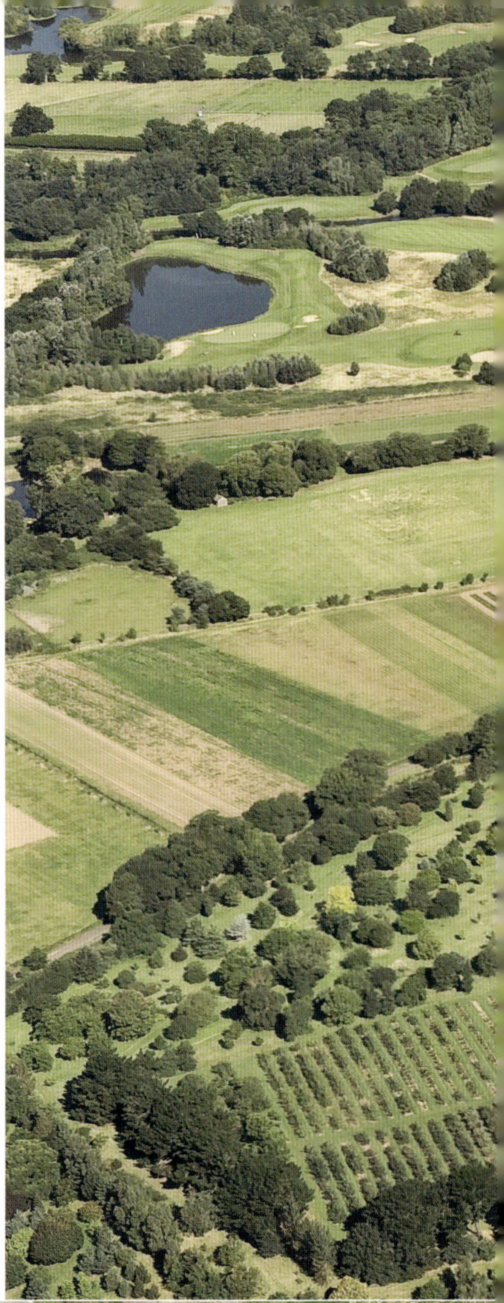

Thorpe Park

One of the UK's first theme parks, Thorpe Park (above) was built in 1979 on a former gravel pit partially flooded to create a water-based leisure park. Located between Chertsey and Egham, the wide range of rollercoasters and proximity to London and the south-east mean that Thorpe Park is the third most popular theme park in Britain after Alton Towers and Blackpool Pleasure Beach, with 1.7m visitors in 2007. Split into eight themed areas, the park contains a number of world firsts including the world's first ten-inversion rollercoaster, the world's first horror movie themed rollercoaster, and the world's first and only backwards in the dark rollercoaster. In October, popular Fright Nights allow visitors to ride rollercoasters in the dark.

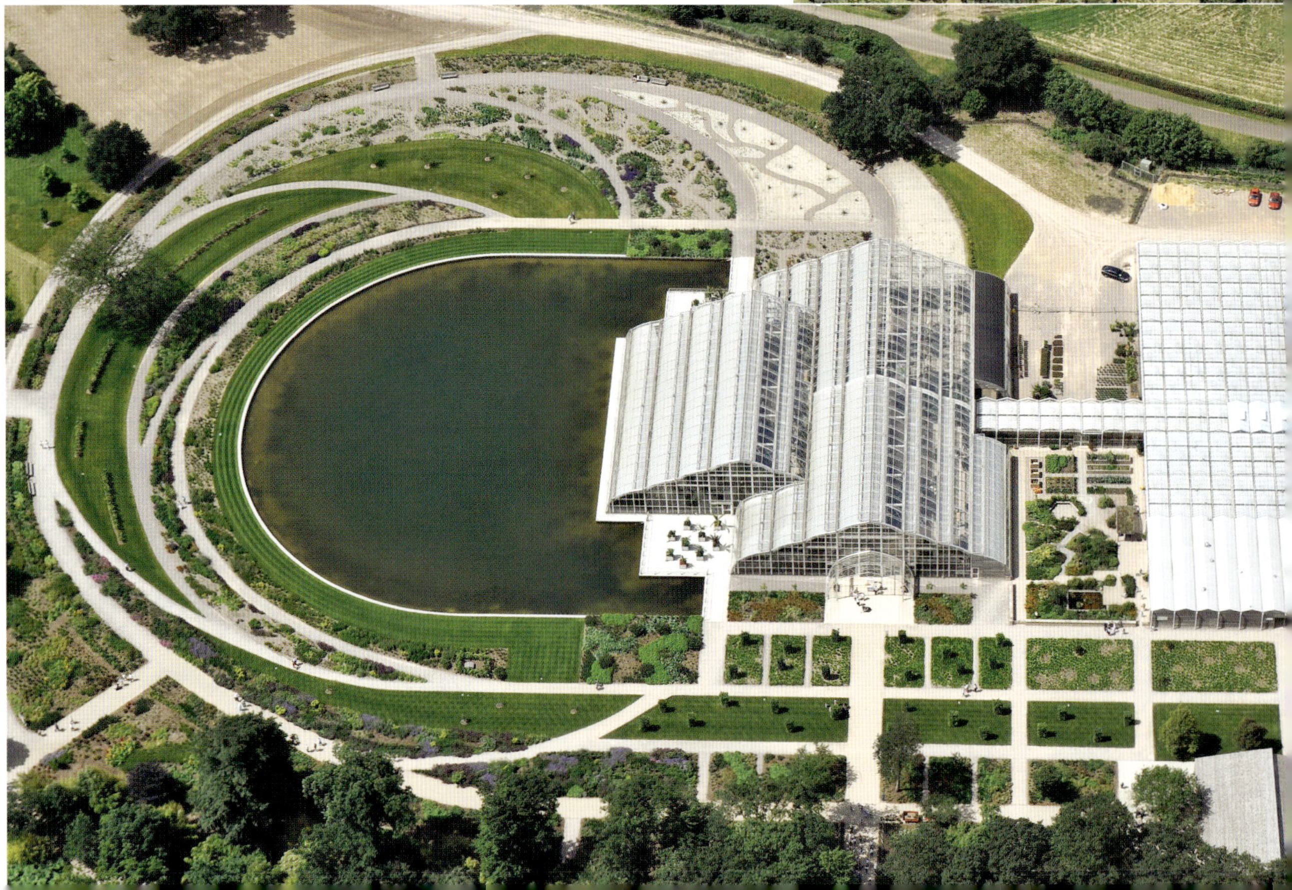

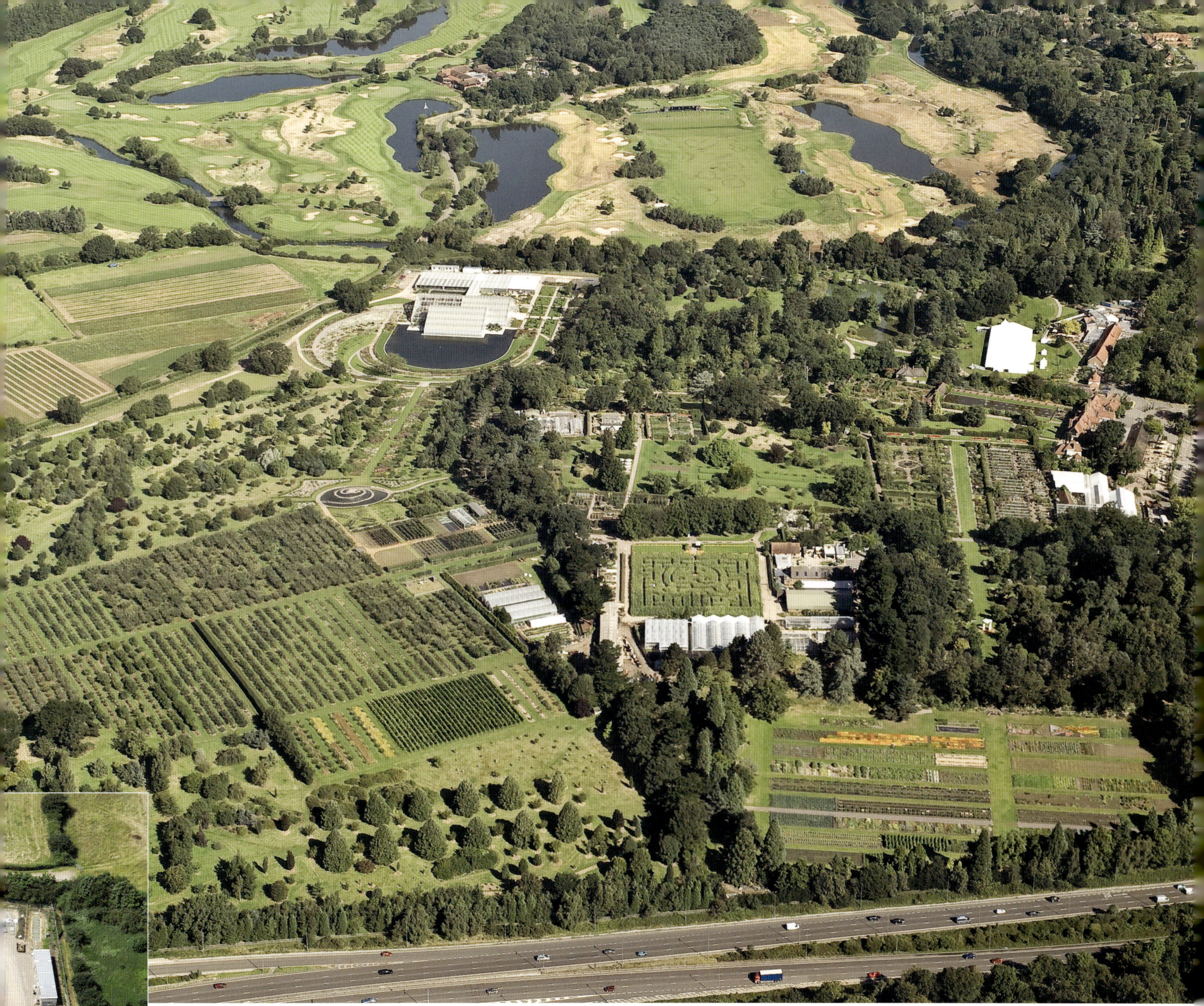

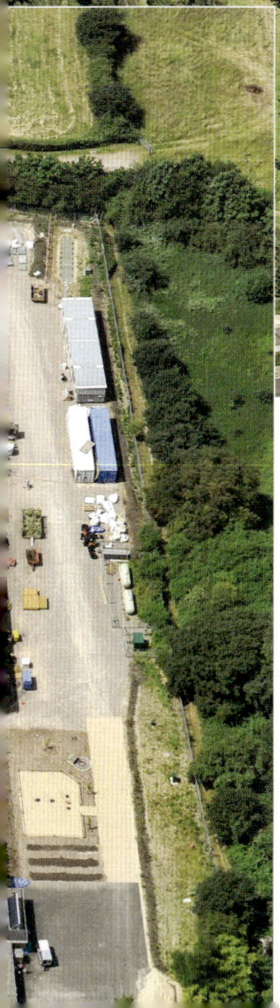

RHS Wisley

The Royal Horticultural Society's gardens at Wisley (left and above) are thought to be one of the great gardens of the world. Spread across a 240 acre site they include an arboretum, a trials field, a number of formal and informal gardens and several glasshouses. Gifted to the Society in 1903, Wisley's facilities also include a scientific and educational laboratory that has trained a number of leading horticulturalists including Robert Fortune, one of the great plant-hunters and Joseph Paxton, later knighted for designing the Crystal Palace. The canal overlooked by the laboratory has one of the UK's largest water lily collections and nearby model gardens show visitors what can be done within an area the size of their own garden. Opened in 2007, the Bicentenary Glasshouse (left) is set beside a lake and within a three-quarter of an acre plot. The glasshouse's design gives a cathedral-like feel. It contains three main planting zones representing tropical, dry temperate and moist temperate climates.

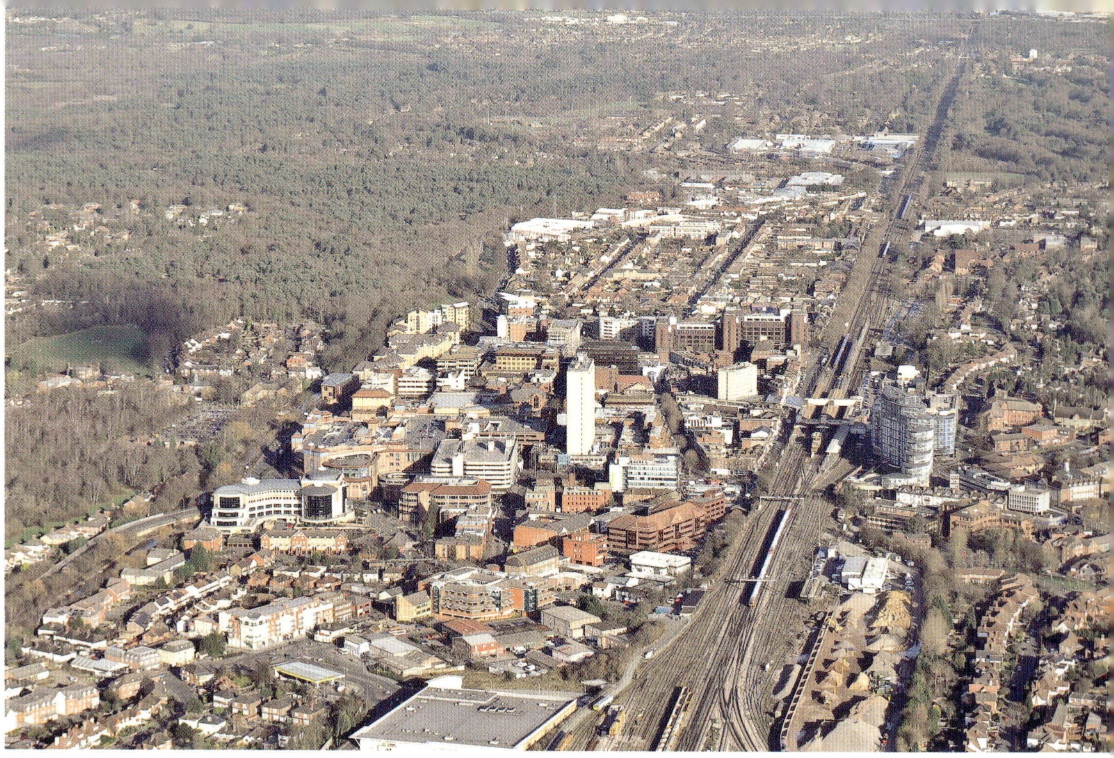

WOKING

A large town on London's commuter belt, Woking's green and leafy surroundings (below and right) were the setting for a Martian invasion in local resident HG Wells' novel *The War of the Worlds*. Built up around the railway station, the town is popular for its convenient shopping and leisure facilities and is the site of the UK's first purpose-built mosque. Woking's Brookwood Cemetery is the UK's largest cemetery and one of the largest in Western Europe, with over 240,000 people buried there. Known as the London Necropolis it was established in 1849 to house the increasing numbers of London deceased and was originally reached by a direct rail line from London's Necropolis Station close to Waterloo. A large number of soldiers from the two world wars are buried here, as well as Muslim scholars and soldiers.

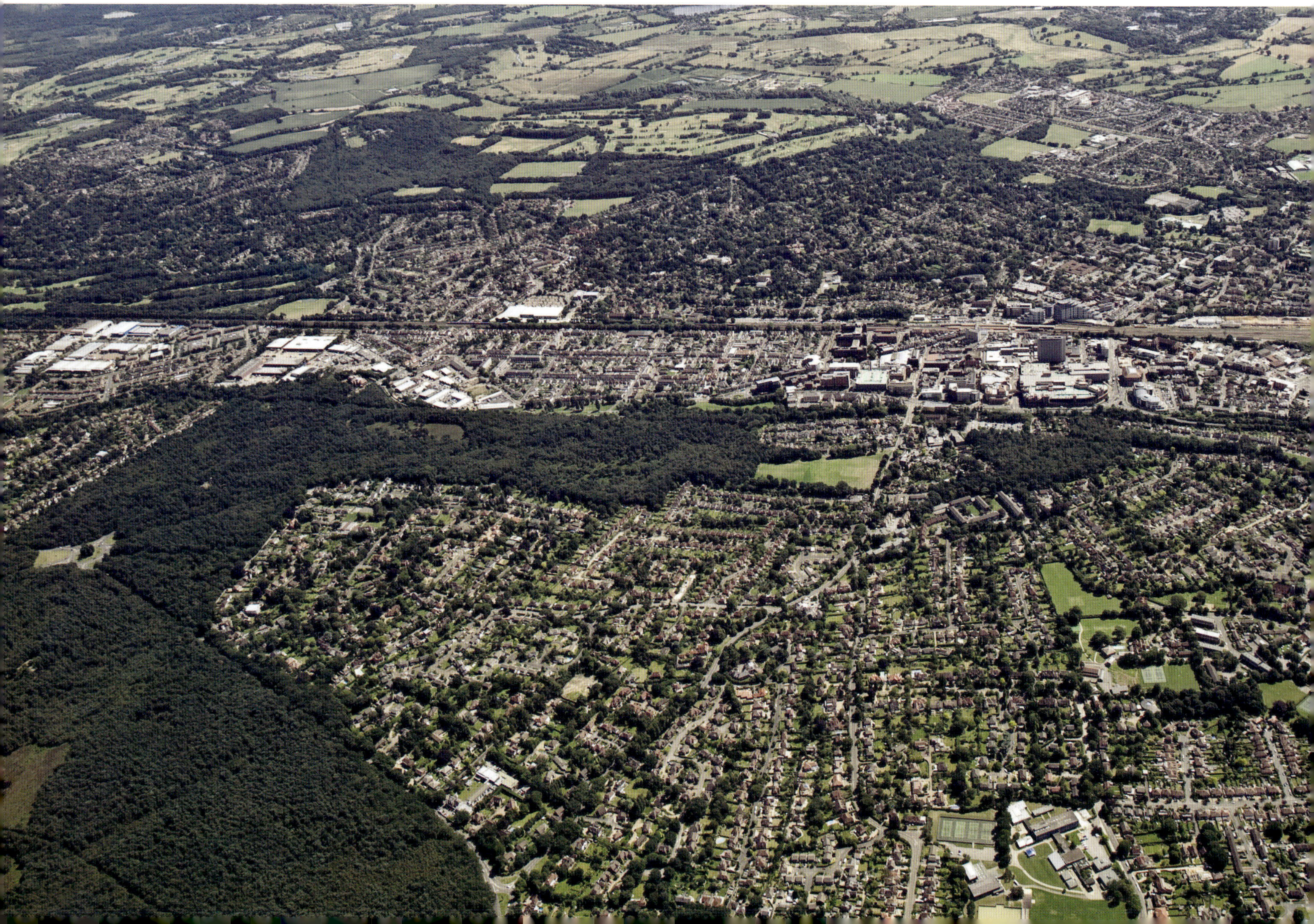

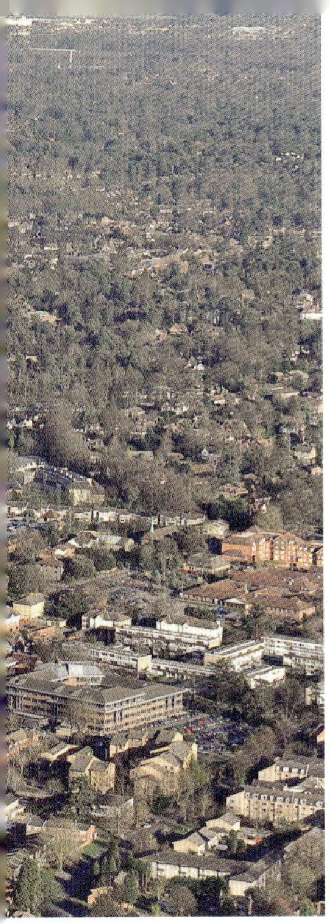

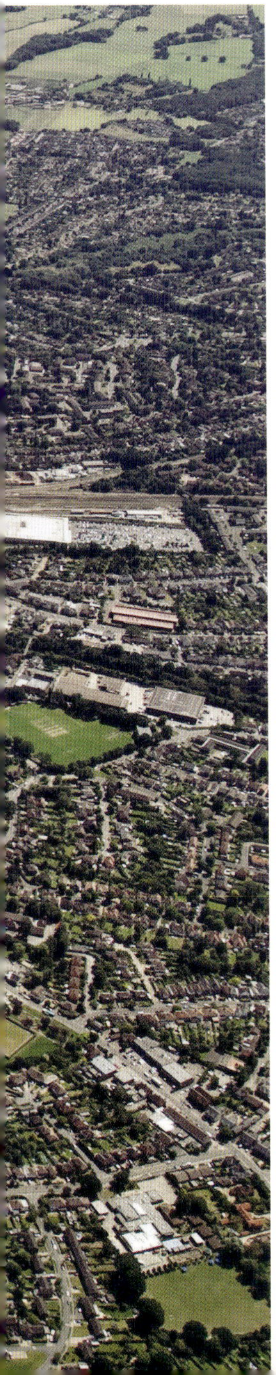

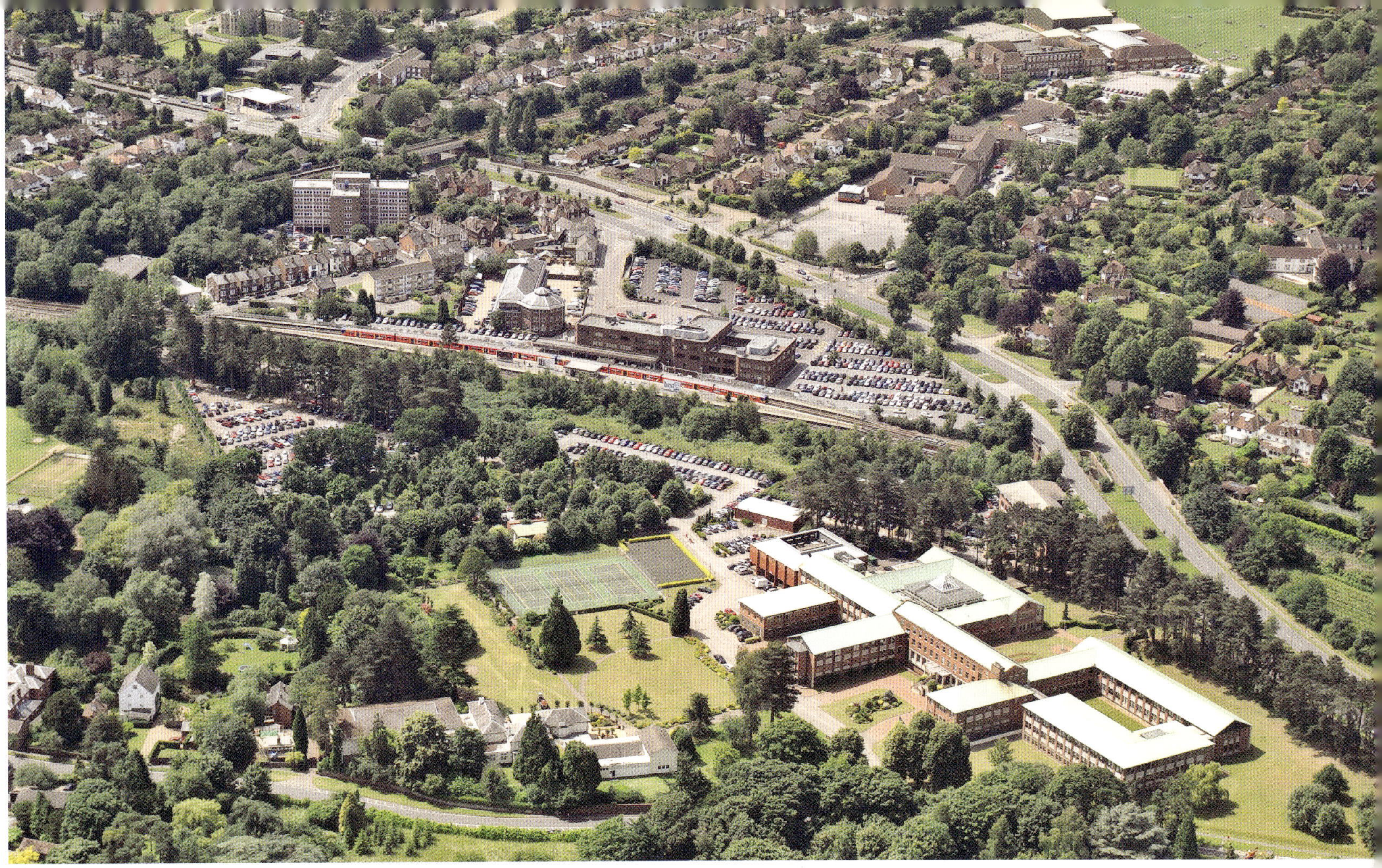

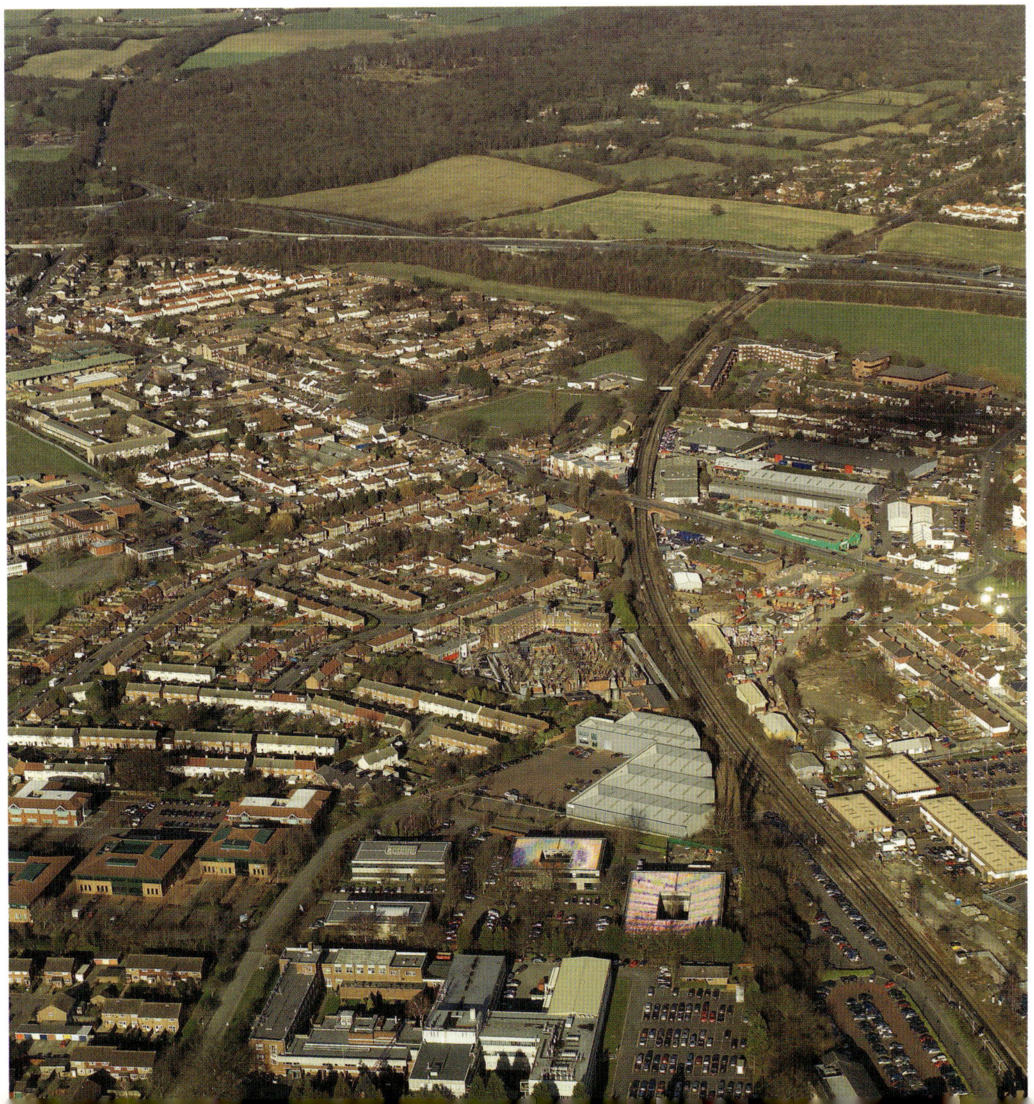

Dorking

Dorking's pleasant setting (above) in the Surrey Hills Area of Outstanding Natural Beauty, and its proximity to beauty spots such as Box Hill, has attracted visitors ranging from Jane Austen and Charles Dickens to EM Forster and John Keats. The market town grew as a transport hub for walkers, riders and coaches following the North Downs or the Roman Stane Street, which connected London to the south coast.

Leatherhead

This market town (left) grew up beside the river Mole close to the Surrey Hills. Before becoming a commercial business centre, Leatherhead was home to industries such as Ronson's Lighters and Goblin Vacuum Cleaners, whose factories were converted to ammunition plants during the Second World War.

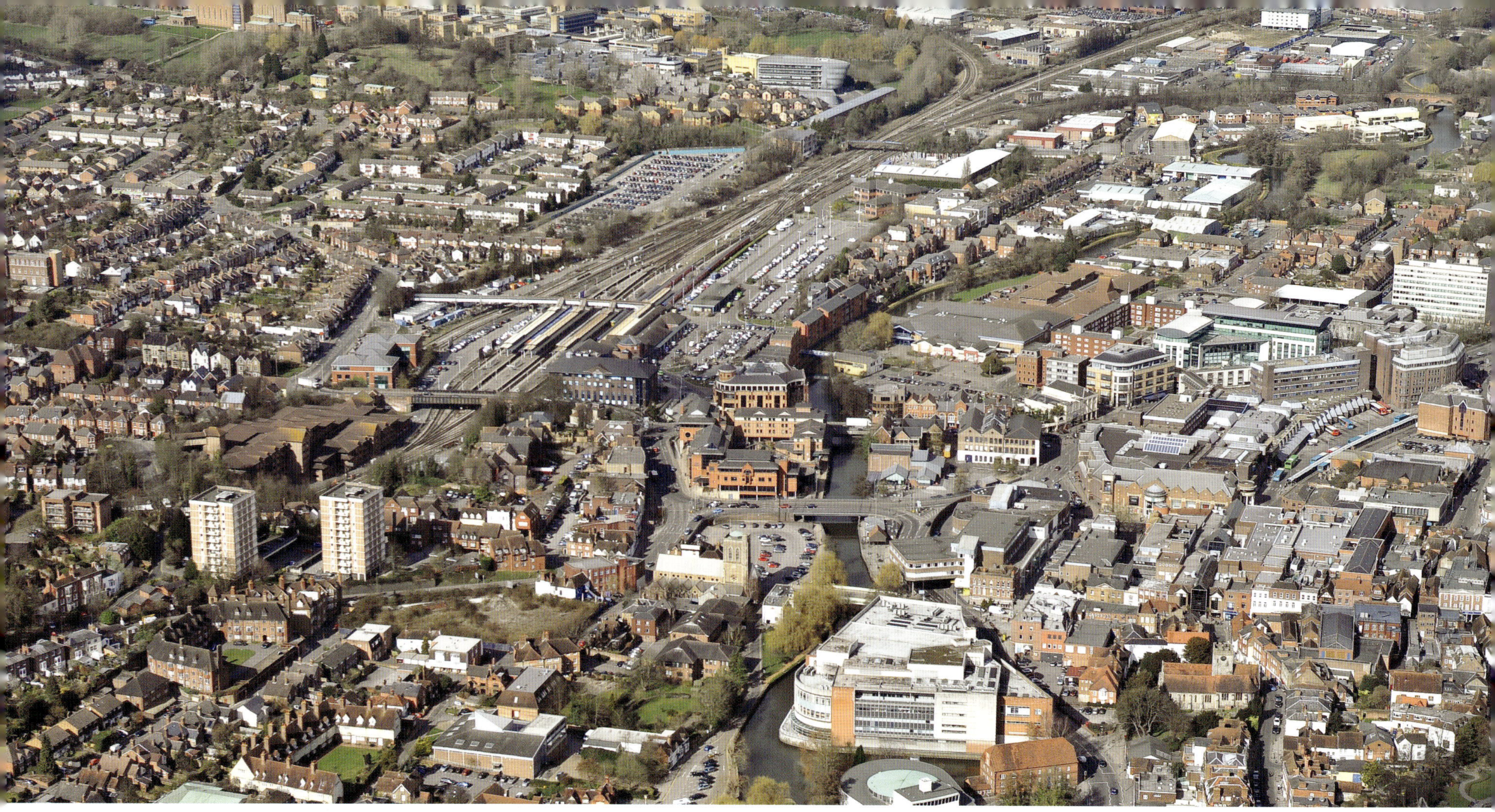

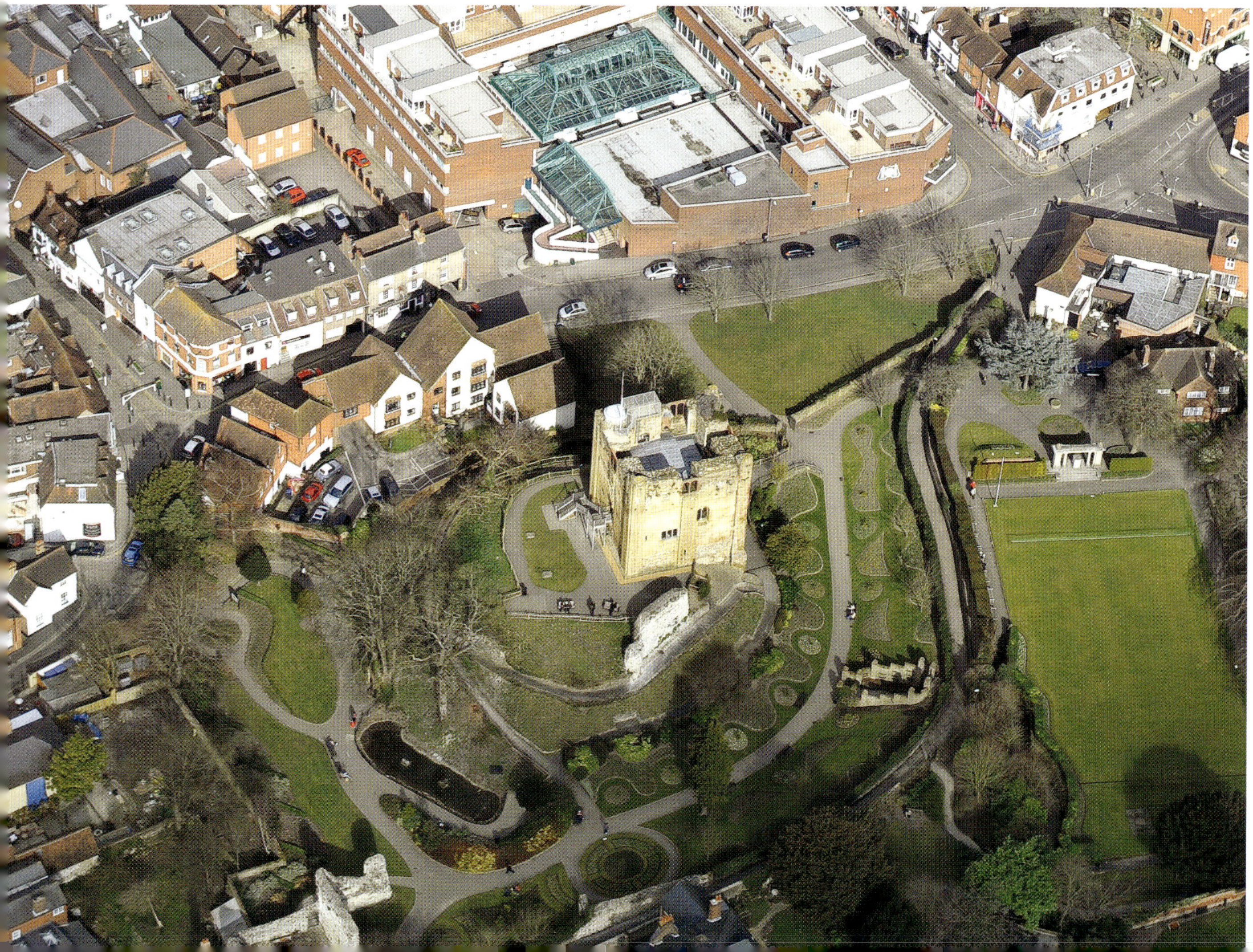

GUILDFORD

The bustling market town of Guildford (above) is a popular shopping centre and one of the most expensive places to live in the UK outside London. The county town of Surrey, Guildford is also home to the campus of the University of Surrey. The Guilfest music festival and the Surrey County Show are held annually in Stoke Park, where there is a prizewinning leisure centre. Famous residents of Guildford include Alan Turing, the mathematician, and Lewis Carroll, author of *Alice's Adventures in Wonderland*. The Norman castle building (left) was constructed by William the Conqueror to prevent rebellion after he sacked Guildford and the countryside after the Battle of Hastings.

Guildford Cathedral

Consecrated in 1961, the Cathedral Church of the Holy Spirit, Guildford stands on Stag Hill (right) overlooking the University of Surrey campus and is used by the university for graduation ceremonies. The cathedral has distinctive red bricks made from Stag Hill clay. Although its construction, to a design by Sir Edward Maufe, began in 1936 building work was interrupted by the Second World War. An Anglican cathedral, the tower is 160ft (49m) high and contains 12 bells and a gilded angel at the top. Scenes from the classic horror film, *The Omen*, were filmed on site.

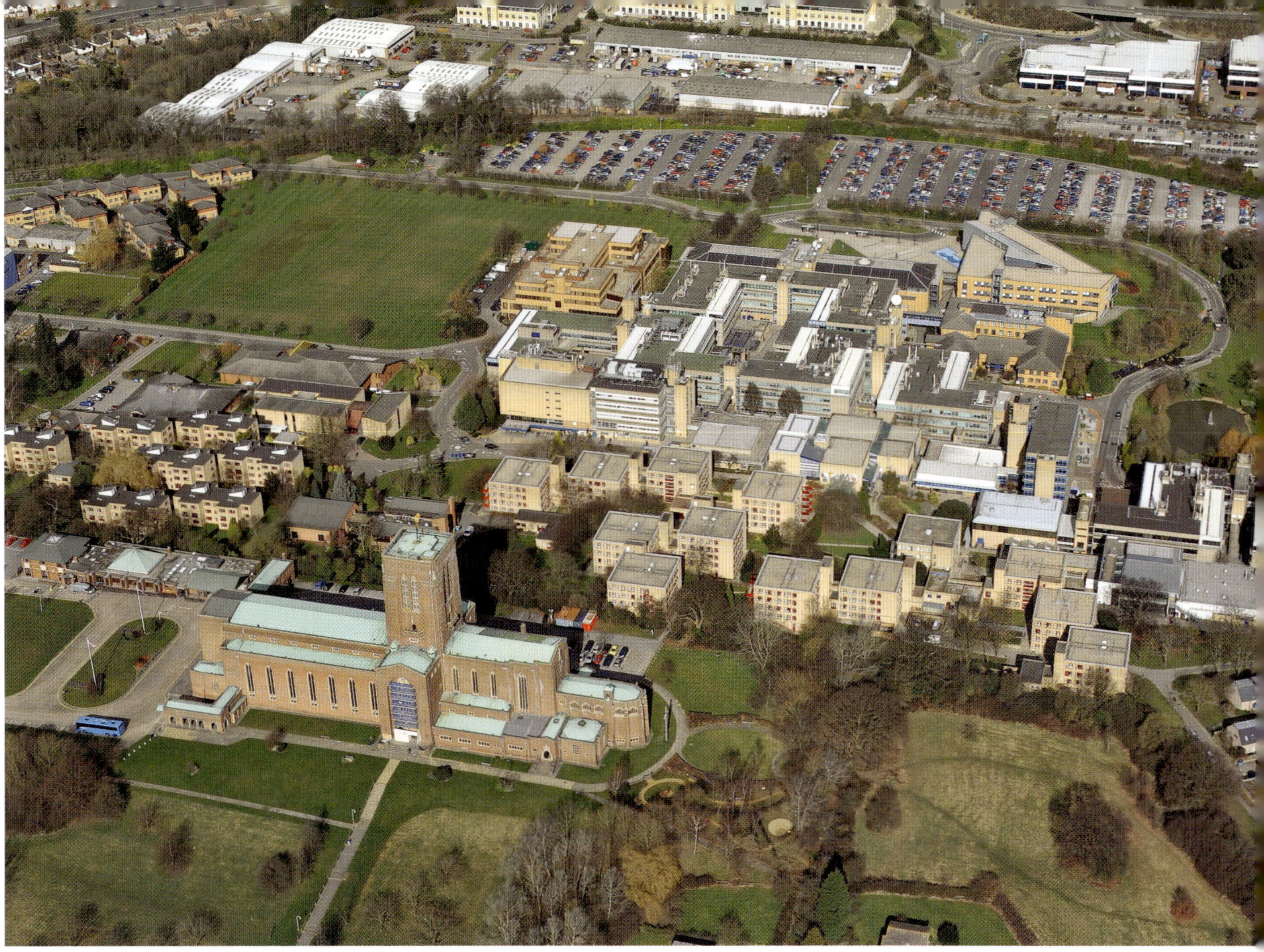

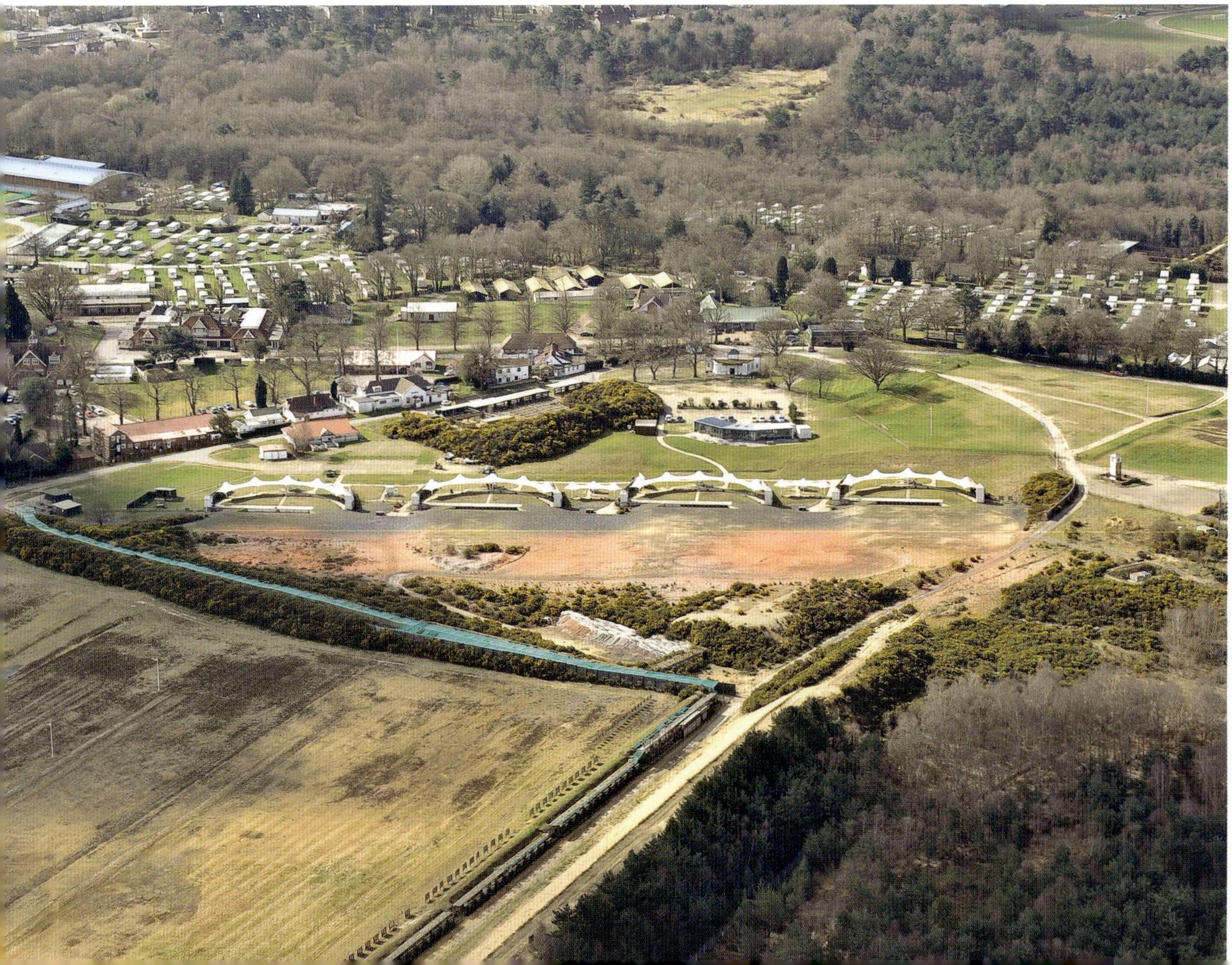

Bisley

The National Shooting Centre at Bisley (left) is the world's best known shooting centre and the headquarters of the National Rifle Association. Set in 3000 acres of Surrey heathland, the centre has some of the most modern shooting facilities in the world and played host to all the shooting disciplines of the 2002 Commonwealth Games. Its colonial style clubhouse buildings date back to the Victorian era when the National Shooting Centre moved from Wimbledon Common. The Pavilion, a former officers' mess, was a music venue in the 1970s and is now a hotel and venue for corporate entertaining.

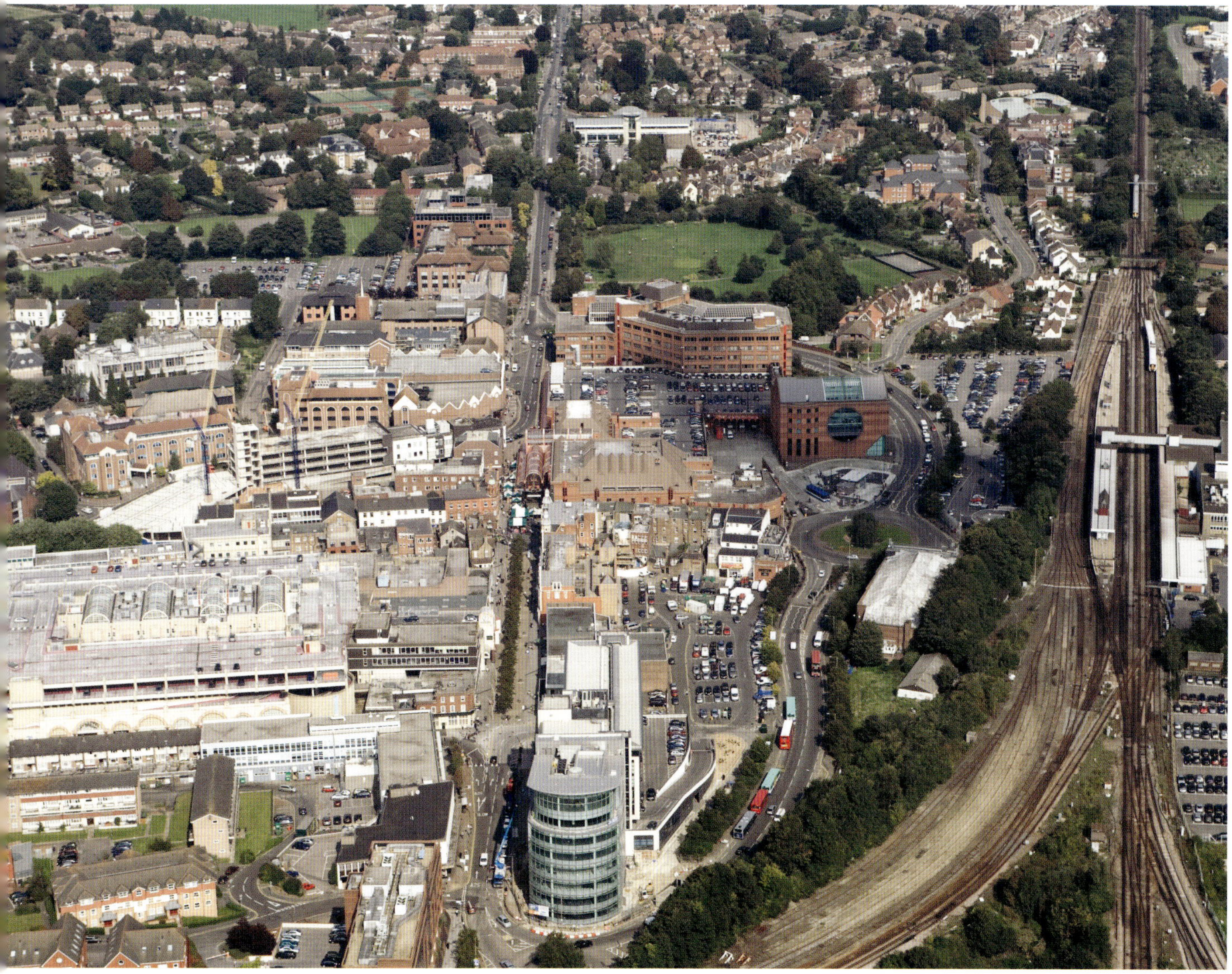

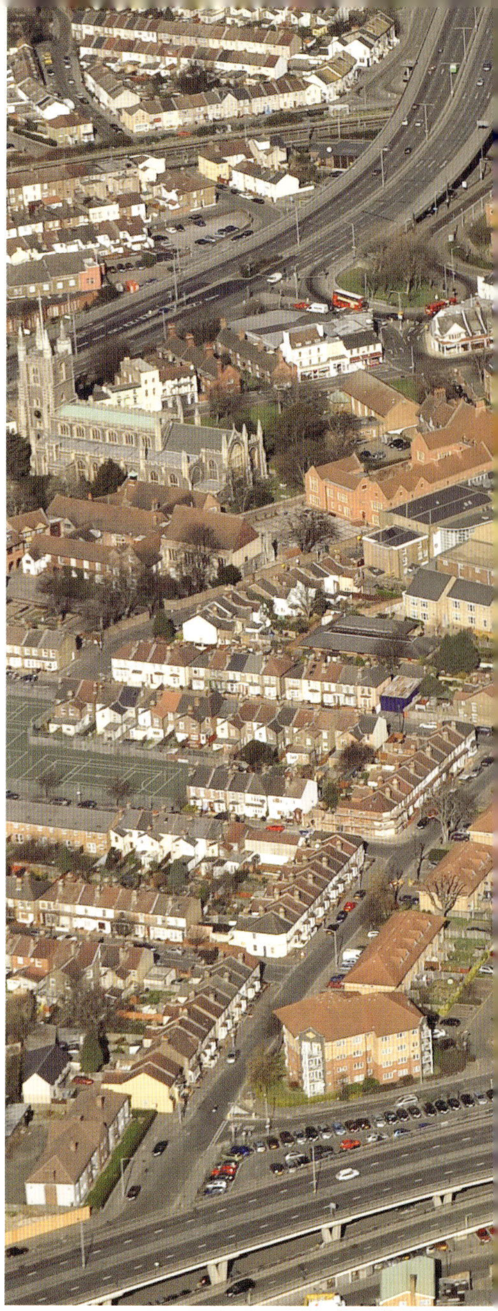

Redhill

At the foot of the North Downs just 20 miles south of central London lie the linked towns of Reigate and Redhill. Reigate is the older of the two towns, first mentioned in the Domesday Book in 1086 as a small settlement, growing up around a late 11th century castle, a priory and an 18th century town hall. Redhill developed in the 19th century and boomed with the arrival of the railway. Now a major shopping centre, Redhill's facilities include the Belfry shopping centre (above) and the redbrick Warwick Quadrant (right) which contains the Harlequin theatre and library.

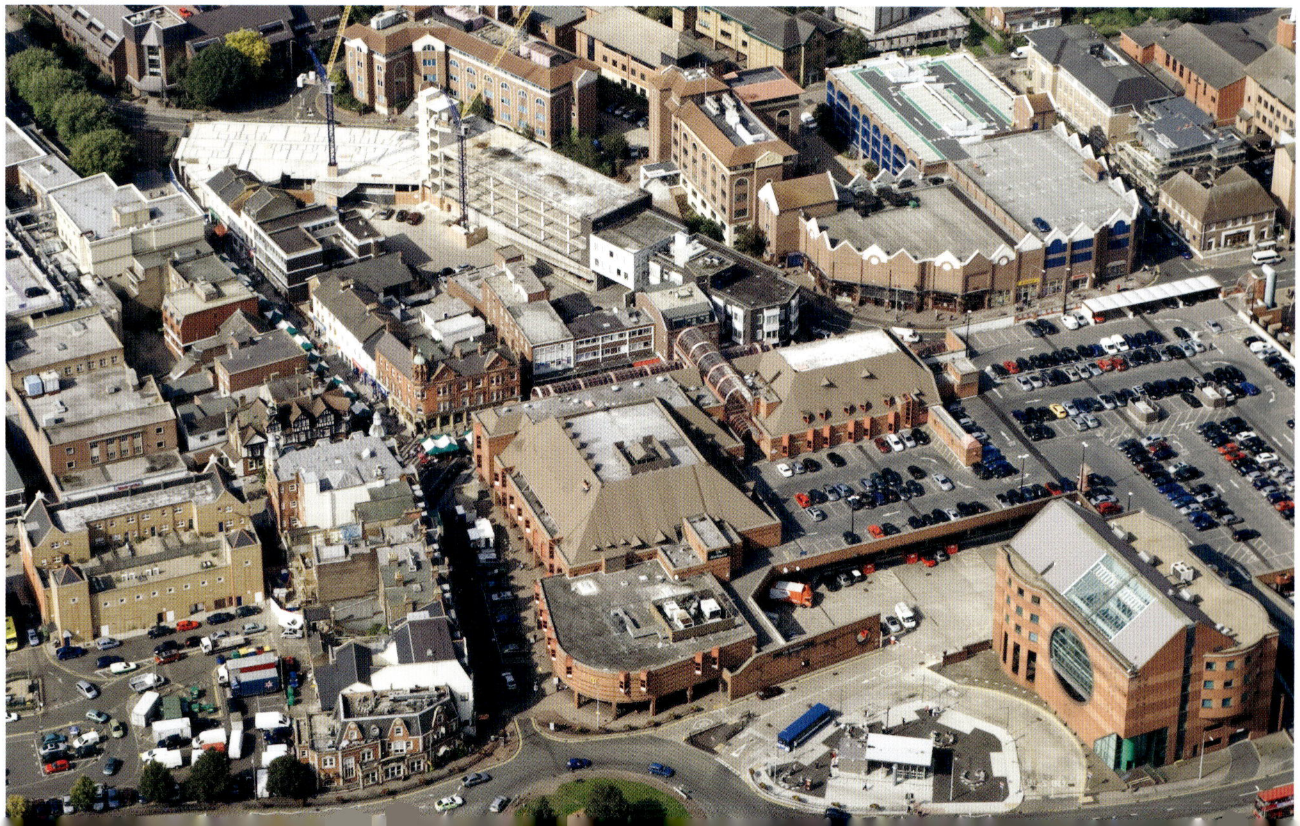

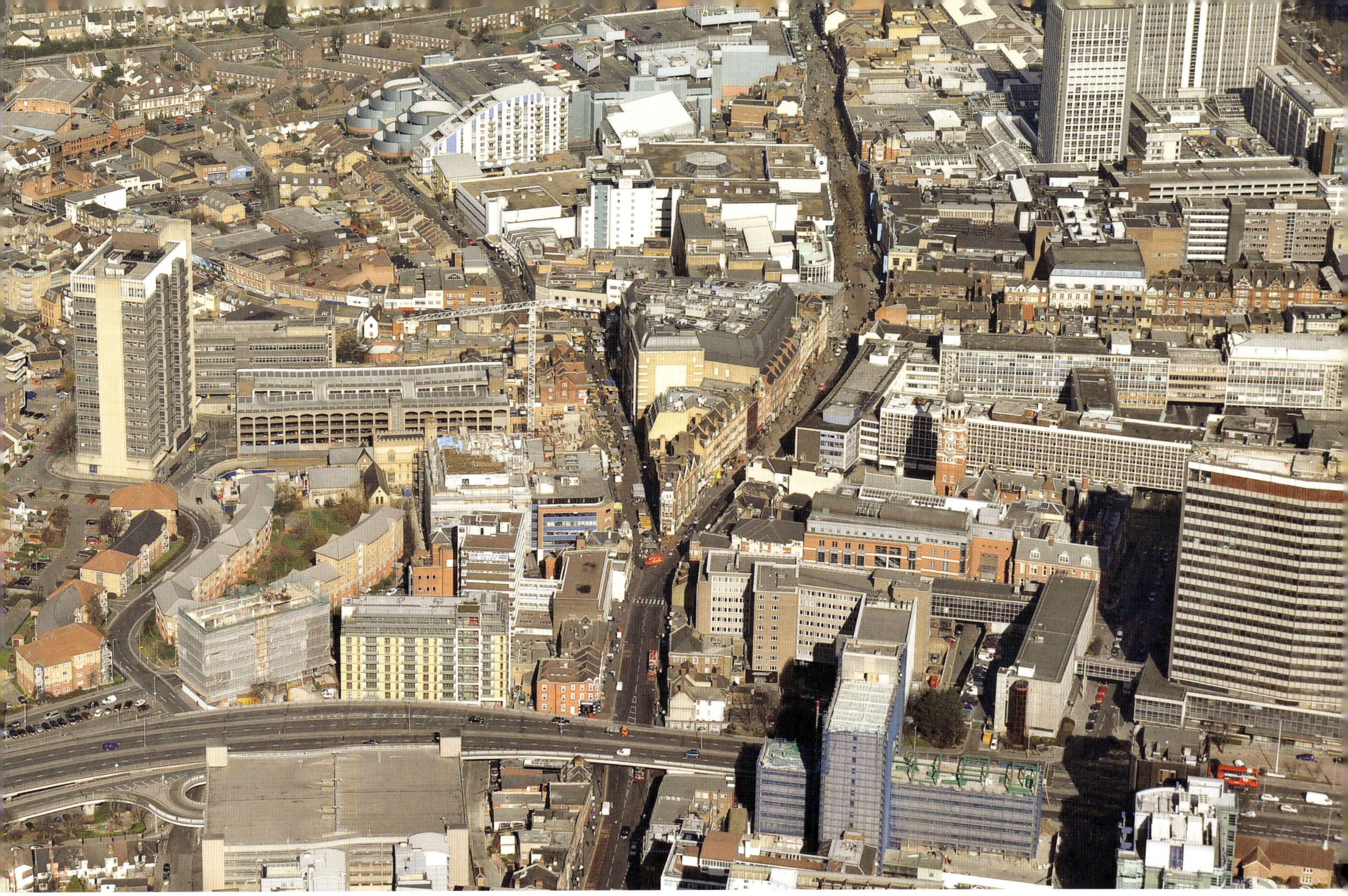

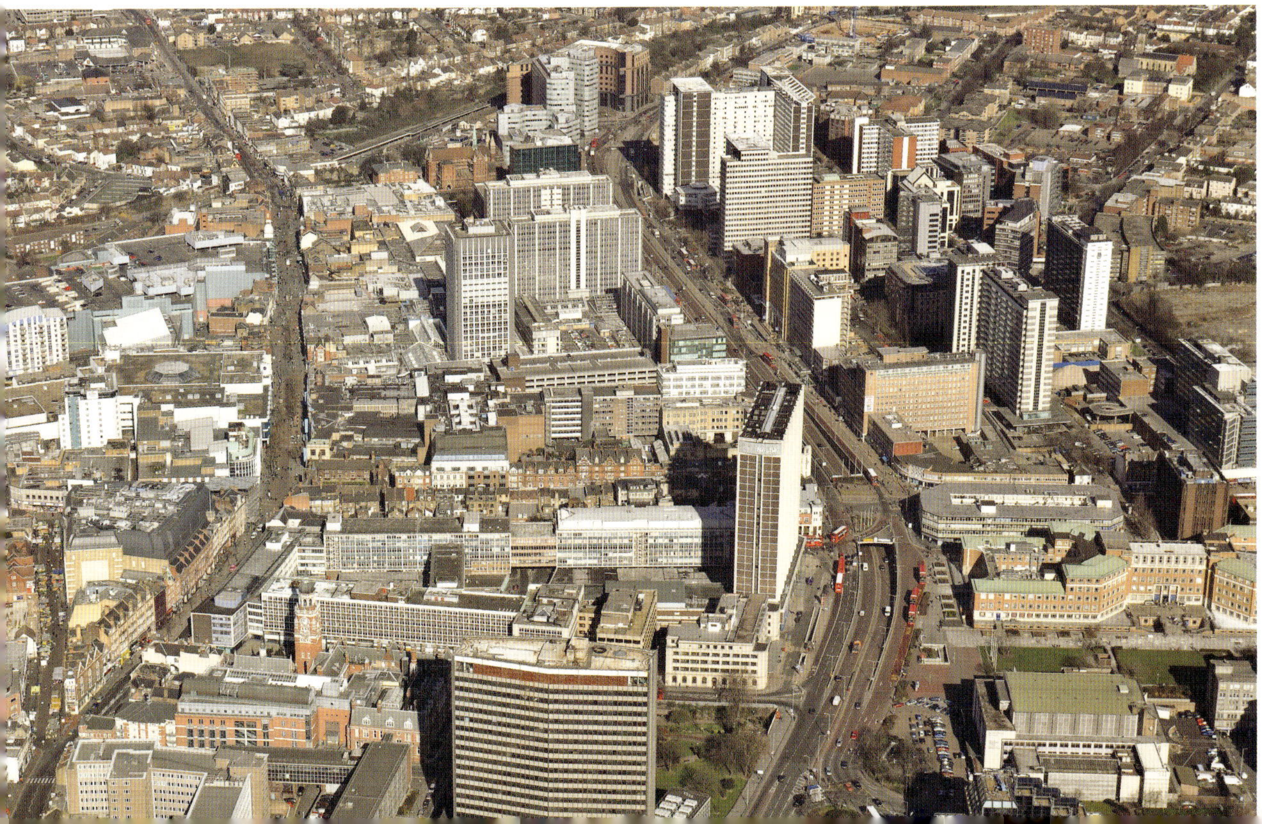

Croydon

Today a major business centre and transport hub, Croydon (above and left) developed during the middle ages as a market town and centre for brewing, leather tanning and charcoal production. In 1803, the world's first horse-drawn railway opened between Croydon and Wandsworth in London, facilitating Croydon's development as a commuter town. Known for industrial production including metalworking and car manufacturing in the early 20th century, mid 20th century redevelopment of Croydon and the relocation of office space from central London brought multi-storey office buildings and facilities. A pedestrianised high street and retail facilities including the Whitgift shopping centre have made Croydon a popular shopping district.

SUSSEX

The chalky South Downs extend from Hampshire to meet the Channel at Beachy Head where they give Sussex its most dramatic outlook. One of Britain's finest unspoilt coastlines, the Sussex Heritage Coast stretches for 6 miles between Eastbourne and Seaford. The Sussex coast is also dotted with seaside resorts such as Brighton, Worthing and Eastbourne that developed in Georgian and Victorian times to enable the wealthy to make the most of the healthy sea air and sunshine. Many continue to cater for tourists and a number of eye-catching Victorian, Edwardian and Art Deco buildings and bandstands evoke the heyday of these seaside resorts. At strategic locations in between the resorts are fortifications ranging from Norman castles, built by William the Conqueror following his victory in the Battle of Hastings, to Martello towers and early 19th century Palmerston forts and follies.

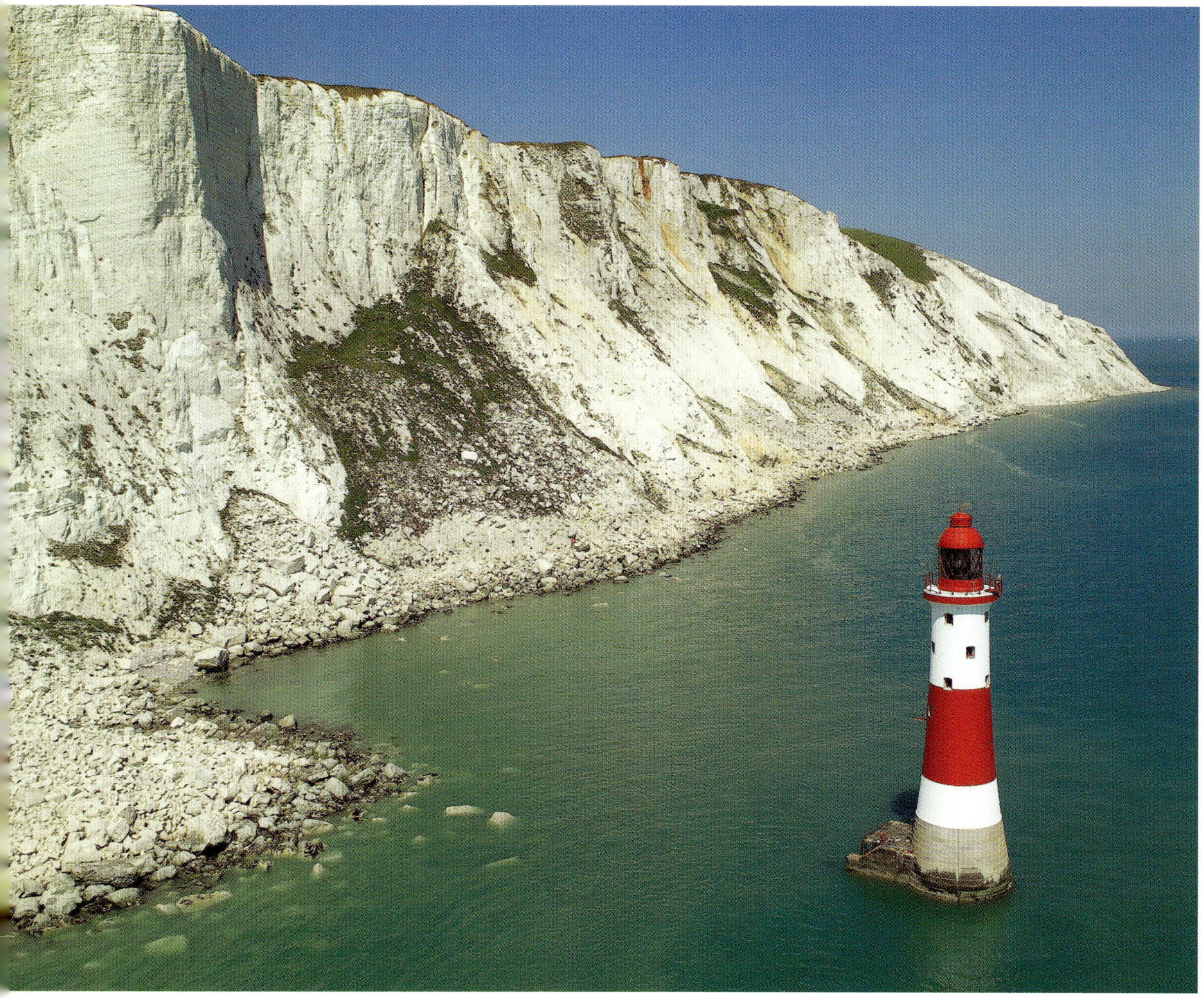

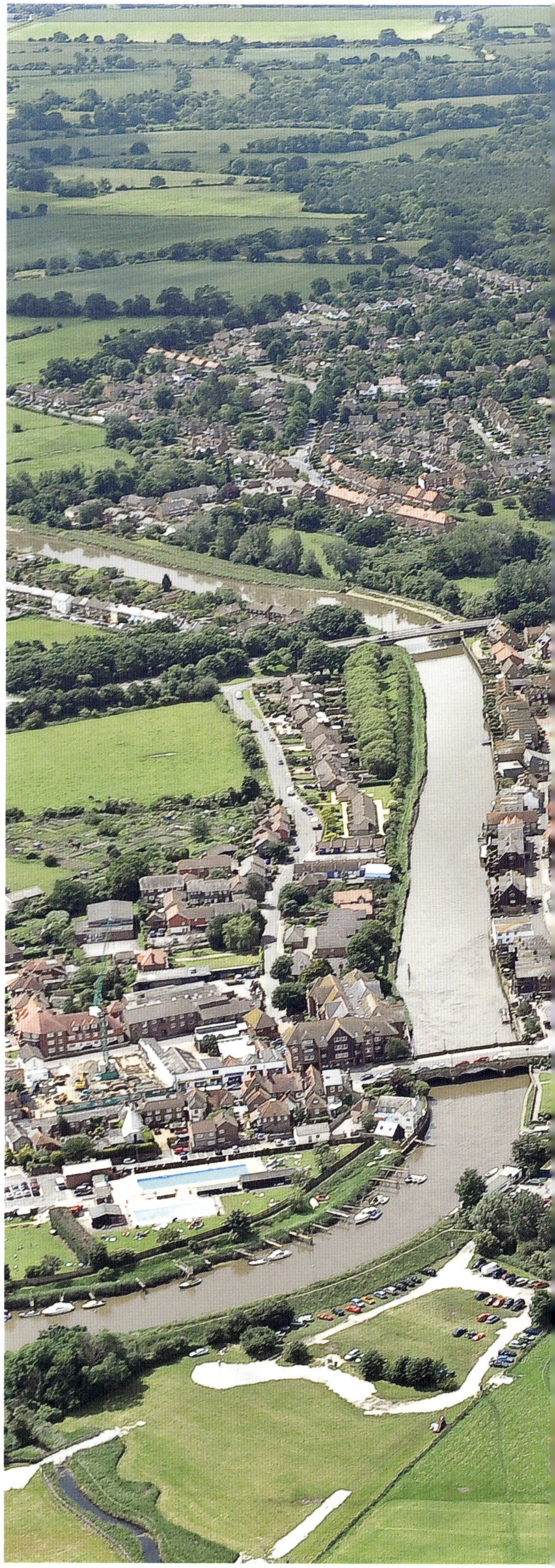

SUSSEX LANDMARKS

The lighthouse at Beachy Head (above) and Arundel's stunning castle and cathedral overlooking the river Arun (right) are among the famous landmarks of the beautiful county of Sussex.

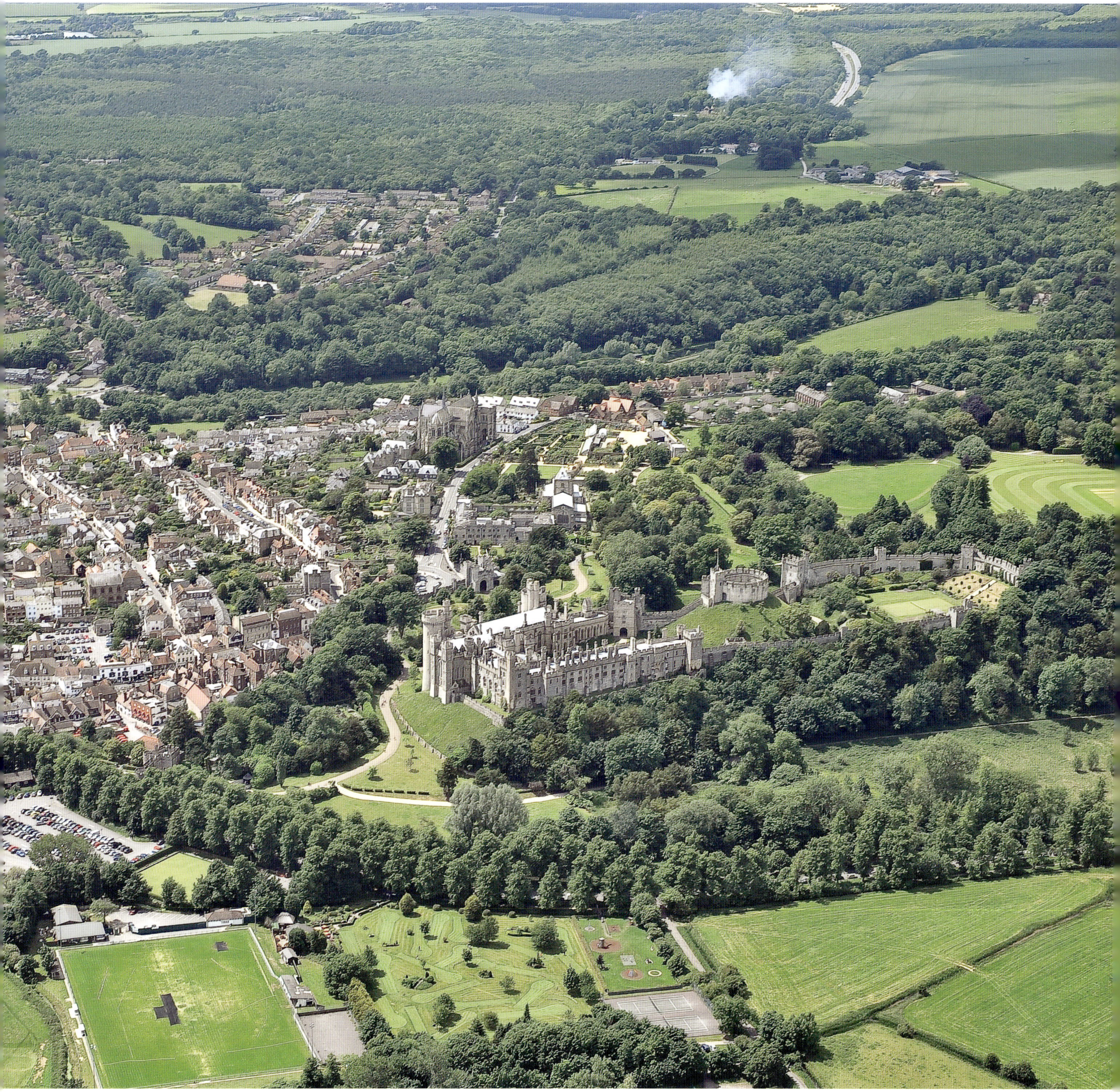

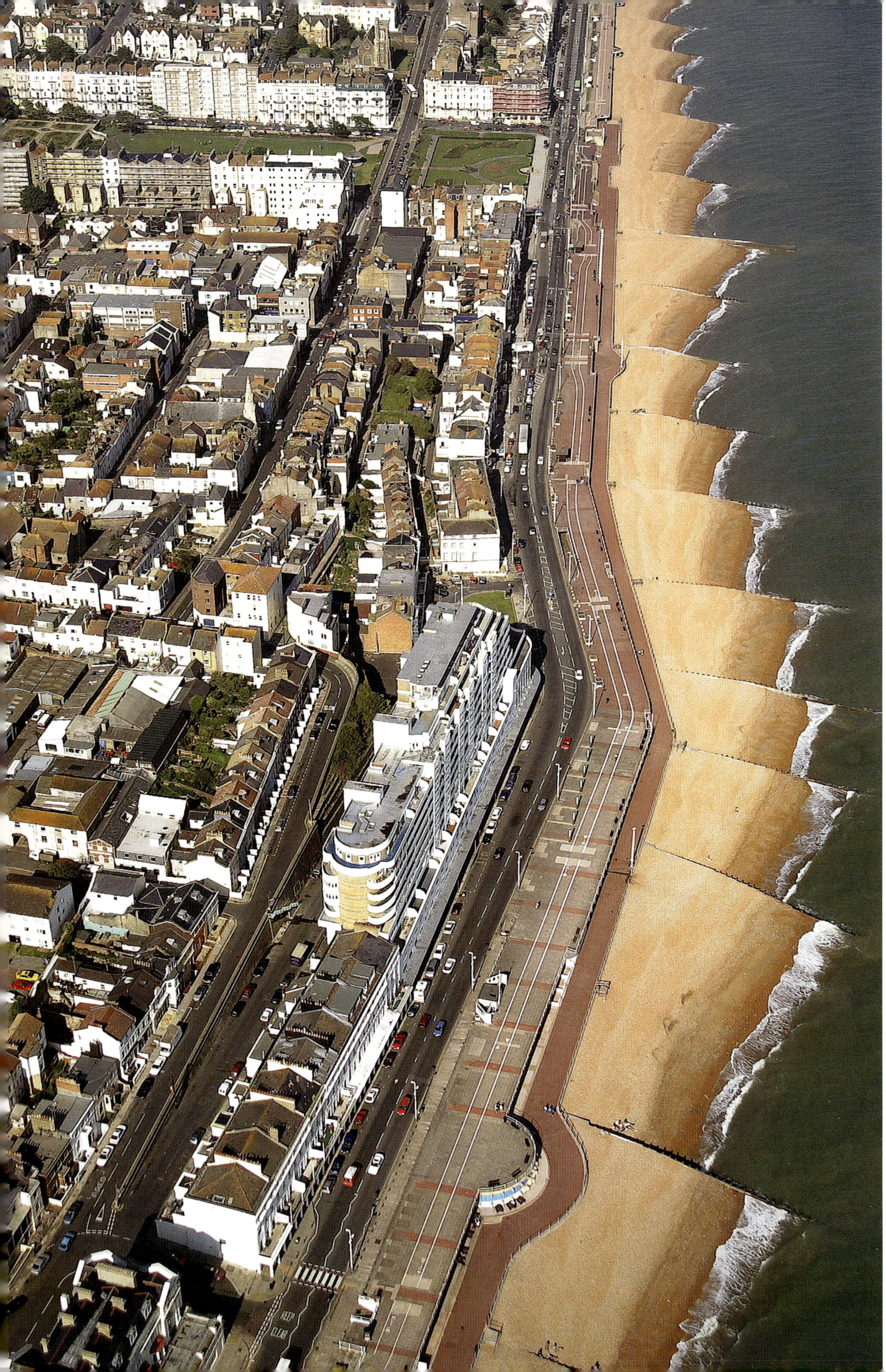

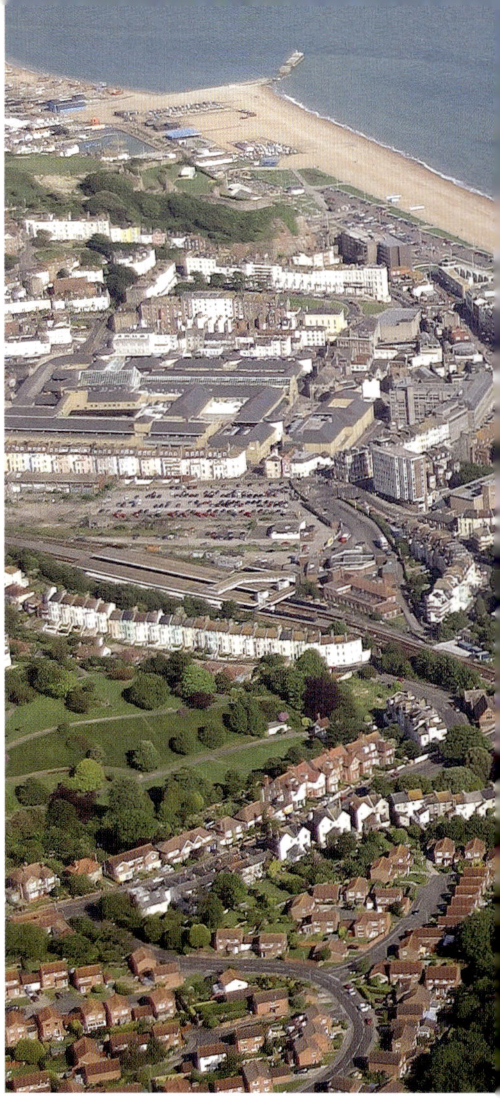

Hastings

This fishing town and seaside resort will be forever famous for the 1066 Battle of Hastings when William of Normandy defeated King Harold, although this historic event actually took place 7 miles inland at Battle. In the later middle ages Hastings became one of the prosperous Cinque Ports. The town's coastal light and clear air attracted artists such as Dante Gabriel Rossetti and Holman Hunt during the late 18th and 19th centuries. Today Hastings still boasts the largest beach-based fishing fleet in England and is undergoing a period of regeneration. A new railway station has opened, as well as an outpost of the University of Brighton.

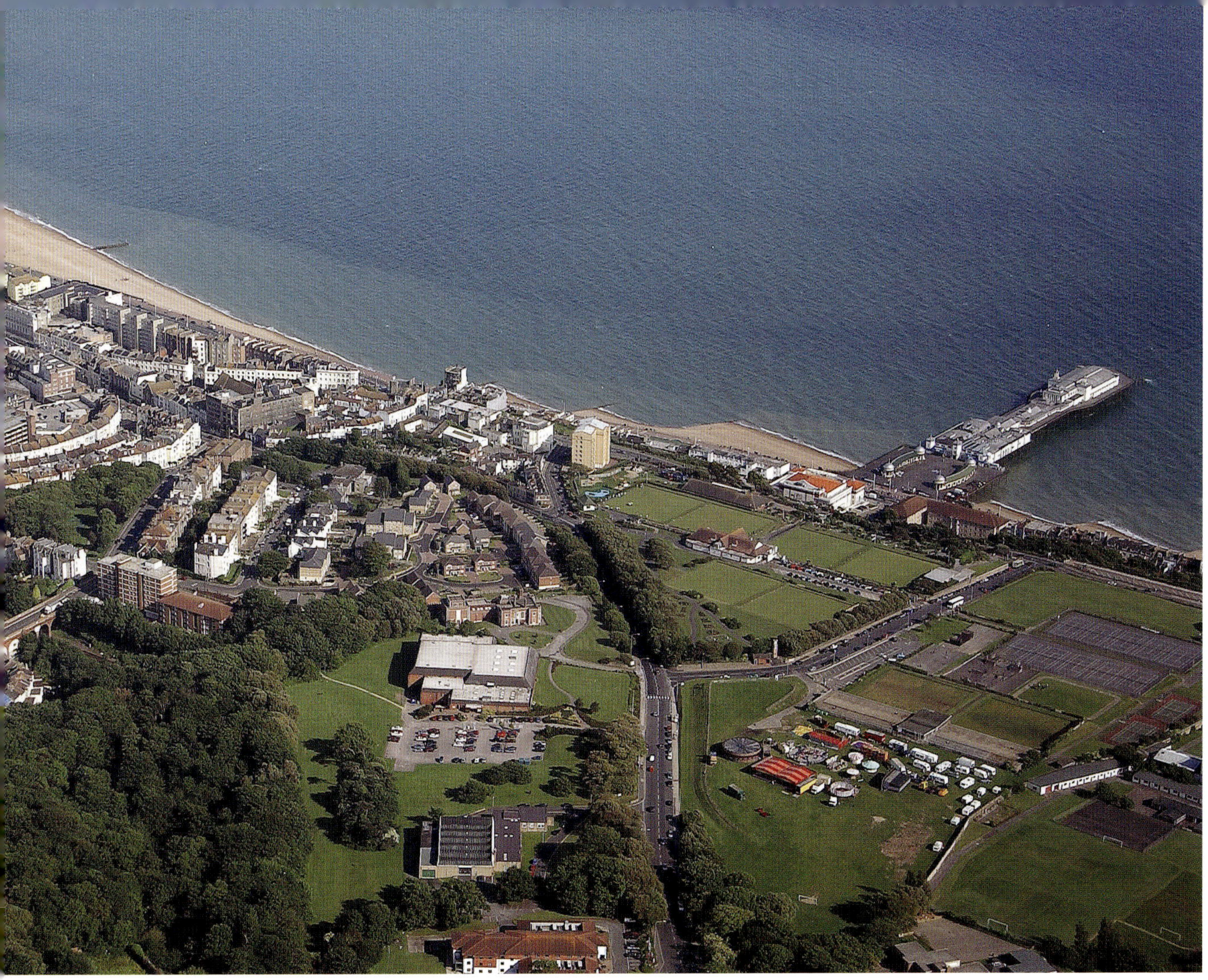

HASTINGS PIER

Opened in 1872, Hastings Pier (left and below) was designed by Eugenius Birch, who also designed Brighton's West Pier. Reaching 910ft (280m), it had a 2,000-seat pavilion that was destroyed by fire in 1917. During the 1960s and 70s the pier was host to concerts by a range of well-known music groups including The Who, The Rolling Stones and Pink Floyd. The pier has been closed since 2006 after storm damage left it unsafe and local residents are campaigning for its restoration.

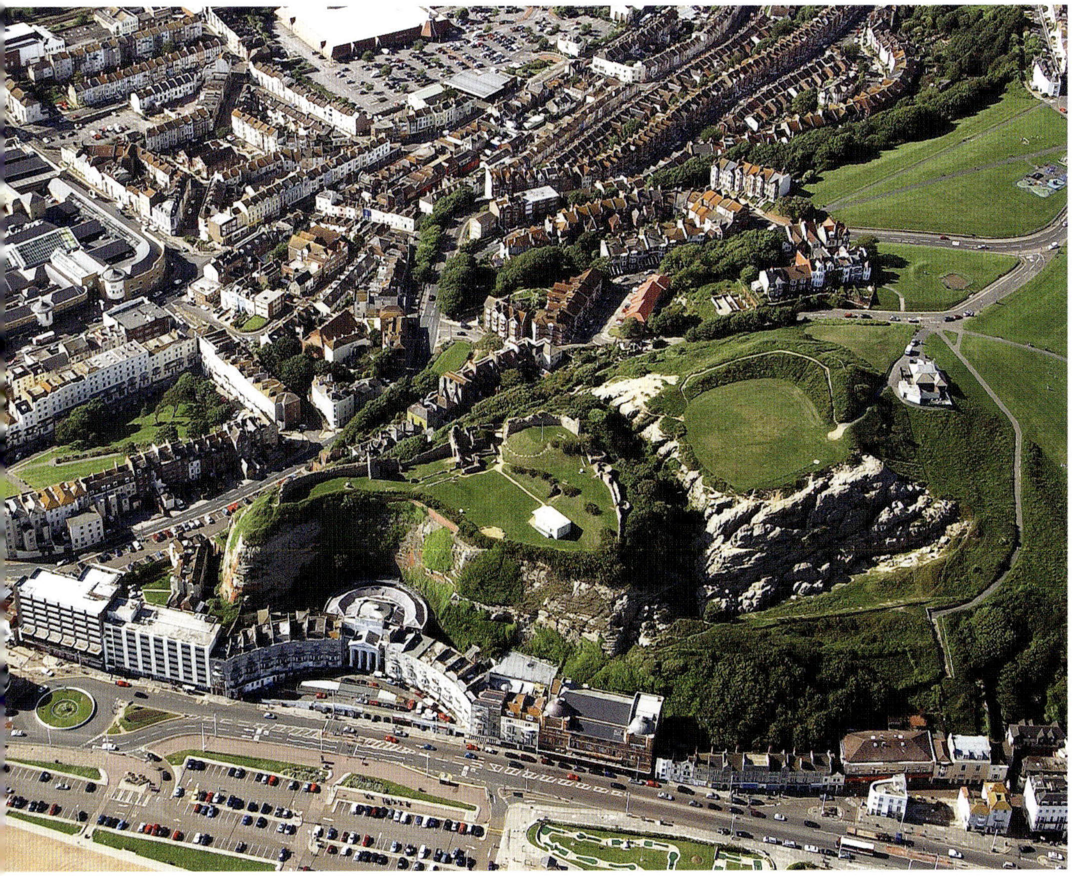

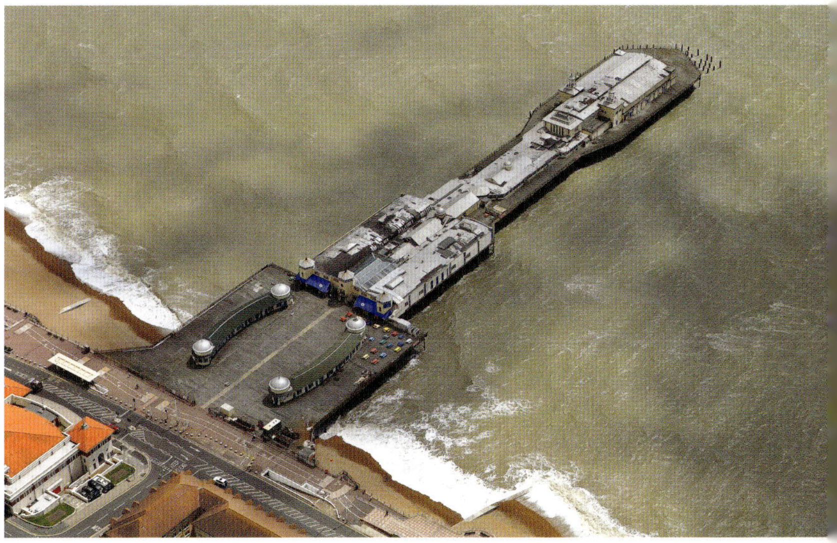

HASTINGS CASTLE

William the Conqueror ordered three fortifications to be built a few days after his victory in the Battle of Hastings: Pevensey Castle, Dover Castle and Hastings Castle. Little remains of Hastings Castle (left) after severe storms in the 13th century, erosion over the centuries and bombing in the Second World War. "The 1066 Story" is a modern attraction at the castle today.

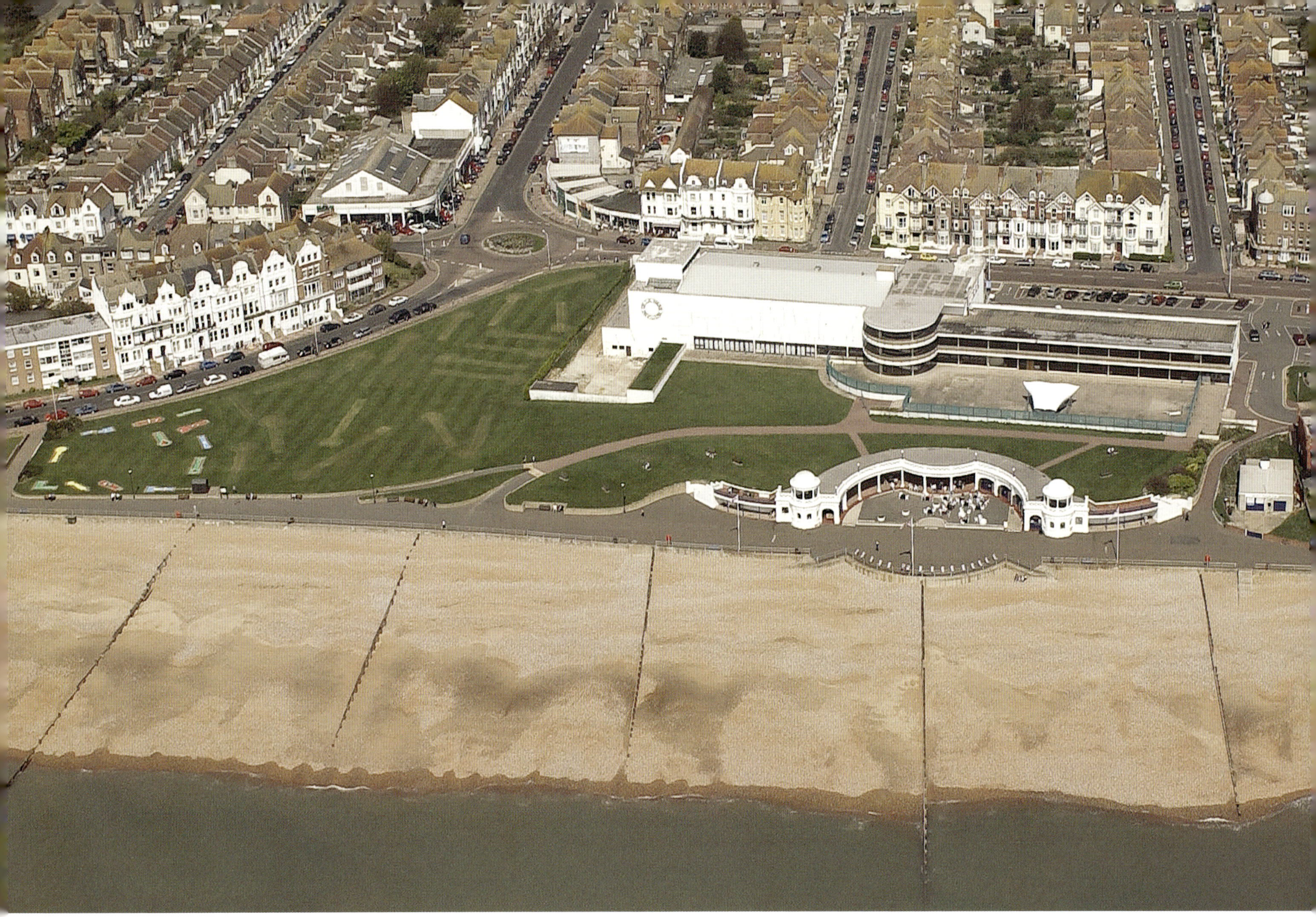

BEXHILL

The rural village of Bexhill was transformed into an exclusive seaside resort by the 7th Earl De La Warr in the 19th century and named Bexhill-on-Sea. He oversaw the construction of the De La Warr Parade, while the luxurious Sackville Hotel, originally including a house for his family, opened in 1890. In 1902 a Royal Charter was granted to Bexhill and delivered by motor car. To celebrate, and to promote the resort, the 8th Earl organised the first ever motor car races along the Parade, making Bexhill the birthplace of British motor racing. It was the 9th Earl who championed the construction of the famous De La Warr Pavilion (above) , which opened in 1935, the first welded steel building in the country and one of the best early examples of the International Modernist style.

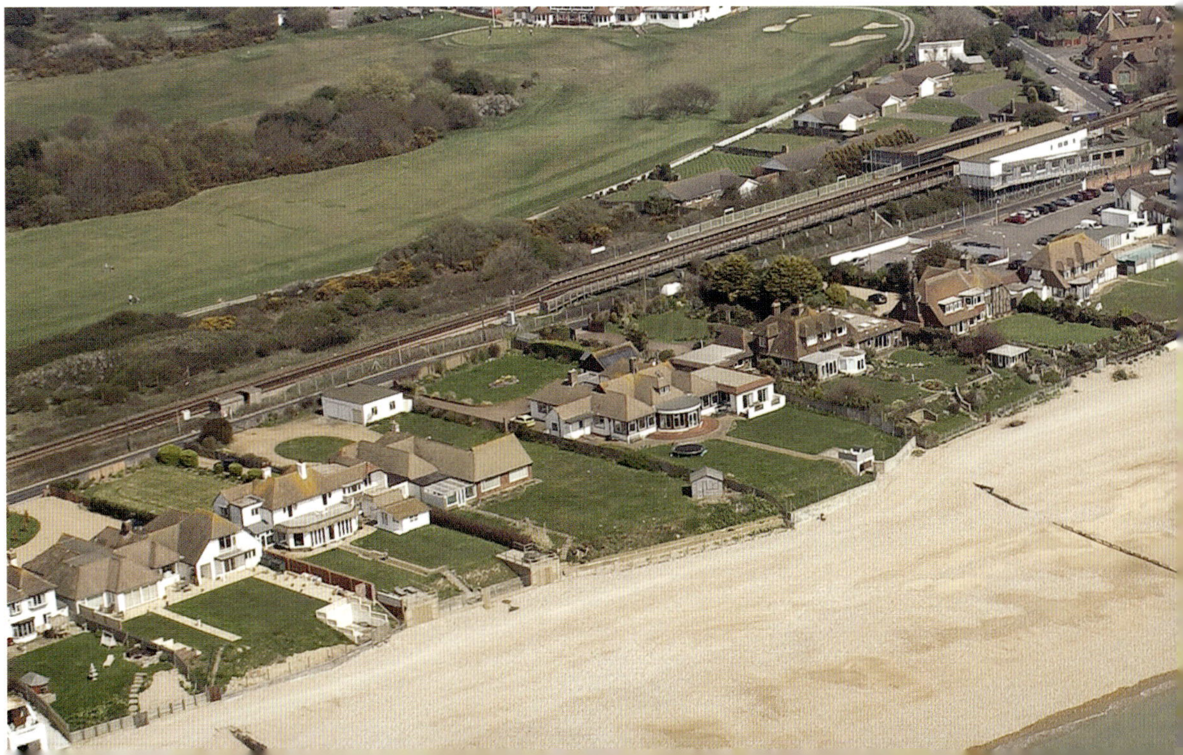

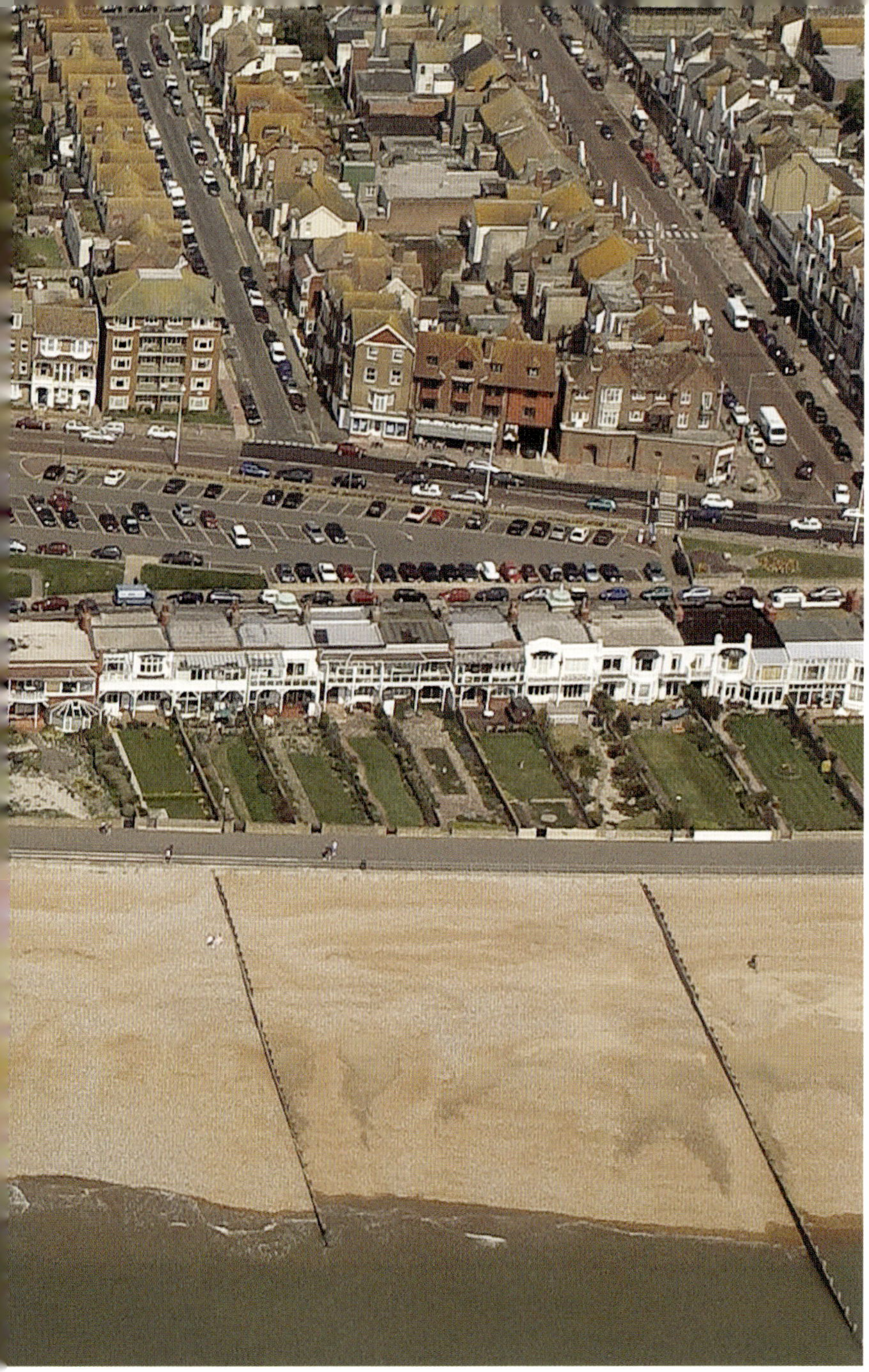

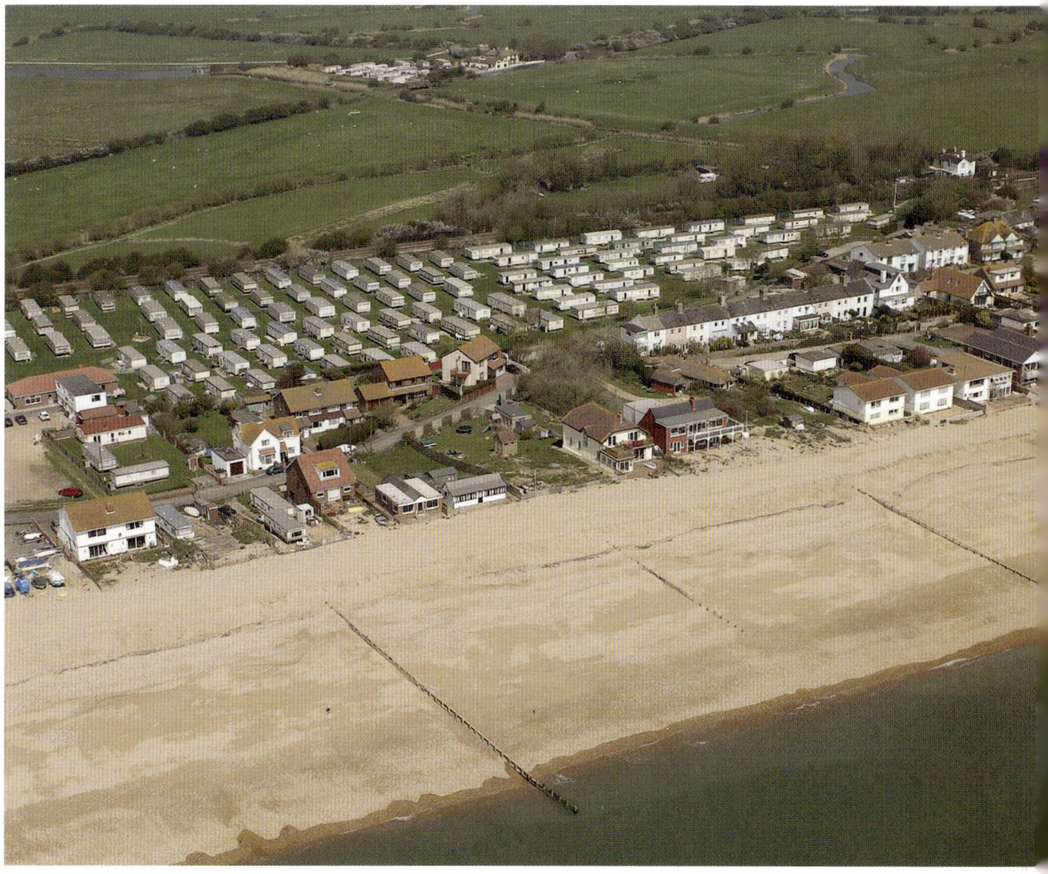

PEVENSEY

Pevensey Bay (above and below left) was a small fishing village founded in the 17th century, but is now a small seaside resort. Pevensey, like many other seaside locations in this area, is littered with fortifications and Martello Towers (below) which were built to resist a potential invasion by Napoleon. Seventy four of these towers were built along the Kent and Sussex coastline from Folkestone to Seaford between 1805 and 1808.

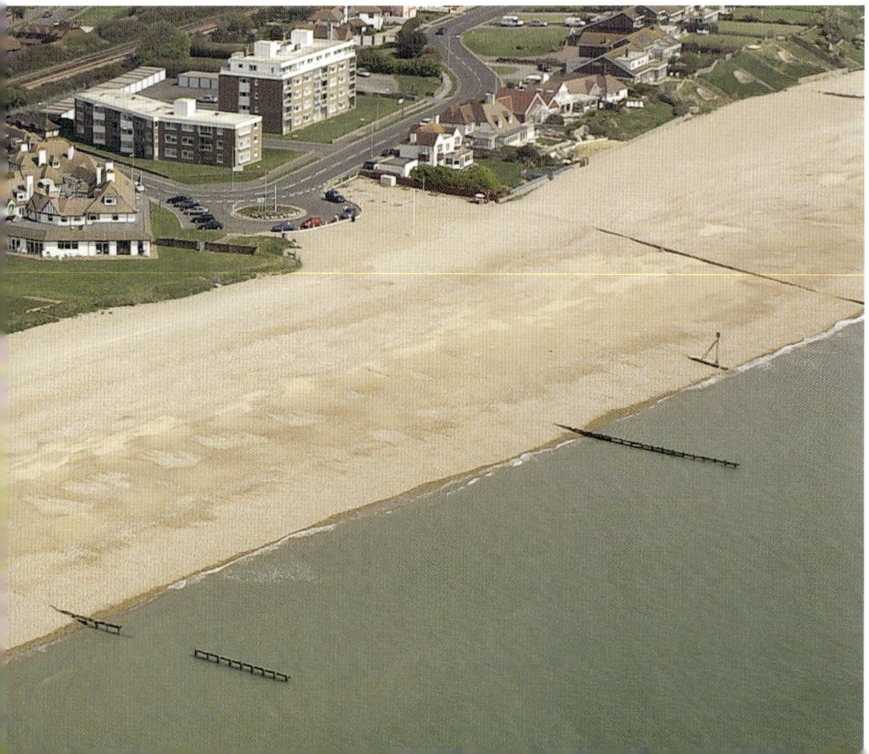

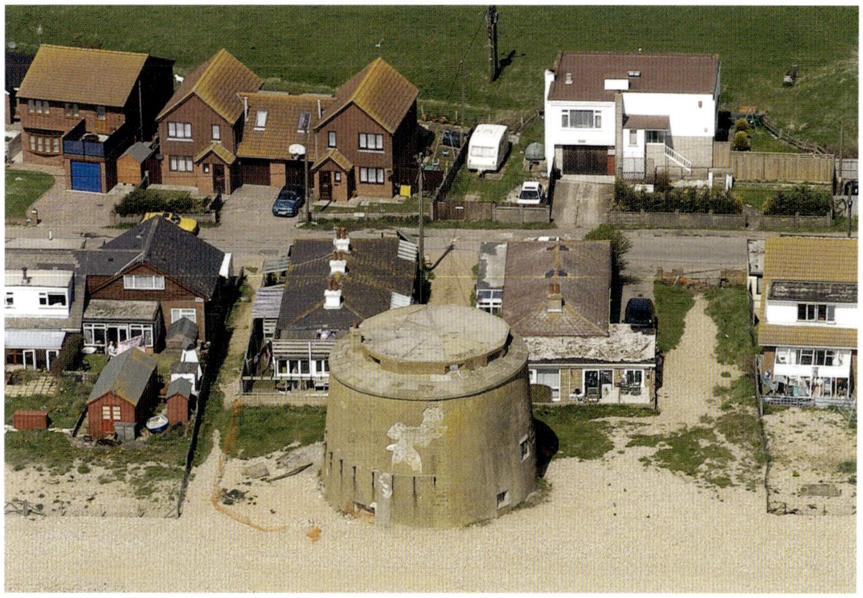

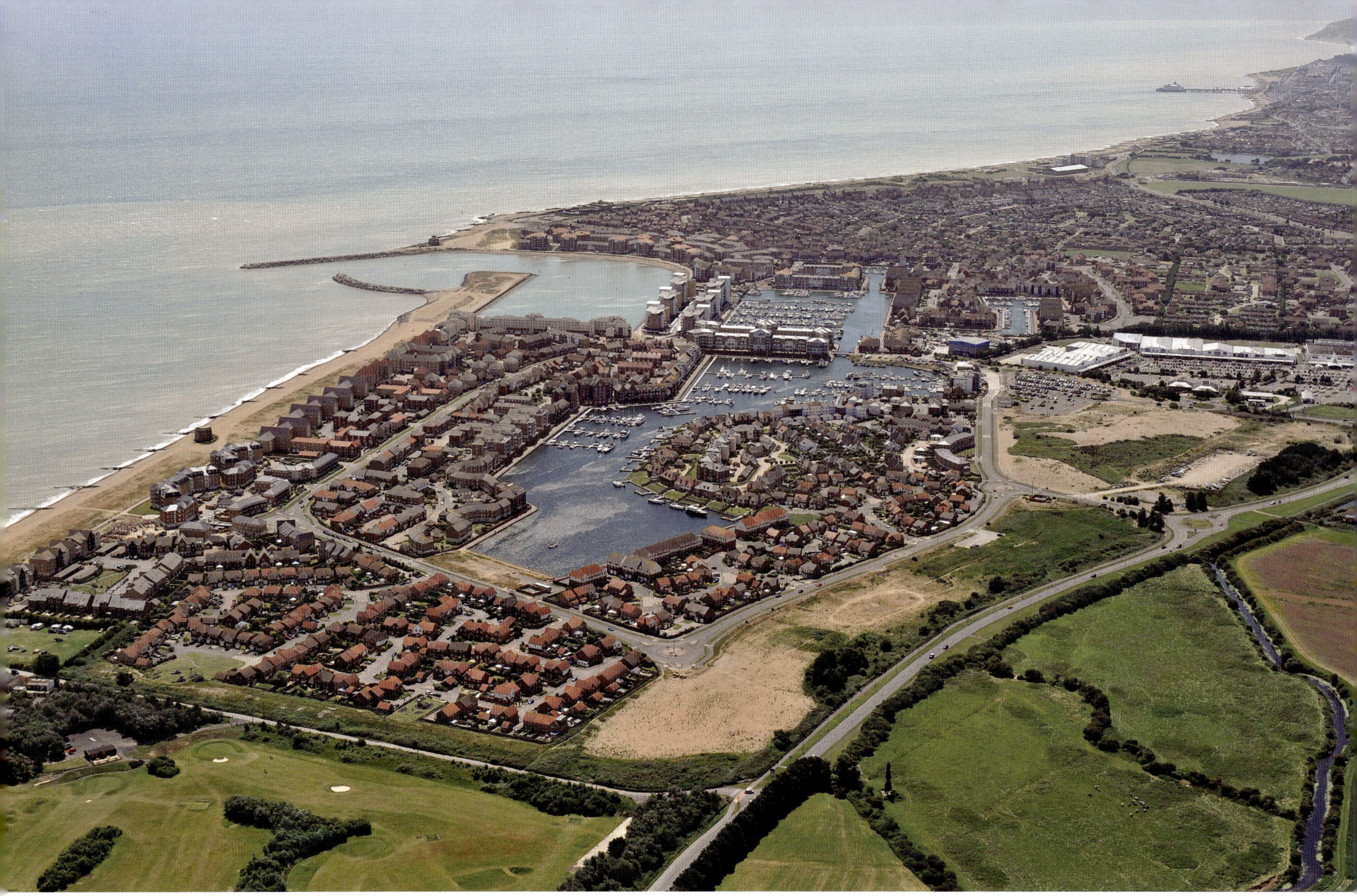

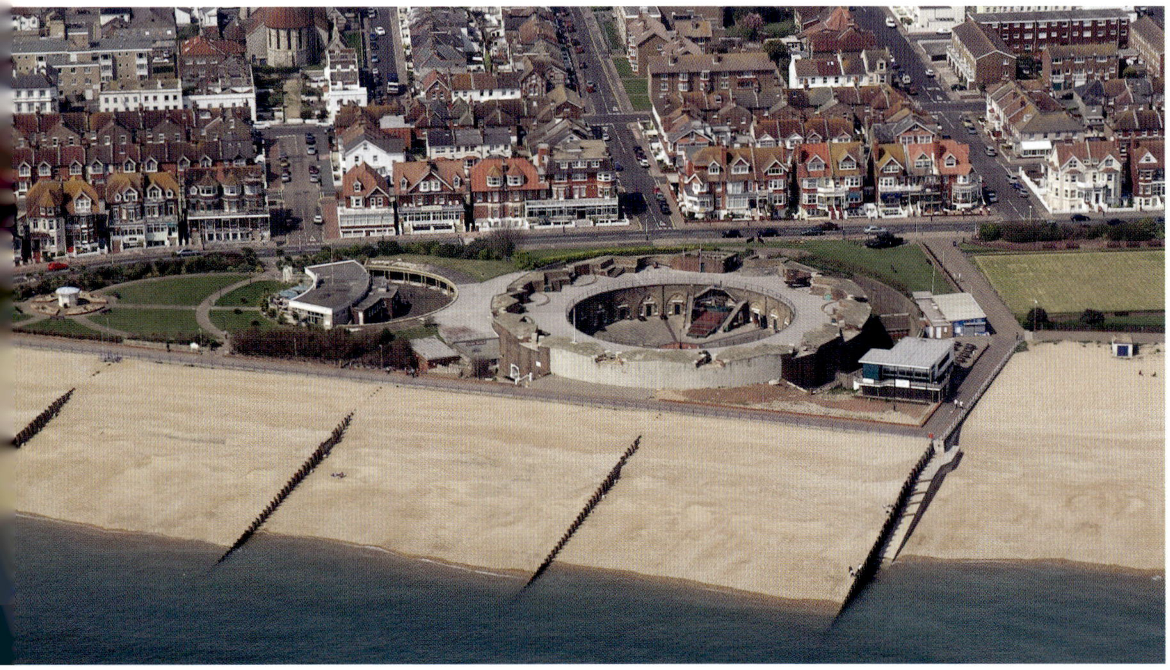

Eastbourne

Eastbourne was conceived by its landowners as a grand resort "for gentlemen by gentlemen" and was visited by four of King George III's children. Set beside Beachy Head, with four miles (6km) of clean, sheltered beach, the town's growth was aided by the arrival of the railway. The Duke of Devonshire planned a wide tree-lined boulevard now known as Devonshire Place and, even today, the front is free of shops. Though Eastbourne suffered badly during the Second World War, growth has continued with the development of Sovereign Harbour (above), which includes a marina, shops, a business park and luxury housing.

Eastbourne continues to derive most of its income from tourism but remains of its military history can still be seen. Fortifications to protect the south coast against Napoleonic invasion include the Eastbourne Redoubt (left) and Martello towers, including the Wish Tower, built in the early 19th century.

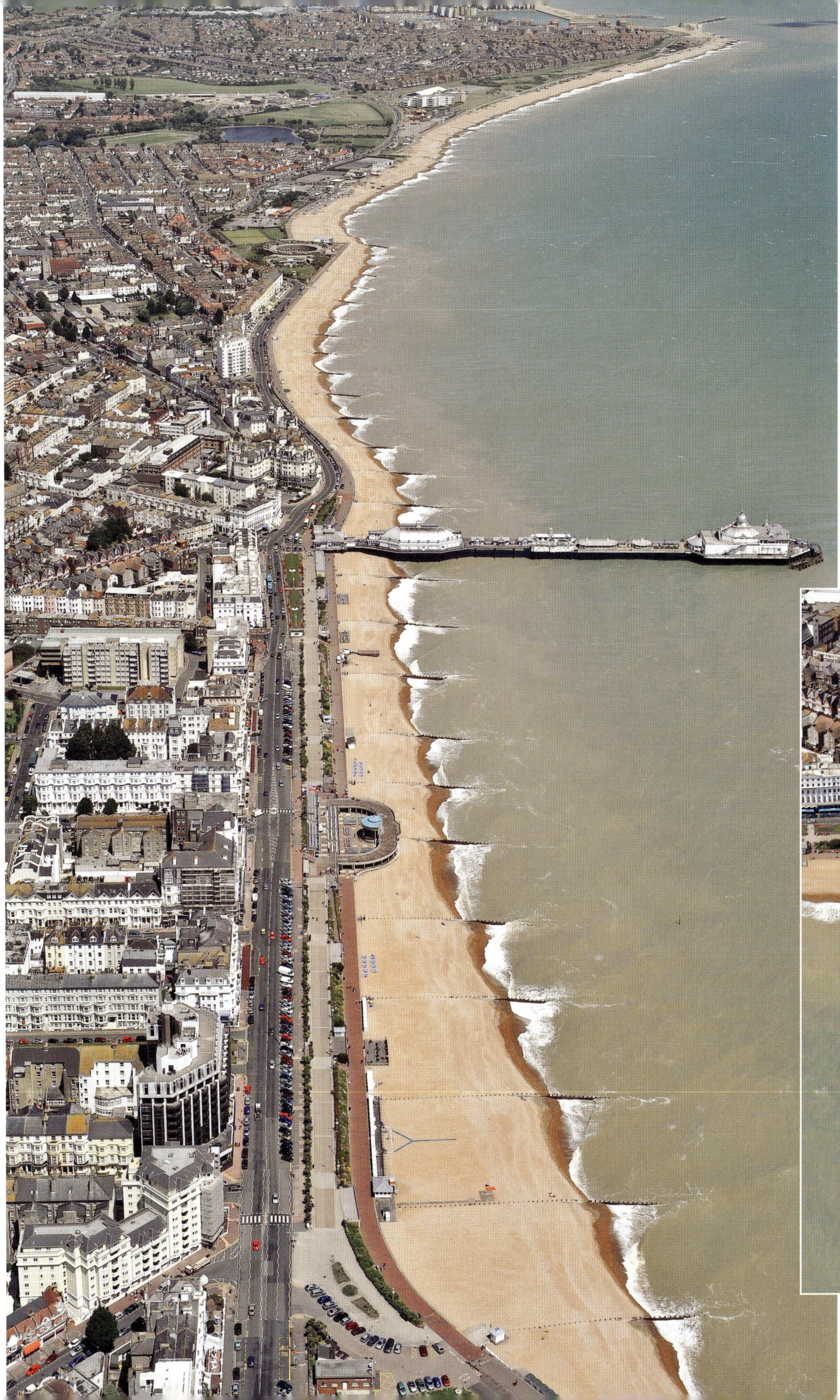

Eastbourne Seafront

The wide seafront promenade (left) that gives Eastbourne much of its character was built in 1872 and is backed by historic hotels and heritage buildings. The parade includes an Art Deco bandstand and award-winning gardens including the Floral Carpet Garden close to the pier. Officially opened in 1870, the pier (below) stretches some 1,000ft (303m) out to sea. A newly restored Victorian camera obscura, designed to give visitors a 360° panoramic view of the seafront, is found at the end of the pier.

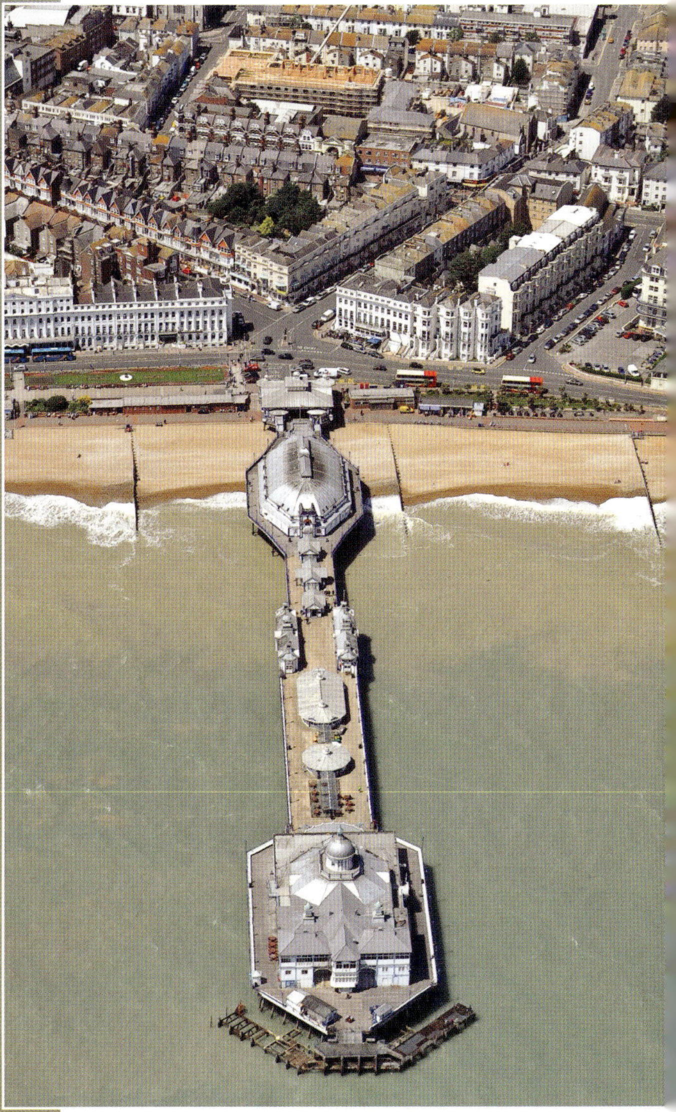

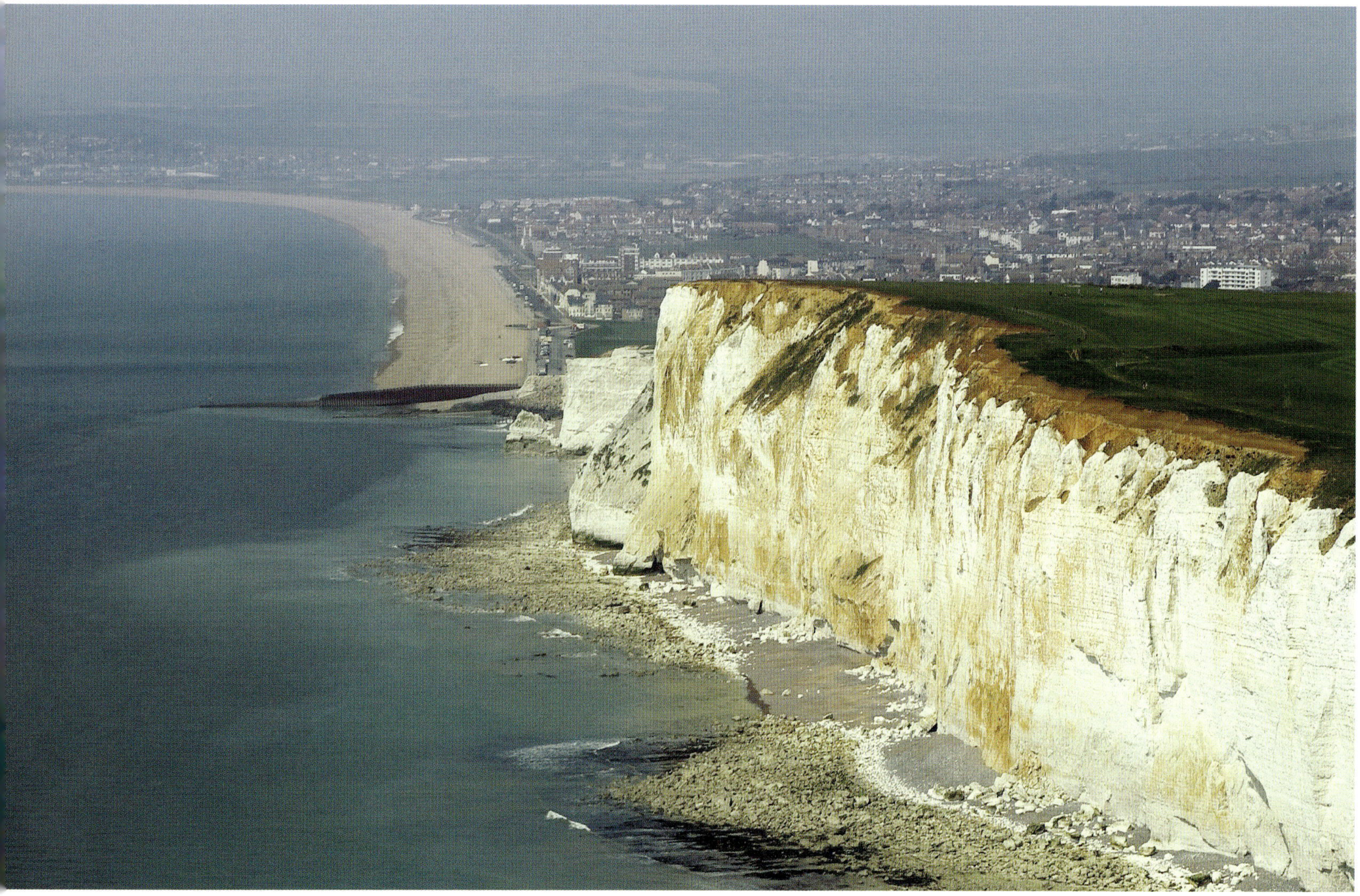

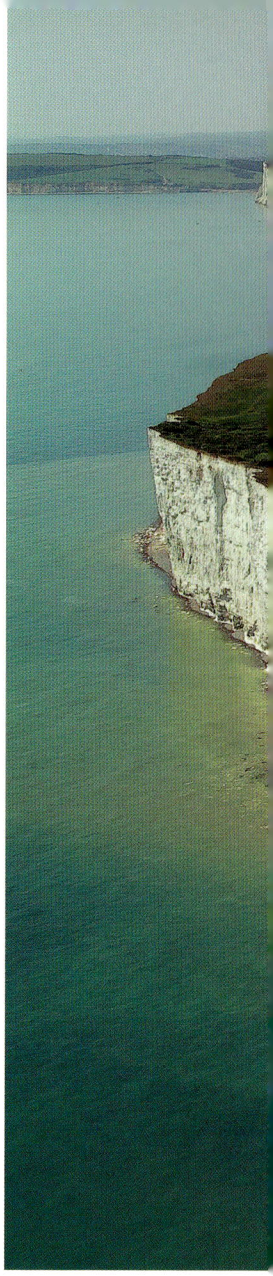

SUSSEX HERITAGE COAST

Beachy Head, with its famous white chalk cliffs, was the first designated Heritage Coast in England and Wales – a recognition by the Countryside Agency of notable natural beauty and scientific interest. The cliffs at Beachy Head and Seaford Head (above) dramatically mark the point where the South Downs meet the sea. This section of the coast is being eroded at an average rate of 30-40cm per year.

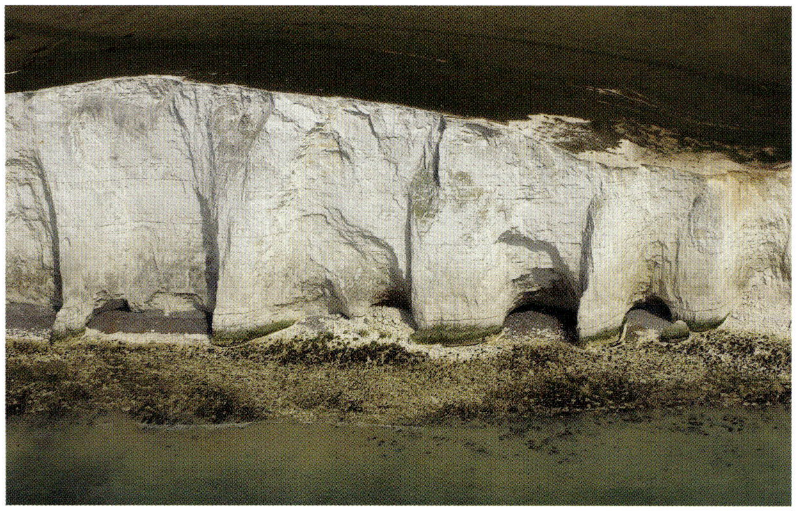

LONG MAN

A little further along the coast on the steep slopes of Windover Hill north-east of Eastbourne, is a famous figure cut into the chalk downland, known as the Long Man of Wilmington (right).

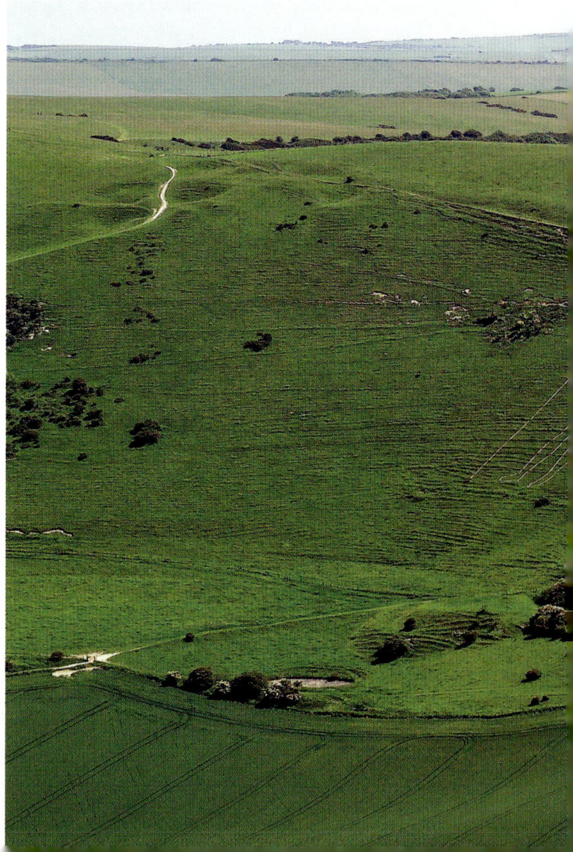

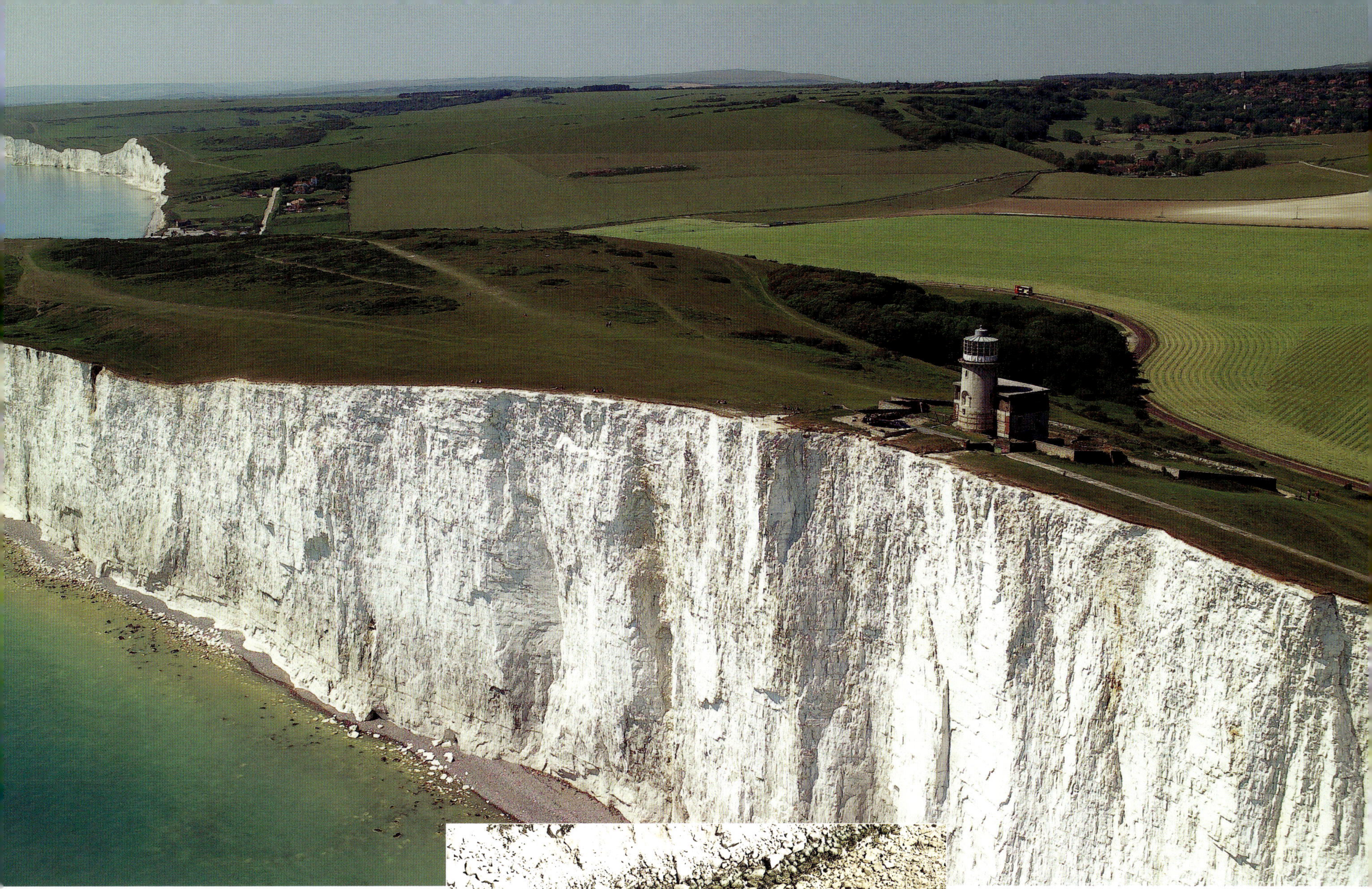

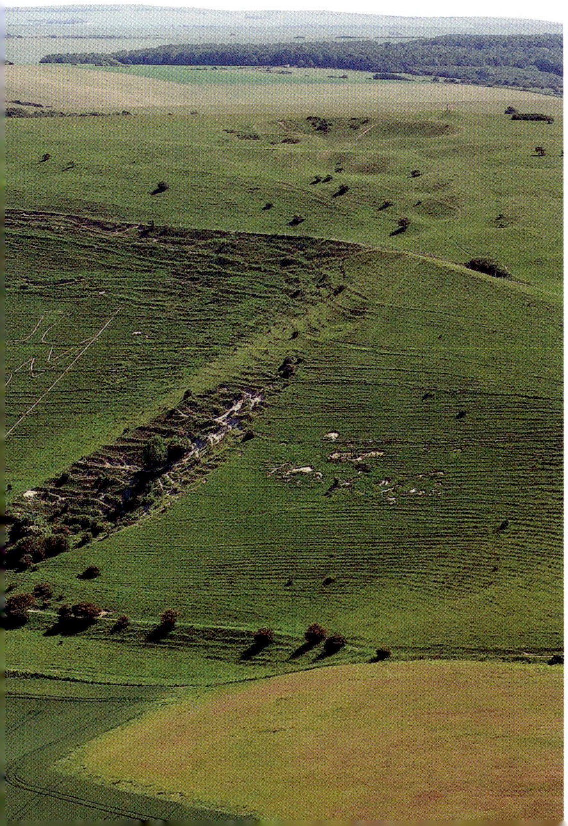

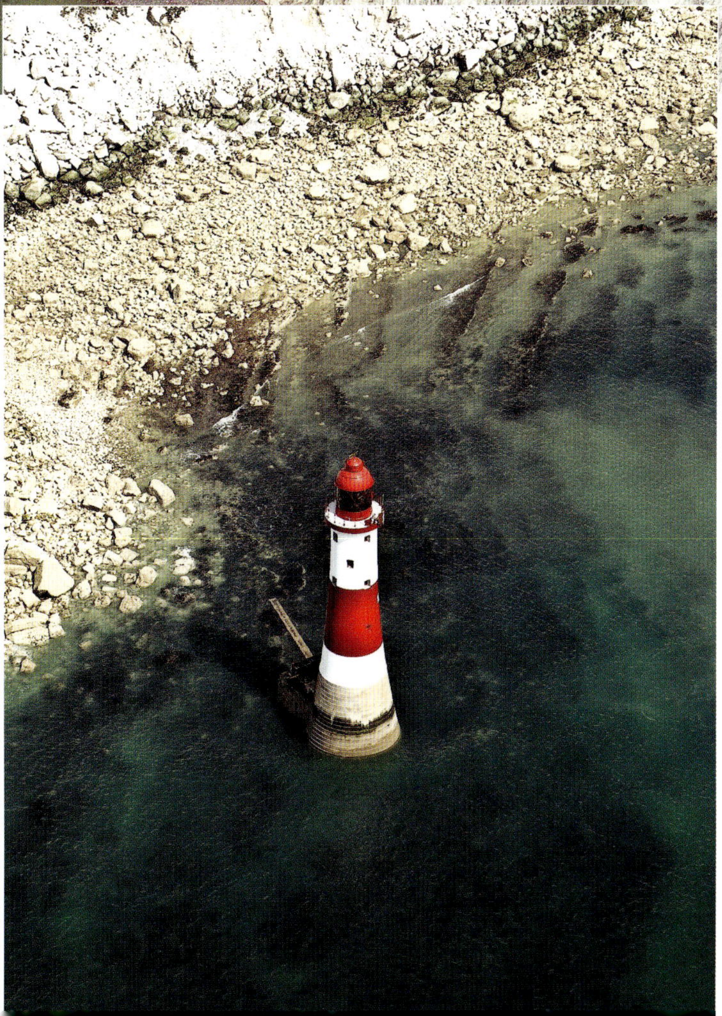

Lighthouses

The first lighthouse at Beachy Head was erected in 1831. Known as the Belle Tout lighthouse, its cliff-top location meant cloud and mist often hid its light. In 1902, the 43m (141ft) high red and white striped lighthouse at the cliff base was constructed and is today fully automated. Due to cliff erosion, the iconic Belle Tout was moved more than 50ft (15m) inland in 1999 in one piece and has recently opened as a hotel.

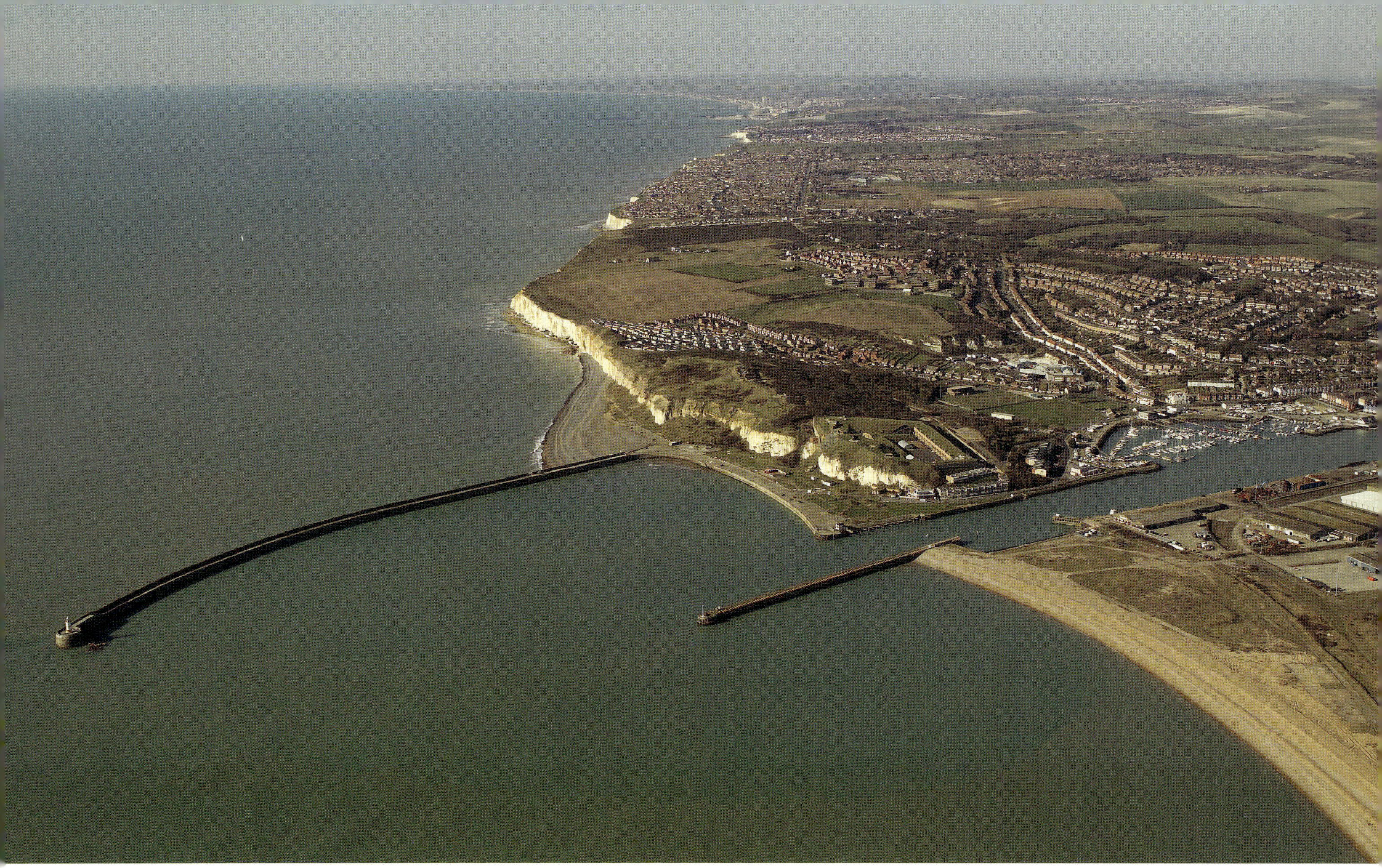

Newhaven

At the mouth of the river Ouse stands Newhaven (above), a port from which passenger ferries and freight ply to and from France. Over the centuries, the river's mouth has migrated between Newhaven and nearby Seaford due to longshore drift. In the mid 16th century a channel was cut in the river below Castle Hill to create a sheltered harbour and in 1790 a breakwater was added. Once the railway arrived in 1847, Newhaven became a major port for cross-channel ferries and a special military area during the First World War. Peacehaven, a town established in 1916, can be seen in the distance above.

Newhaven Fort

Designed by Lieutenant John Charles Ardagh at the age of 22, Newhaven Fort (right) fits the contours of the surrounding land and was the first military fortification to be built with concrete. Completed in 1871, the fort played an important role in the two world wars protecting the harbour at Newhaven but later fell into disrepair. In 1988 it re-opened as a heritage museum.

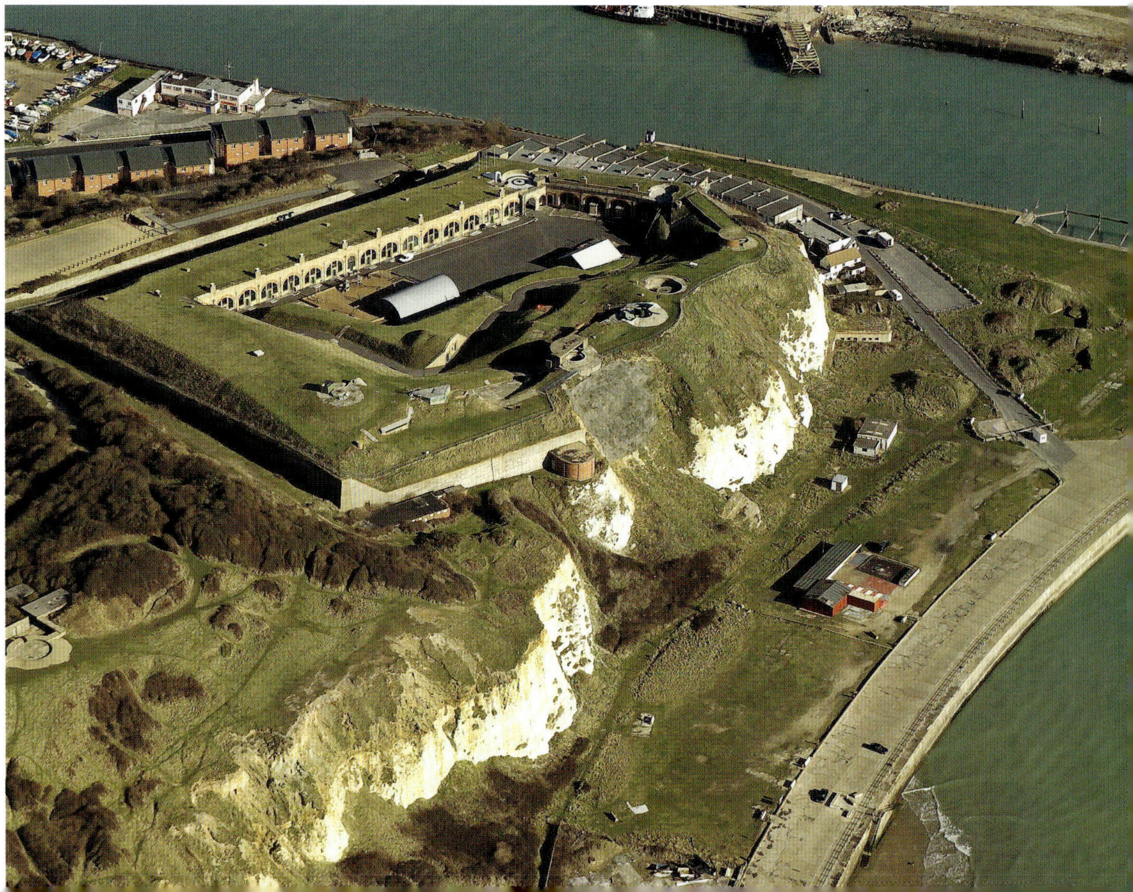

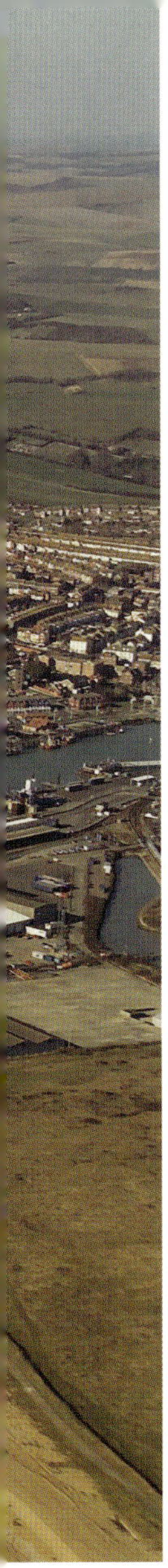

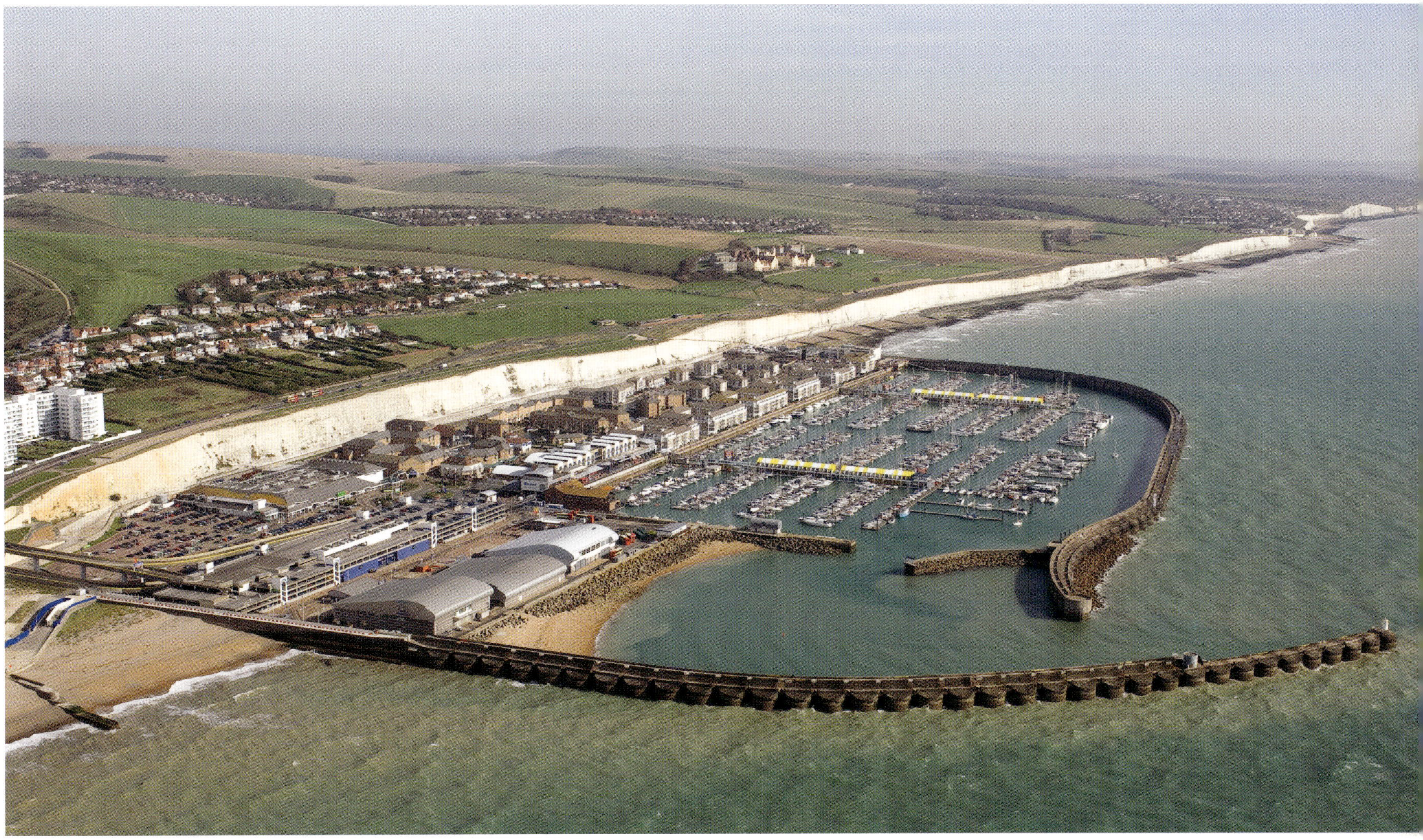

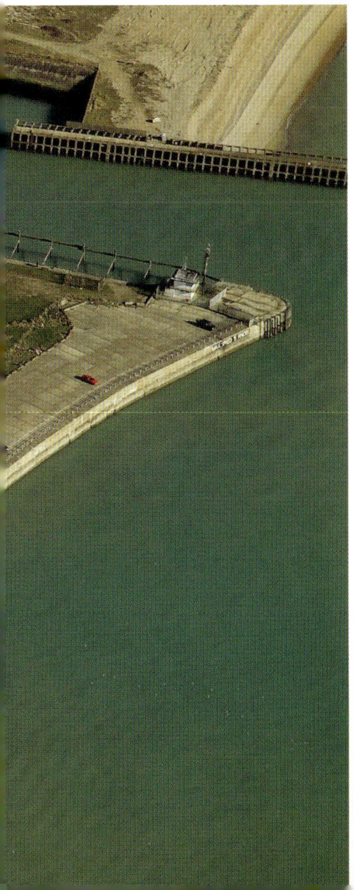

EAST BRIGHTON

Brighton Marina (above) is the largest purpose-built harbour for yachts and sailing boats in the UK. All sizes of craft from dinghies to luxury yachts have 24-hour access to the sea through the deep water entrance while charter boats use the marina as a base for fishing and diving expeditions.

Money for Brighton's racecourse (right) was raised through subscription and the first race took place in 1783. The racecourse has had a chequered history with, in 1848, a riot, whirlwind and invasion of the grandstand all within one week.

The campus of the University of Sussex is situated to the east of Brighton. Founded in the 1960s, it is one of Britain's leading universities.

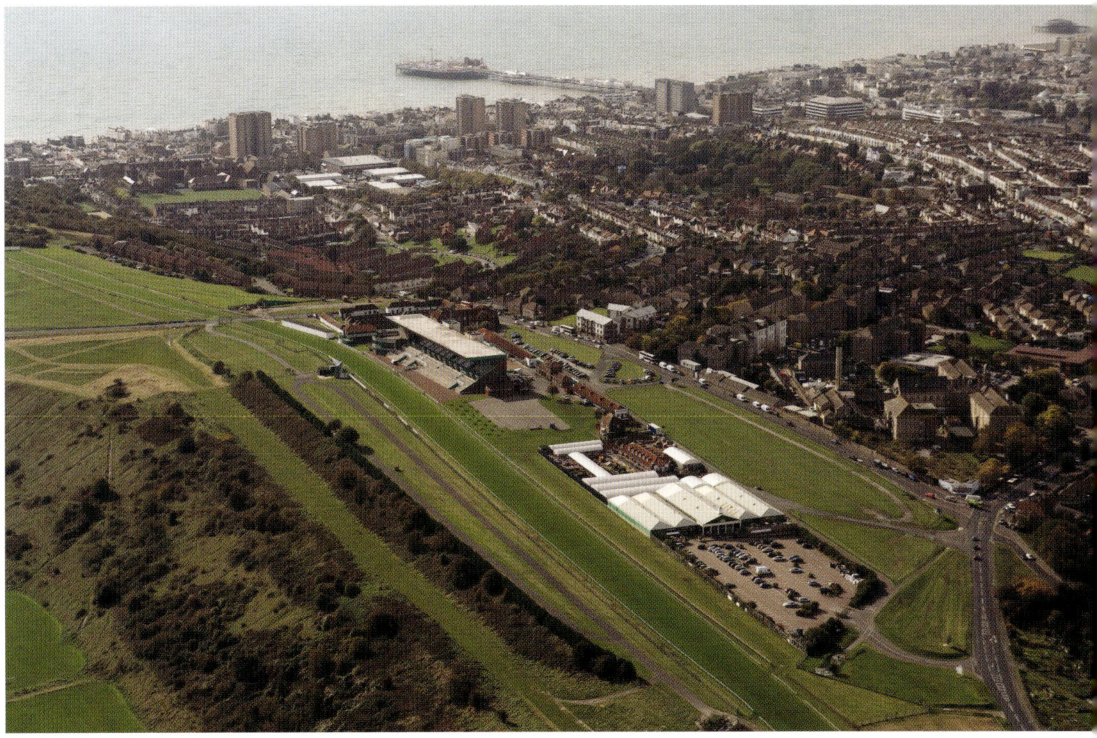

Brighton & Hove

Brighton began as a small fishing village but grew in the mid 18th century when it became fashionable to visit the seaside. Dr Richard Russell of Lewes set up a spa in the town as the sea water was thought to be particularly beneficial and the influx of wealth is reflected in the Regency terraces built in the 1780s. Today, Kings Road along the seafront gives access to the beach bars, restaurants, nightclubs and amusement arcades. Just an hour from London, the Blue Flag shingle beach is popular with day-trippers. Once a neighbouring town, Hove is now part of a single conurbation with Brighton which was granted city status in the year 2000. As Brighton grew in popularity, developers sought cheaper land and less demanding local taxes and found Hove a suitable site.

The Palace Pier (below), known as Brighton Pier, is one of two piers. Opened in 1899 it was one of the last British piers to be built. At 1,760ft (536m) long it included a 1,500 seater pavilion at the seaward end and is a theme park and fairground attraction today.

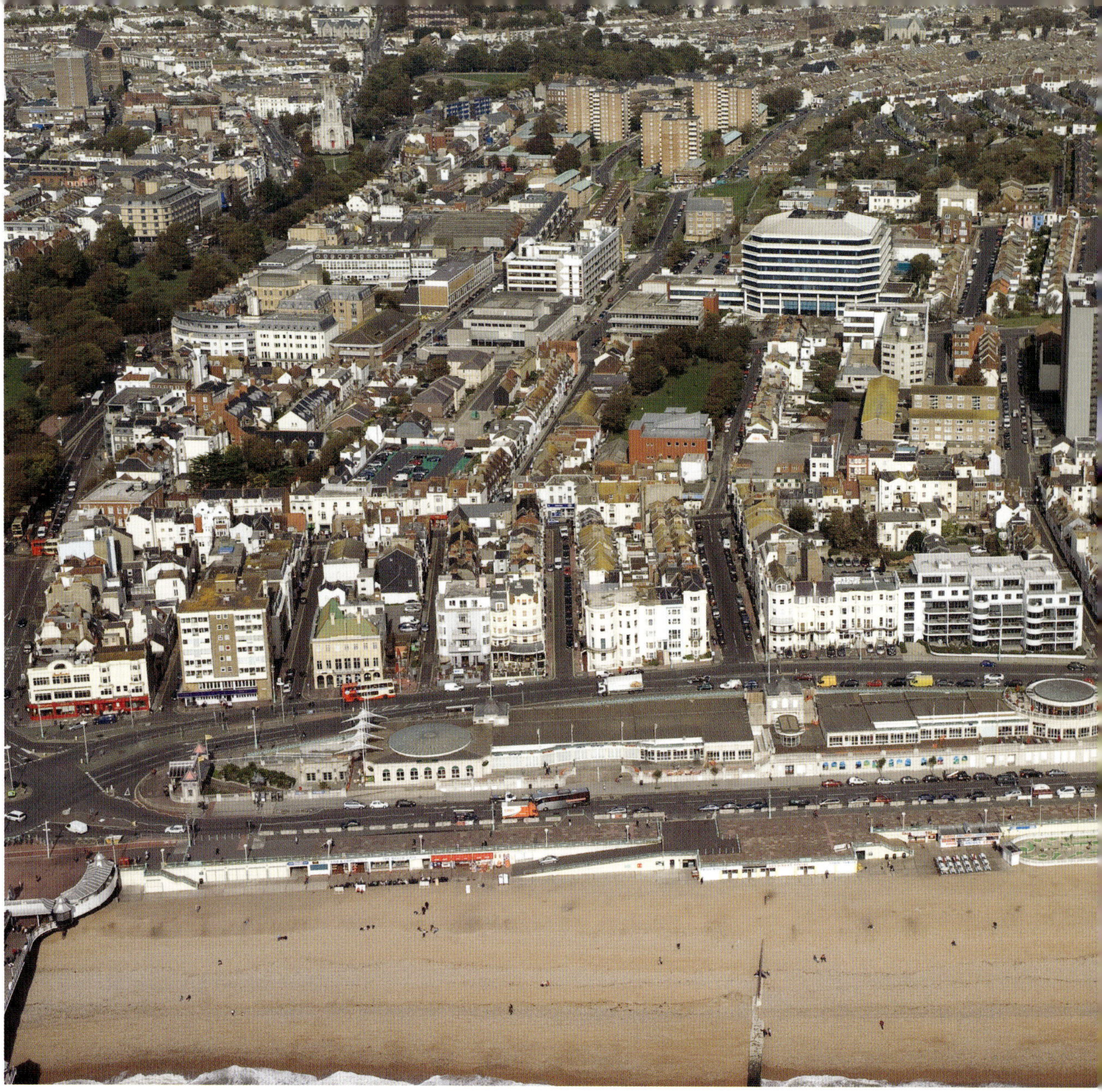

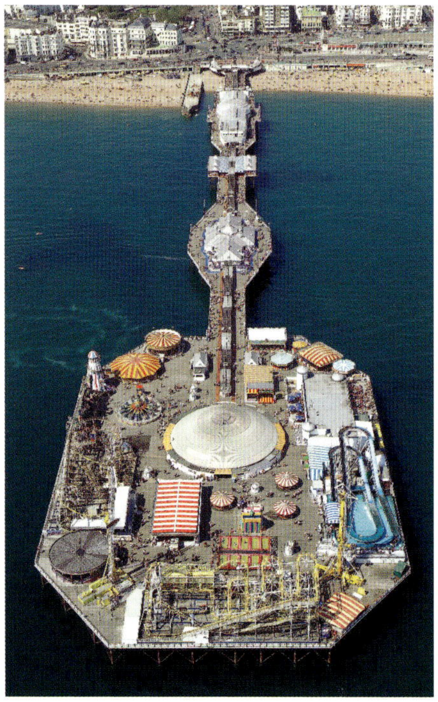

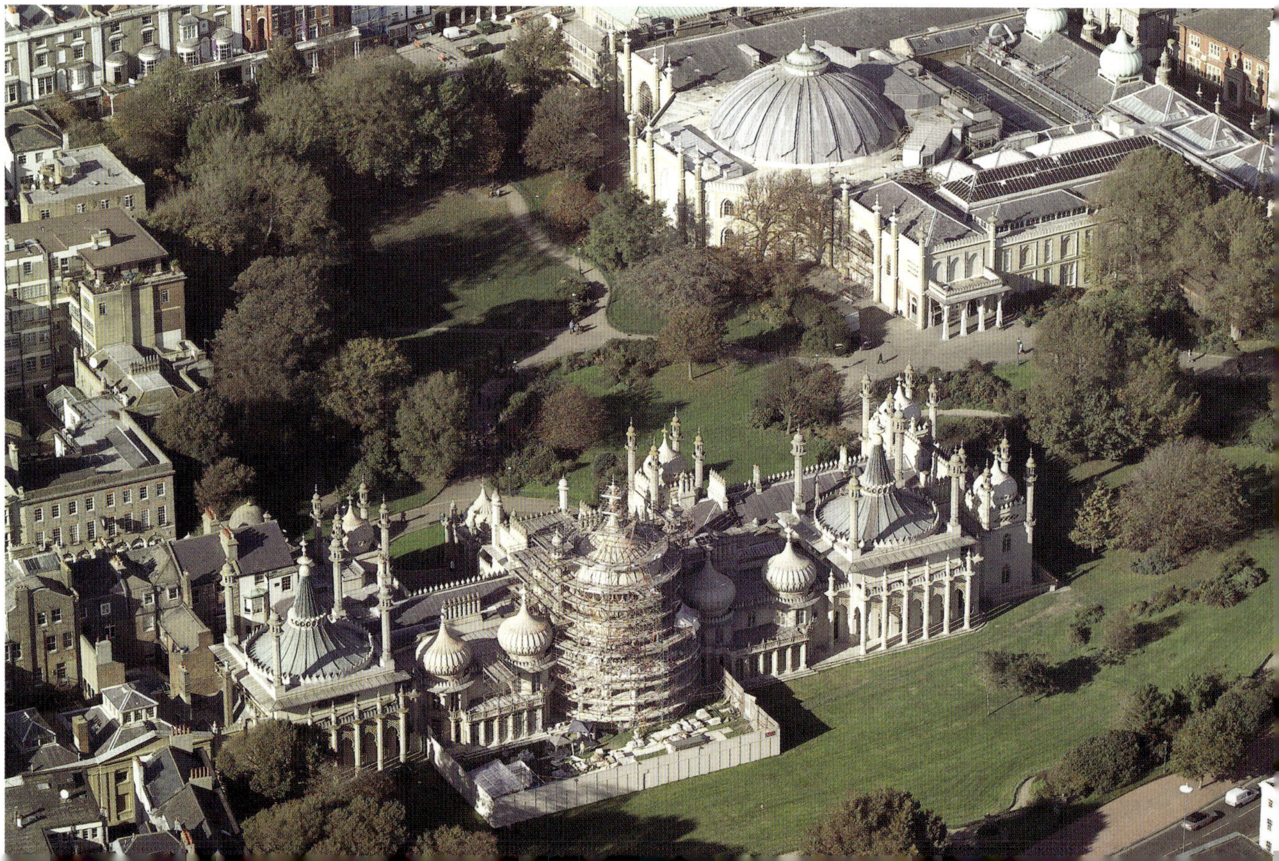

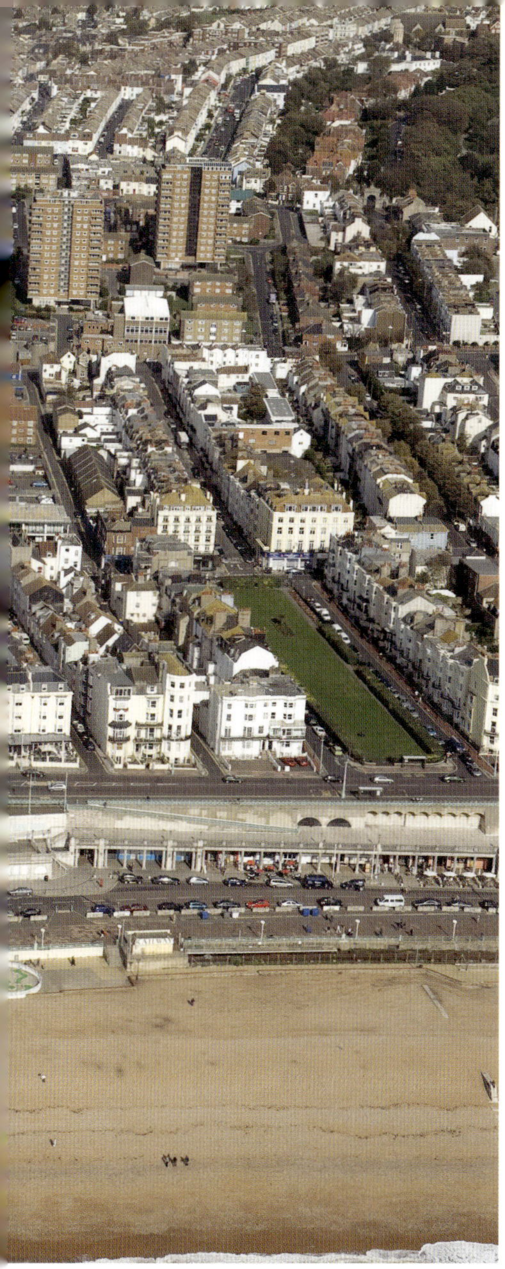

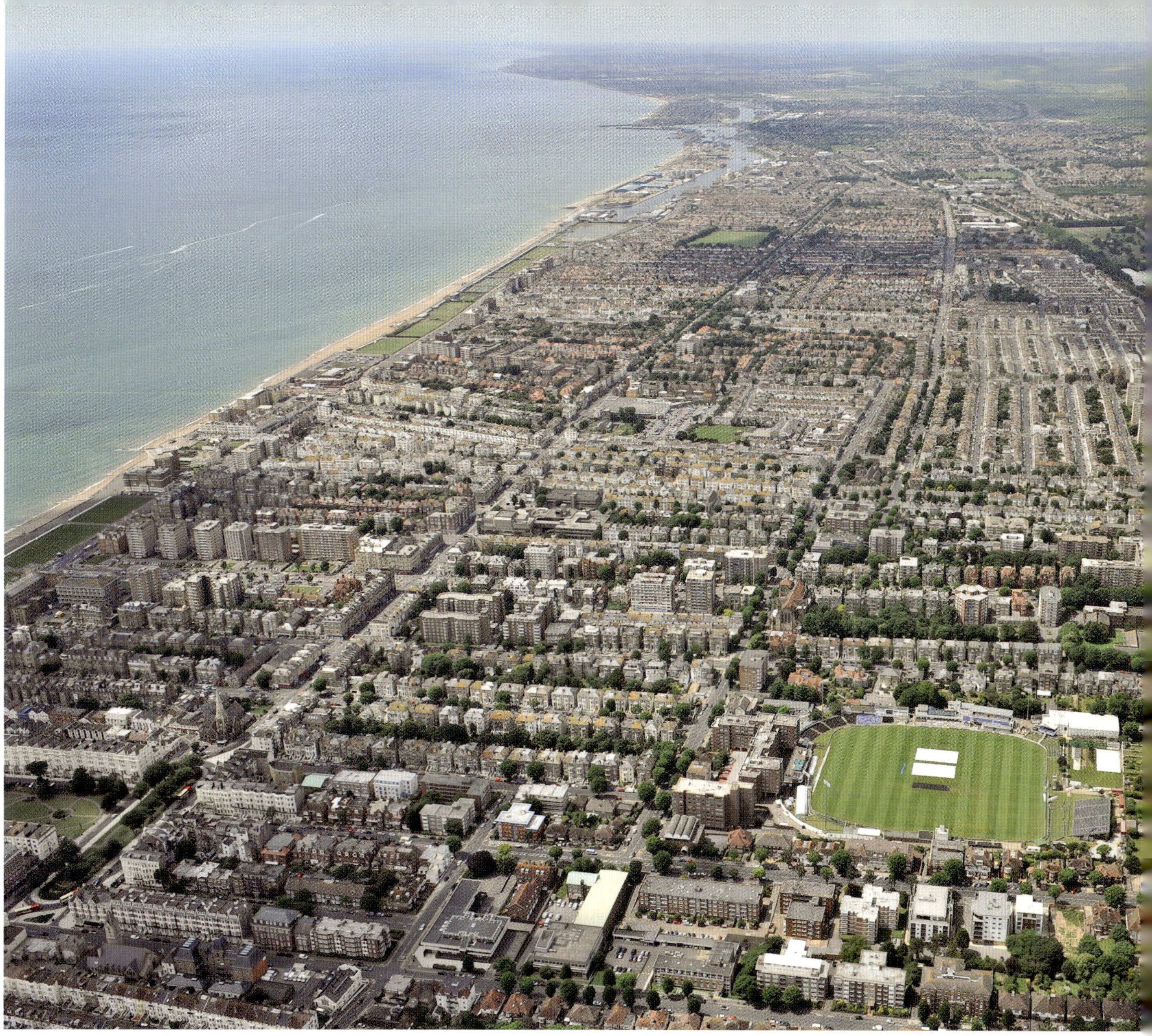

Brighton & Hove's streetscape

As well as rows of elegant Regency terraces, Hove in particular was the result of careful town planning. Charles Augustin Busby's work on the Brunswick estate in the early 19th century led to the neat grid system found in the town today. Palmeira Square (right) was built in 1855 as an extension to Adelaide Crescent which was completed in 1850. A glass and cast iron conservatory was intended for the site but the building collapsed a day after it was completed. Opposite Brighton's Palace Pier is Marine Parade and Brighton's esplanade. Beyond lies the Old Steine Road area with its green gardens which, in Brighton's early days, were the social centre of the city. The Prince Regent (later King George IV) became a regular visitor to Brighton and built the Royal Pavilion (left) as his grand seaside residence. Originally designed by Henry Holland, it was John Nash who gave the building its "maharajah" look when he took over, with the second phase completed in 1822. During the First World War the Pavilion was used as a military hospital.

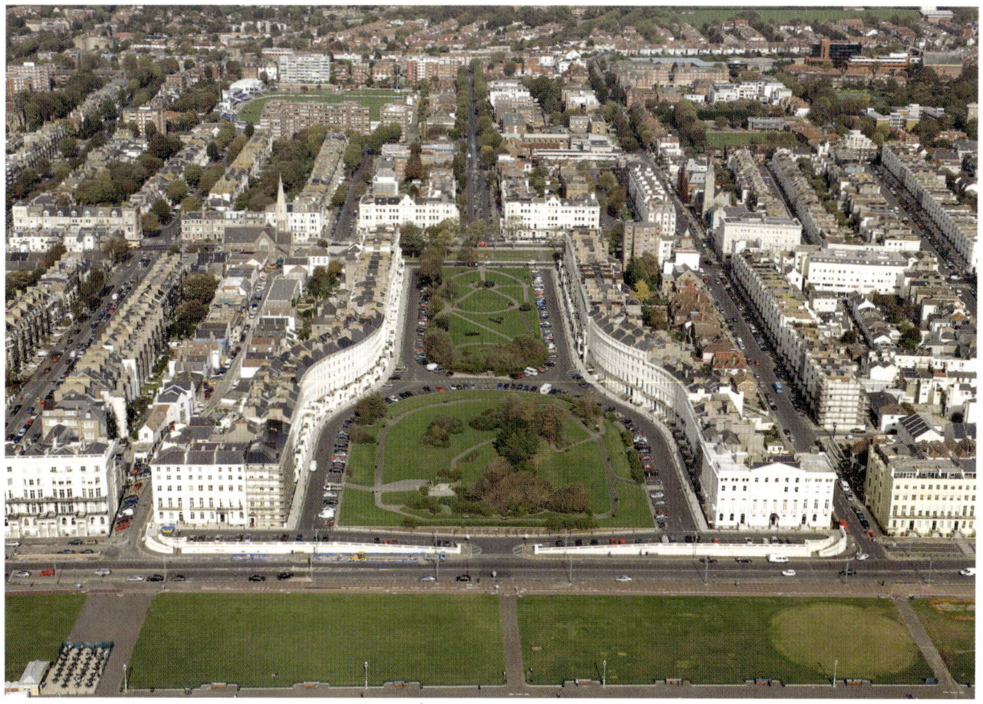

Shoreham

Situated five miles west of Brighton and Hove with its shingle beach and natural harbour is Shoreham-by-Sea. A safe haven since Norman times, the town has grown up around the 11th century church of St Mary de Haura (St Mary of the Harbour). The 12th century Marlipins Museum is one of the oldest non-ecclesiastical buildings in the UK. With the arrival of the railway in the 19th century the port grew rapidly and several shipyards were established. A commercial and cargo port today, trade includes aggregates, sawn timber, steel, oil, locally-grown cereals and scrap metal. The RNLI have maintained a lifeboat in the harbour since 1865, which can be found alongside the yachts and fishing boats. An experimental fort built in 1857 sits at the head of the harbour spit. After decommissioning at the end of the 19th century it was used as a film studio.

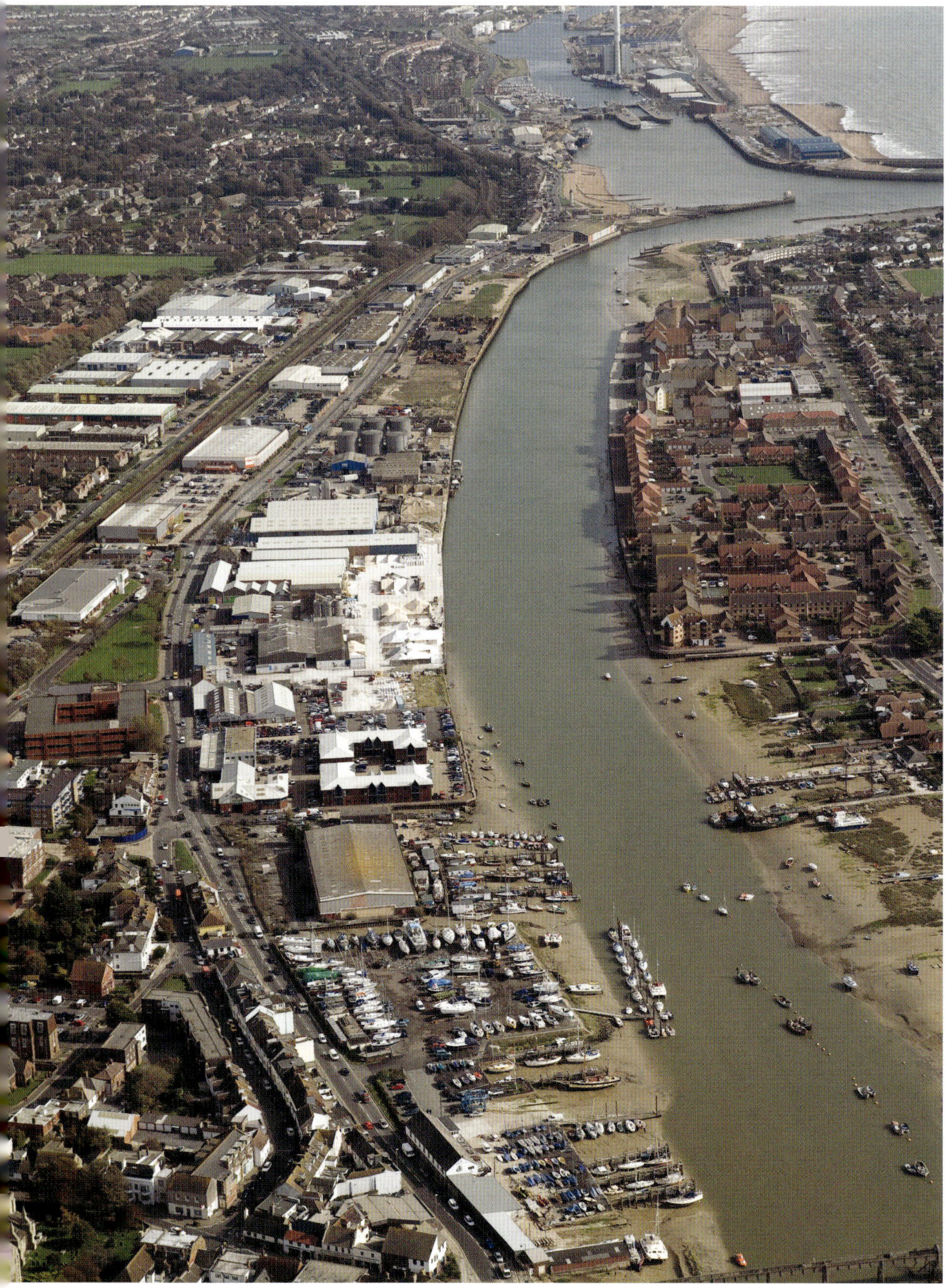

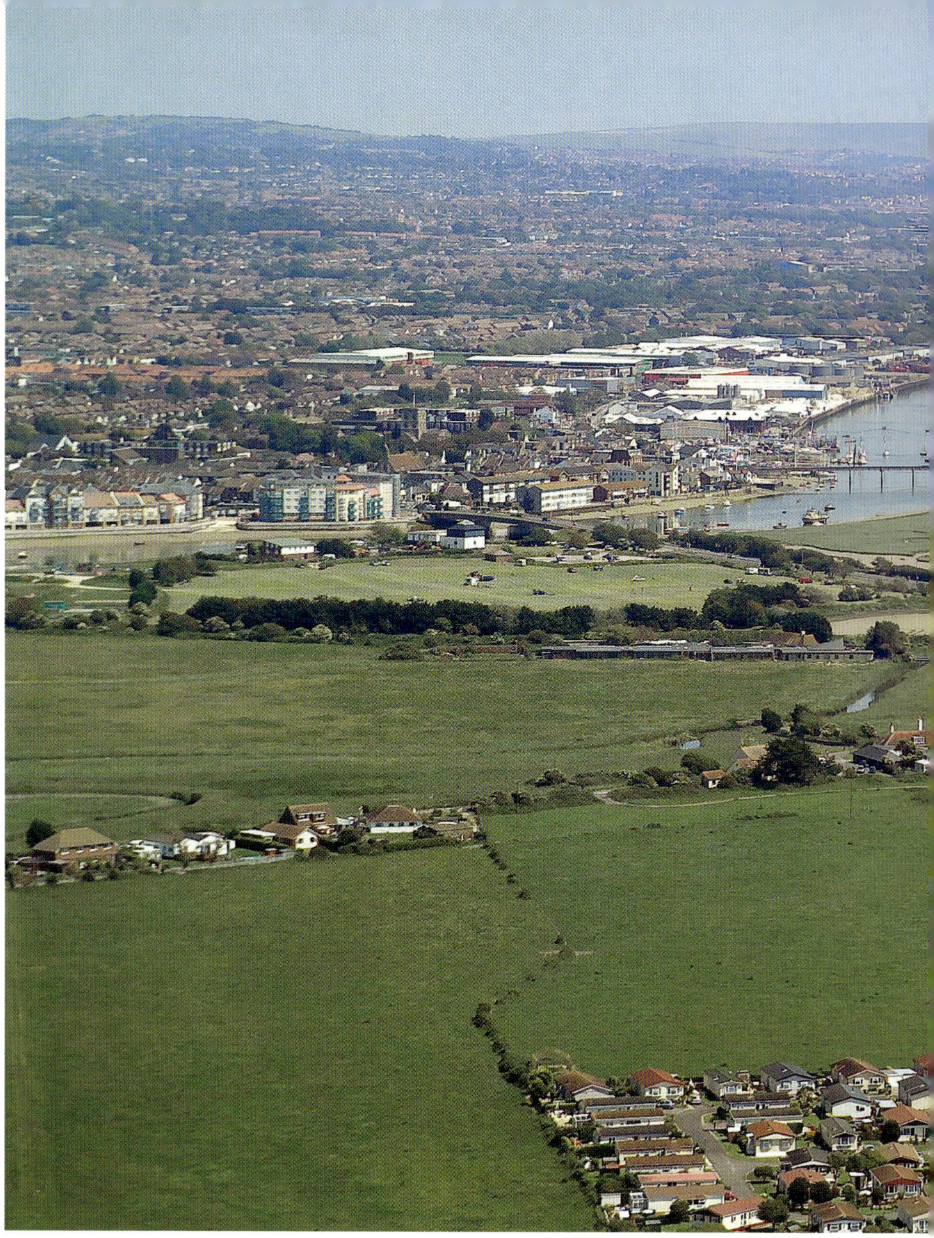

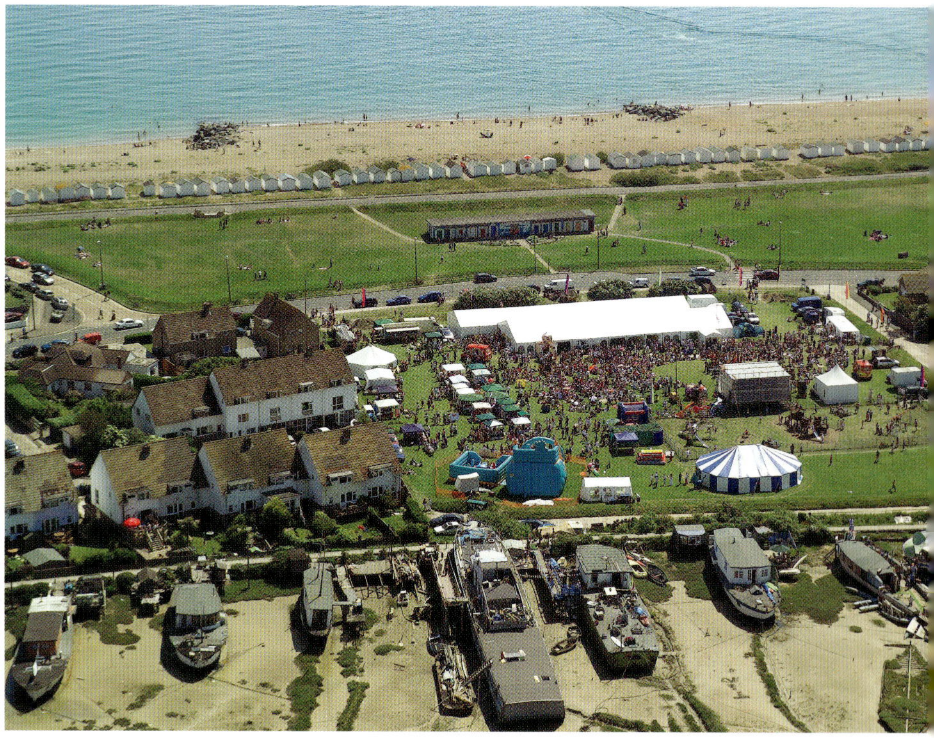

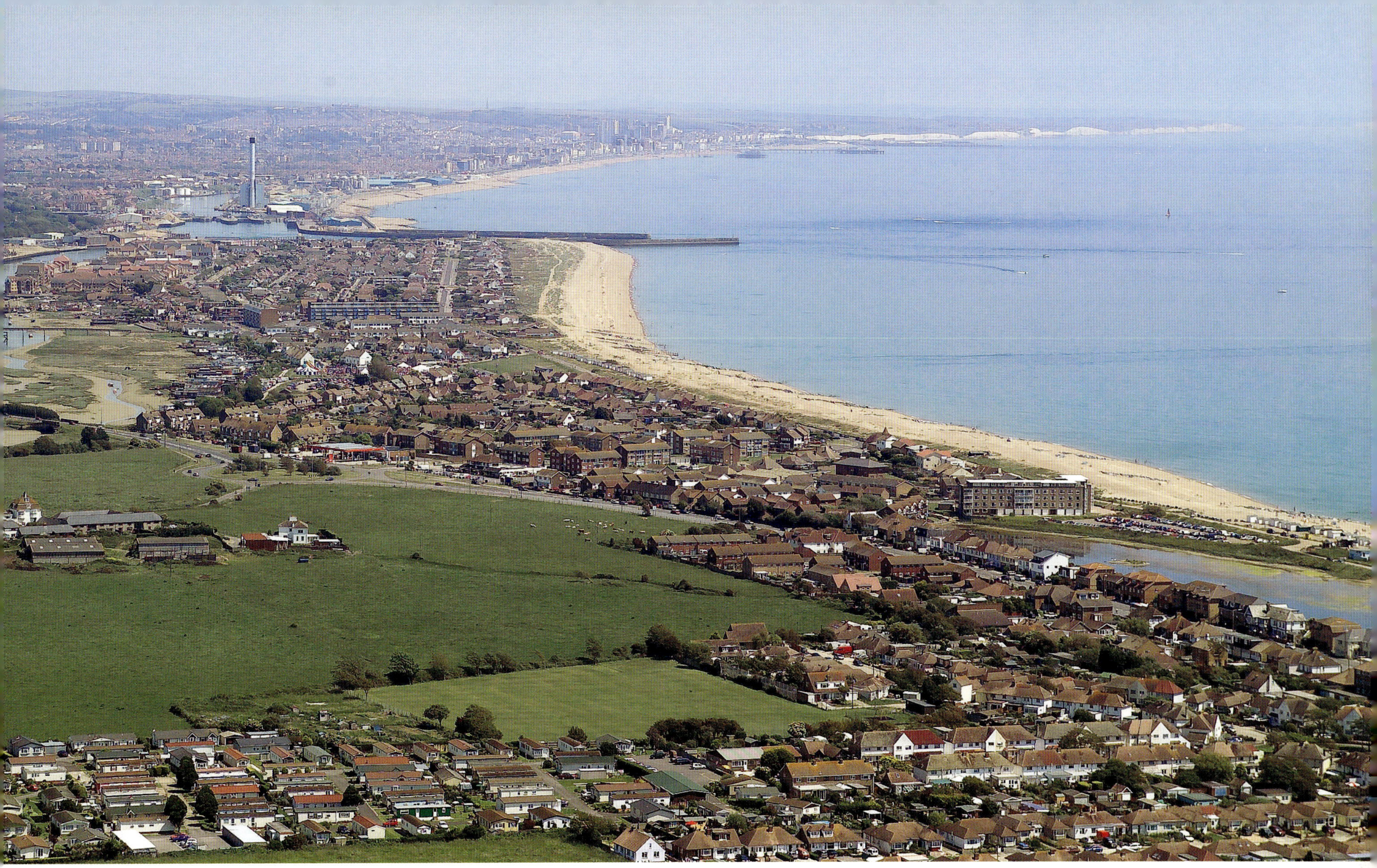

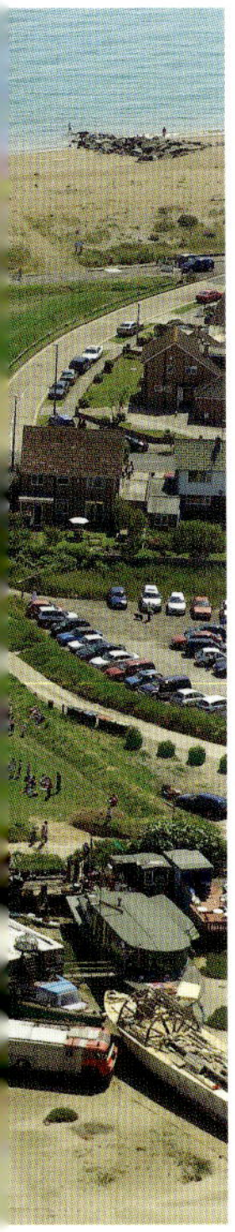

SHOREHAM SIGHTS

Founded in 1910 and the oldest licensed airport in Britain, Shoreham Airport's Art Deco terminal (right) is a listed building and has been used for the filming of an Agatha Christie *Poirot* story and scenes in the film *The Da Vinci Code*. The community festival Beach Dreams is held on Shoreham's Beach Green (left). Mudflats along the river Adur beside the green are home to a collection of beached houseboats including converted barges, tugs, and minesweepers that float at high tide.

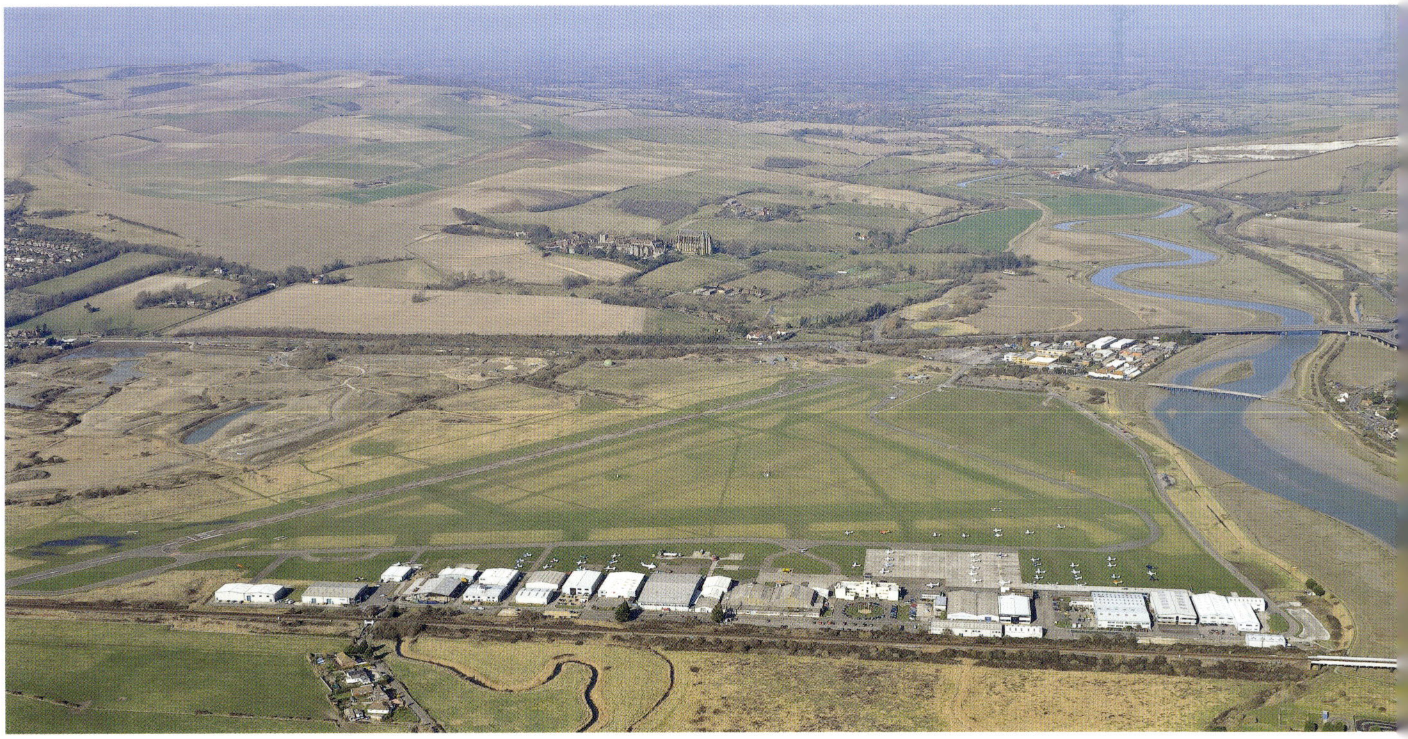

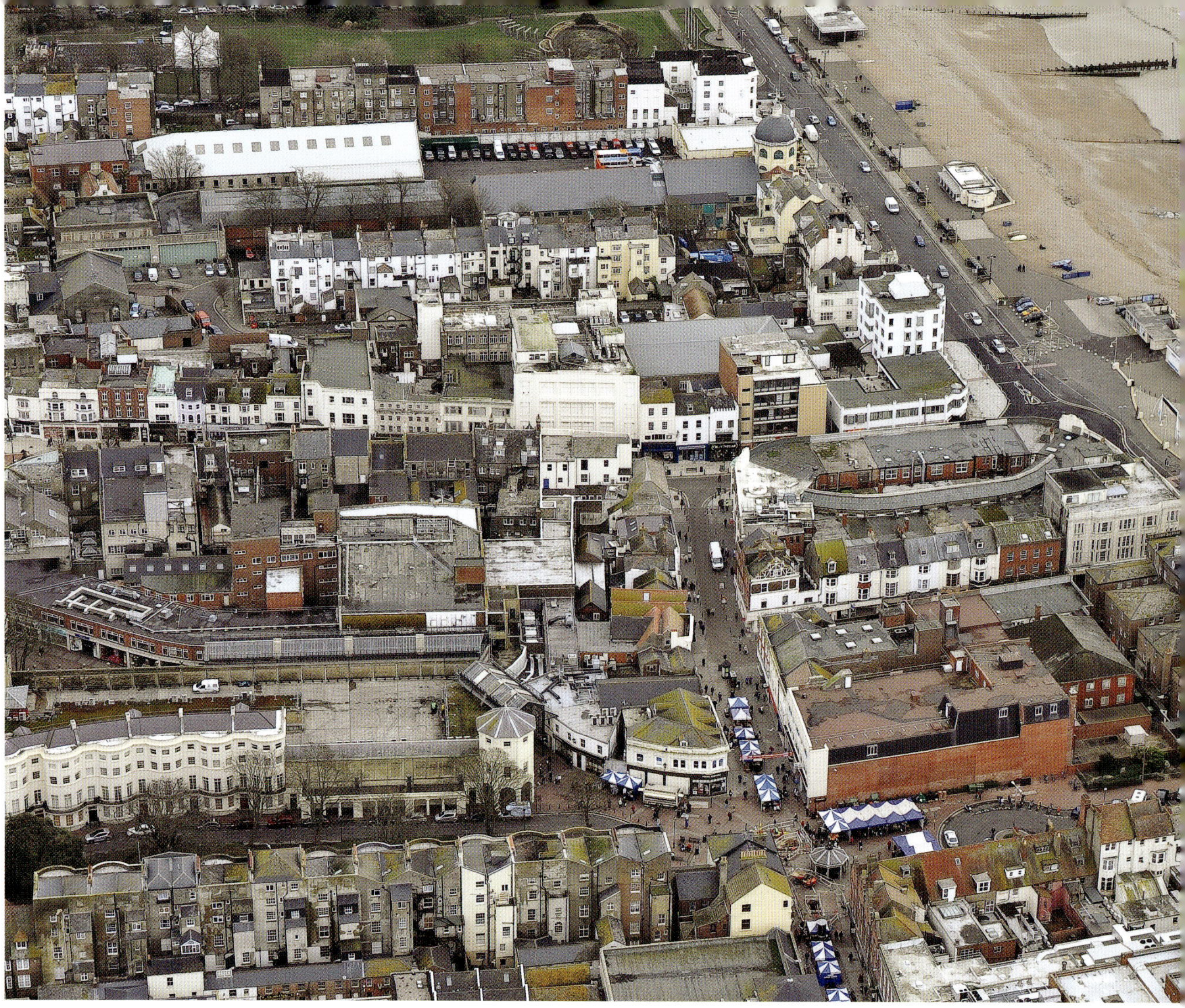

Worthing

With the popularity of sea bathing in the 19th century, Worthing (right) grew rapidly from a small fishing and farming community into a large town. George III sent his daughter Amelia to Worthing in 1798 in the hope that the sea would improve her damaged knee while keeping her distant from her elder brother and his entourage in Brighton. The pier was originally built in 1861-2 and two pavilions were added in 1888 and 1926. Although part of it was blown down in 1913, and a fire destroyed the original pavilion in 1933, the pier is still operating. Between 1884 and 1892 there was significant violence in the town as the so called Skeleton Army – formed in Worthing and made up of toughs recruited by pub and brothel-owners – confronted the Salvation Army, disrupting its rallies and beating up its members. Oscar Wilde wrote his satirical play *The Importance of Being Earnest* in Worthing and named the main character, Ernest Worthing, after the town.

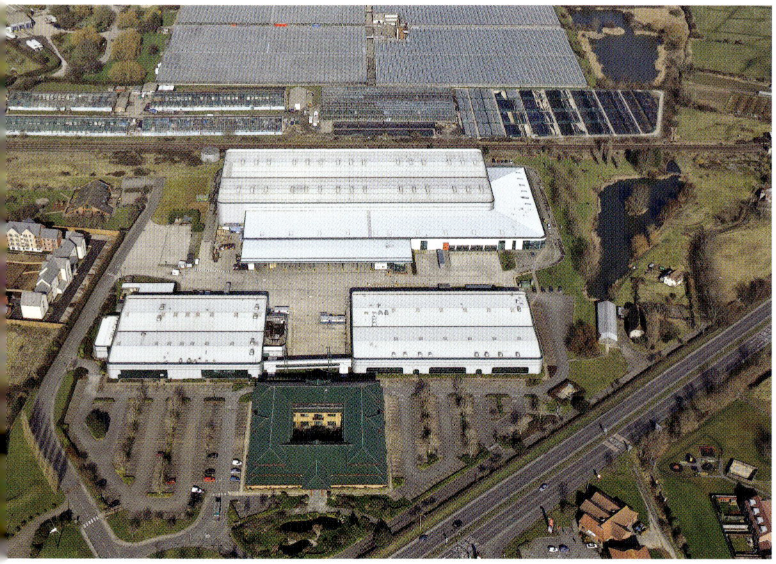

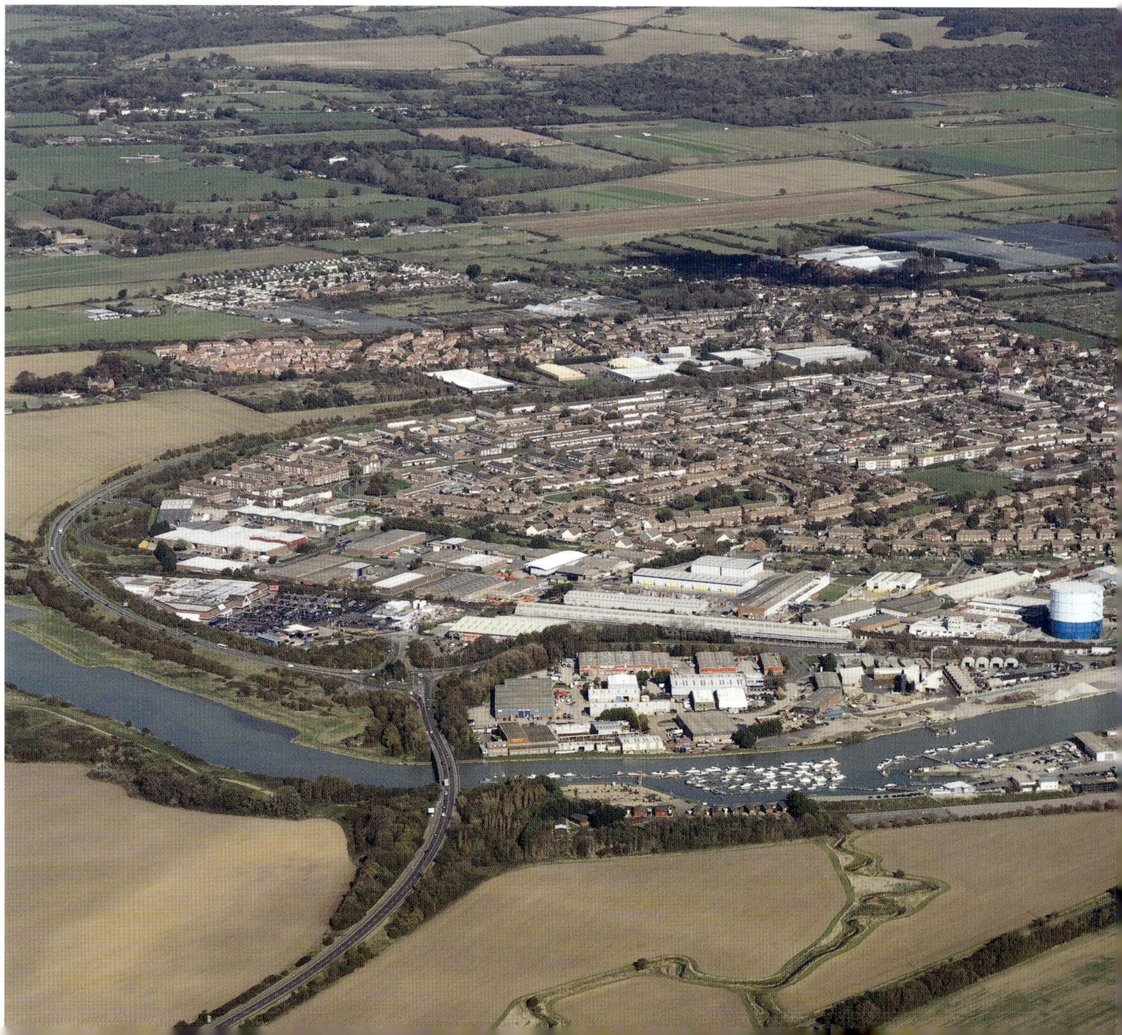

Littlehampton

This seaside resort (right) was once famous for the construction of warships, as Henry VIII's dockyards were located here. Today, shipbuilding continues with Littlehampton known for its yacht-building. The Body Shop's international headquarters and factory are based in the town (above).

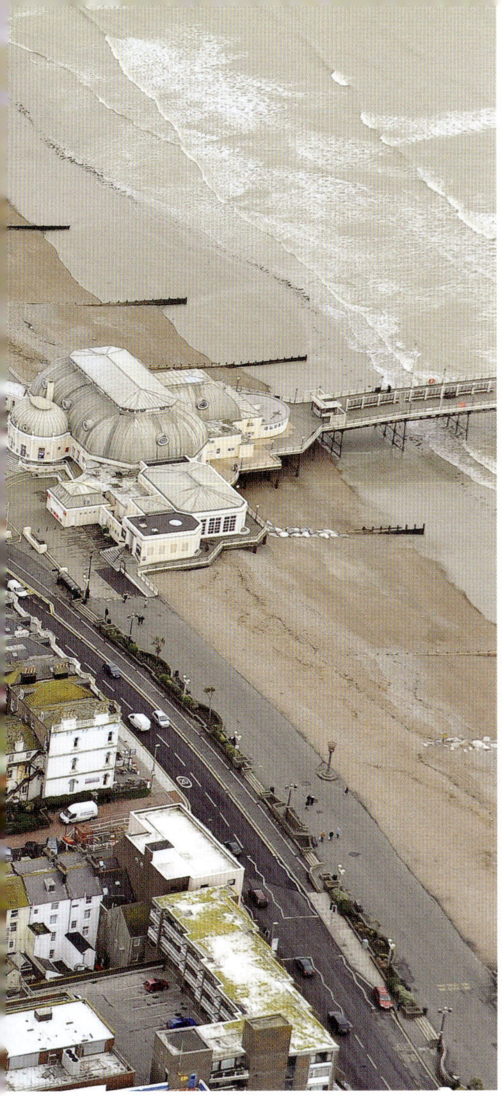

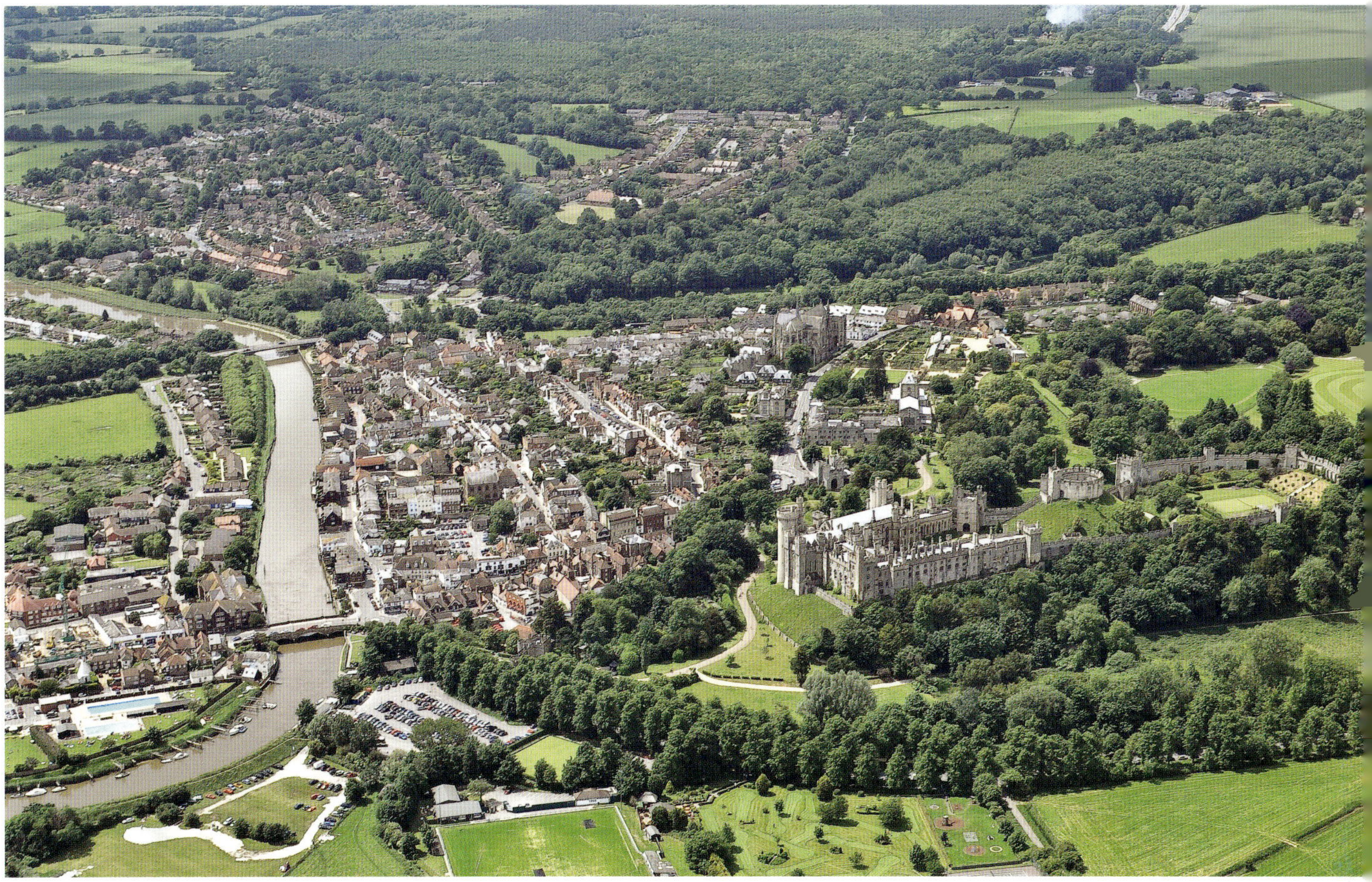

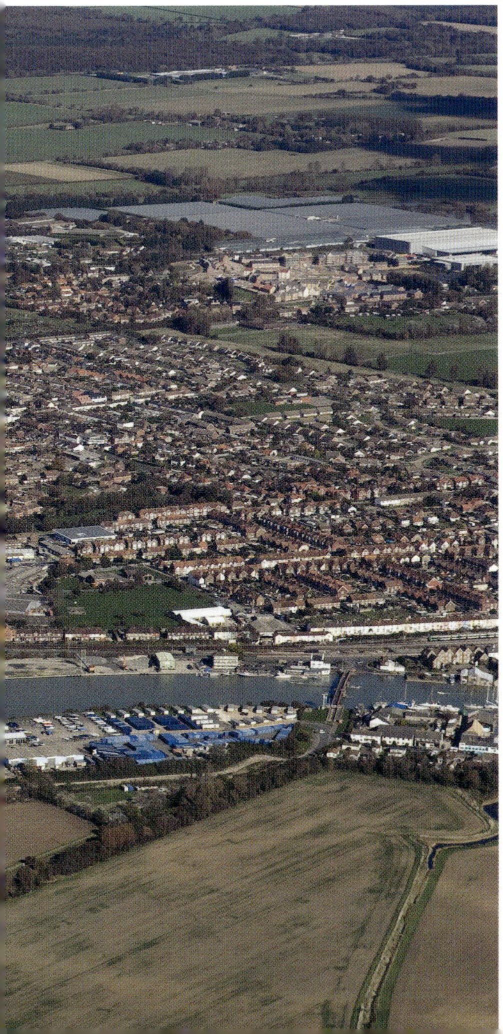

Arundel

Located next to the river Arun from which it takes its name, Arundel is famous for its 11th century castle and Catholic cathedral. The castle was extensively restored in the 19th century and is the residence of the Dukes of Norfolk. With its priceless works of art and over 40 acres (16 ha) of grounds and gardens, the castle is a major visitor attraction. The French Gothic-style cathedral was commissioned in 1868 by Henry Fitzalan-Howard, the 15th Duke of Norfolk, and completed in 1873. Designed by Joseph Hansom, the inventor of the hansom cab, it is built in brick with Bath stone cladding.

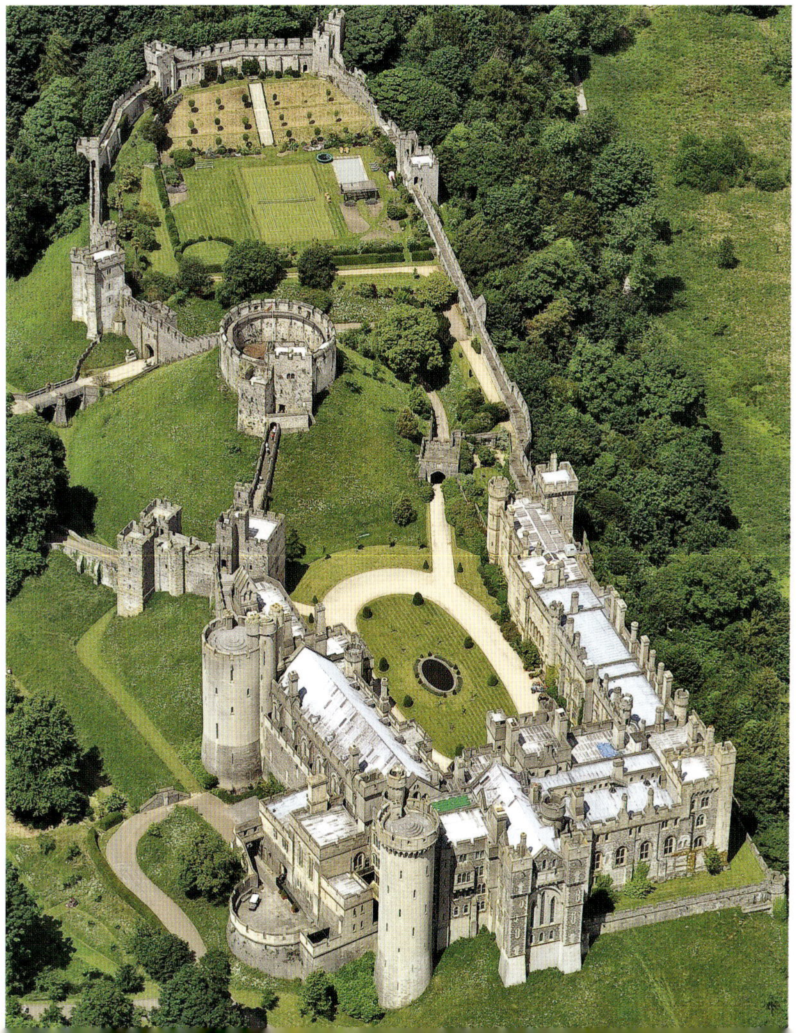

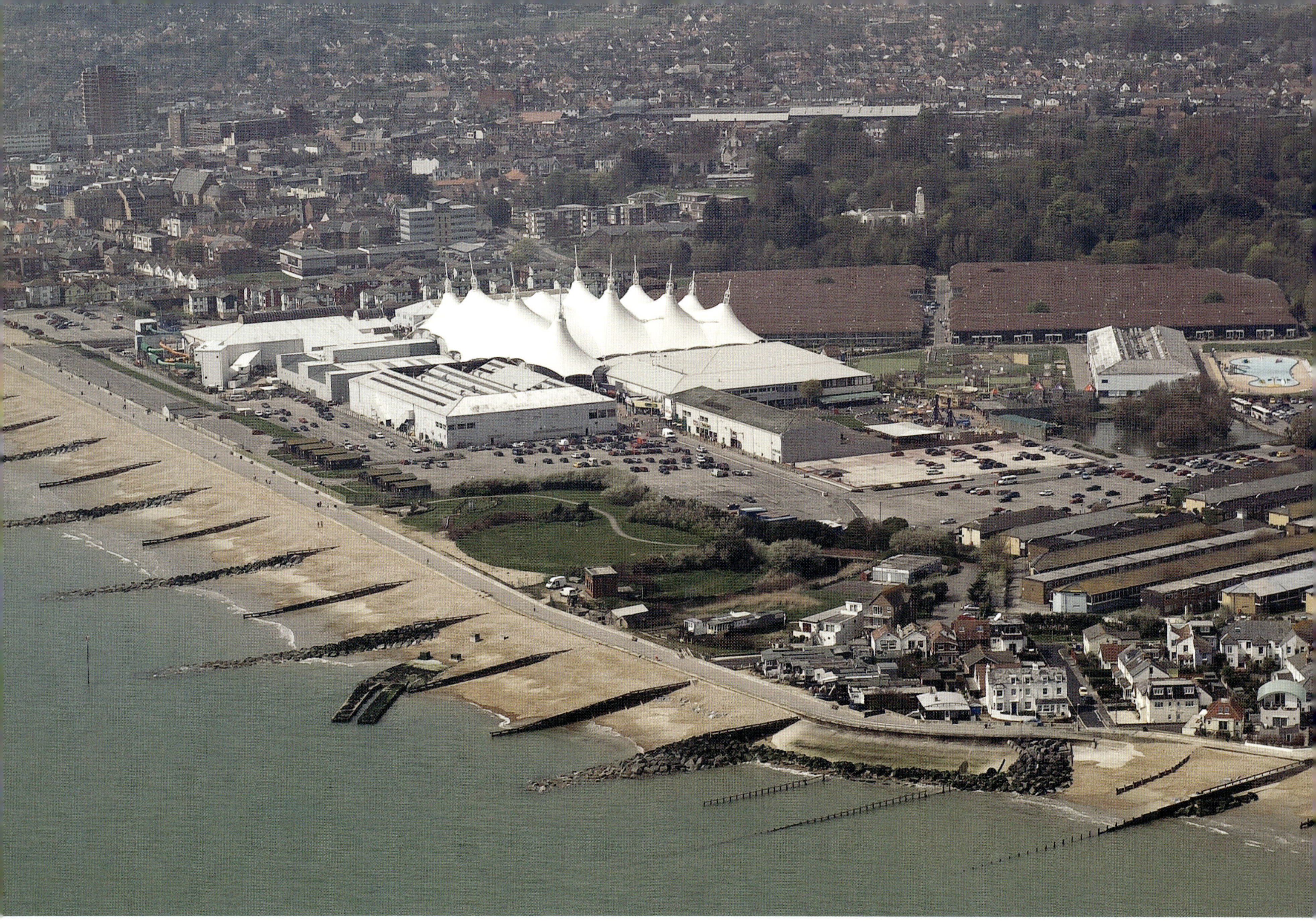

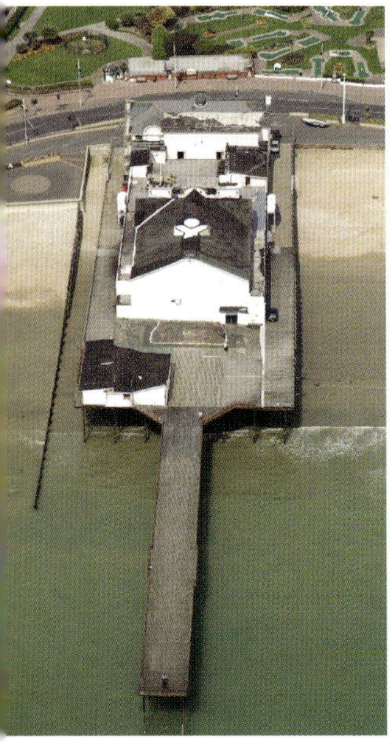

Bognor Regis

Bognor was developed into a seaside resort by the 18th-century property developer Sir Richard Hotham, and after King George V convalesced here in 1929 the town gained its Regis suffix. The Bognor Regis Butlins (above and right) is one of three remaining holiday camps established by Billy Butlin and was opened in 1960. The "Skyline Pavilion" at the centre of the camp plays host to a number of activities organised by the famous "red coat" entertainment officers. A 160-room luxury hotel set in landscaped gardens was recently completed (right). Costing £10m, the Shoreline's Art Deco design in the shape of a cruise ship recalls some of the south coast's most iconic buildings.

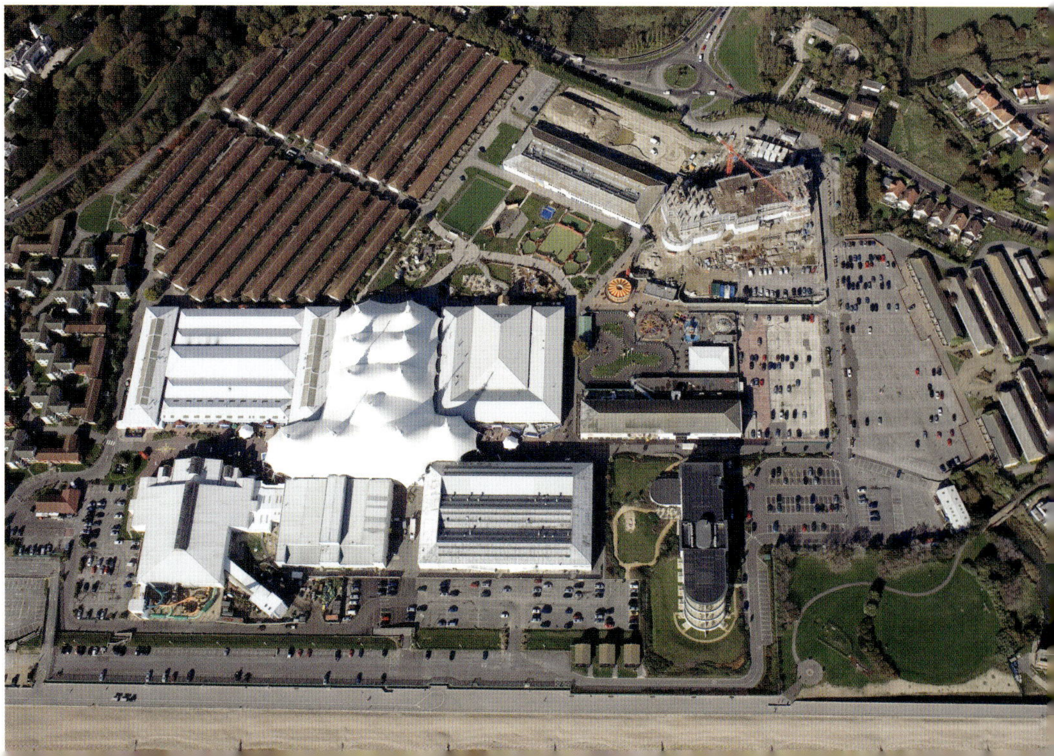

Chichester

Historic Chichester (right) contains some of the oldest buildings and churches in Britain. Its elegant 12th century cathedral is unusual in having a separate medieval bell tower and is the only cathedral visible from the sea. Within the cathedral there is a medieval tomb of a knight and his wife, the inspiration of the poem *An Arundel Tomb*, by Philip Larkin. The nearby village of Fishbourne is home to the Fishbourne Roman Palace, built in the 1st century AD shortly after the Roman conquest of Britain. A museum protects the building, which is the largest known Roman residence north of the Alps. Chichester is also a popular sailing centre with the second largest marina in Britain set in an extensive natural harbour. Chichester has a vibrant cultural life thanks in part to its annual drama festival.

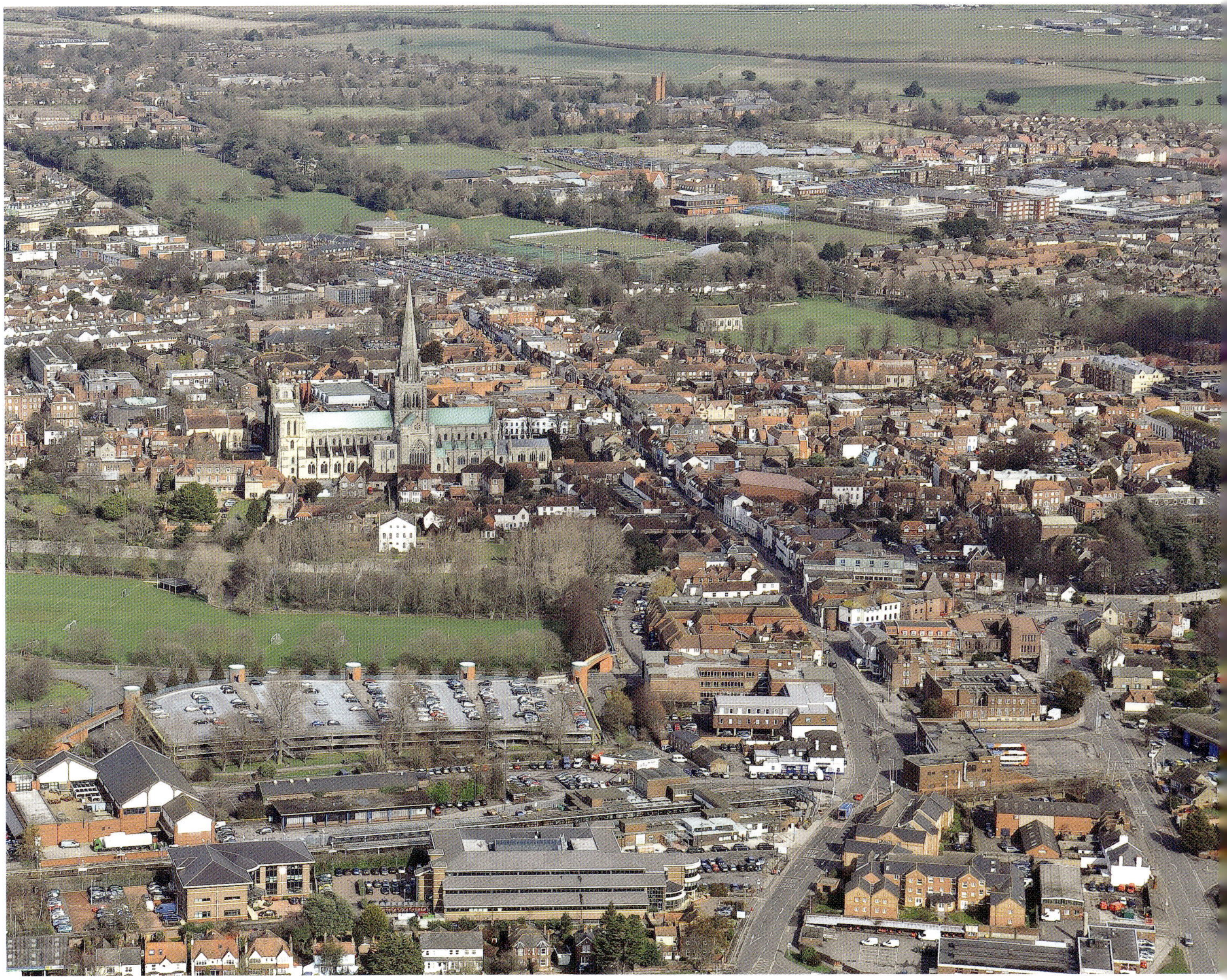

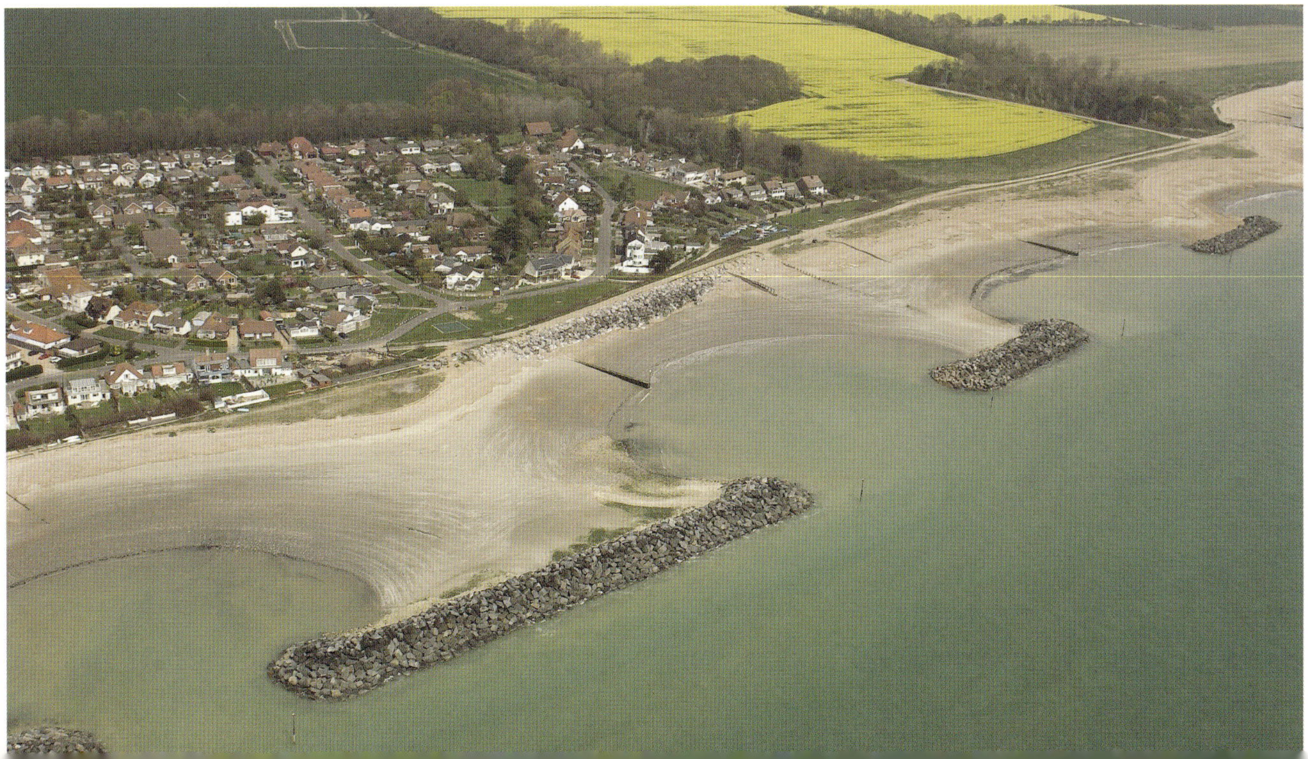

Coastal Erosion Management

Rapid coastal erosion in this stretch of the south-east's coastline has been partially halted by the use of sea walls and wooden groynes. In Elmer, a village on the outskirts of Bognor Regis, severe storms in 1989-90 caused damage to the sea defences and flooding of the hinterland. New offshore breakwaters (left) were constructed that run parallel to the shore. Sediment has built up behind the rocks to create rock islands accessible at low tide.

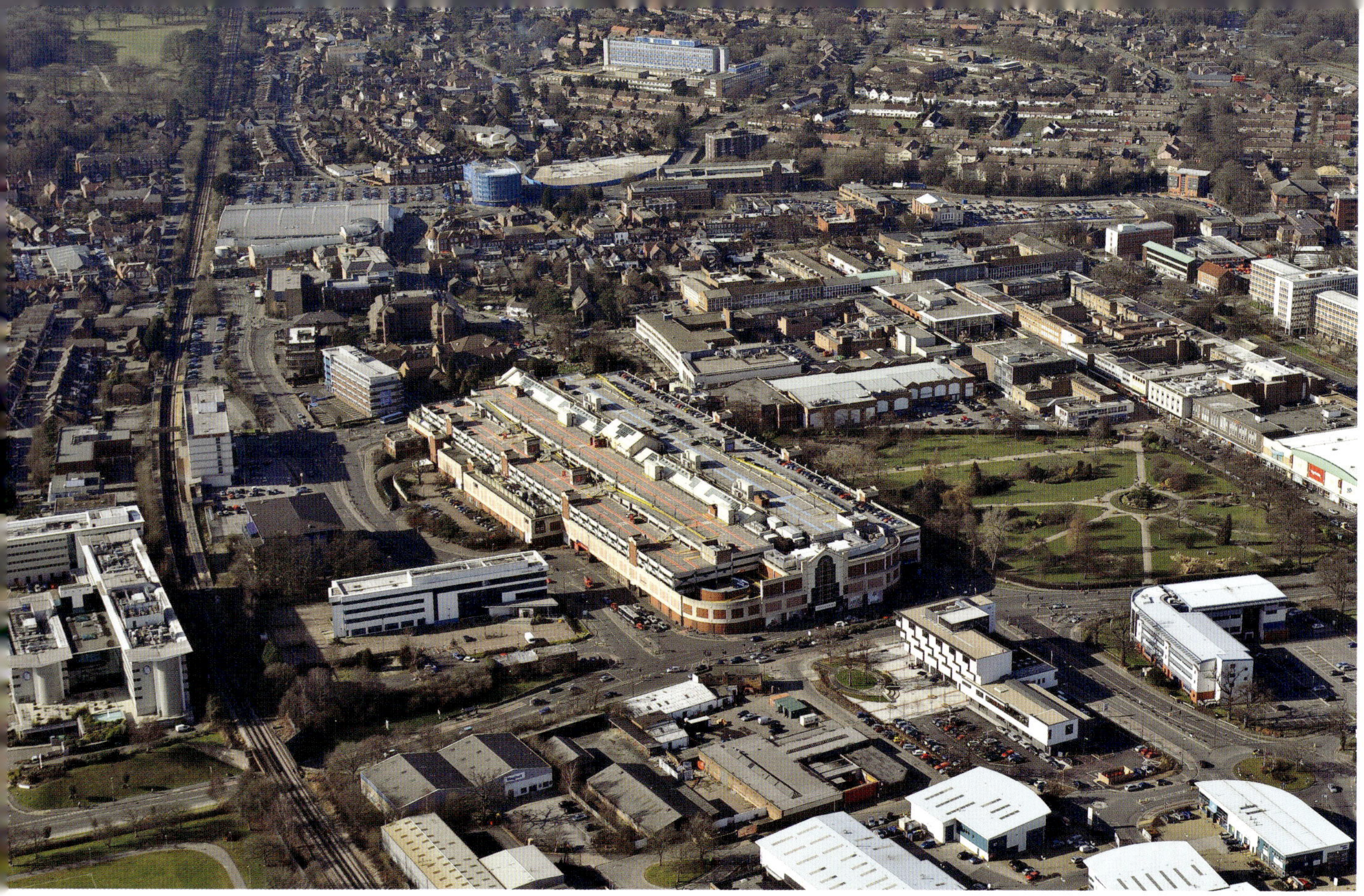

CRAWLEY

Located on the main road between London and Brighton, Crawley (left) developed as a market town with coaching inns from the 13th century onwards. Following the Second World War, Crawley was developed as a New Town to rehouse thousands of people from the centre of war-damaged and overcrowded London. Homes and employment opportunities were created so that despite a population rise from 9,500 in 1949 to 51,700 in 1960 only 70 people were registered as unemployed. Crawley's proximity to Gatwick has seen the rapid development of industrial and commercial businesses that support the airport.

BLUEBELL LINE

One of the largest tourist attractions in Sussex is the Bluebell Line Railway (right), which runs for nine miles (14 km) between Sheffield Park and Kingscote along the border between East and West Sussex. The line is the UK's first preserved standard gauge steam-operated passenger railway and operated its first services in 1960. The railway is managed and run largely by volunteers and has the UK's largest collection of steam locomotives outside the National Railway Museum in York. More than 30 locomotives are resident on the line, which is also a popular filming location for dramatisations and films such as *The Railway Children* and *Miss Potter*.

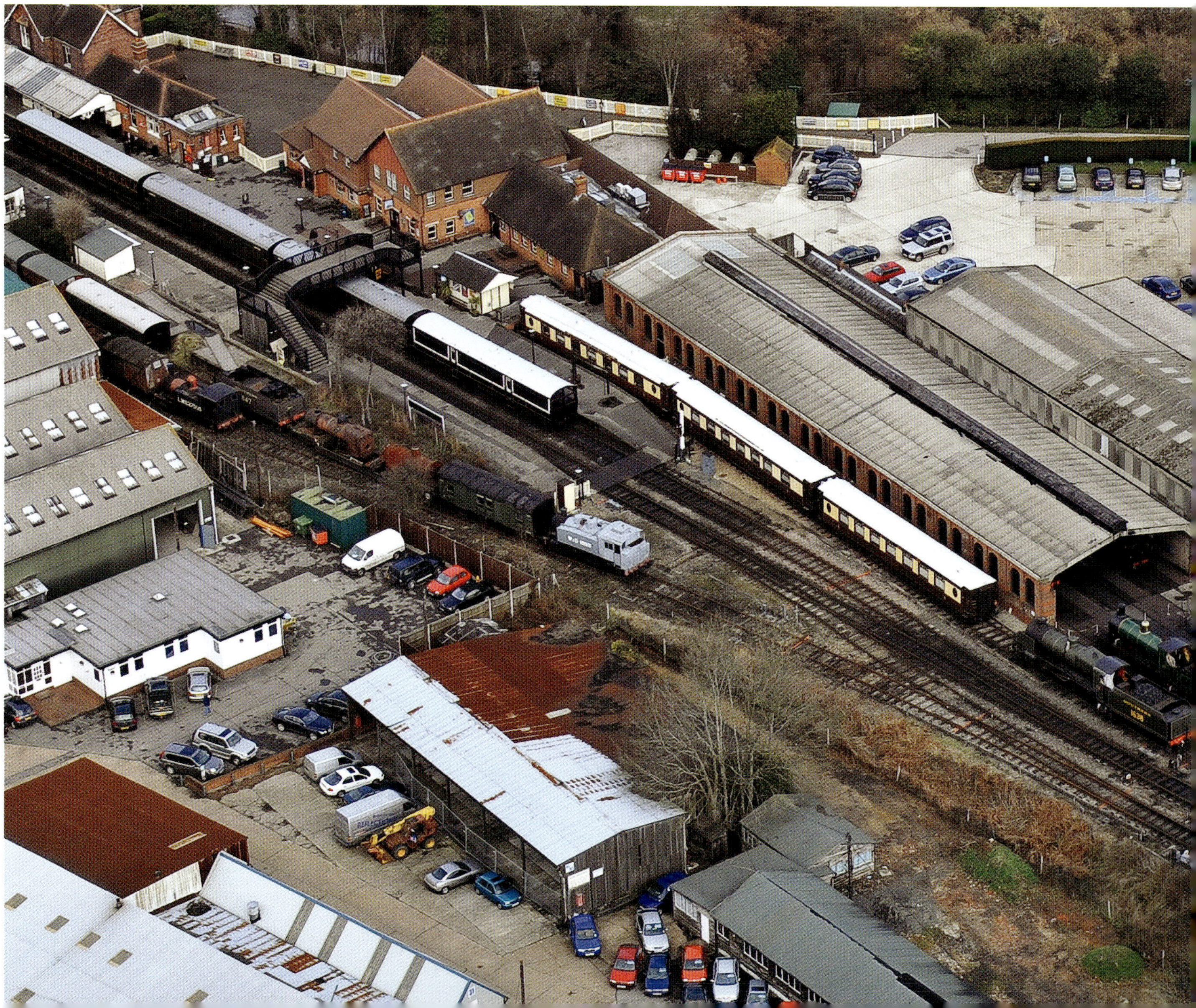

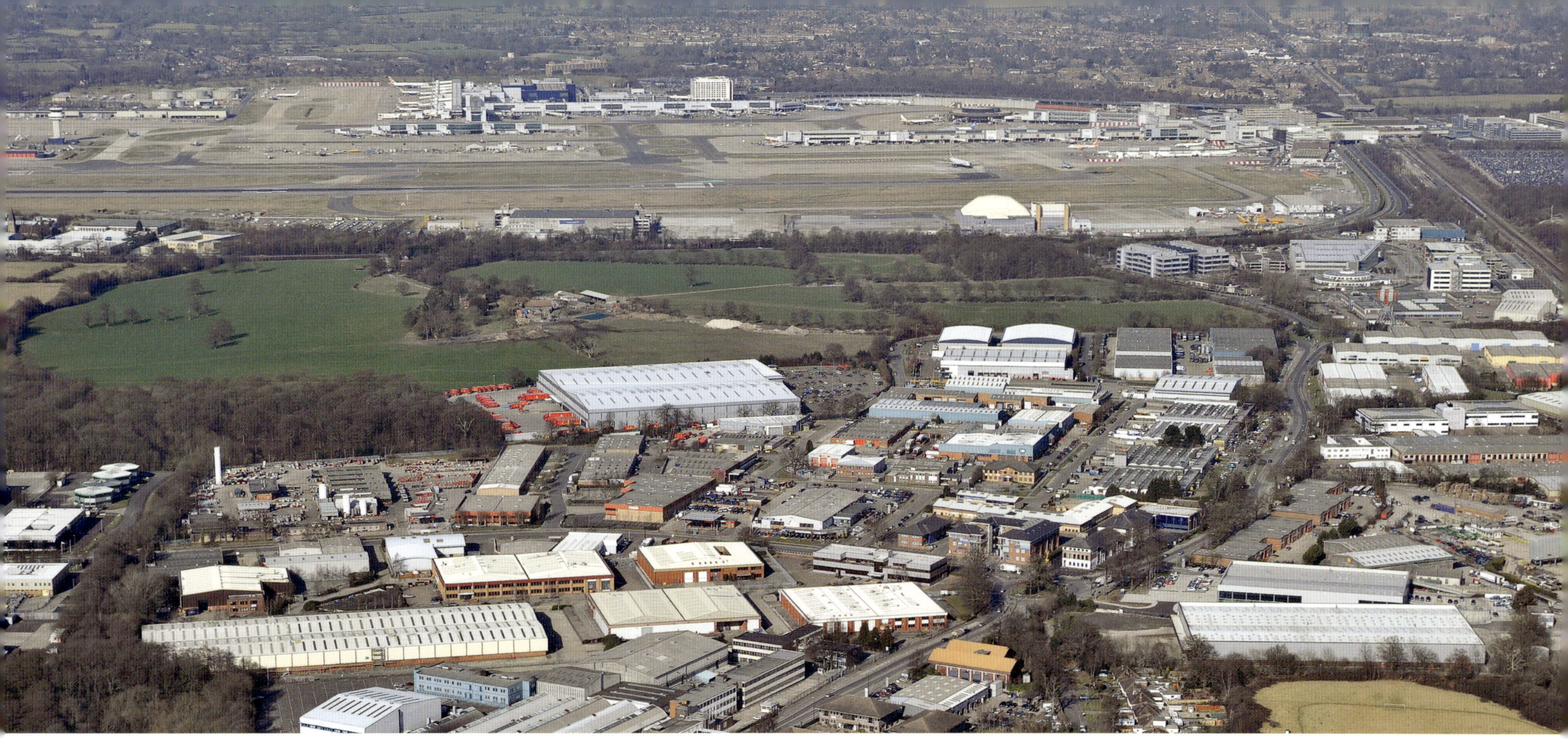

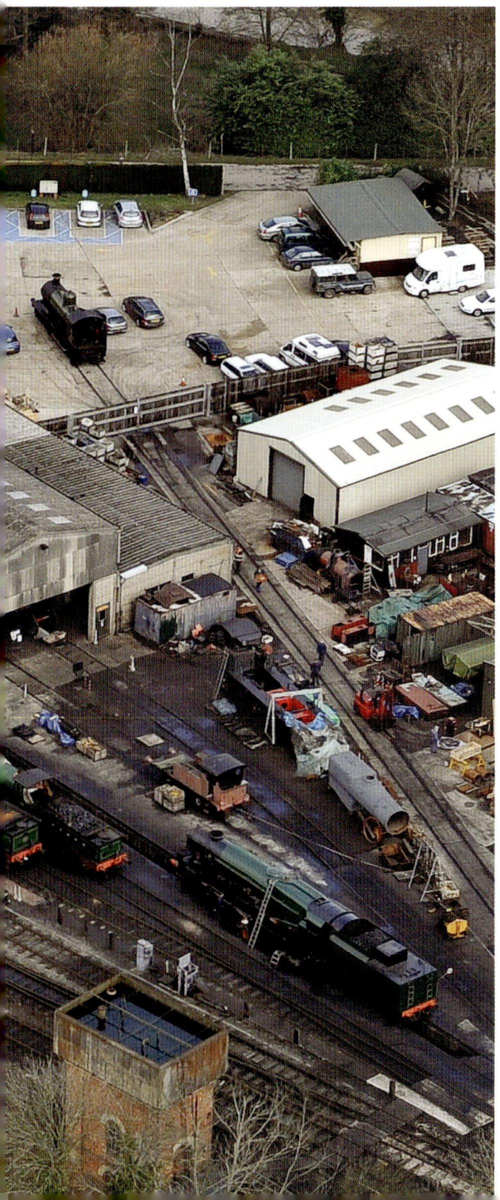

Gatwick

As Britain's second busiest airport, more than 30m passengers pass through Gatwick (above and below) each year travelling on a range of full service, charter and "no frills" flights. Originally developed as an airport for flights to British and European destinations, aircraft now fly to destinations all over the world from Gatwick's North and South terminals. The two terminals are linked by a 0.75 mile (1.21km) two-way automated monorail opened in 1983 as the UK's first people mover system. Gatwick's life began in 1931 as a private airfield with a unique subway and covered walkway linking the airport with the nearby railway station. As an RAF base during the Second World War the airfield grew substantially but the runway remained unpaved. In 1953 Gatwick was designated as London's second airport and was transformed into a modern facility over a three-year period with a 2,000ft runway (609m) and the UK's first covered walkway linking the terminal with the aircraft. Today, Gatwick has the world's busiest single-use runway.

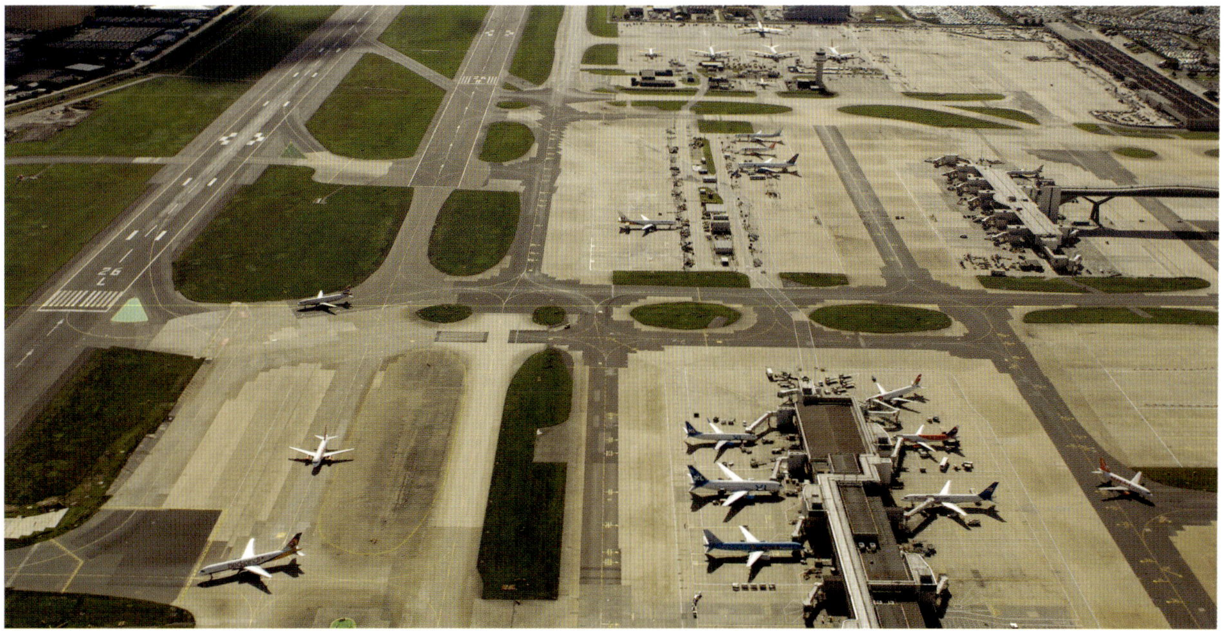

Berkshire and the Thames Valley

The Thames Valley region has a mainly urban population living in towns such as Reading, Maidenhead and Slough, but there's plenty of rolling countryside with wooded areas including Windsor Great Park and Bracknell Forest. Many settlements developed along the Great Western Road from London to Bristol or as river ports delivering timber and grain to London. The arrival of the Great Western Railway in the 19th century saw a massive population increase and the Thames Valley is still the UK's fastest growing region, with a working population of one million people. Berkshire is known as the Royal County of Berkshire due to the presence of Windsor Castle. The royal family's influence can be seen in Henley-on-Thames's Royal Regatta and Ascot racecourse's world famous Royal Ascot race meeting.

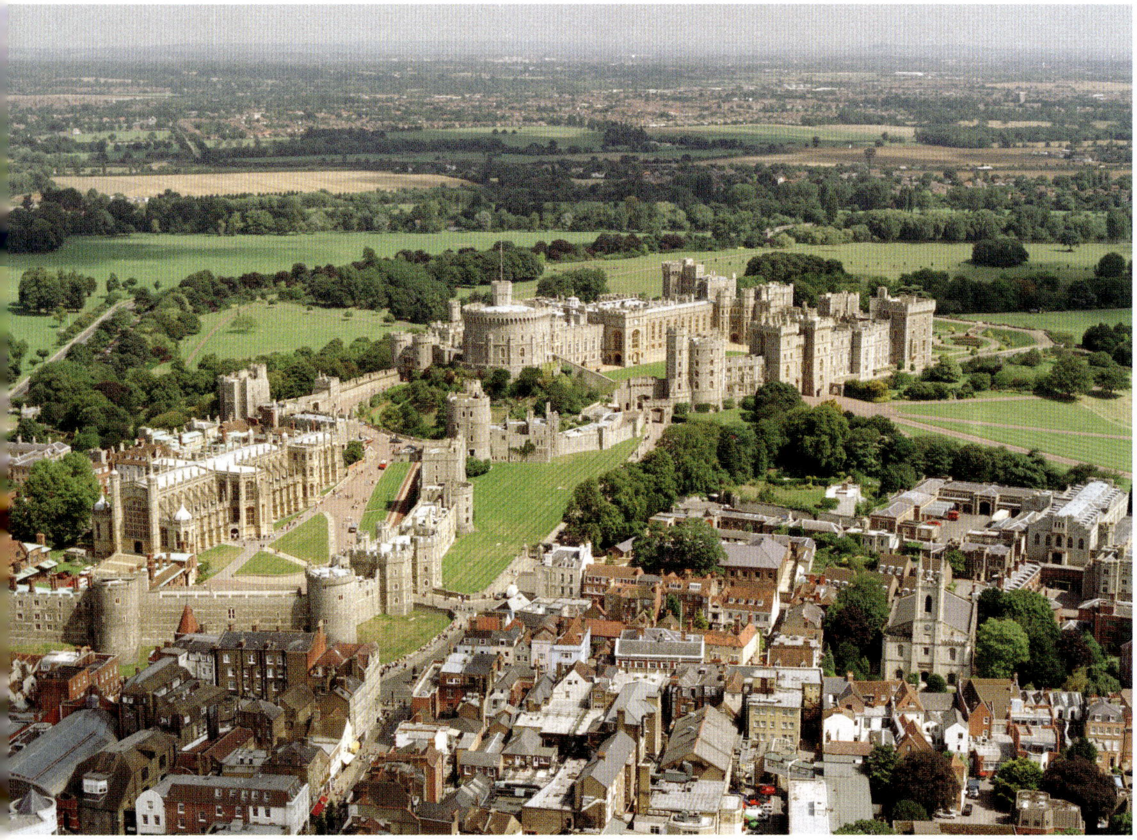

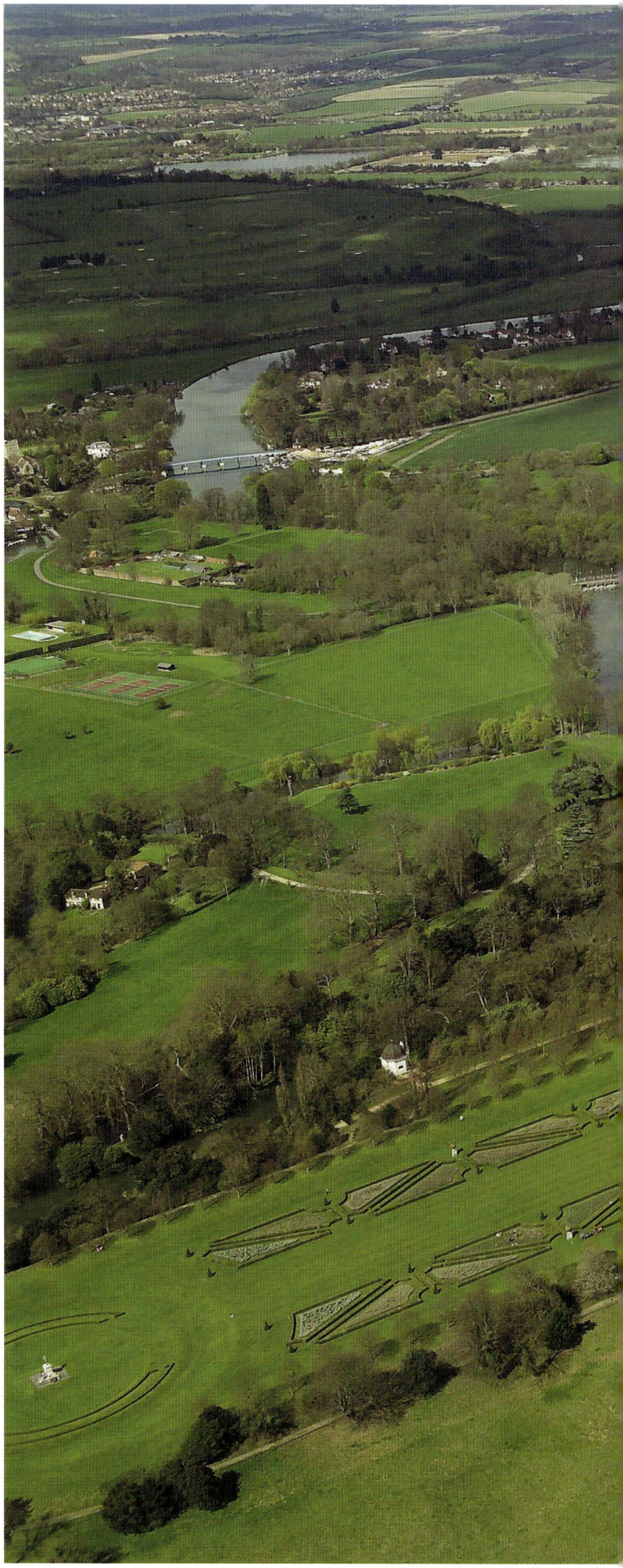

Homes to the Rich and Famous

Attractive views of the river Thames and surrounds can be seen from Windsor Castle (above), one of the official royal residences of the British monarch, and Cliveden (right), an Italianate stately home at Taplow, once owned by American billionaire William Waldorf Astor.

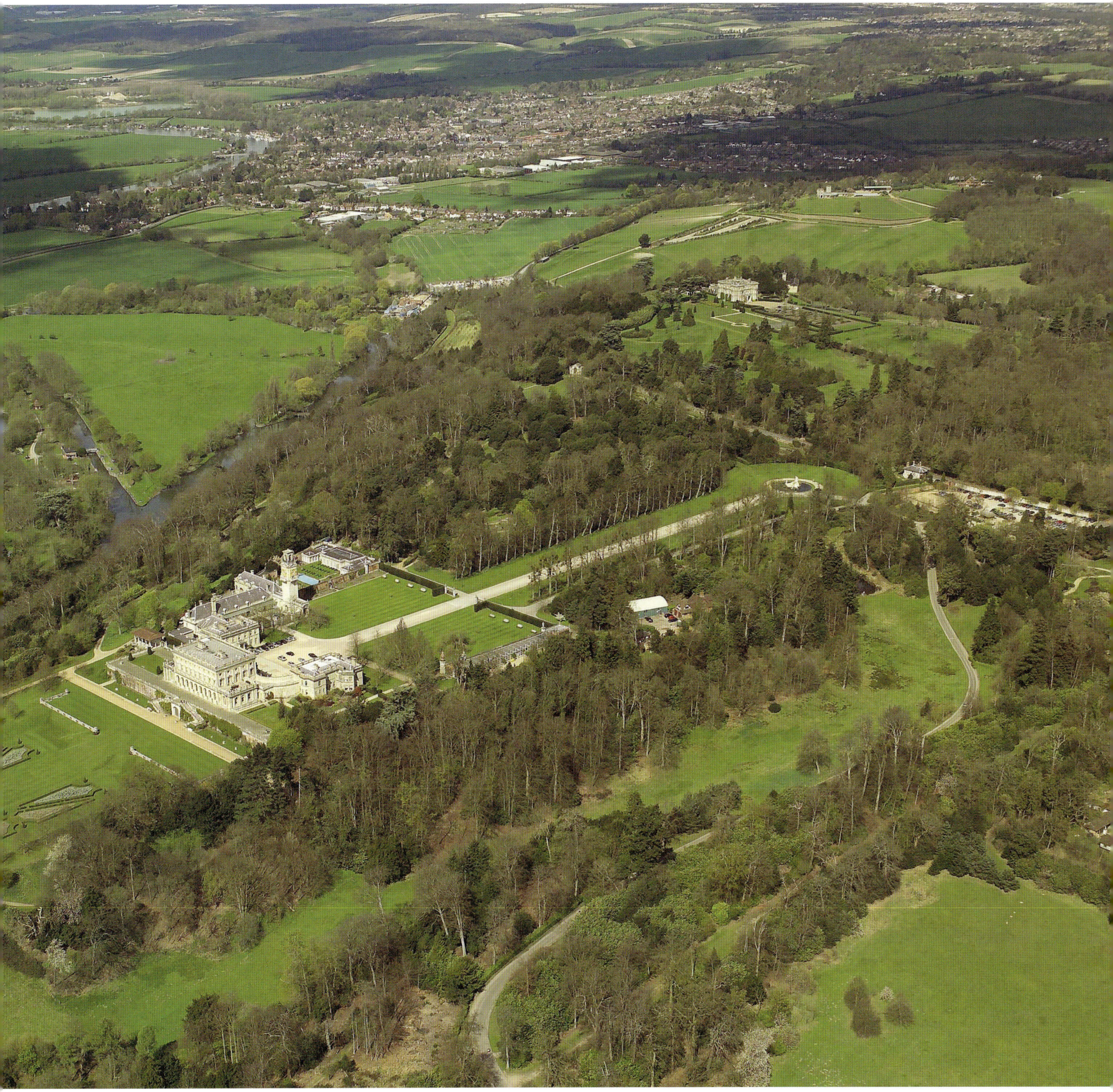

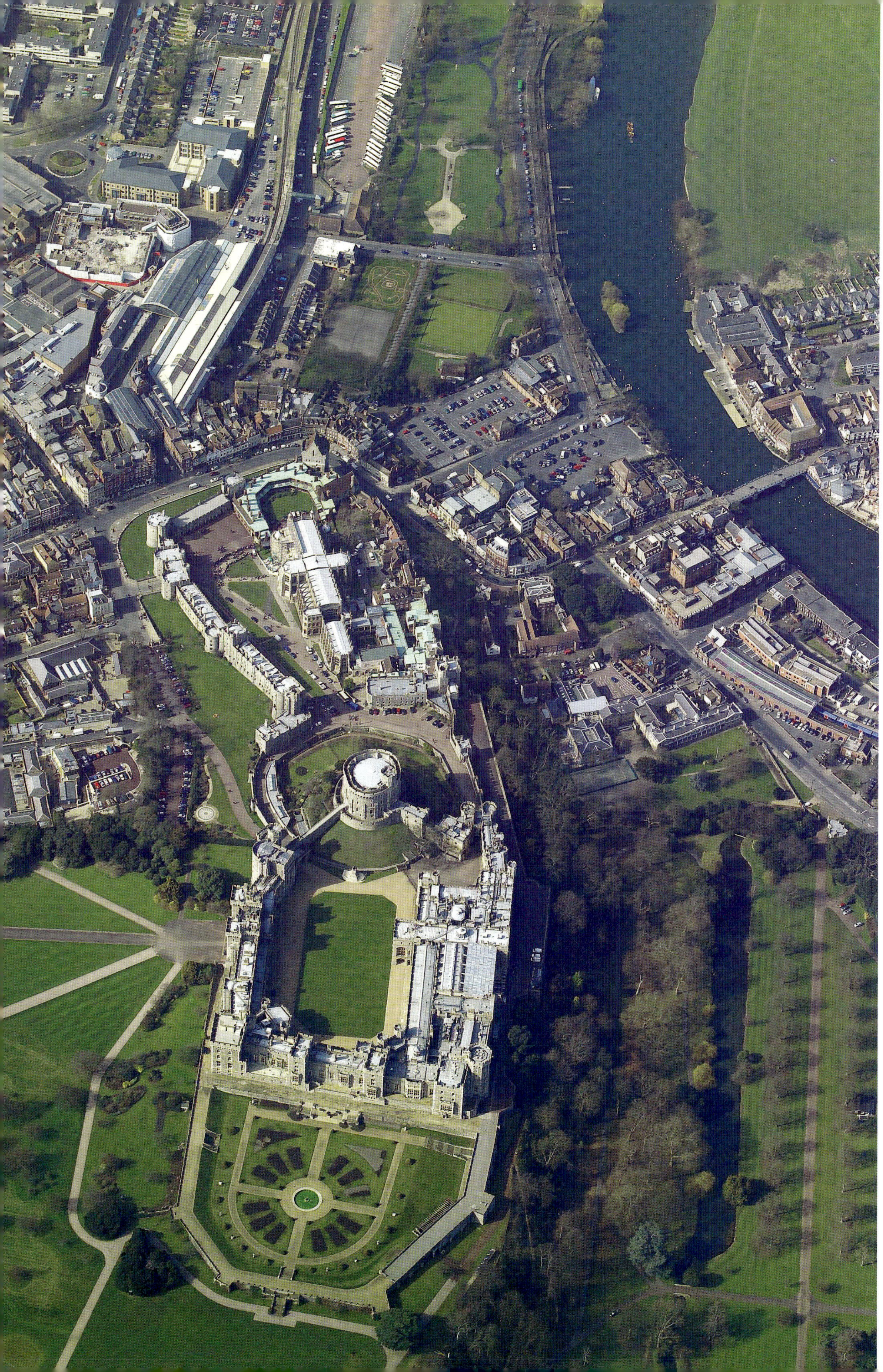

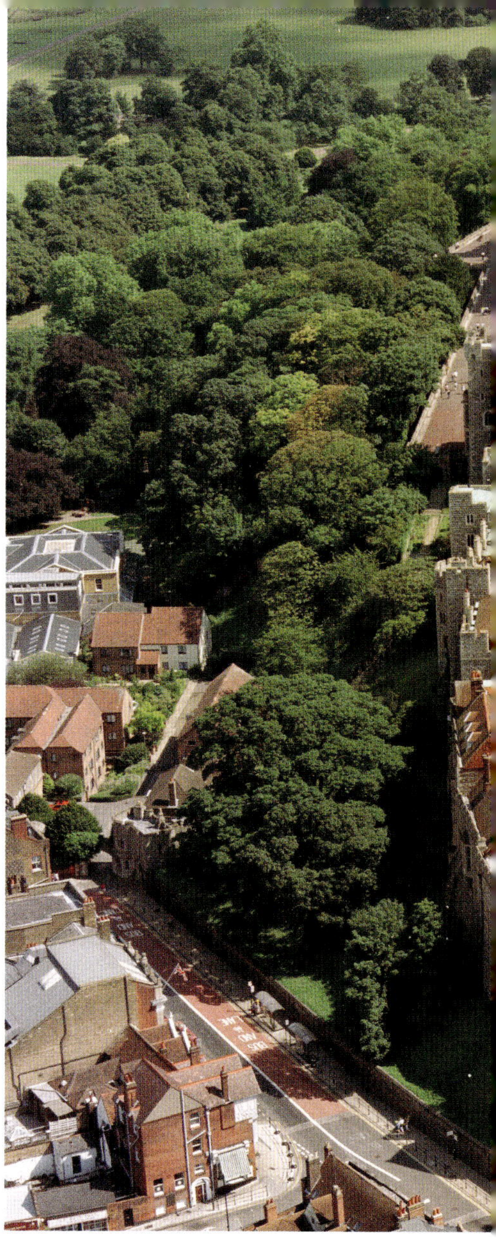

WINDSOR

The town of Windsor is a major tourist destination with a wide range of attractions including Windsor Castle, Eton College, Legoland, the Ascot and Royal Windsor Racecourses, Virginia Water and the Savill Garden. Boat trips can be taken along the river Thames and horse-drawn carriage rides are available through the largely Georgian and Victorian town. The area has an abundance of greenery with 1,000 acres of National Trust land and 4,800 acres owned by the Crown Estate. Some of the UK's most expensive and desirable housing is found close by.

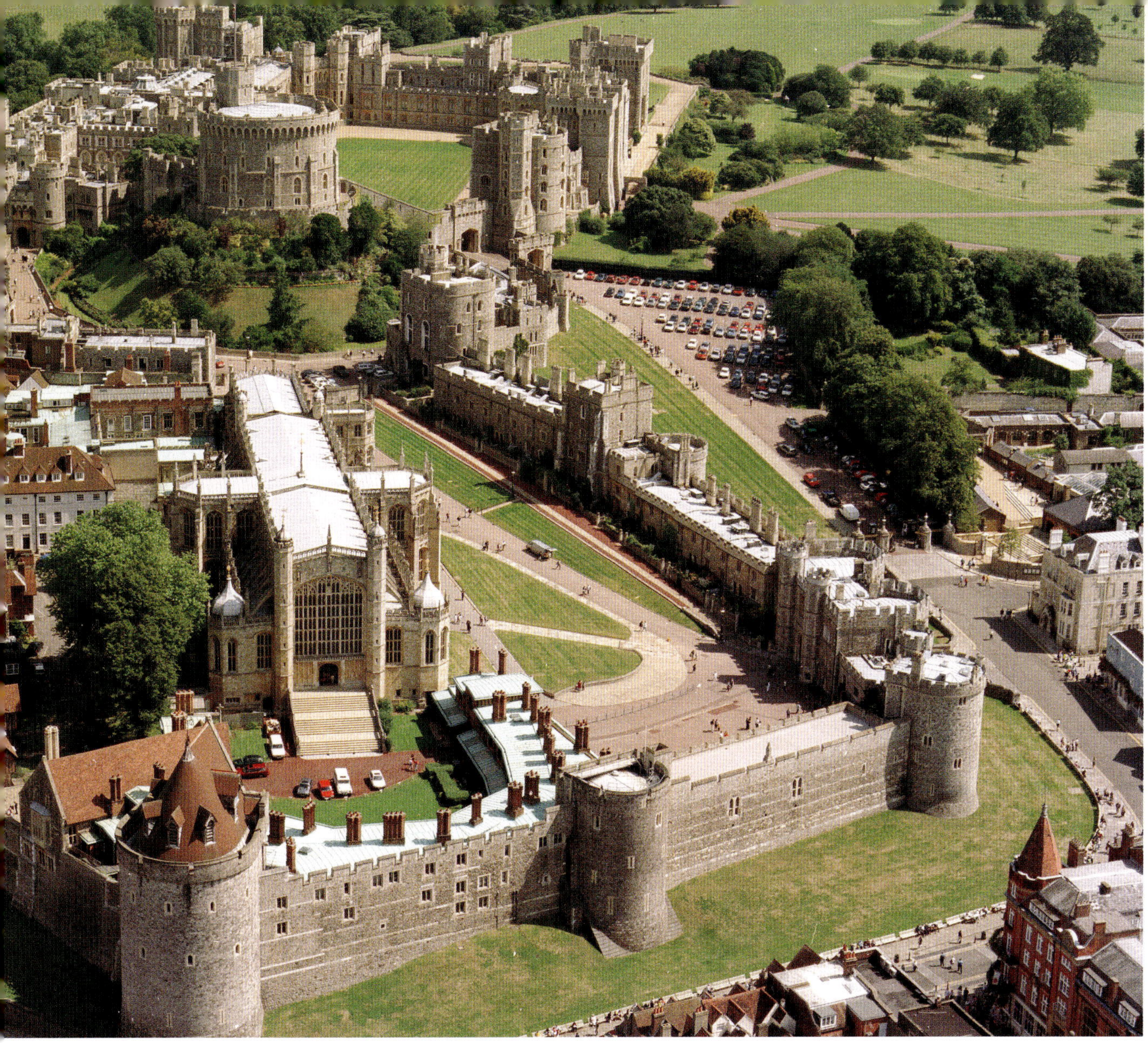

Windsor Castle

Windsor Castle is one of the Queen's official residences and has been in continuous use for over 900 years. William the Conqueror first built a wooden motte and bailey castle on the site between 1070 and 1086, and it was later rebuilt in stone. Most of the kings and queens of Britain have added to the building in some way, developing the fortress into a royal palace. The Gothic style seen today is largely the work of Sir Jeffry Wyattville in the 1820s, during the reign of George IV. St George's Chapel (below) is the burial place of 10 monarchs. It is also the home of the Order of the Garter and the setting for many royal weddings. In June 1999 Prince Edward, now the Earl of Wessex, married Sophie Rhys-Jones in St George's Chapel and the marriage of the Prince of Wales to Camilla Parker Bowles was dedicated there following a civil ceremony in Windsor's Guildhall in April 2005.

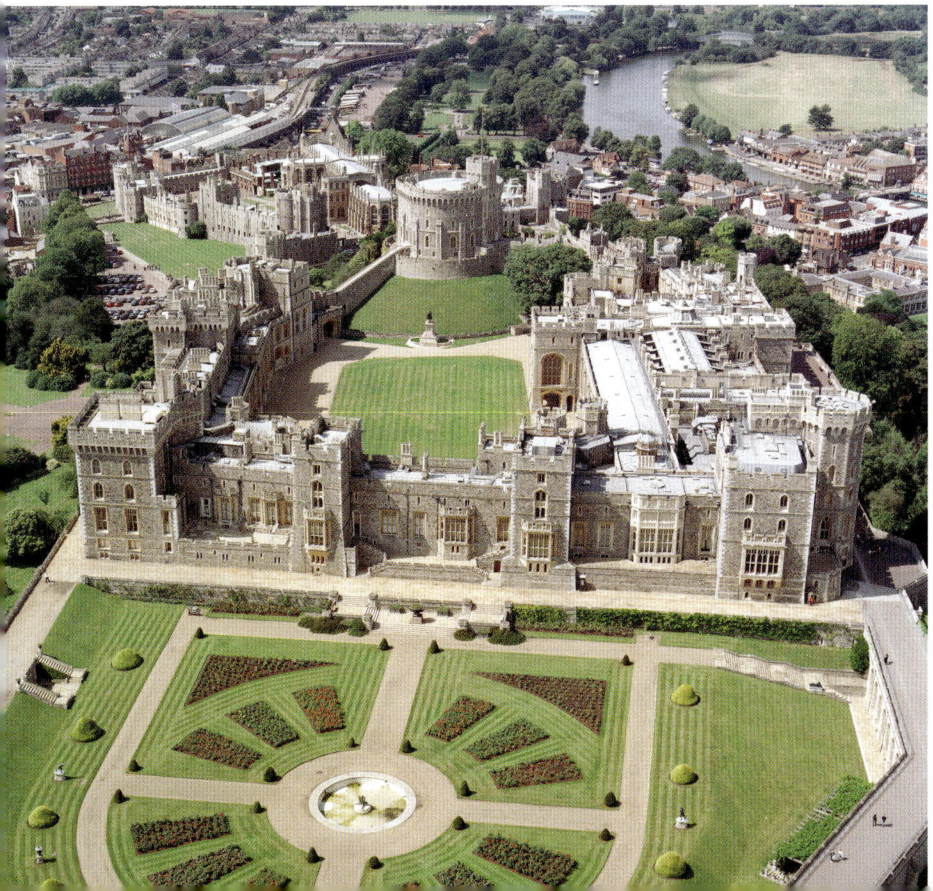

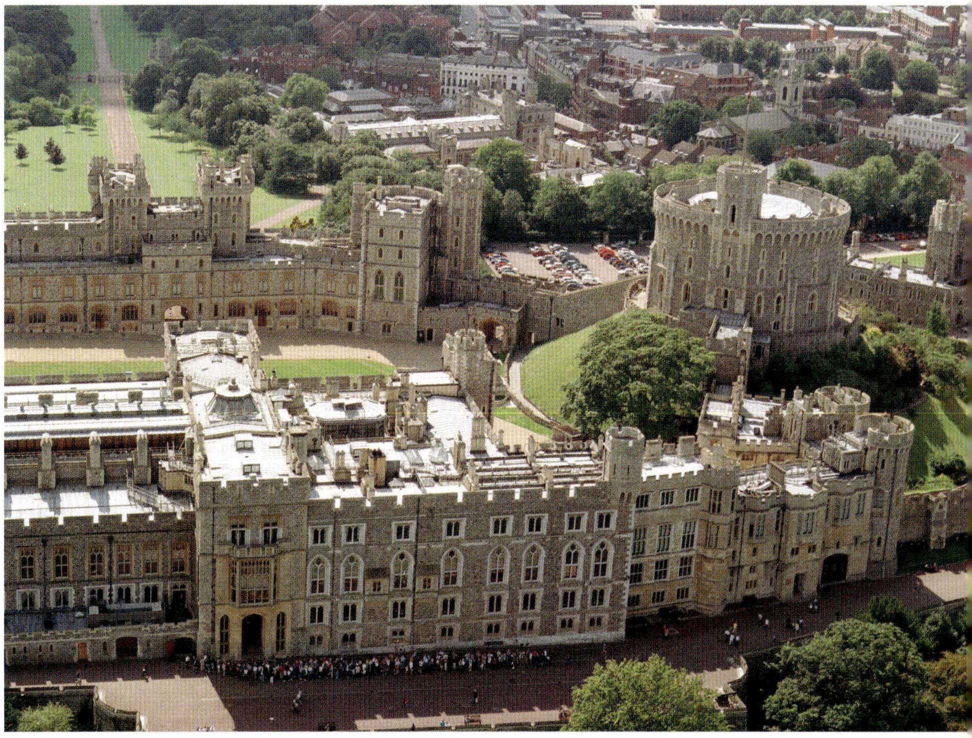

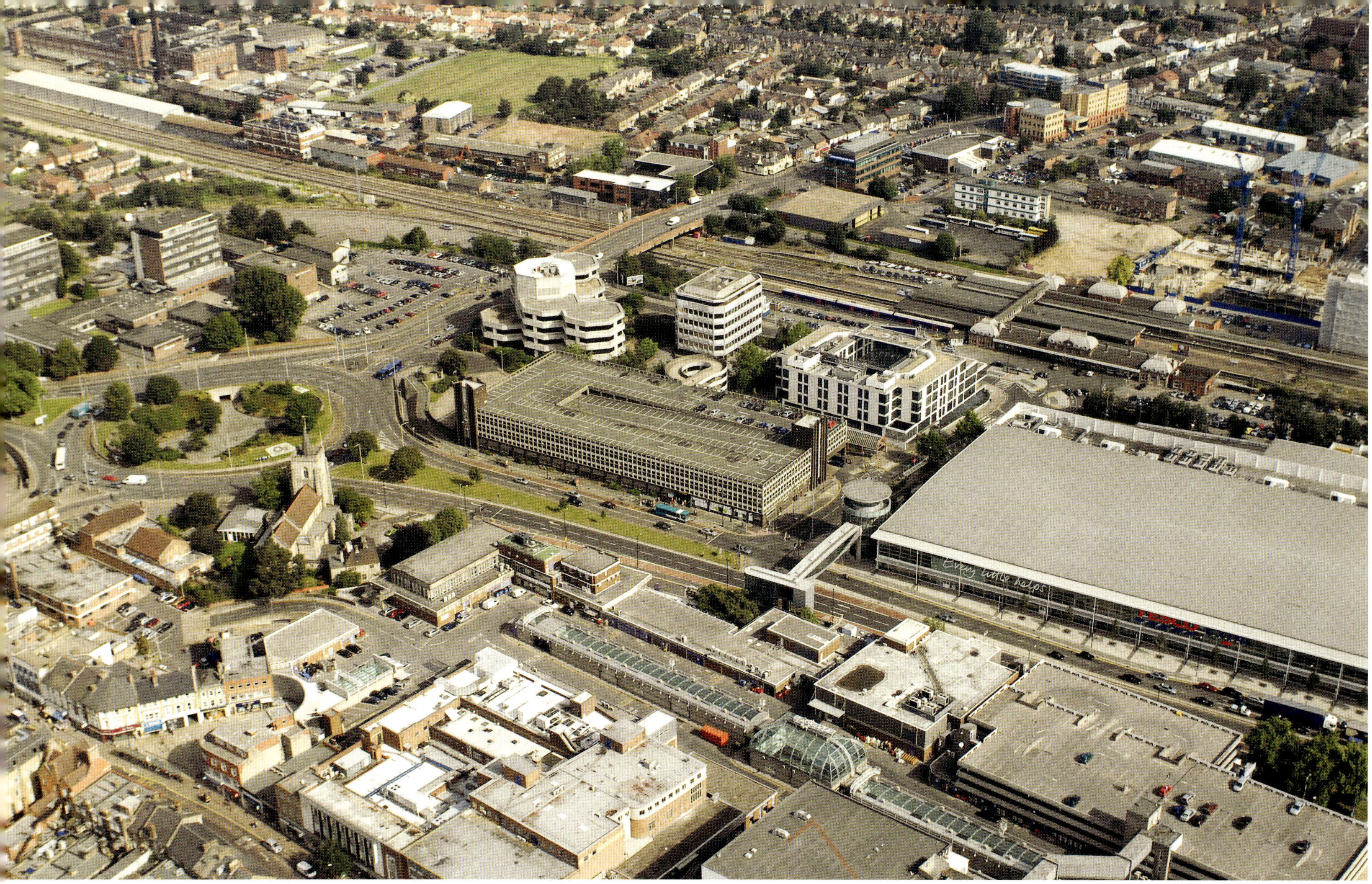

Slough

Close to London and major transport routes, Slough (above and right) has developed as a major business centre. The Slough Trading Estate, founded in 1920, is the largest industrial estate in single private ownership in Europe with over 600 buildings, its own power station and a working population of about 20,000. The BBC comedy series *The Office* is set on the trading estate featuring fictional paper merchants Wernham Hogg. Slough is unfairly thought of as an industrial wasteland, perhaps following John Betjeman's well-known poem *Slough* written in 1937 to protest about the opening of 850 factories in a former rural area. Slough is the most ethnically diverse local authority outside London and there has been major redevelopment of the town centre in recent years.

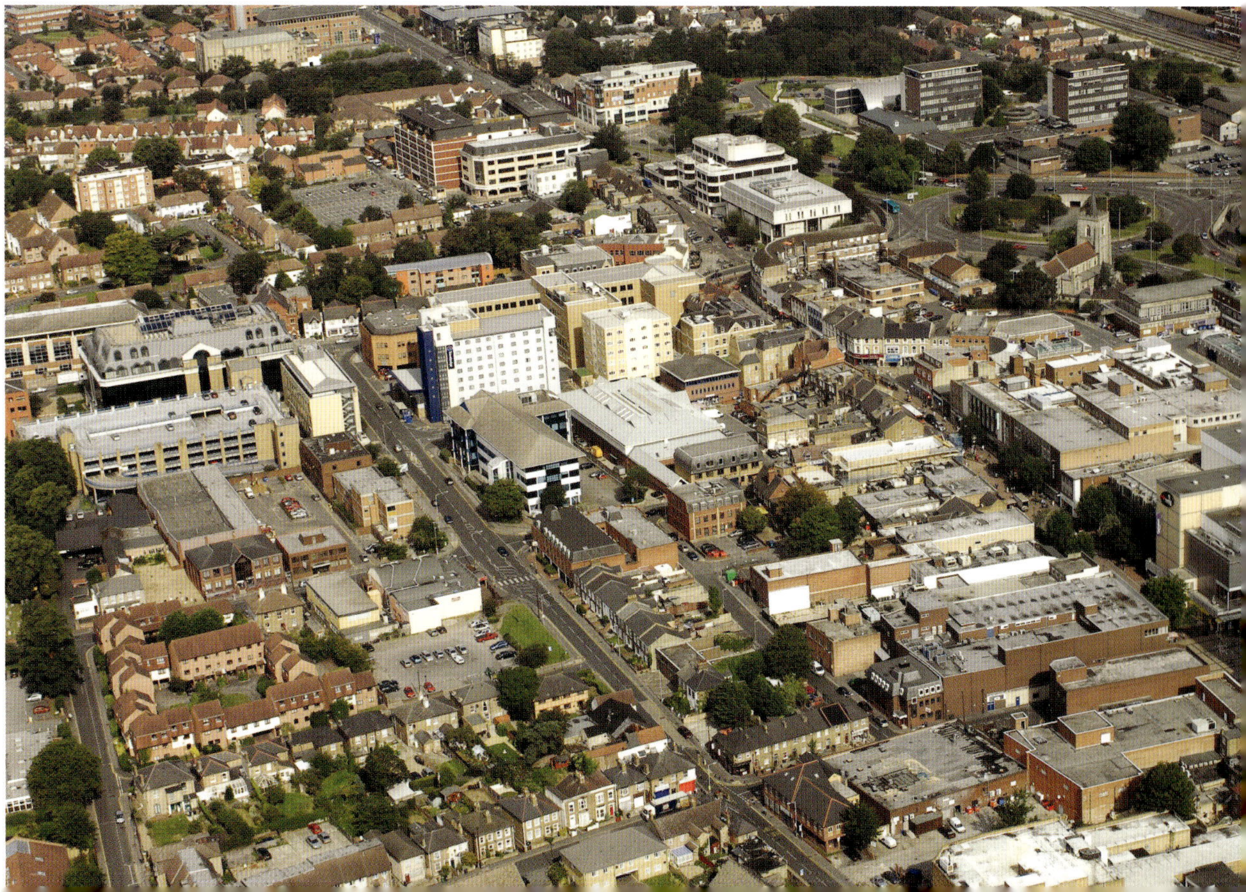

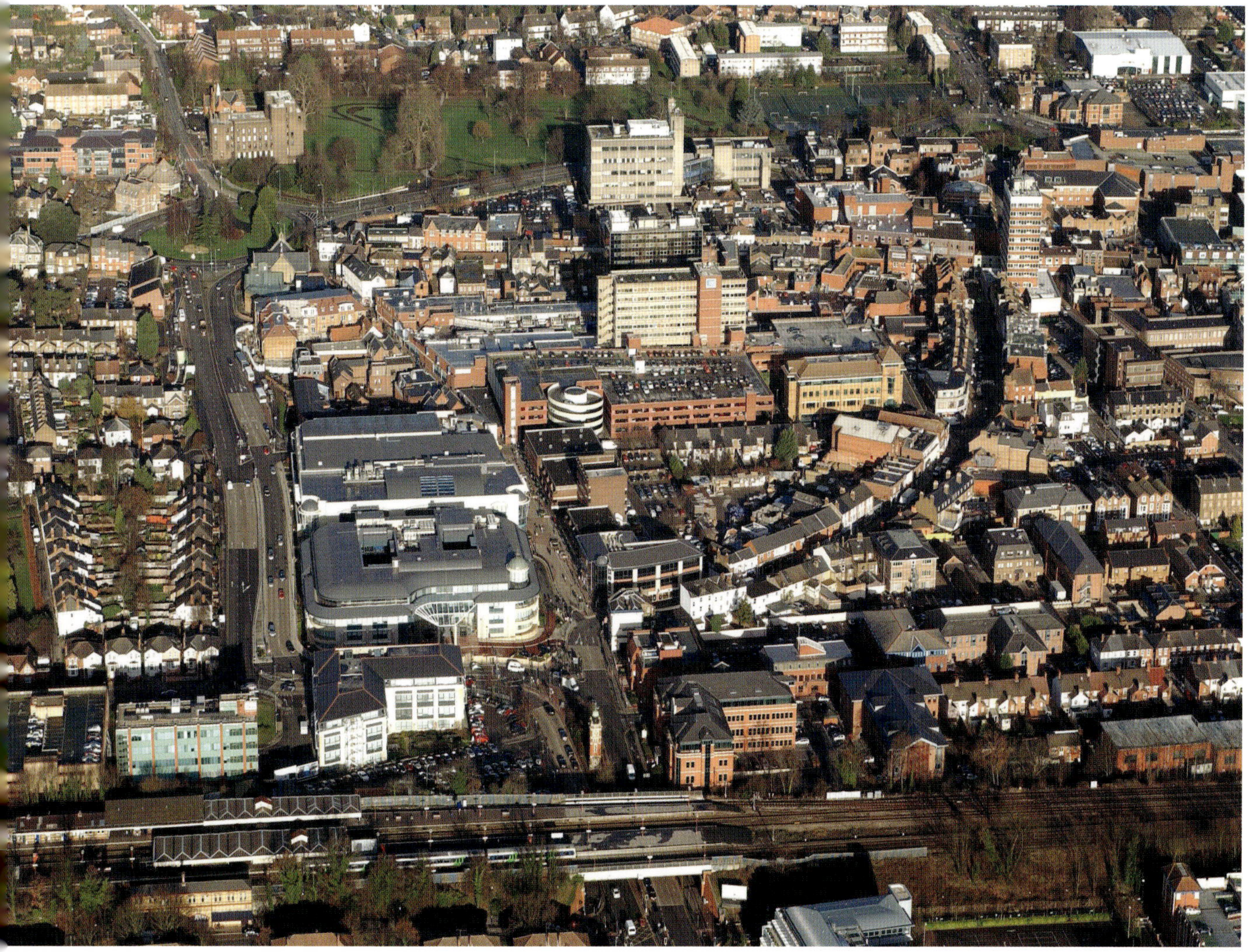

Maidenhead

Situated on the Great Western Road between London and Bath, Maidenhead (left and below) was a stopping off point for stagecoaches and provided ample refreshment for travellers from its four breweries close to the river Thames. Middle-class commuters arrived with the construction of the railway in 1838, and Isambard Kingdom Brunel's brick-built Maidenhead Railway Bridge spanning the Thames, which offered quick and easy links with London and Bristol. Known to locals as the Sounding Arch because of its spectacular echo, the bridge was painted by Turner in 1844. Today Maidenhead sits in England's "Silicon Corridor" and provides employment in industries such as computer software, plastics and pharmaceuticals. The nearby M4 motorway also offers easy transport along the Thames valley to nearby towns such as Swindon and Reading.

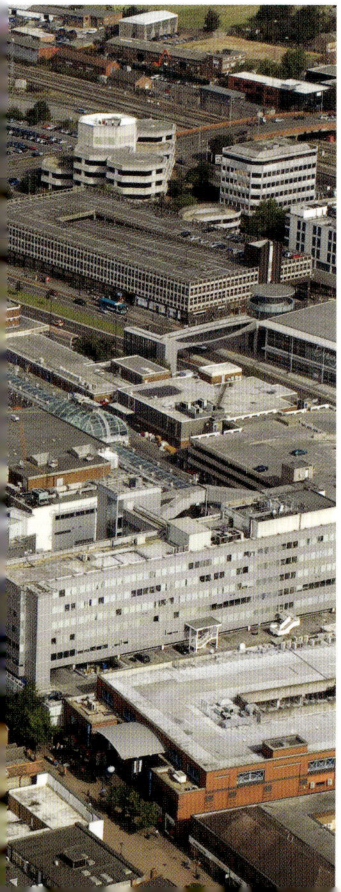

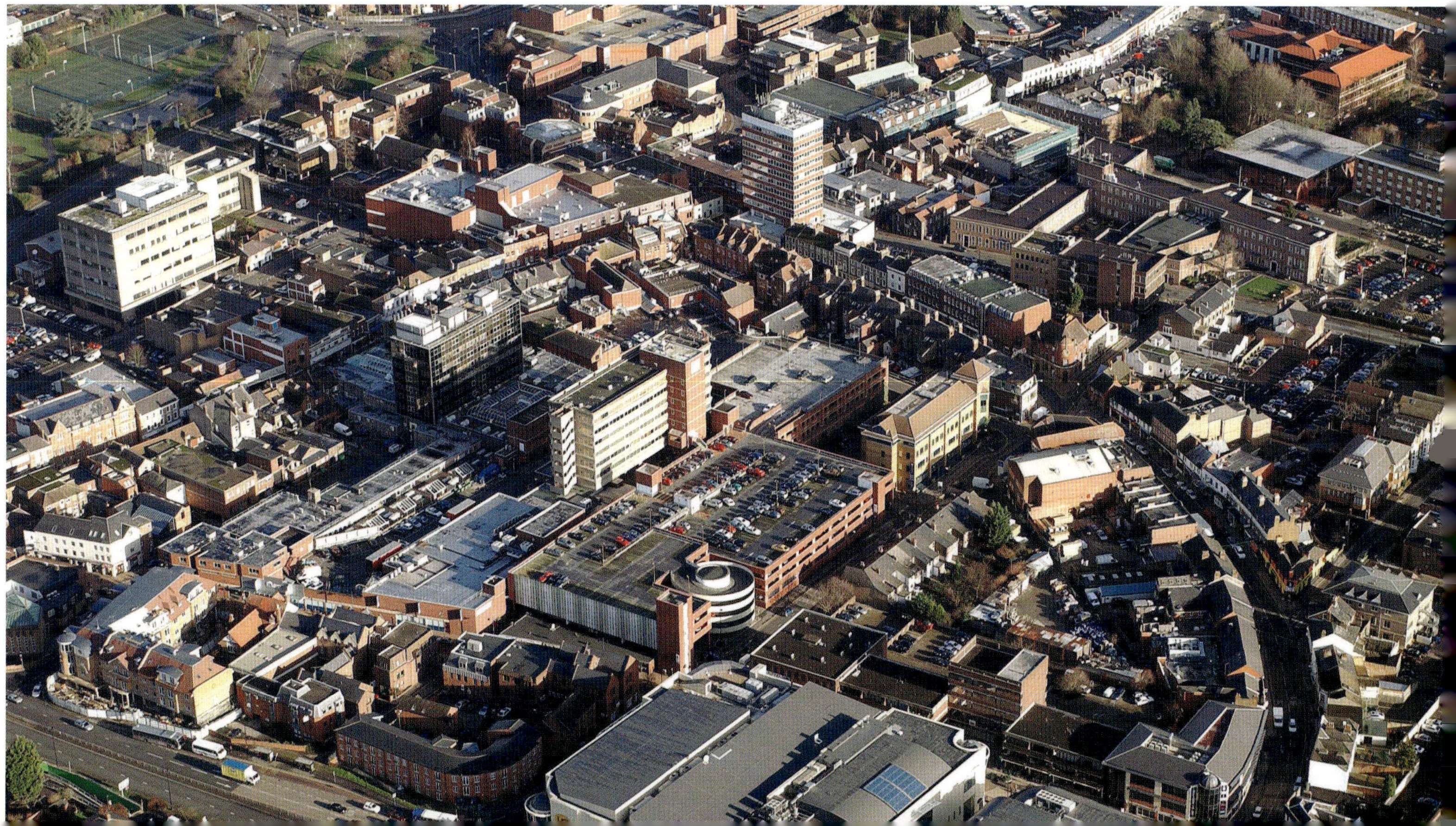

Reading

The county town of Berkshire was once famous for the three b's – beer, bulbs and biscuits – but Reading is now often referred to as the commercial capital of the Thames Valley. Company headquarters for a wide range of businesses including IT and insurance are located in business parks around the town. Once a river port, situated on a low ridge between the rivers Thames and Kennet, Reading's position on the Great Western Railway and proximity to the M4 has helped the population grow to over 145,000 today. Reading is a popular shopping location with the pedestrianised Broad Street, and the Oracle shopping and leisure centre, built in 1999. Named after the 17th century workhouse that was once on the site, its three storeys of shopping have provided 4,000 jobs. Reading has a large student population as it is home to the University of Reading and a campus of the Thames Valley University. The Reading Festival, a major music event, has been held in the town each year since 1971.

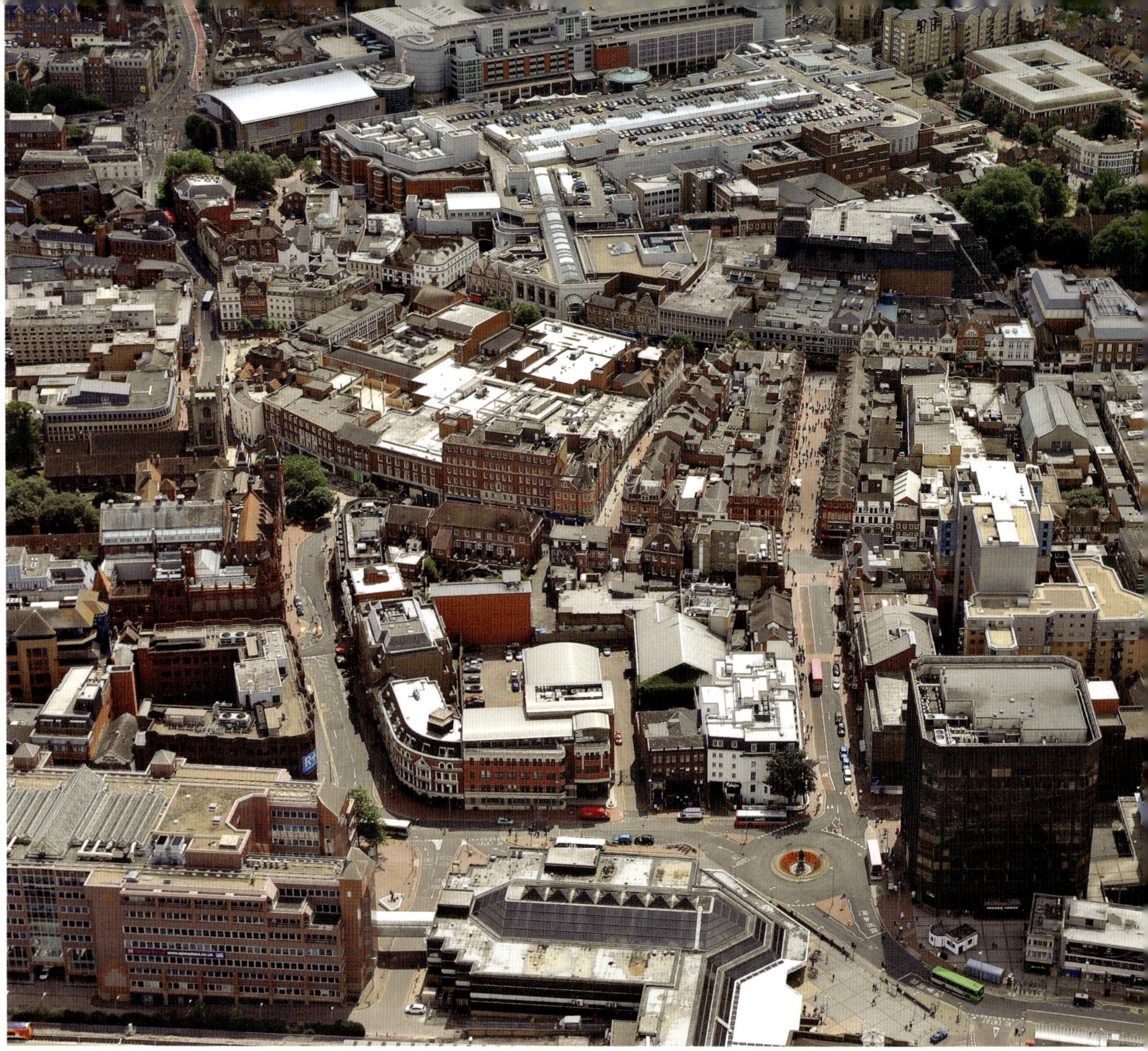

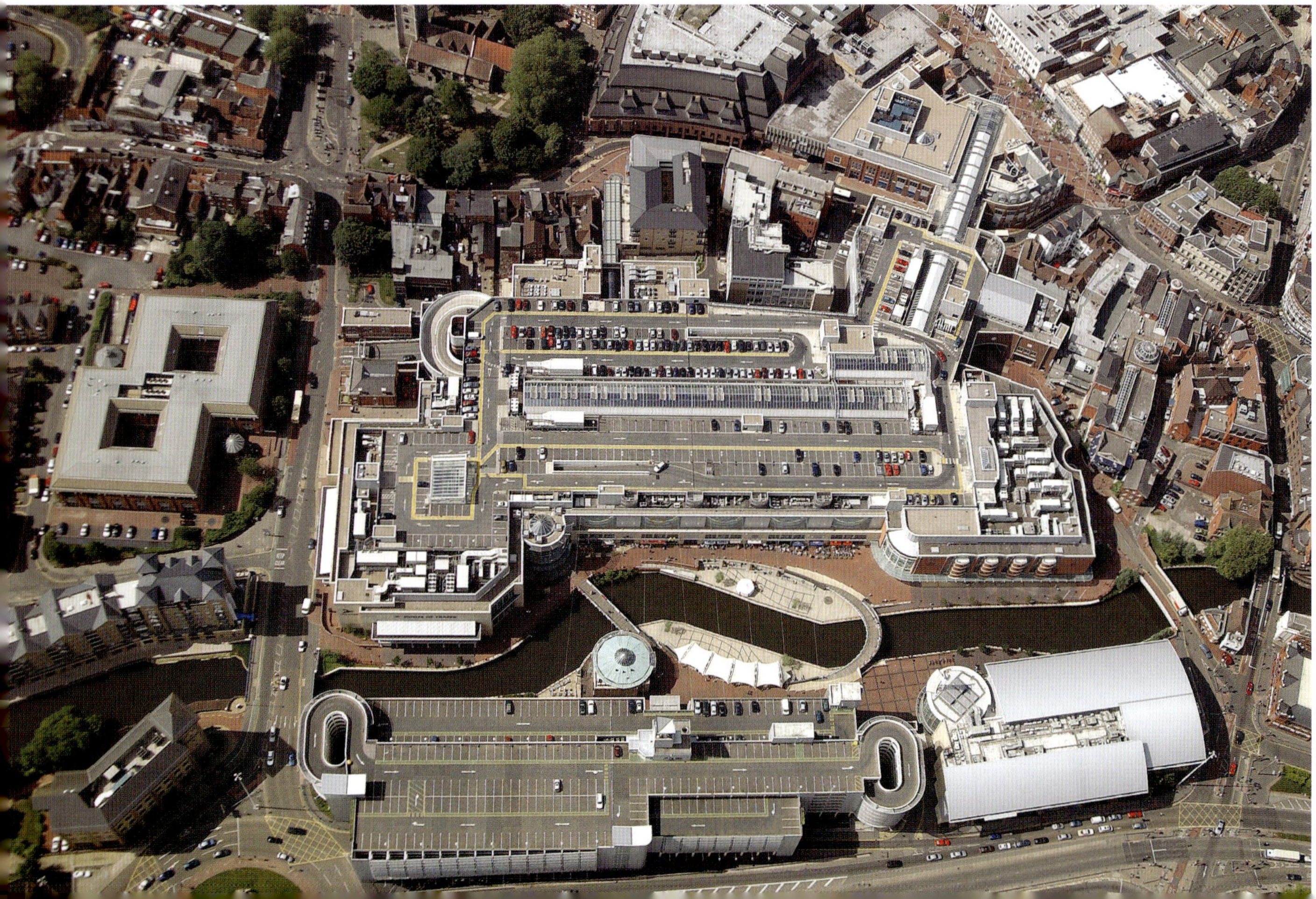

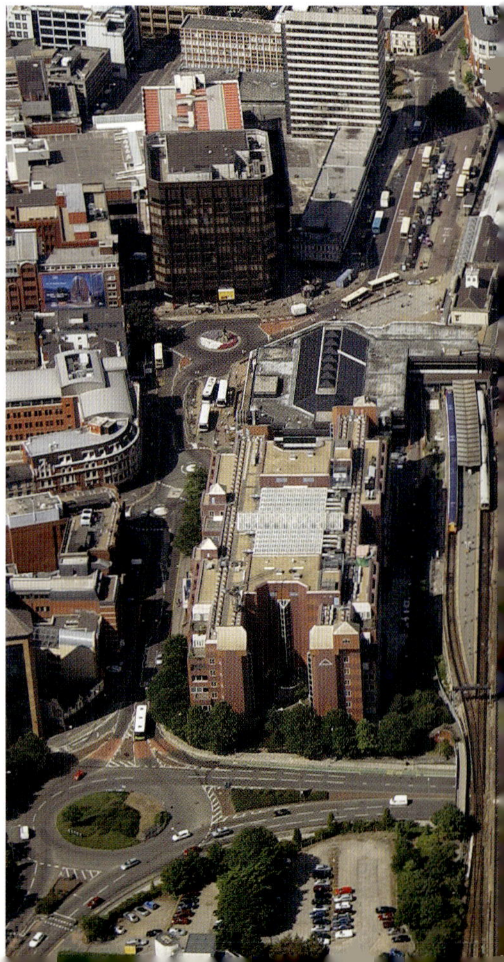

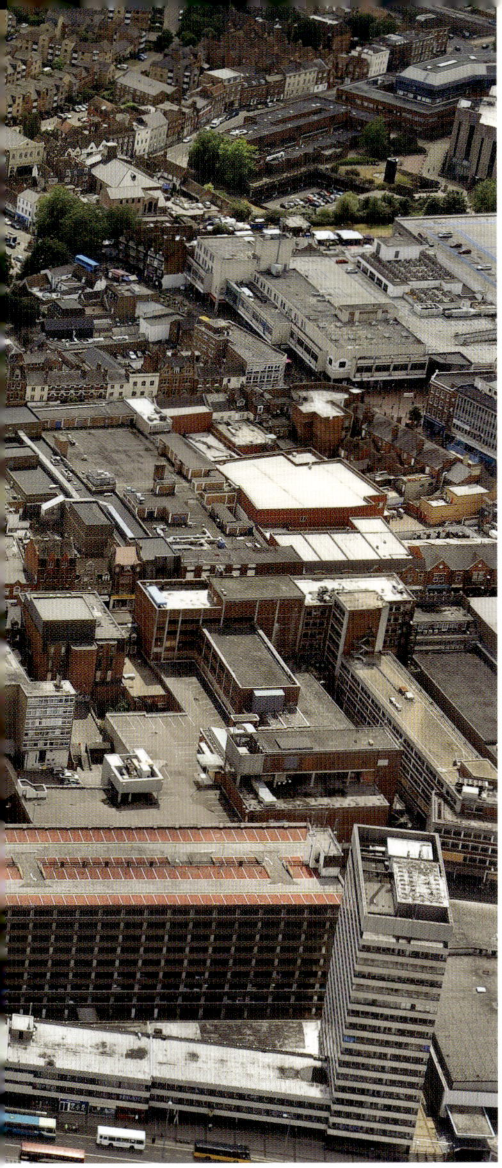

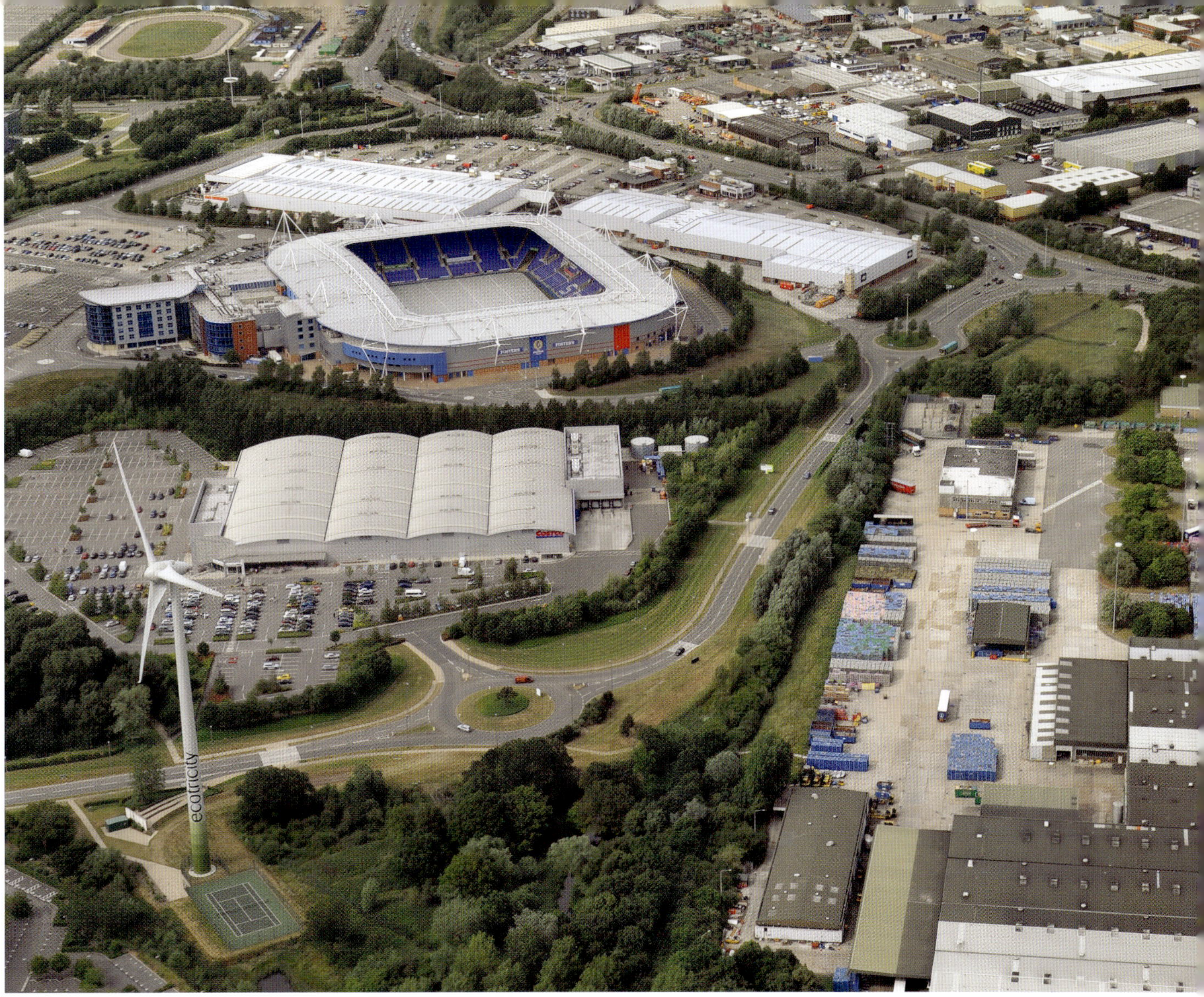

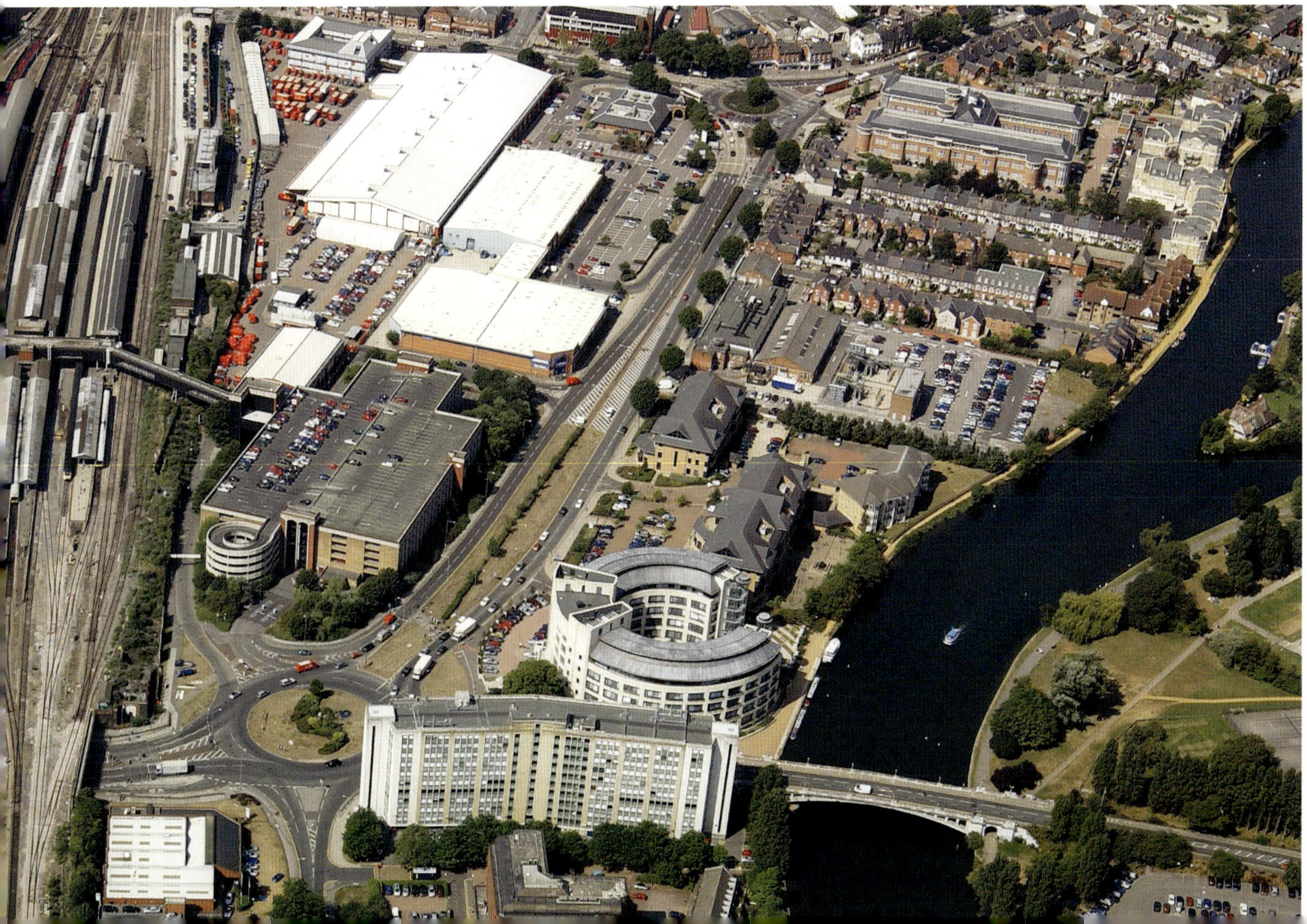

The Madejski Stadium

Nicknamed The Royals after the Royal County of Berkshire, Reading Football Club play at the £50m Madejski Stadium (above). Named after the club's chairman, Reading businessman Sir John Madejski, the stadium has a capacity of 24,161. Built on the site of a former household waste dump, Reading Borough Council sold the land to the club for £1, and the stadium incorporates methane gas vents to accommodate the underground build-up of gases. Madejski contributed £25m of his own personal wealth towards the stadium's construction and owns 98% of the club, who went on to enjoy top-flight football in the 2006-7 season.

Aldermaston

Located in west Berkshire, the quiet rural village of Aldermaston is famous for its close proximity to the Atomic Weapons Establishment (AWE), which provides and maintains the warheads for Britain's nuclear deterrent, Trident. Established on the site of the former RAF Aldermaston airfield in 1950 (right), the AWE has attracted protest since 1958 when several thousand people marched from Trafalgar Square to Aldermaston to demonstrate their opposition to nuclear weapons. Organised by the Campaign for Nuclear Disarmament, the Aldermaston Marches were held regularly until 1963, with revivals in 1972 and 2004. The 50th anniversary of the event was marked on March 24, 2008. There is currently a monthly women's peace camp held outside the Establishment.

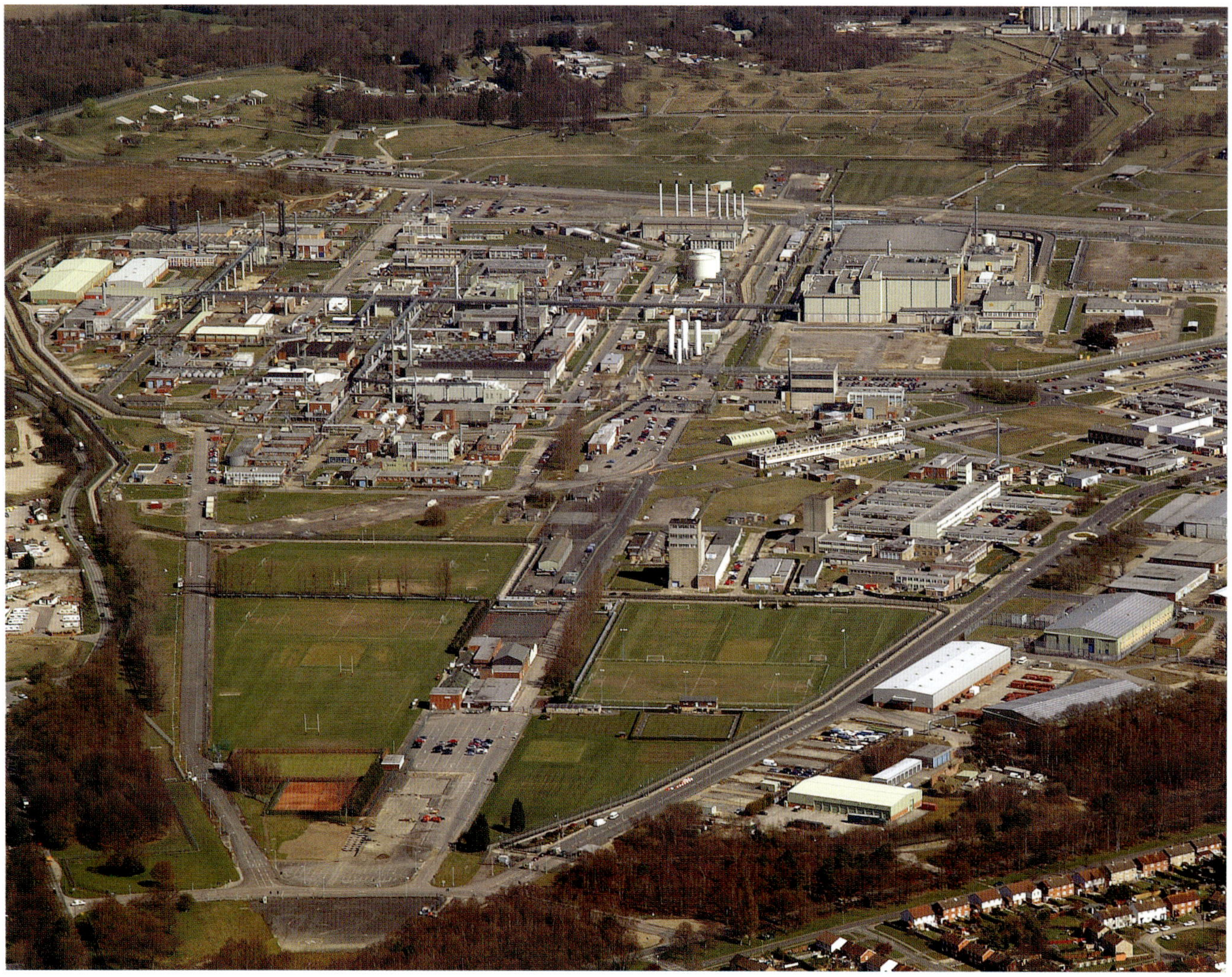

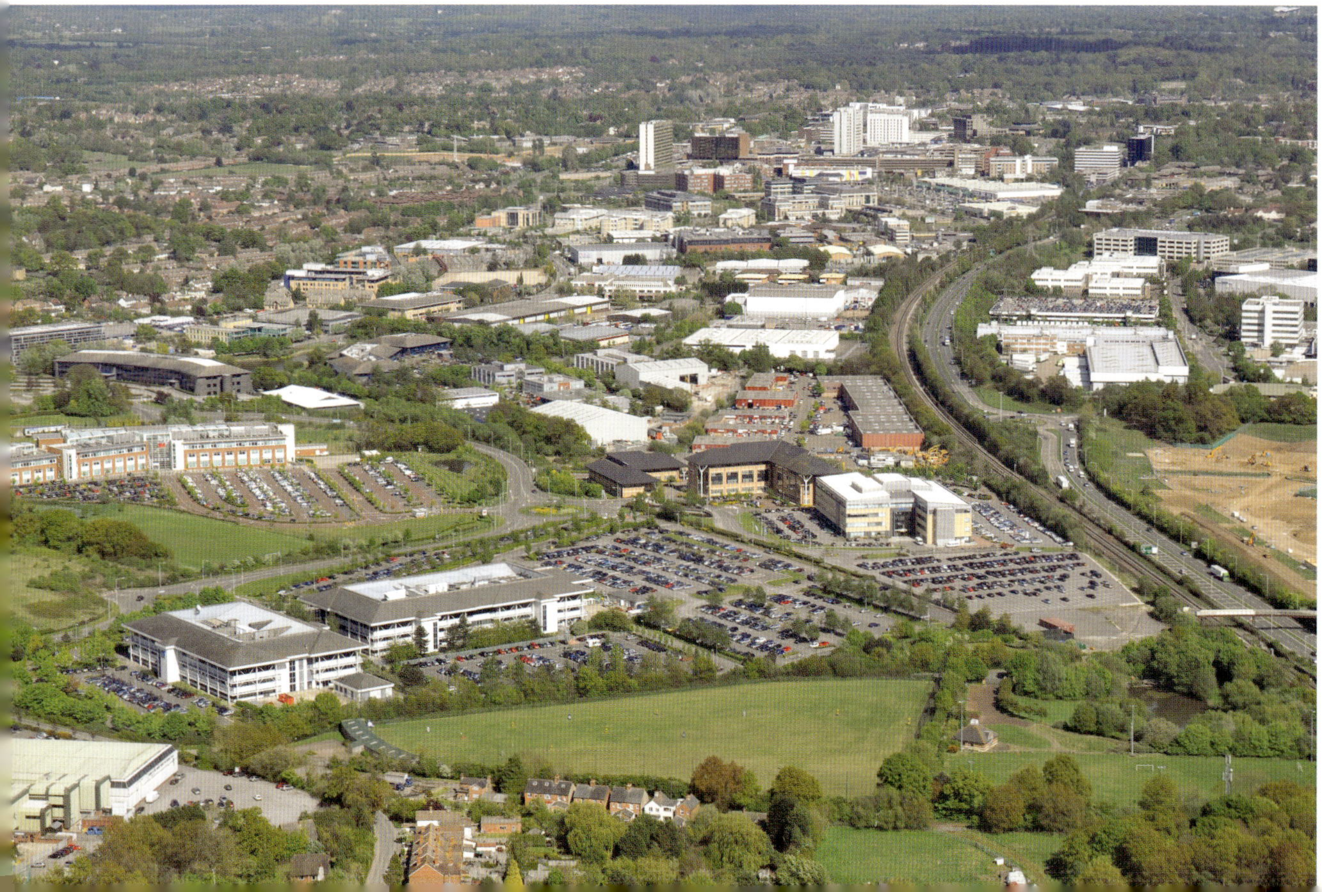

Bracknell

A designated New Town intended for 20,000 people, Bracknell's population now exceeds 50,000. Home to high-tech industries and IT firms situated close to the M4 corridor, Bracknell (left and right) was a centre for brickmaking in the late 19th and early 20th century. The Thomas Lawrence brickworks were famous for the "red rubber" bricks used in the Royal Albert Hall and Westminster Cathedral. The New Town was developed in three phases between 1945 and 1999, with a pedestrianised town centre surrounded by multi-storey car parks completed in the 1970s. Bracknell's modern high-rise buildings have been used by film producers to recreate New York City.

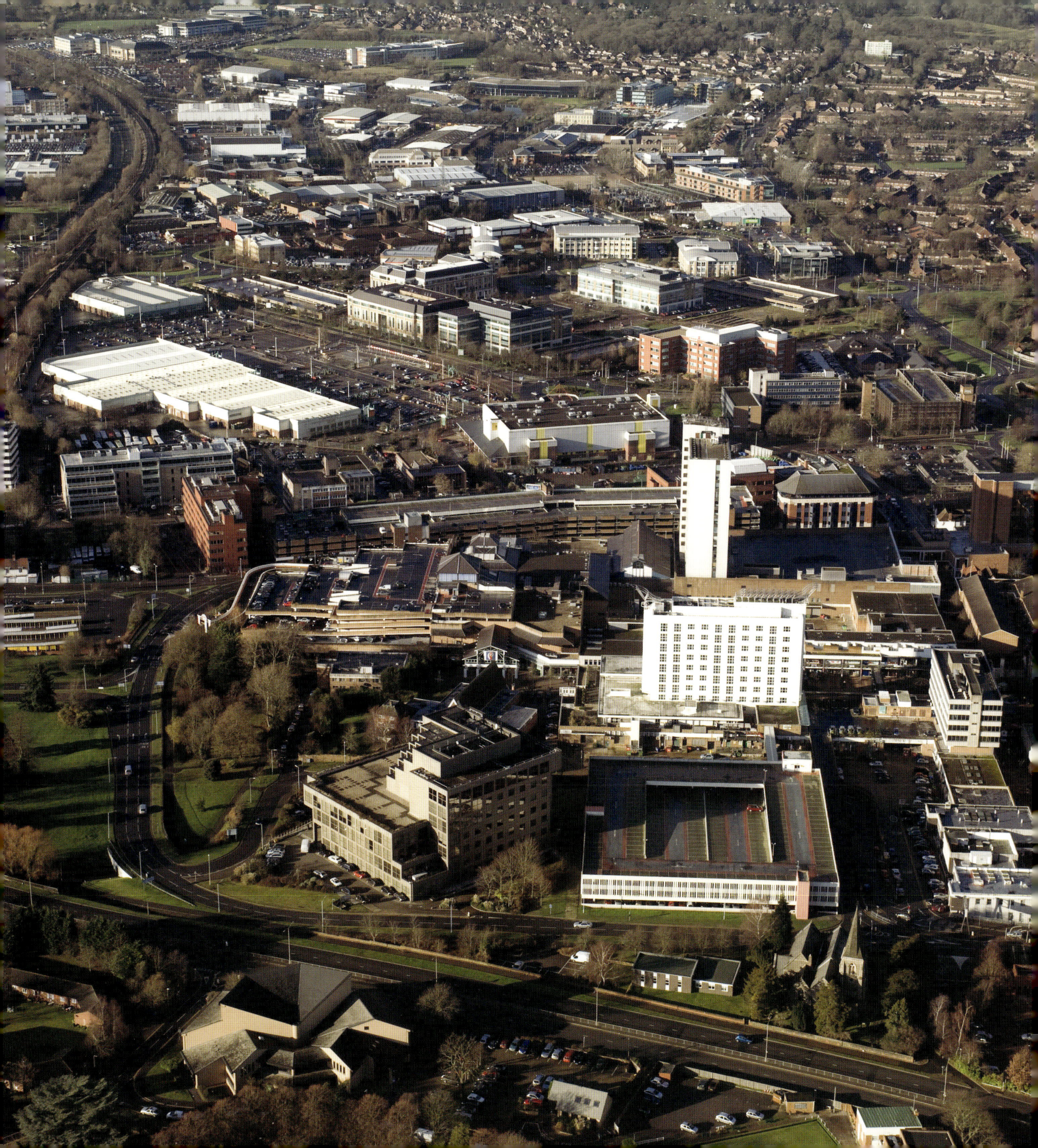

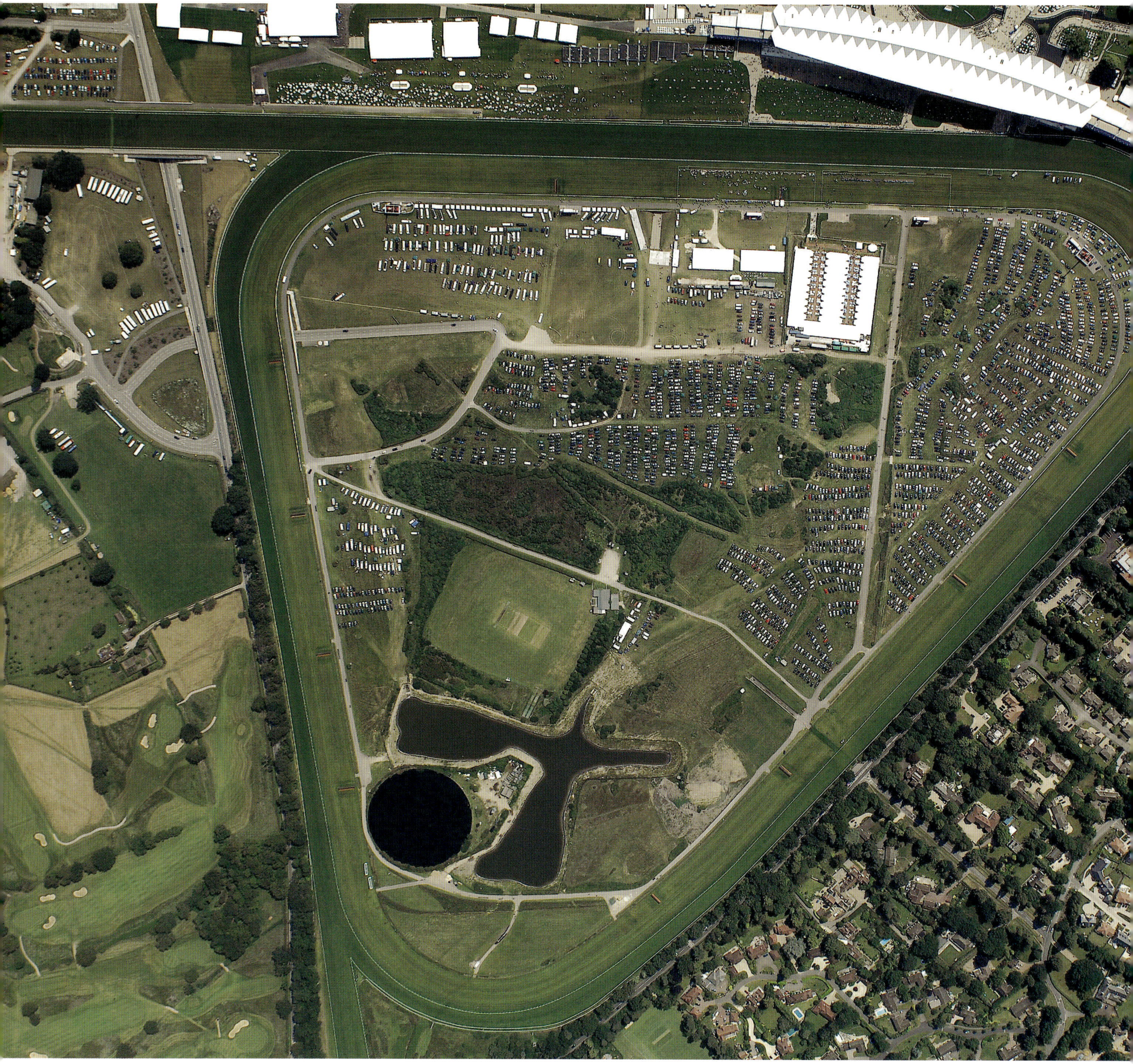

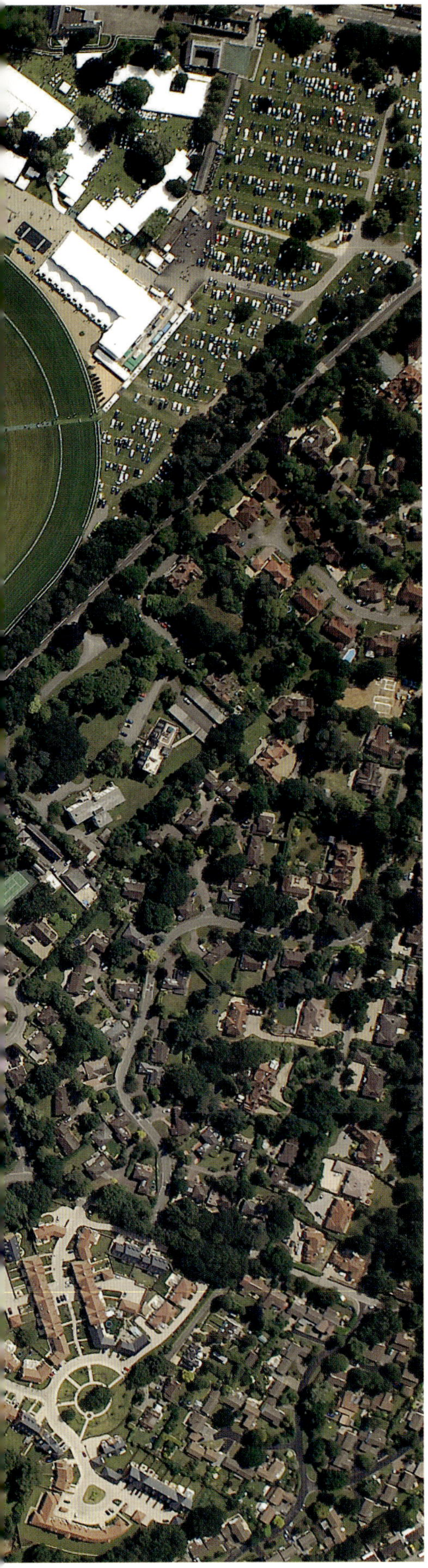

Ascot

Just six miles from Windsor Castle, Ascot racecourse (left and right) is owned by the Crown Estate and has close ties with the Royal Family. One of the country's leading racecourses, Ascot stages 25 days of racing each year including the Royal Meeting. Held in June, the third day of the Meeting is usually the day of the Gold Cup, Britain's most prestigious long-distance race. Horses complete a race of 2 miles and 4 furlongs (4,023m) and the winner's trophy is presented by the Queen. Referred to as Ladies' Day, the day of the Gold Cup is an important event in the social calendar and attracts widespread media attention for the spectacular hats and fashionable clothes worn by the women attending.

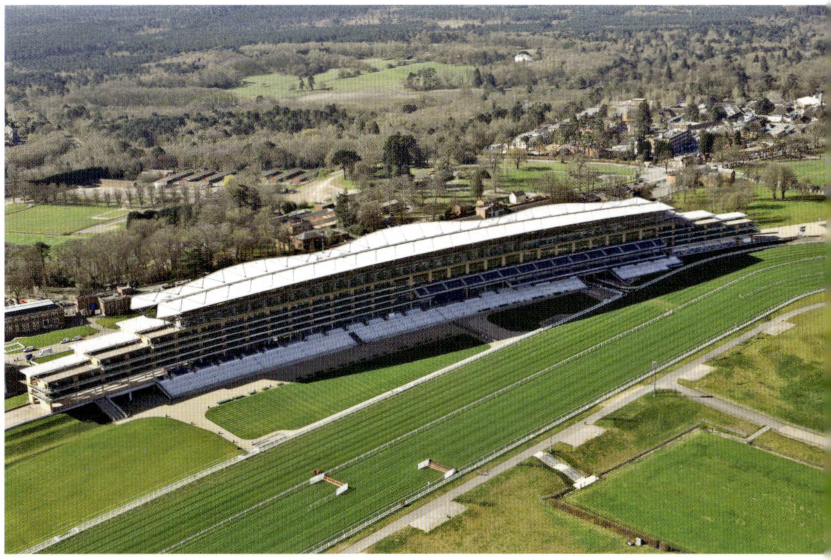

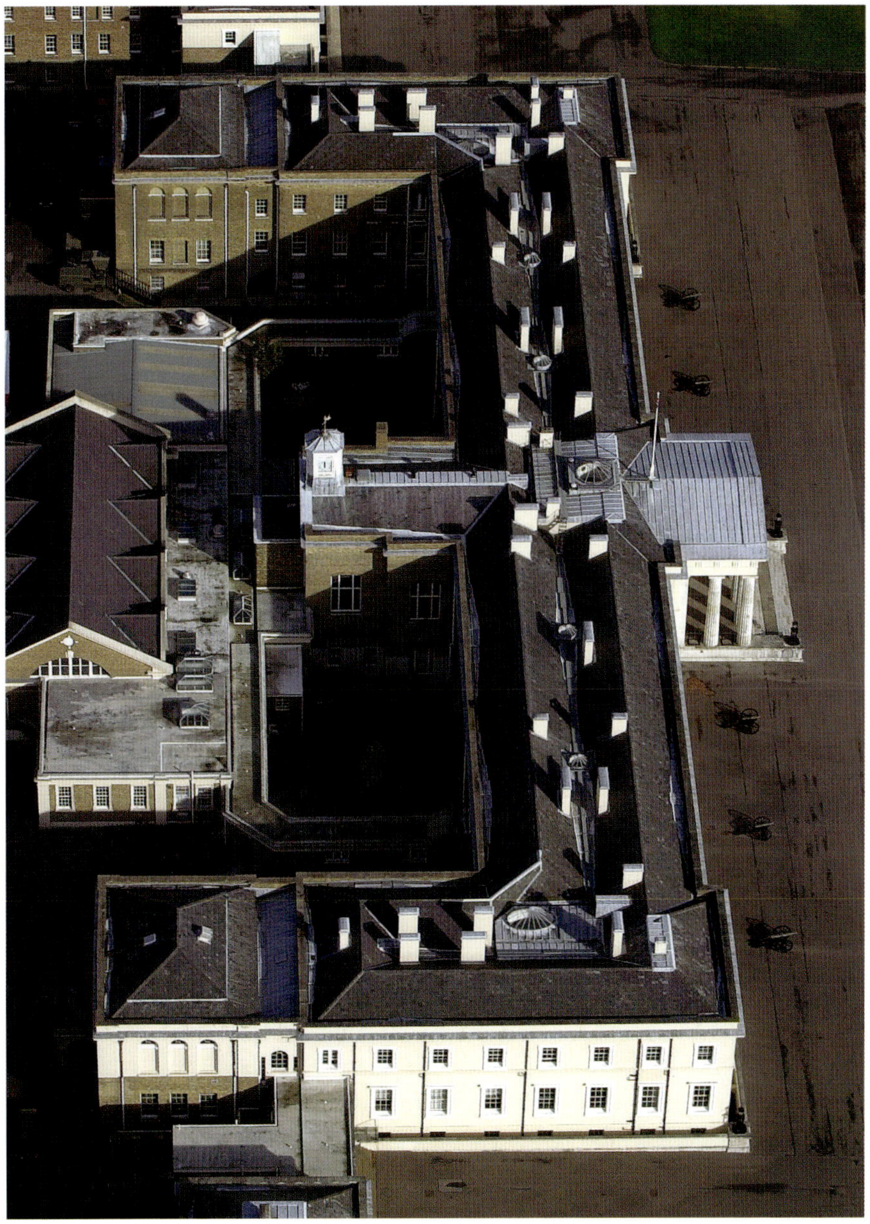

Sandhurst

The Royal Military Academy at Sandhurst (left) is the initial training centre for British army officers. Formed in 1947 from a merger of the Royal Military Academy at Woolwich and the Royal Military College of Sandhurst, the Old College building dates from the early 19th century. Army officers who have successfully completed the arduous 44 week Commissioning Course march up the steps of the Old College to be commissioned as officers. It is also a renowned academic facility. Famous graduates include Prince William, Prince Harry, Sir Winston Churchill and James Blunt, the musician.

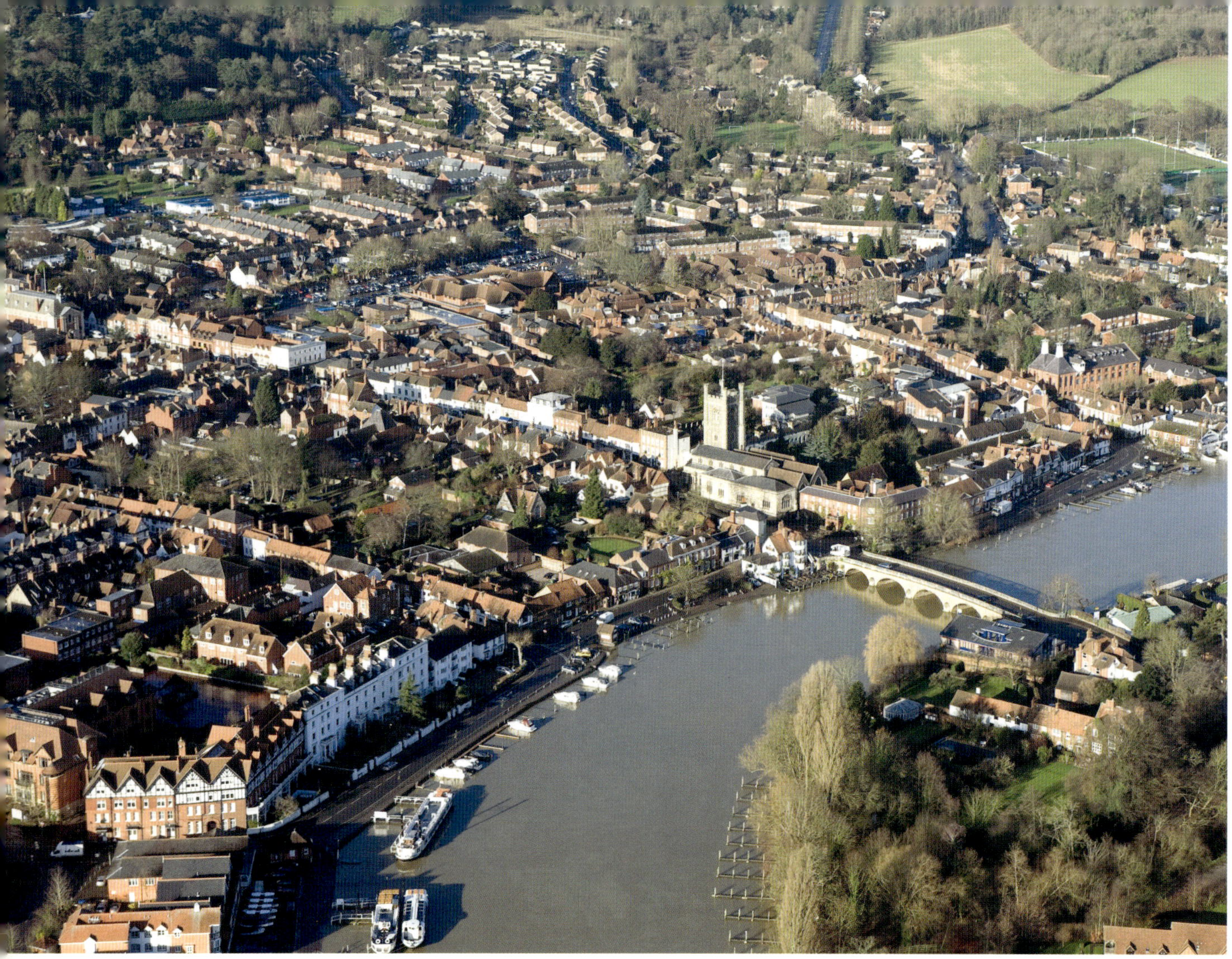

CLIVEDEN

Designed in 1851 by the architect Sir Charles Barry, Cliveden (below and right) is a classic Italianate house owned by the National Trust and set in 376 acres of formal gardens and parkland. America's richest man, William Waldorf Astor, bought Cliveden in 1893 and gave it to his son, Waldorf, as a country retreat. Waldorf's wife, Nancy Astor, was a prominent society hostess and went on to become Britain's first woman MP. Cliveden became the centre of high society in the early 20th century with house guests including Charlie Chaplin, George Bernard Shaw, Winston Churchill and Theodore Roosevelt. In the 1960s Cliveden was at the centre of the political whirlwind known as the "Profumo Affair" which led to the resignation of the then Secretary of State for War. Today the house is run as a luxury hotel.

HENLEY-ON-THAMES

This picturesque town is situated on the edge of the Chiltern Hills beside the Thames. Founded as a river port in the 12th century, Henley (above) has become famous for its rowing heritage and the annual Royal Regatta. A River and Rowing Museum in the town opened in 1998; it commemorates the international sport and includes statues of Olympic rowers Sir Steve Redgrave and Sir Matthew Pinsent. Boat trips down the Thames are a popular excursion for visitors, and historic buildings include the 16th century church of St Mary, a 15th century Chantry House and the 18th century Henley Bridge.

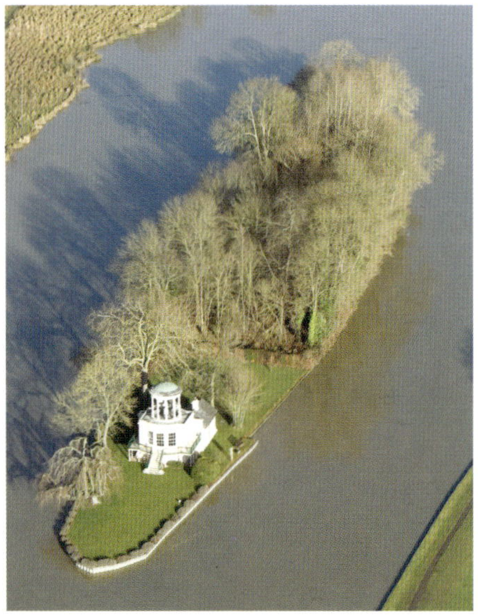

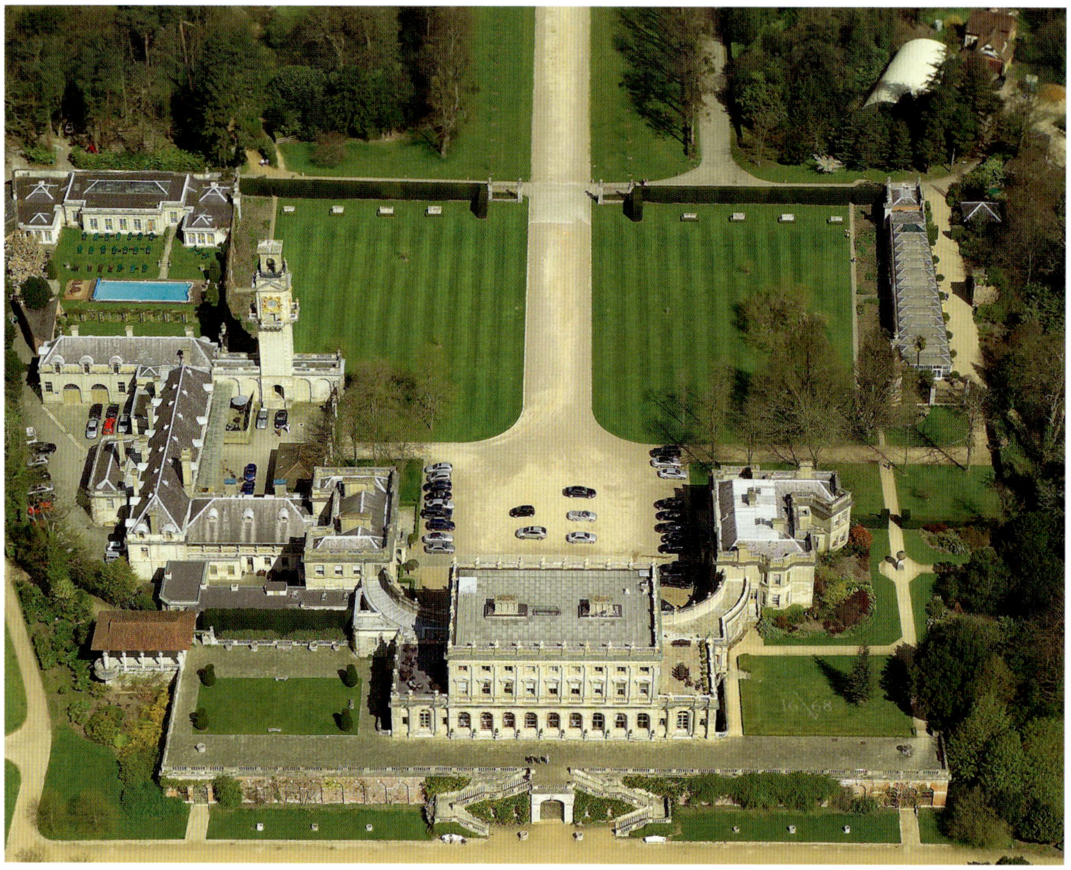

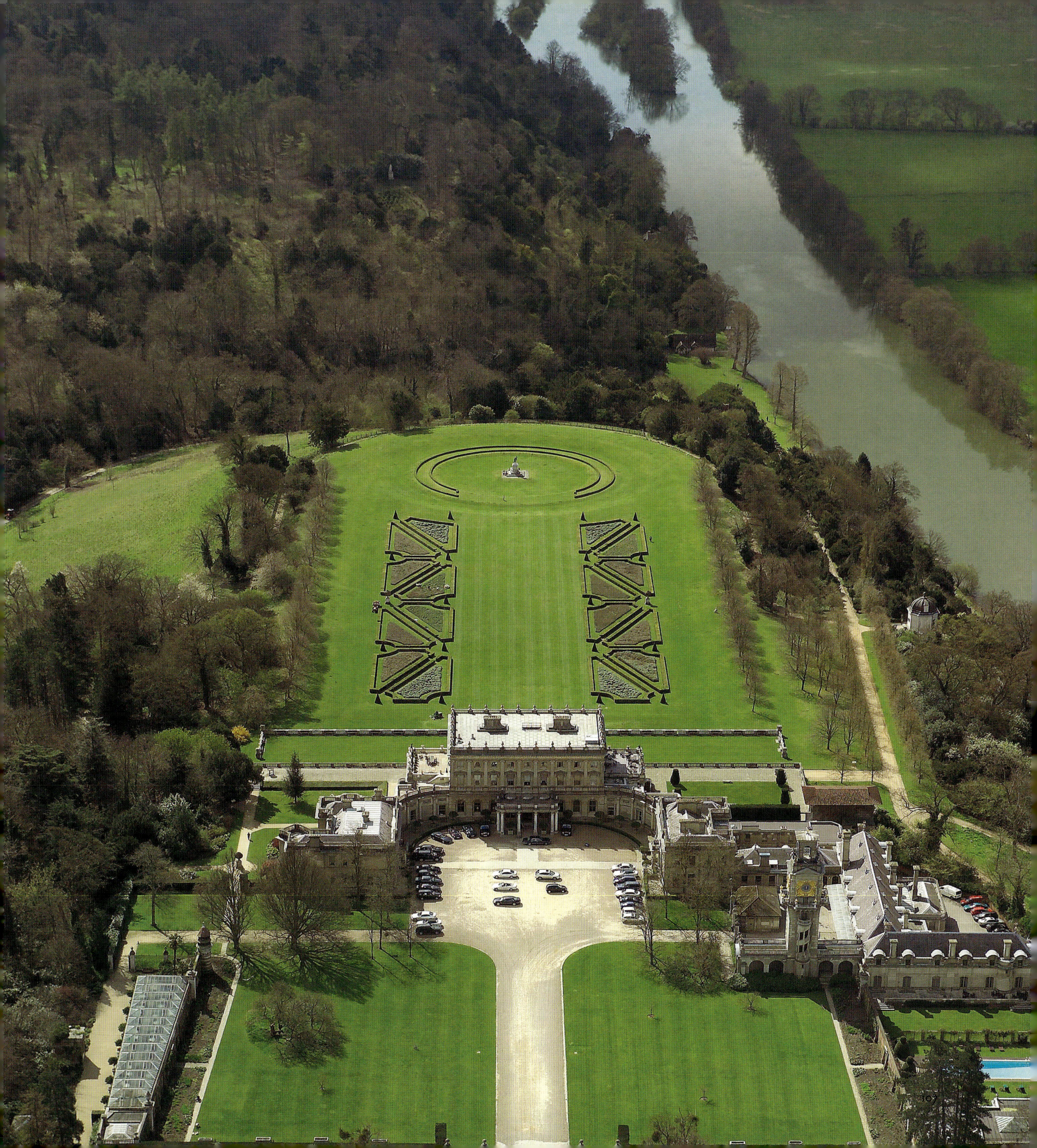

The Northern Home Counties

The northern Home Counties are defined by the chalky Chiltern Hills that stretch from Oxfordshire and Buckinghamshire, where they overlook the Vale of Aylesbury, to the low hills of Hertfordshire. One of the oldest roads in Britain, the Icknield Way, follows the line of the hills at their base, and a major Roman town, *Verulamium*, was built near modern-day St Albans. This area today forms part of London's commuter belt, with Buckinghamshire's leafy towns and villages particularly attractive to wealthy residents. Much of this area was once owned by the nobility and aristocracy and a rich legacy of historic homes and manors can be seen. The industrial era brought the Grand Union Canal to the region, connecting London and the Midlands, while the 20th century saw the development of planned towns such as Letchworth Garden City and Stevenage New Town.

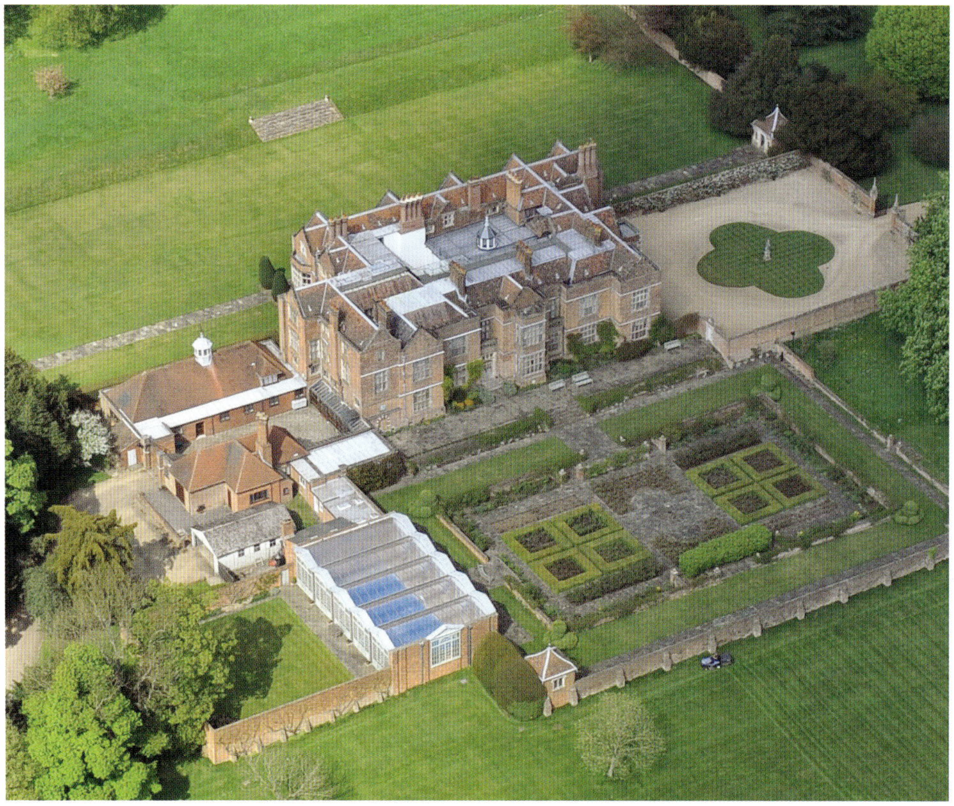

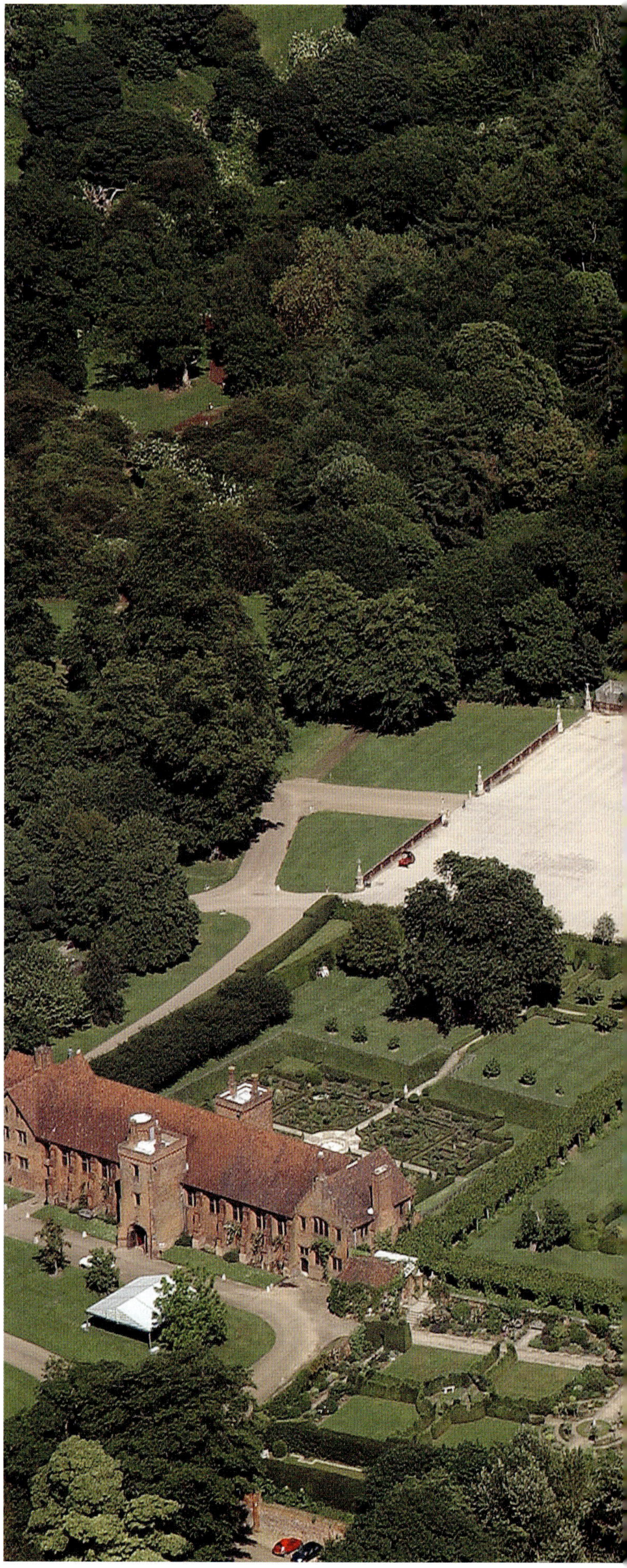

Historic homes

Some of the region's historic homes include the prime minister's Tudor retreat at Chequers (above), and Hatfield House (right), the home of Queen Mary I and Queen Elizabeth I for much of their childhood.

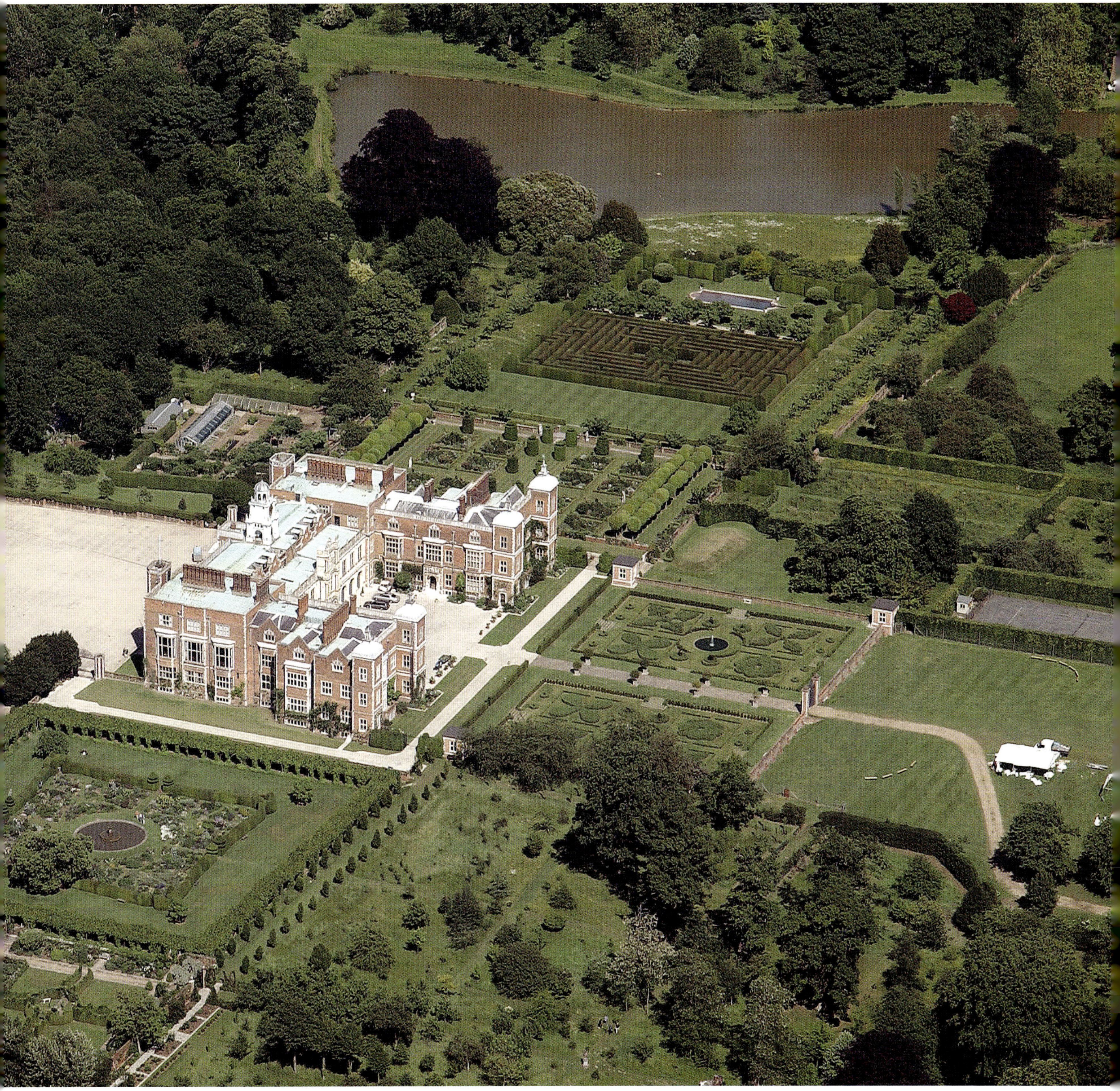

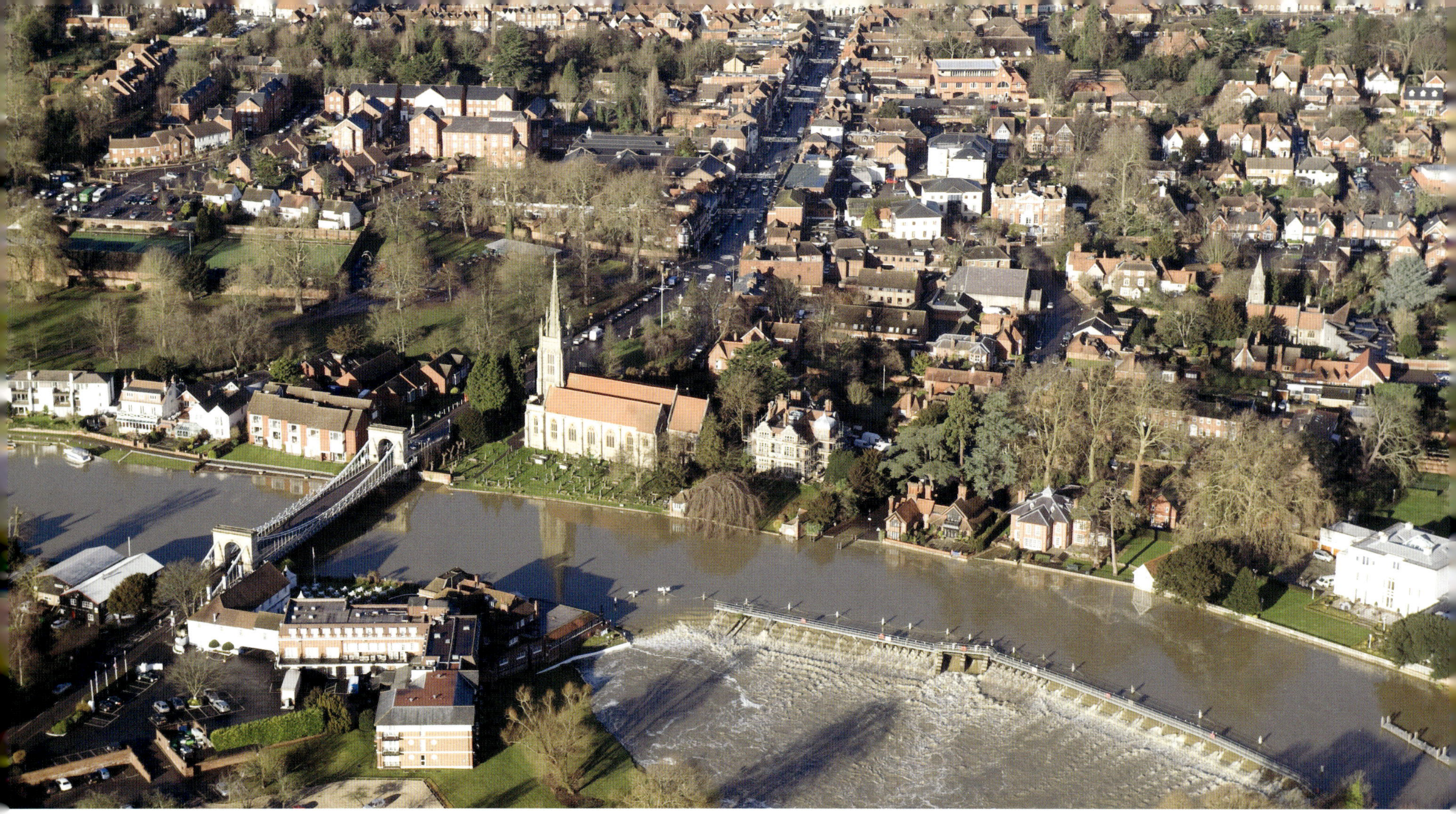

Marlow

This historic riverside town (above) has been the home of a number of famous authors including Mary Shelley, who finished writing *Frankenstein* here, her husband Percy Bysshe Shelley, Jerome K Jerome and TS Eliot. Today's most famous resident is Sir Steve Redgrave, Britain's most successful Olympian and rower; appropriately, the town hosts two regattas. The river Thames is crossed by the Marlow suspension bridge, designed by William Tierney Clark in 1832, and by the weir at Marlow, which is recorded in the Domesday book and today forms part of Marlow Lock.

Chequers

The country residence of the British prime minister has been Chequers Court (right) since 1921. Situated near Ellesborough, at the foot of the Chiltern Hills, Chequers, as it is more commonly known, is a Tudor mansion created by William Hawtrey. The country retreat was a family home until the First World War, when it became a hospital and then a convalescent home for officers. Chequers was gifted to the nation in 1917 by Lord and Lady Lee of Fareham so that British prime ministers could entertain foreign dignitaries and relax from the affairs of state.

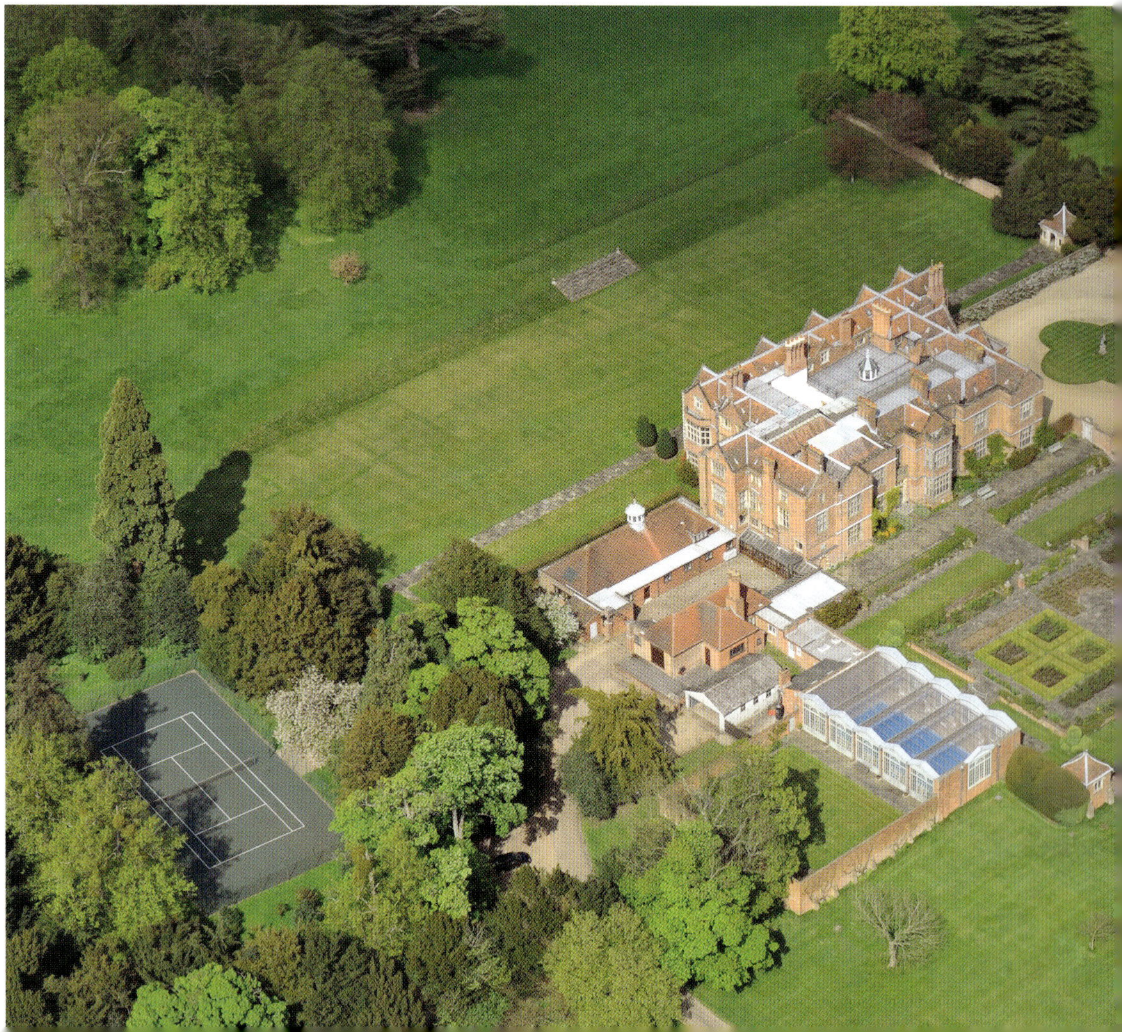

HIGH WYCOMBE

In the middle ages High Wycombe (right) was a mill town producing lace and linen, and then became a centre of the paper industry in the 17th and 18th centuries. However, with its ready access to the beech forests of the Chilterns, the town is best known for its 19th century furniture factories. In 1875, it was estimated that 4,700 chairs were made there every day, but furniture manufacture declined in the 1960s. The town centre was redeveloped at this time with shopping centres, car parks, flyovers and roundabouts and has since undergone regeneration. High Wycombe boasts two famous political residents – the Earl of Shelburne was MP for the town and prime minister Benjamin Disrael (1804-1881) lived at the beautiful Hughenden Manor, two miles from the town centre.

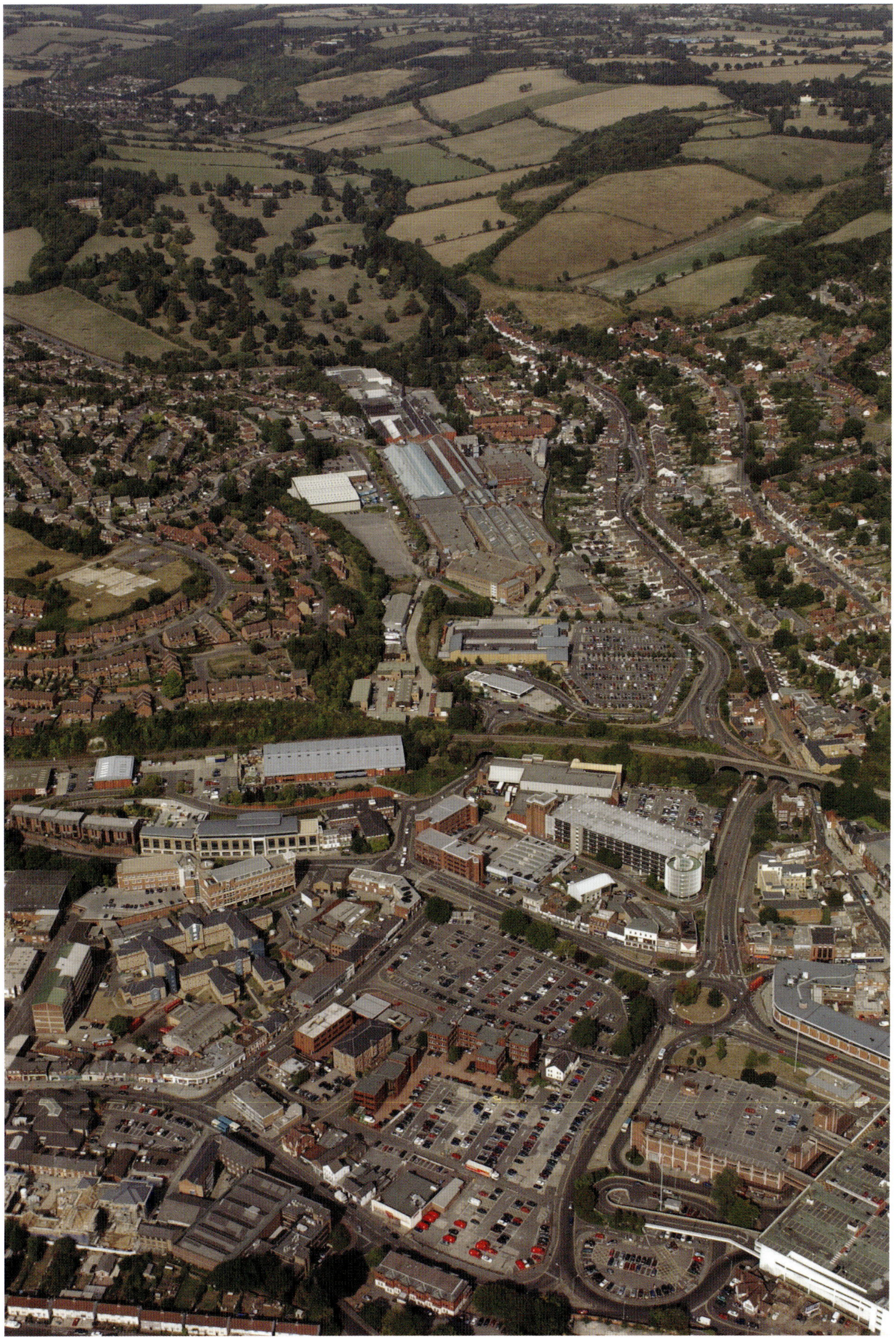

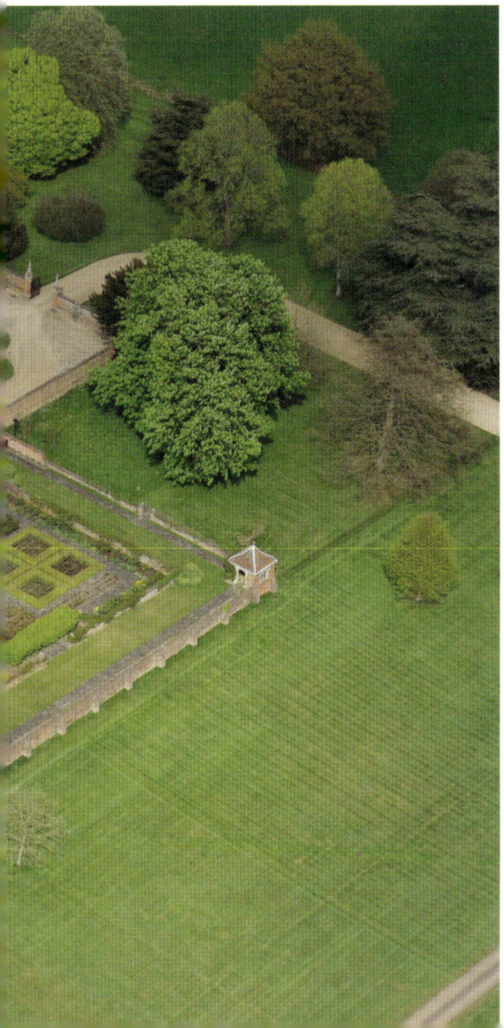

ST ALBANS

This sought-after commuter town (below) was once the site of the second largest Roman town in Britain after *Londinium*. Named *Verulamium*, it was the first major town on Watling Street. Although much of the settlement is unexcavated agricultural land, city walls, a theatre, mosaics and underfloor heating systems are some of the visible remains. St Albans was established in medieval times and named after the first British Christian martyr, Saint Alban, who was thought to have been beheaded locally some time before AD 324. St Albans Abbey marked the spot and its Norman abbey church became St Albans Cathedral in 1877. The town had a rural feel until the 20th century, when it expanded rapidly for Londoners displaced by the war bombings.

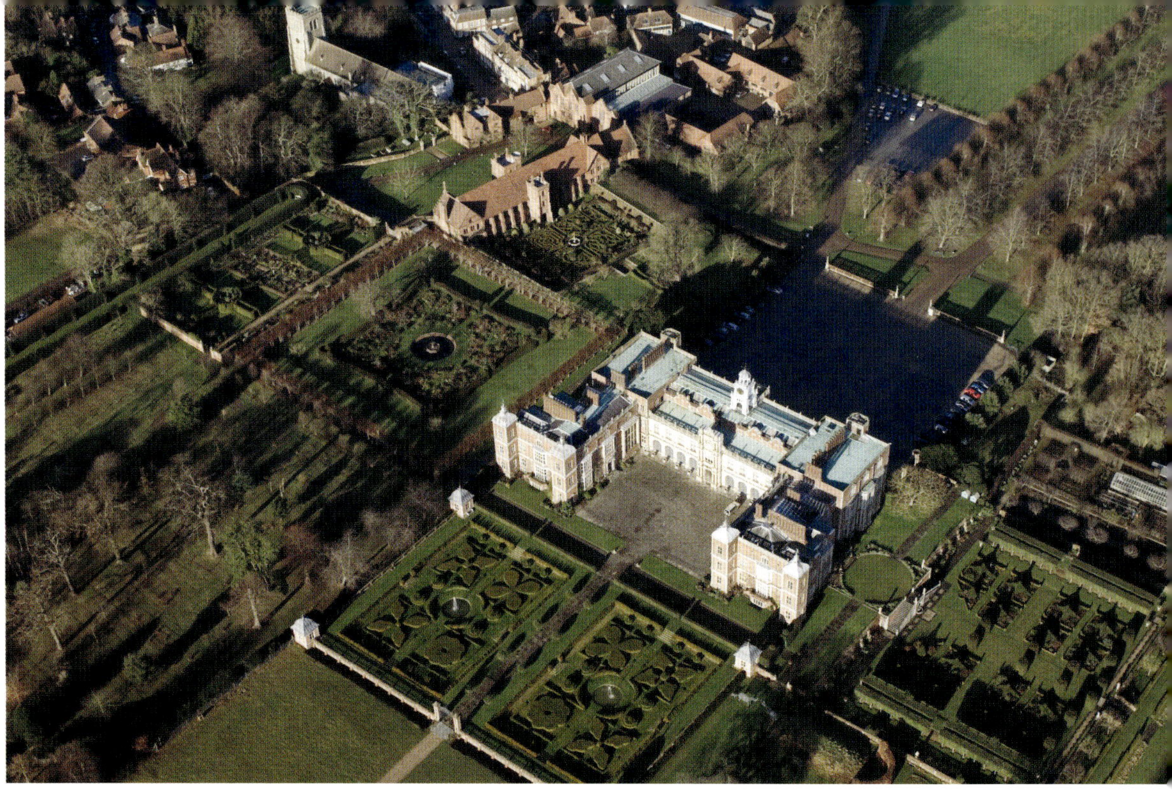

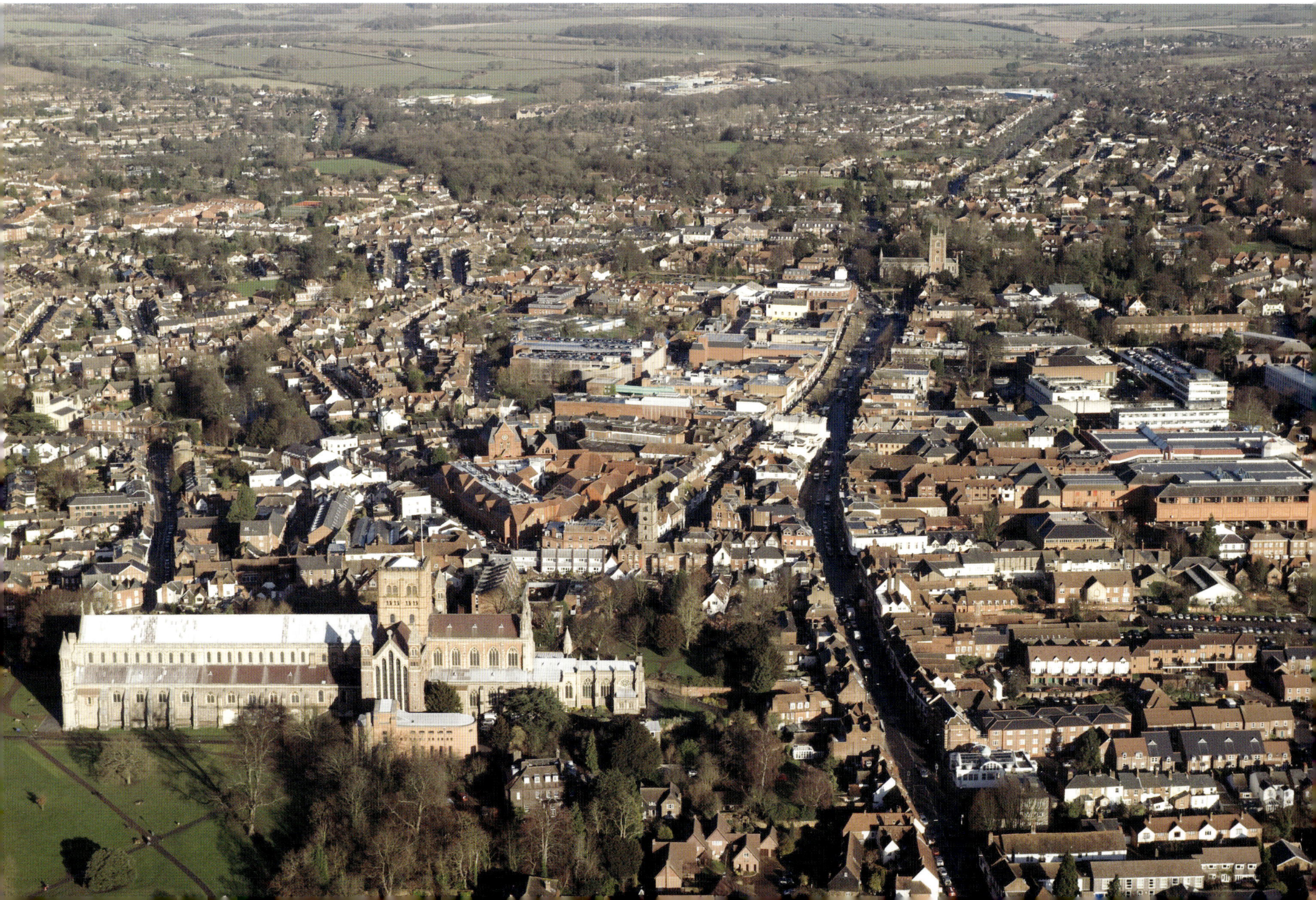

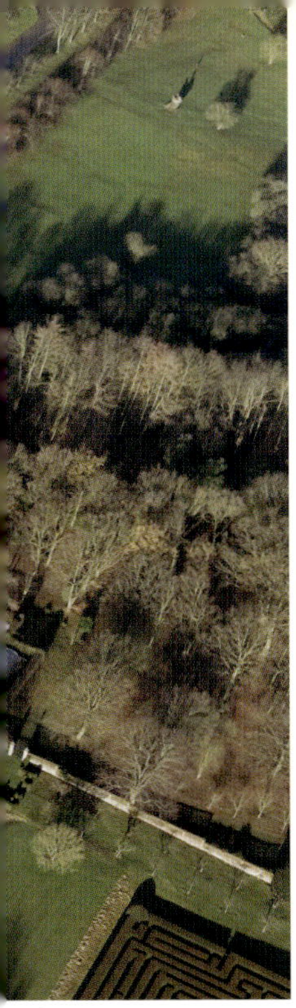

HATFIELD HOUSE

Built by Robert Cecil in 1611, Hatfield House (left) is a fine Jacobean house set in spectacular countryside known as the Great Park. Open to the public in the summer months, the house has many objects related to Queen Elizabeth I who spent her childhood, with her older sister Queen Mary I, in the Hatfield Royal Palace, part of which still stands. The gardens date from the early 17th century when Robert Cecil employed John Tradescant the Elder to collect plants from Europe for his home. The extensive parkland includes an oak tree marking the place where Princess Elizabeth heard of her accession to the throne.

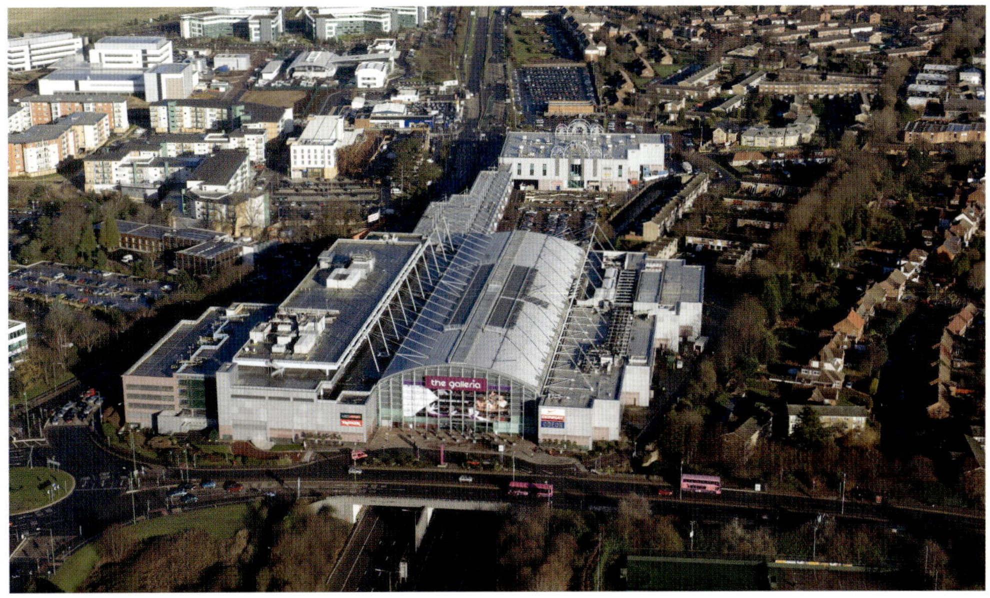

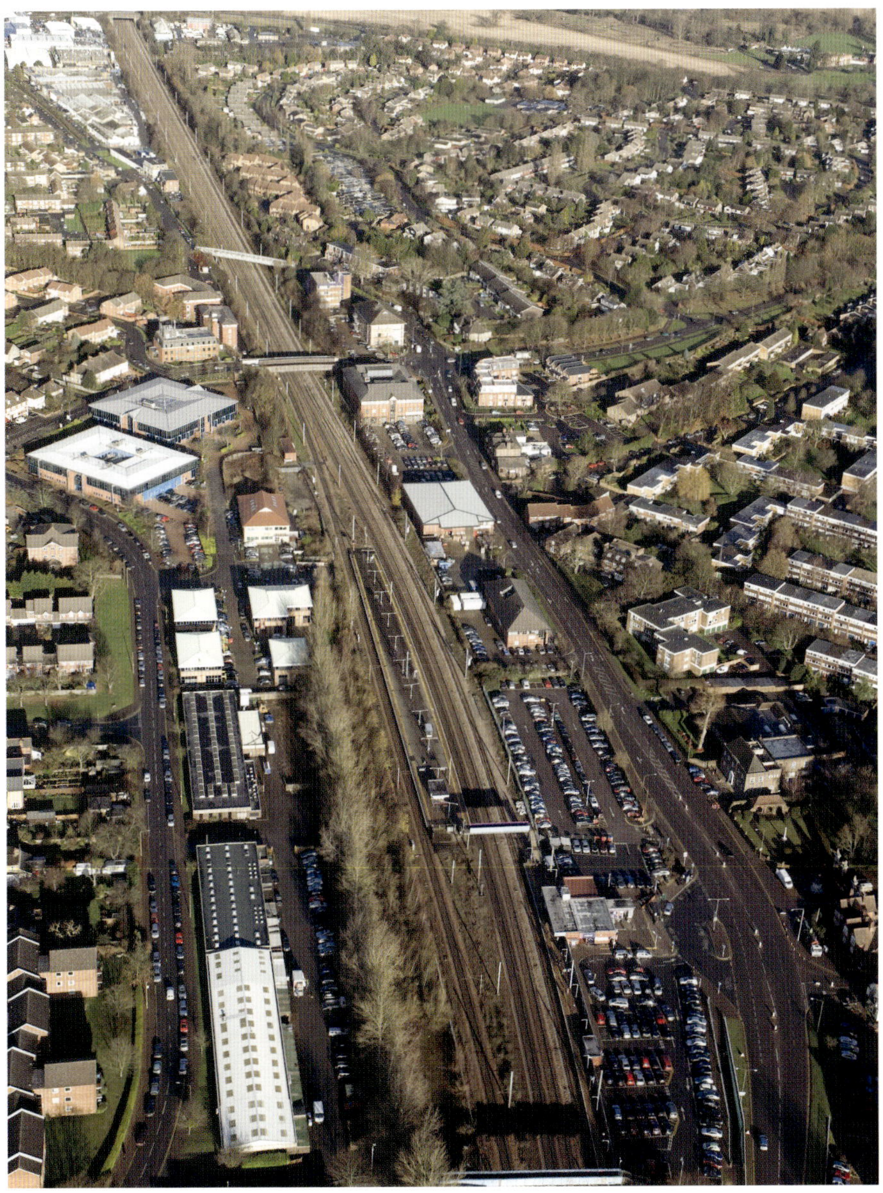

HATFIELD

The original village of Hatfield developed around the gates of Hatfield House, but the construction of the Great North Road in Victorian times led to a new settlement to the north-west. Hatfield grew again with the arrival of the de Havilland aircraft factory and airfield prior to the Second World War. The de Havilland Company, later known as British Aerospace, was Hatfield's biggest employer until 1992. The company name lives on in the £120m de Havilland campus of the University of Hertfordshire (formerly Hatfield Polytechnic). Designated a new town in 1946, Hatfield's population is still rising with the expansion of Hatfield Business Park alongside redevelopment of the airfield. Hatfield Galleria is a popular shopping centre in the town situated above the A1(M) motorway, which passes underneath in the Hatfield Tunnel.

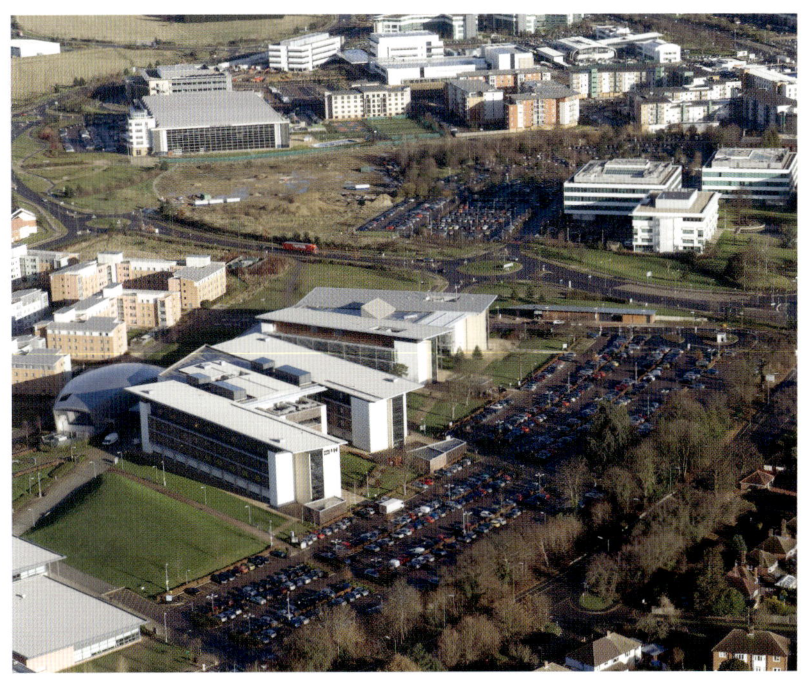

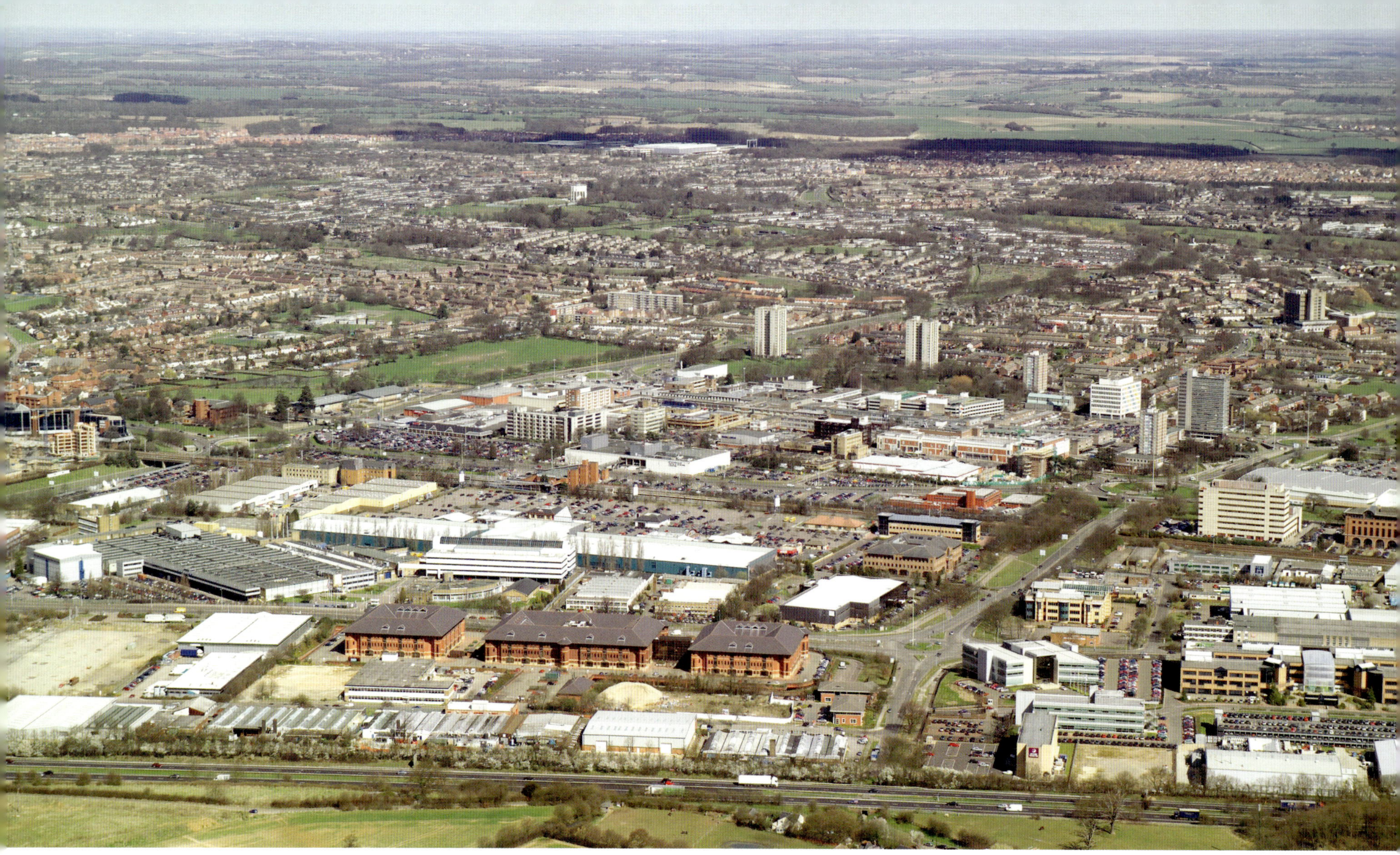

Stevenage

The village of Stevenage grew slowly until, in the aftermath of the Second World War, it was designated as the first ever New Town despite local opposition. Planned with six self-contained neighbourhoods, Stevenage (above and below) boasts the first purpose-built traffic-free town centre in Britain, officially opened by the Queen in 1959. Much of Stevenage's architecture dates from the 1960s and 1970s and the Industrial Area is separate from the residential neighbourhoods. For many years British Aerospace was the biggest employer, but today GlaxoSmithKline has a large research laboratory complex in the town. Stevenage's position on a fast rail link to London, as well as proximity to scenic countryside and the A1(M) motorway have all contributed to its success as a new town.

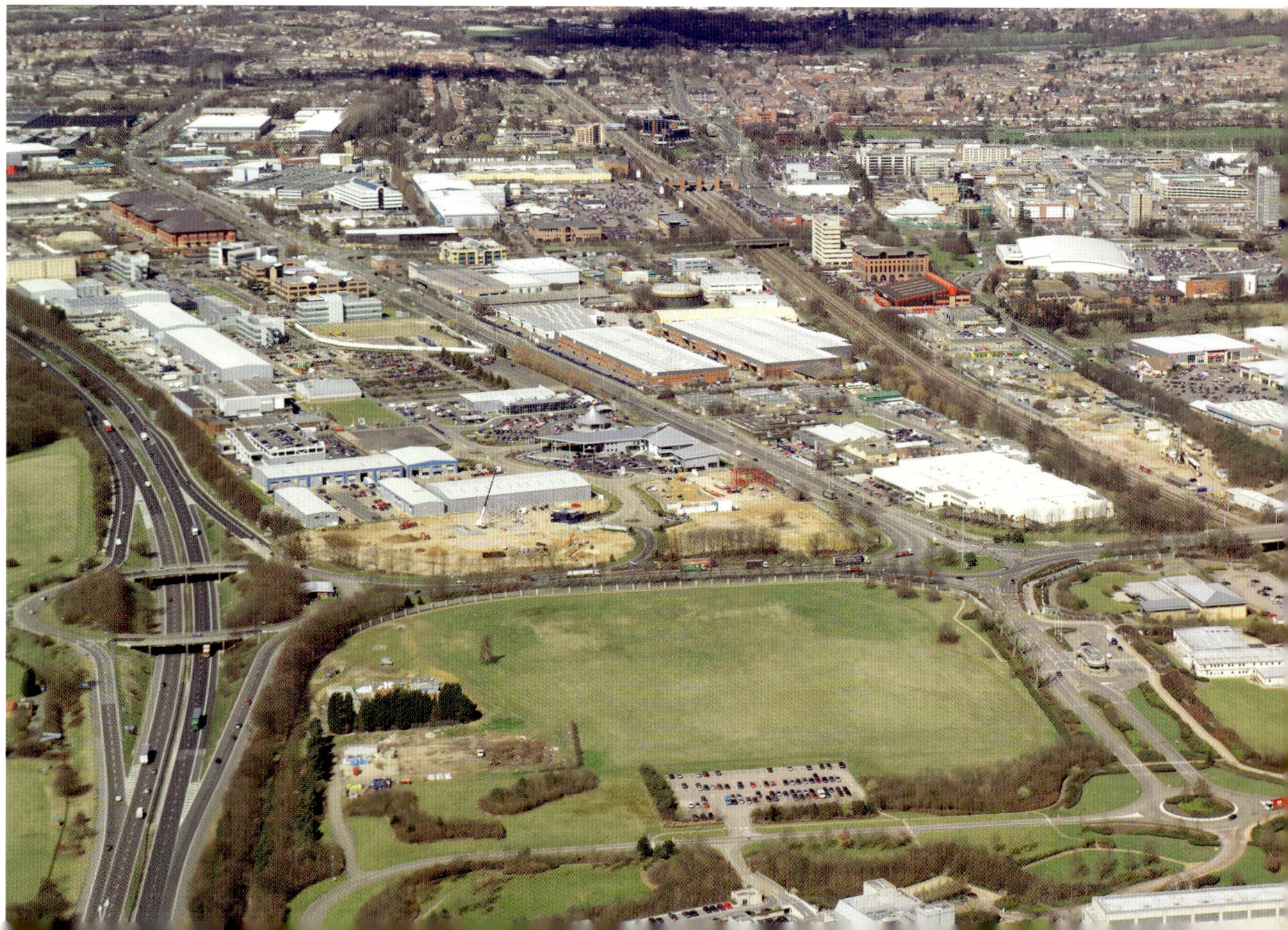

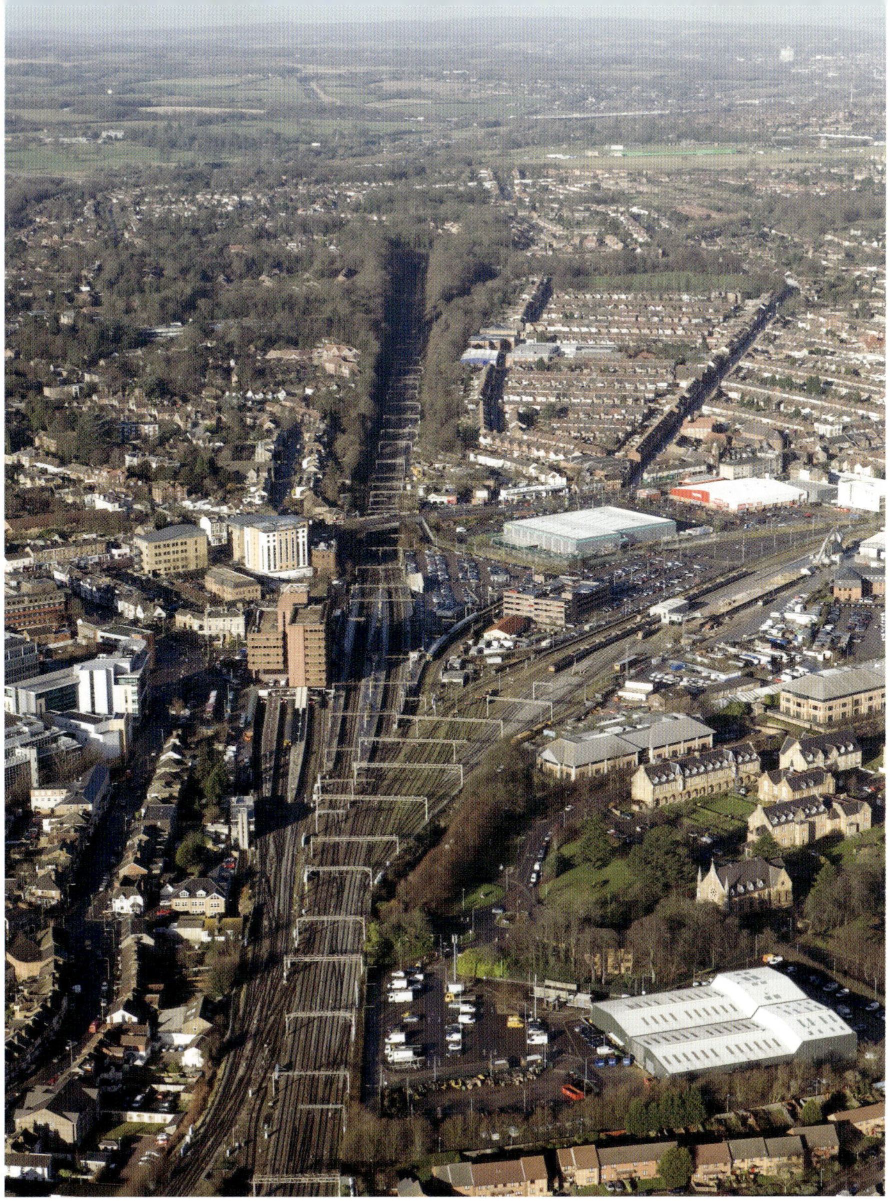

Watford

Located at a low point in the Chiltern Hills where the river Colne was forded, Watford lies on a natural route between London and the Midlands. Though the main road and Grand Union Canal passed through Watford, concerns over smoke pollution meant the railway station (left) was built east of the town at Watford Junction. A major business and commercial centre, Watford is home to company headquarters and good retail facilities. Officially opened in 1992, the Harlequin Shopping Centre (bottom) is a large purpose-built indoor mall with over 140 shops, restaurants and cafes. Watford Football Club (below) play at Vicarage Road. Famous for reaching the FA Cup Final in 1984, Sir Elton John is a keen, long-term supporter of the club and a former chairman.

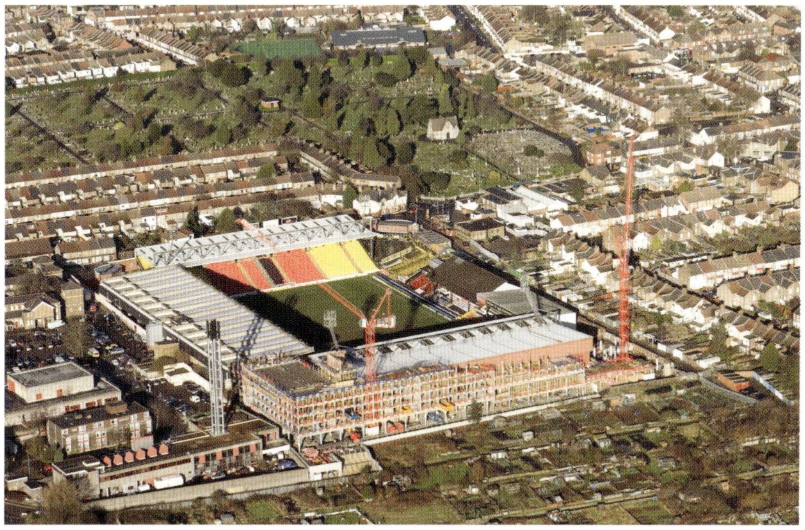

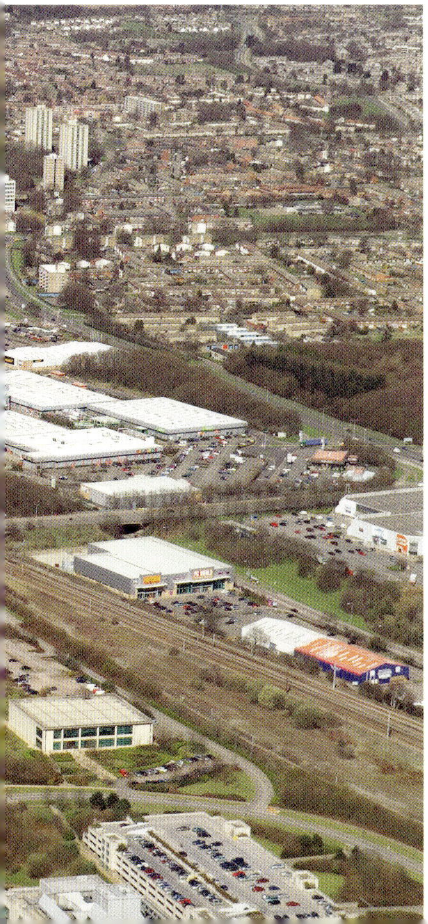

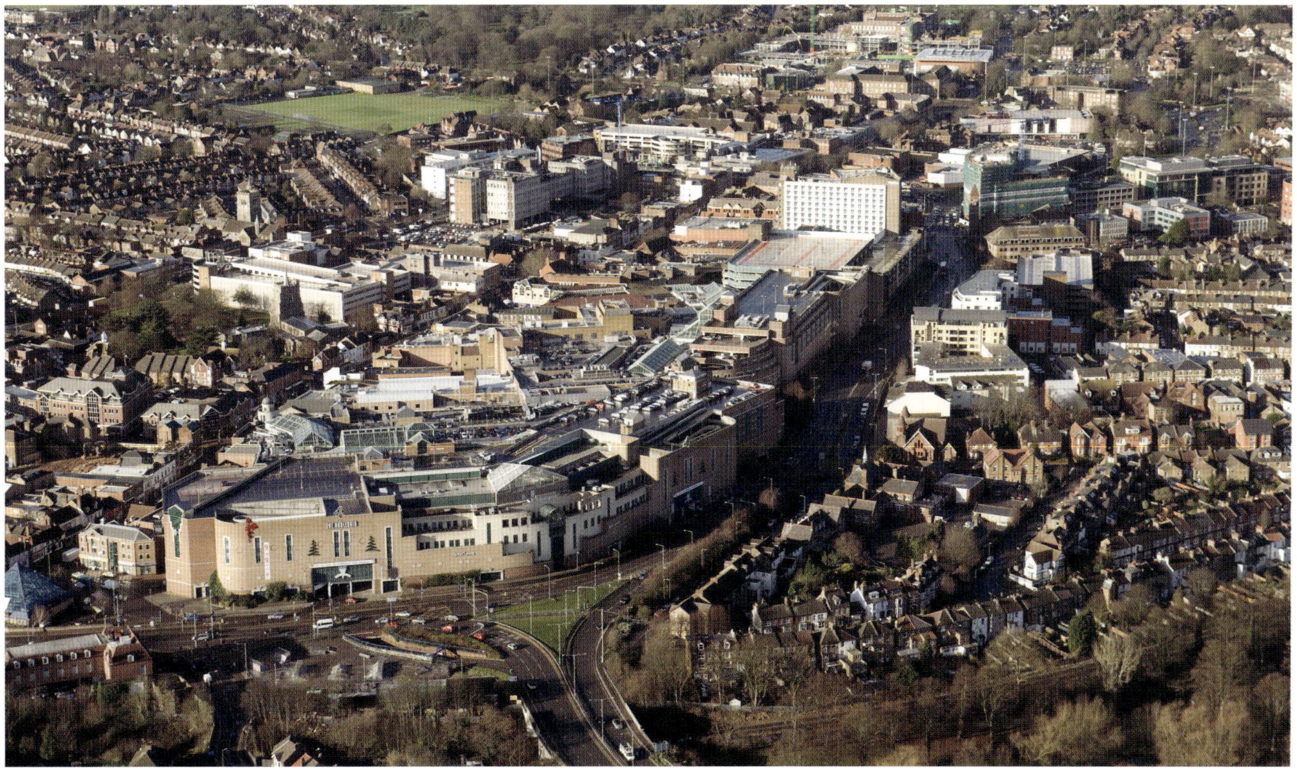

Essex

Bounded by the river Thames and its estuary to the south, Greater London and its green belt to the west, and the river Stour to the north, low-lying Essex combines rural villages surrounded by agricultural land with industrial hubs and coastal shipping centres. Established in ancient times as the Kingdom of Essex, the county was home to a number of Roman settlements, none more important than Colchester, the Roman capital of Britain until its sacking by Boudica in AD61. Today a garrison town, Colchester is the largest town in Essex, and is situated close to scenic river estuaries. Many of Essex's settlements close to London provide homes for commuters, who visit Thurrock's Lakeside Shopping Centre in their millions each year. Resorts such as Southend and Clacton-on-Sea have attracted London day-trippers since the advent of the railways, but much of Essex's attractive marshy coastline remains relatively undiscovered.

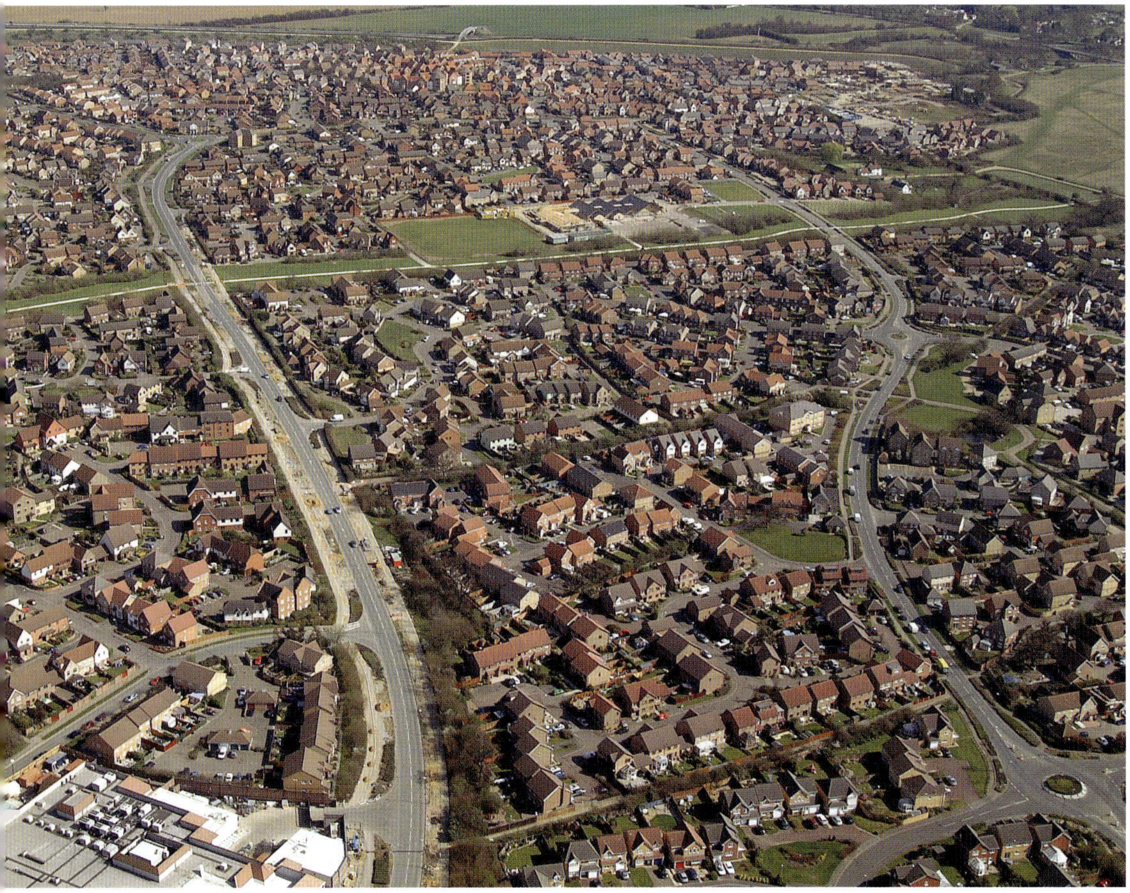

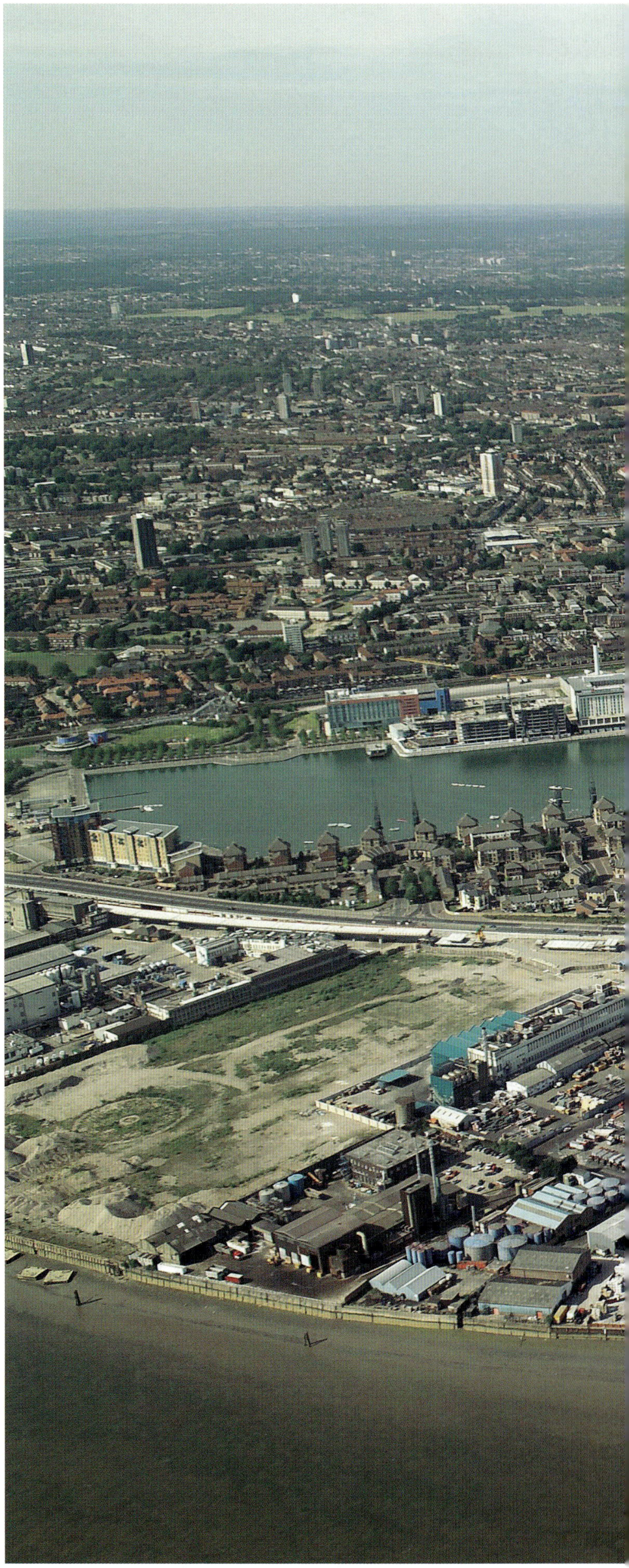

New towns

Essex is home to two New Towns, Basildon and Harlow (above), built to accommodate those moving from the war-damaged and increasingly crowded East End of London that has itself been reinvented as Docklands (right).

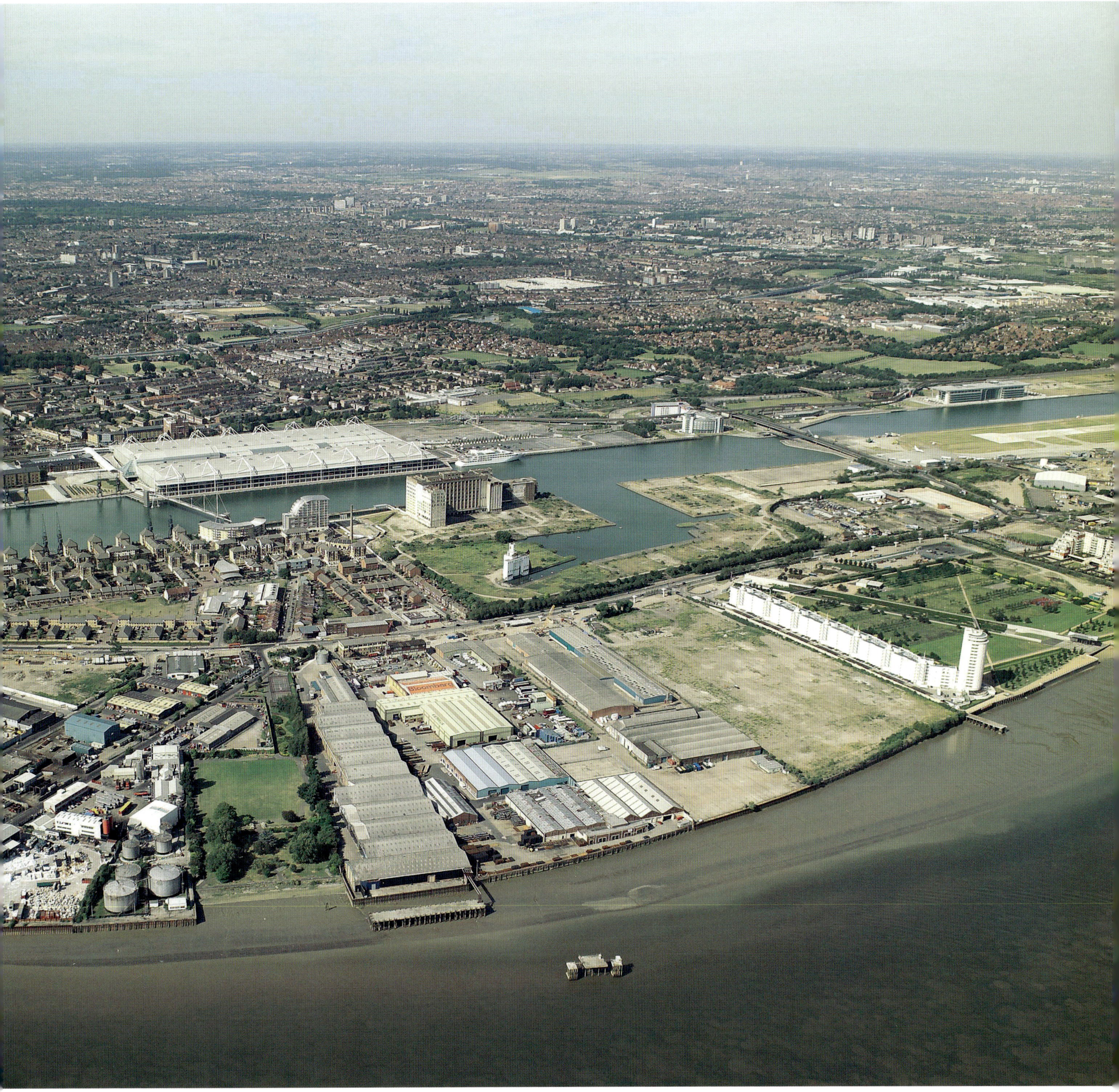

Chelmsford

Chelmsford (right and below) is the county town of Essex and a popular commuter town for London's City workers. Once the site of a Roman settlement, Chelmsford was granted a Royal Charter to hold a market in 1199 and developed as an agricultural and market town. Following work to create a canal from the rivers Chelmer and Blackwater in 1797, it developed as a base for industry and light engineering. The world's first "wireless" factory was established by Guglielmo Marconi in 1899, leading Chelmsford to be described as the birthplace of radio. Marconi's New Street factory of 1920 still stands today. Chelmsford cathedral is the second smallest in England. Dedicated to St Mary the Virgin, St Peter and St Cedd it contains 19th century stained glass and contemporary works of art.

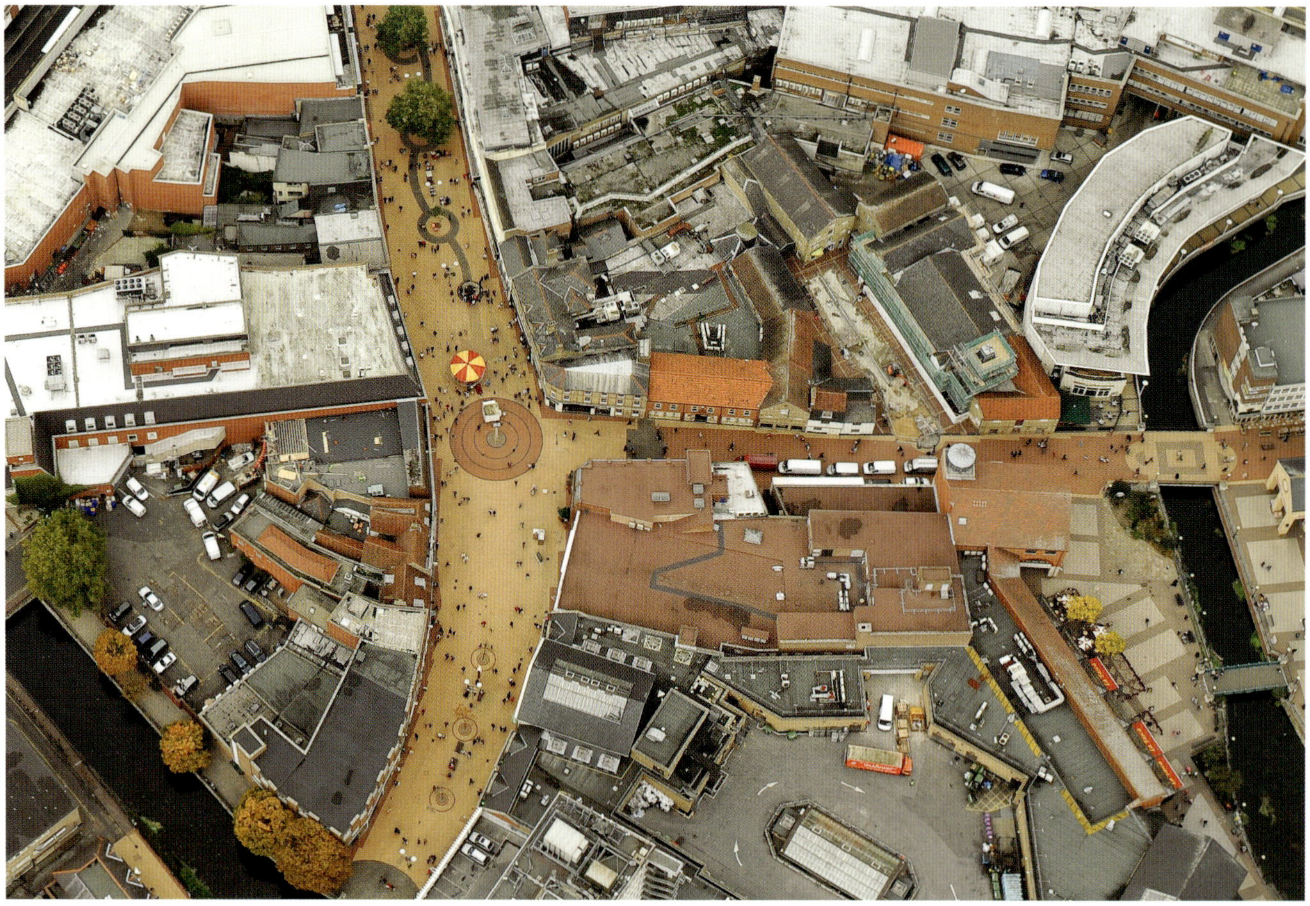

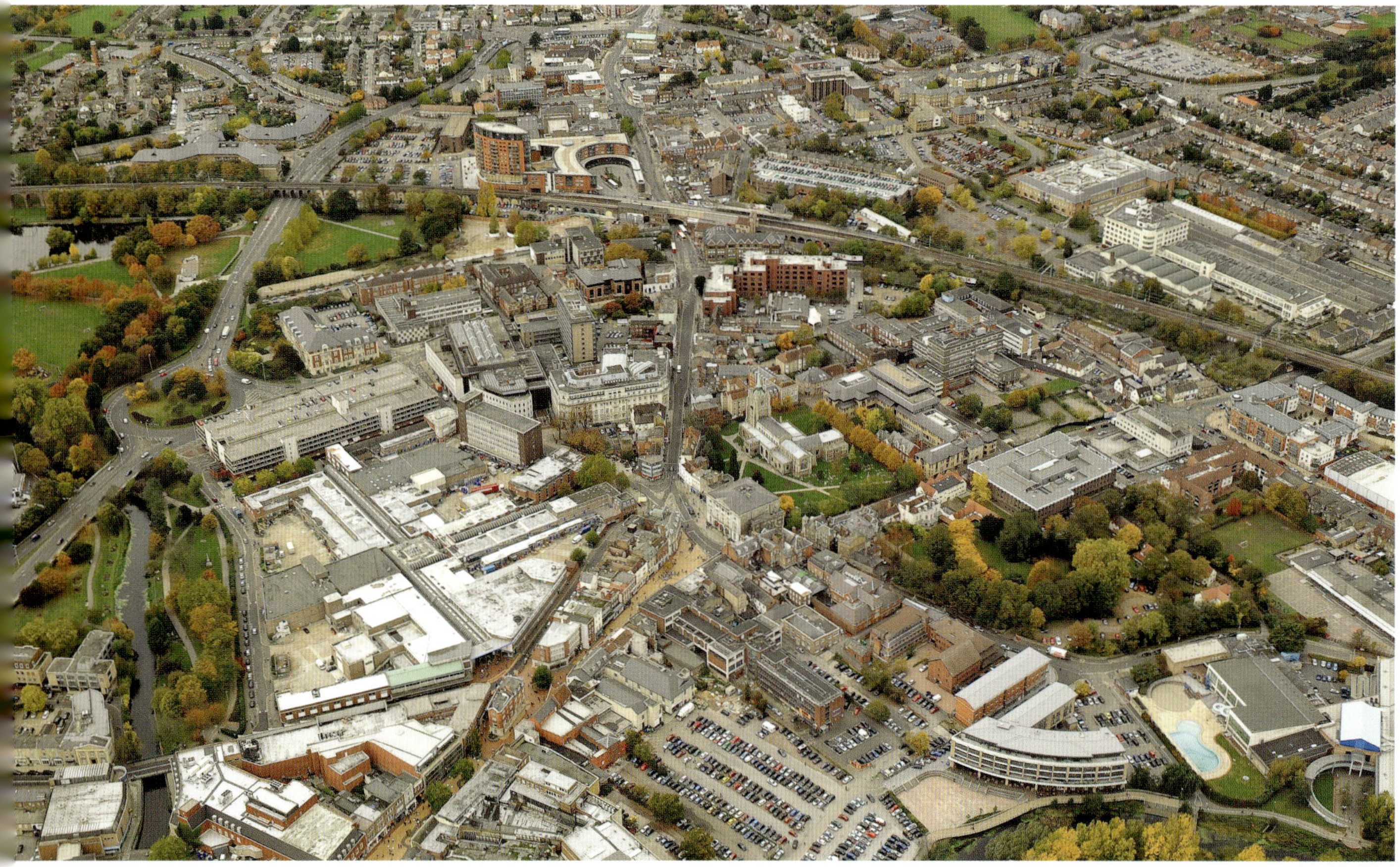

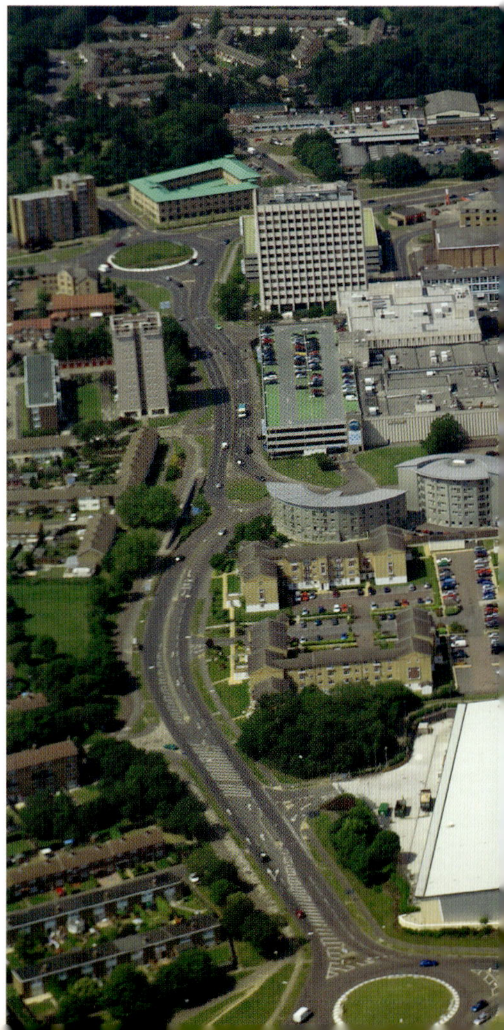

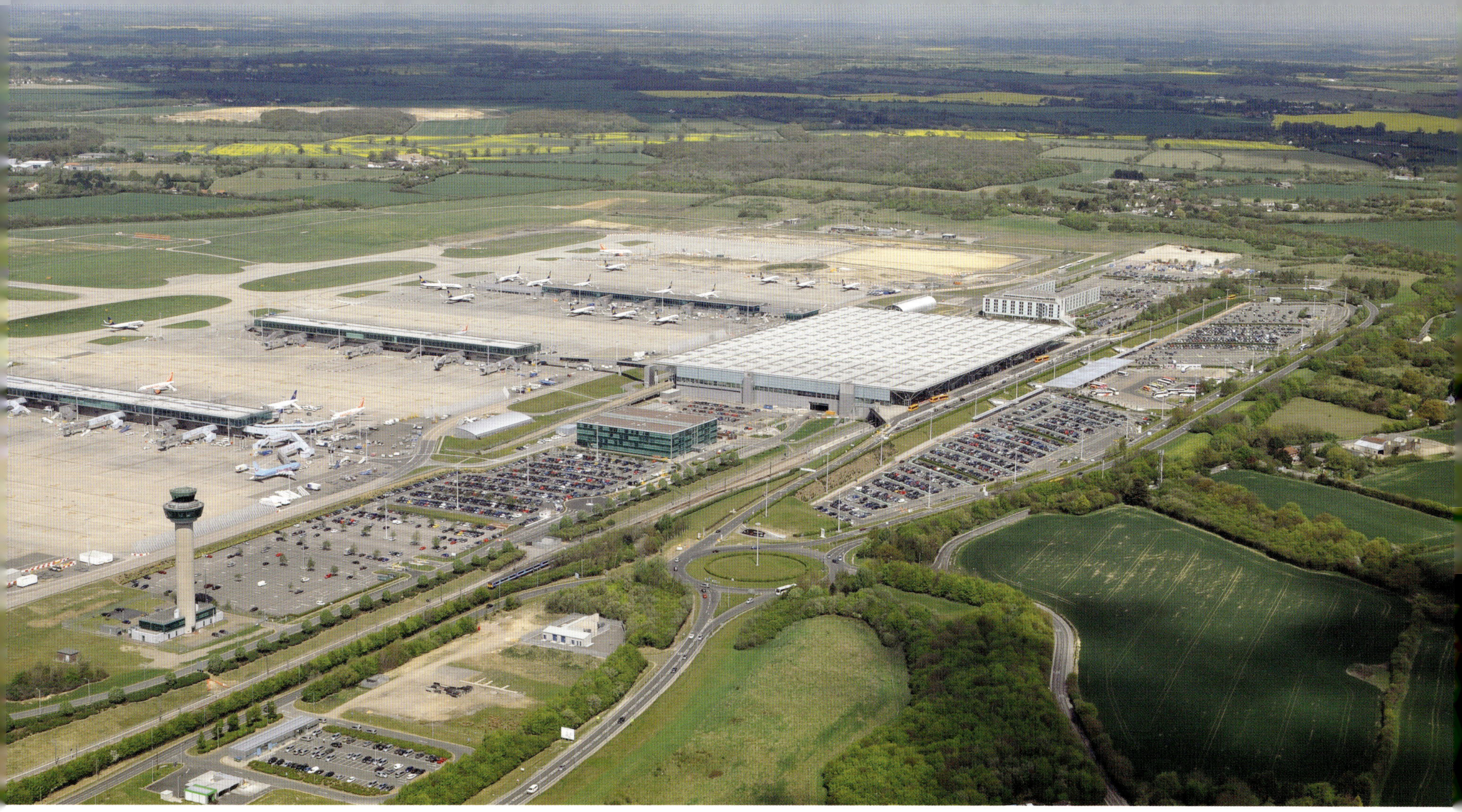

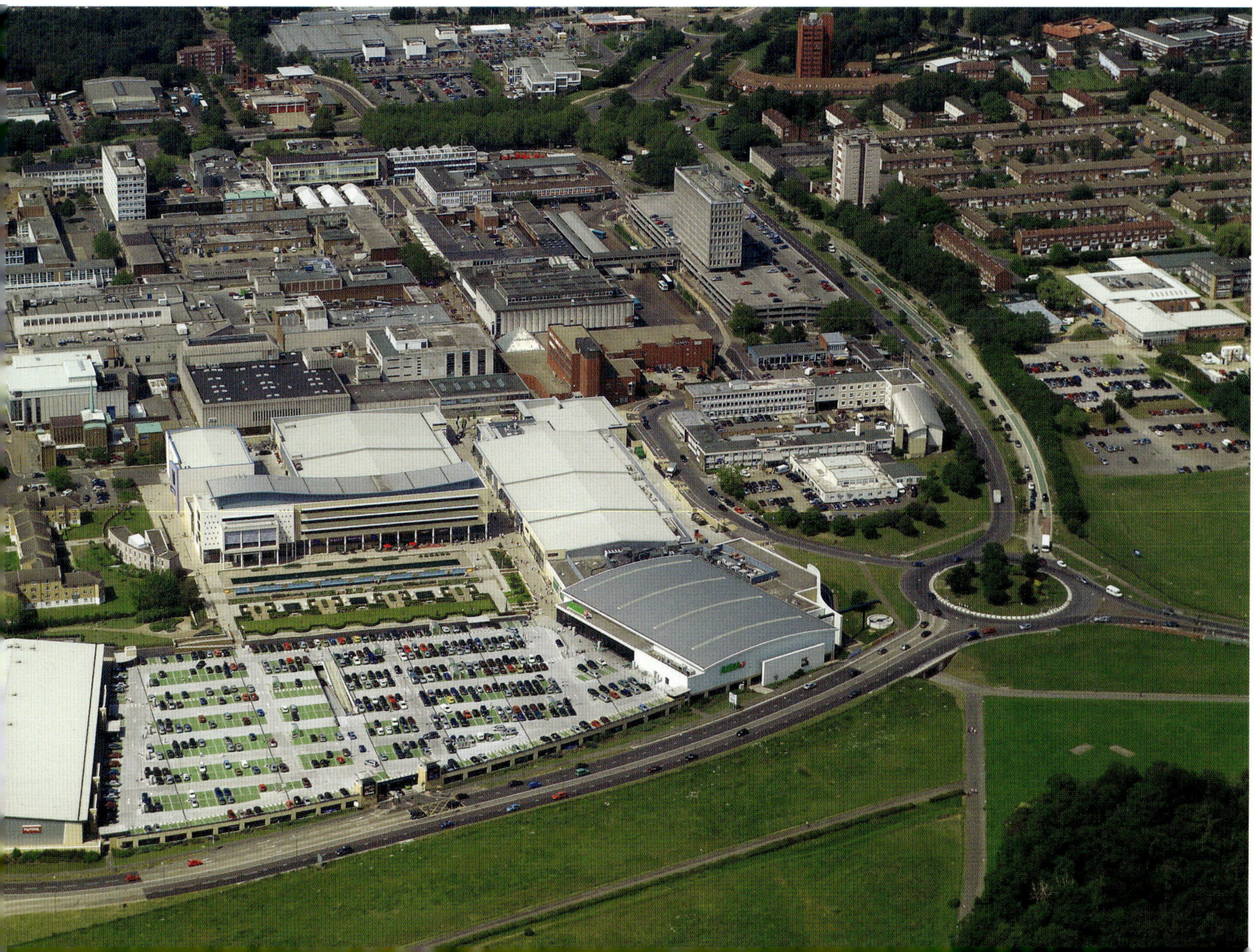

STANSTED

Stansted Airport (above) is the UK's third busiest after Heathrow and Gatwick with over 20m passengers a year. The base for a number of low-cost airlines, Stansted passengers travel from the terminal to gates in satellite hubs by transit trains. The main terminal building, designed by Foster Associates, is made of glass and features a "floating" roof.

HARLOW

One of the original New Towns, Harlow (left) was designed by Sir Frederick Gibberd to provide homes and jobs for 60,000 people leaving London. Gibberd drew up a plan in 1947 to create self-providing neighbourhoods with their own facilities, each separated by green space. He became the only architect to live in a town of his own design.

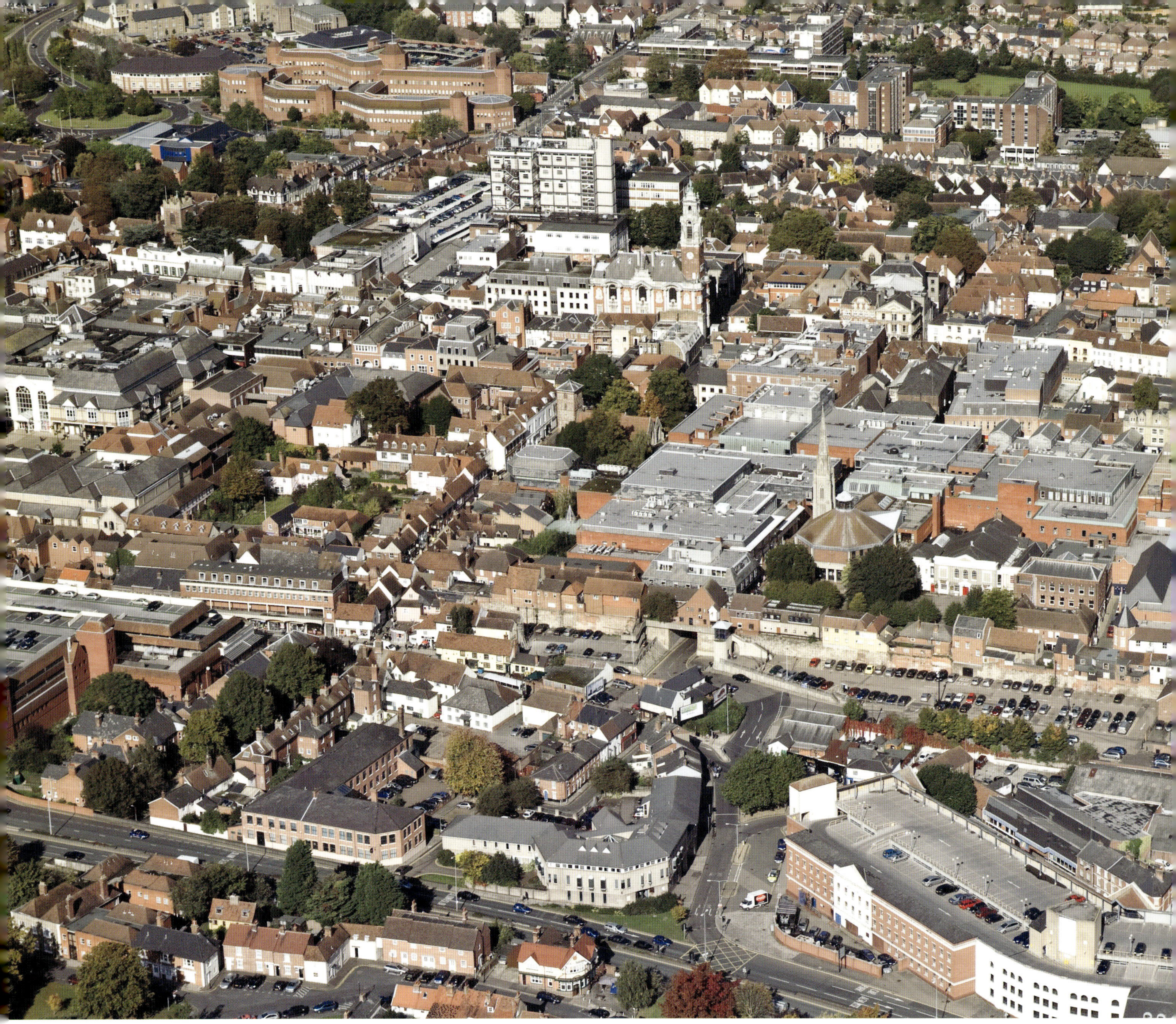

Colchester

Britain's oldest recorded Roman town sits close to beautiful river estuaries and the Dedham Vale area of outstanding natural beauty that inspired artists such as Constable and Gainsborough. Colchester was for a time the capital of Roman Britain. The largest surviving Roman gateway in Britain can still be seen, as well as mosaic flooring and 1.5 miles (2.5km) of Roman wall. Colchester Castle's Norman keep was used as the blueprint for the Tower of London and was the first Royal Castle in Britain. The largest surviving Norman keep in Europe, it was built on the foundations of the temple of Claudius. During the English Civil War in 1648, Colchester was under siege for 11 and a half weeks; the siege ended with the execution of Royalists in the castle. Today, the castle boasts a fascinating museum charting the history of Colchester from the Stone Age to the Civil War.

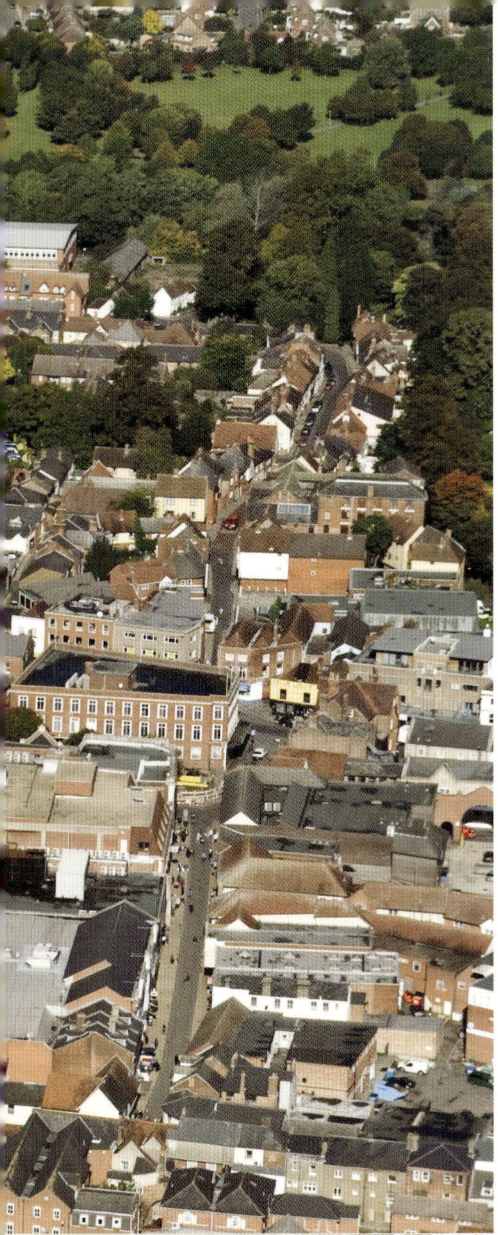

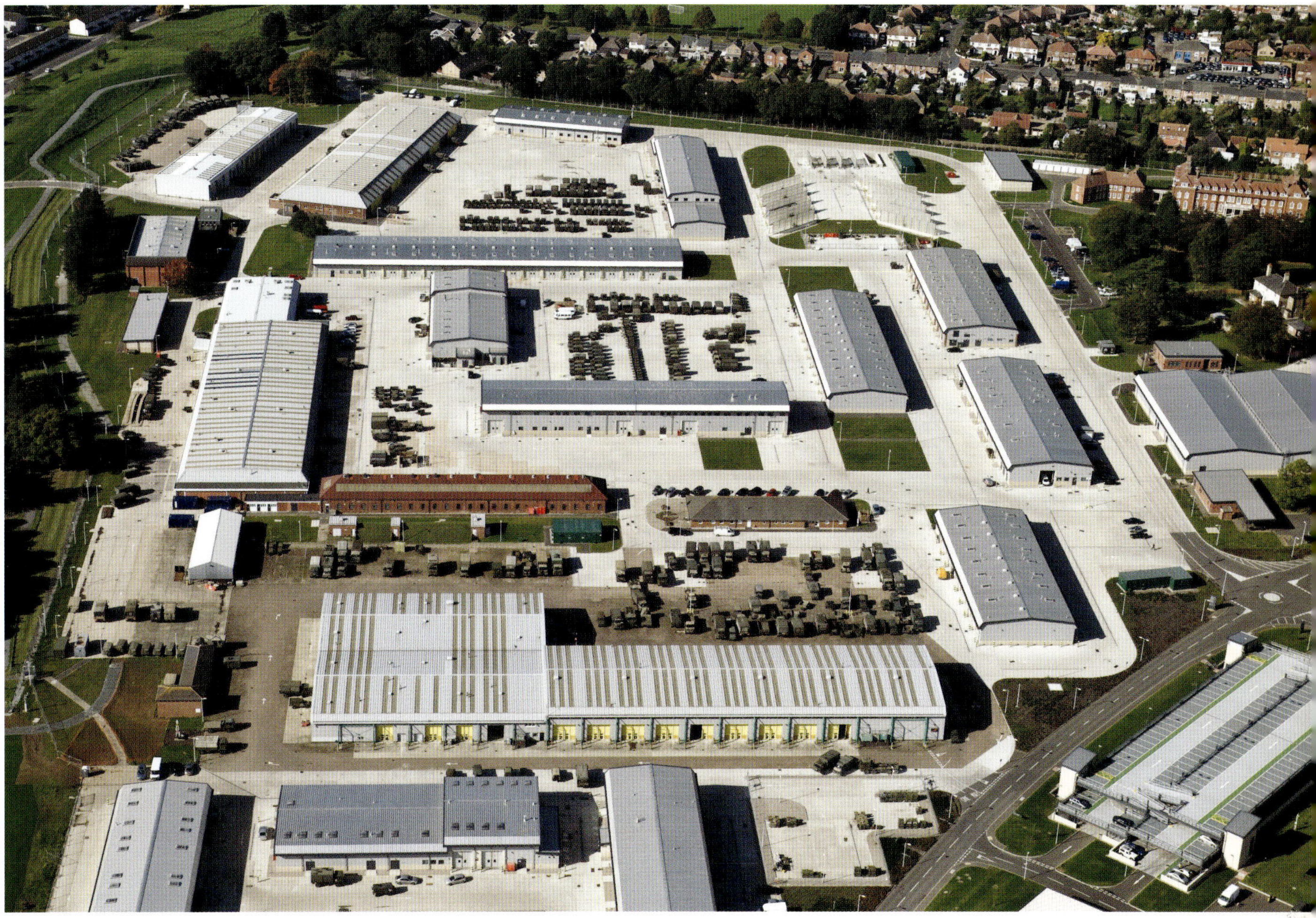

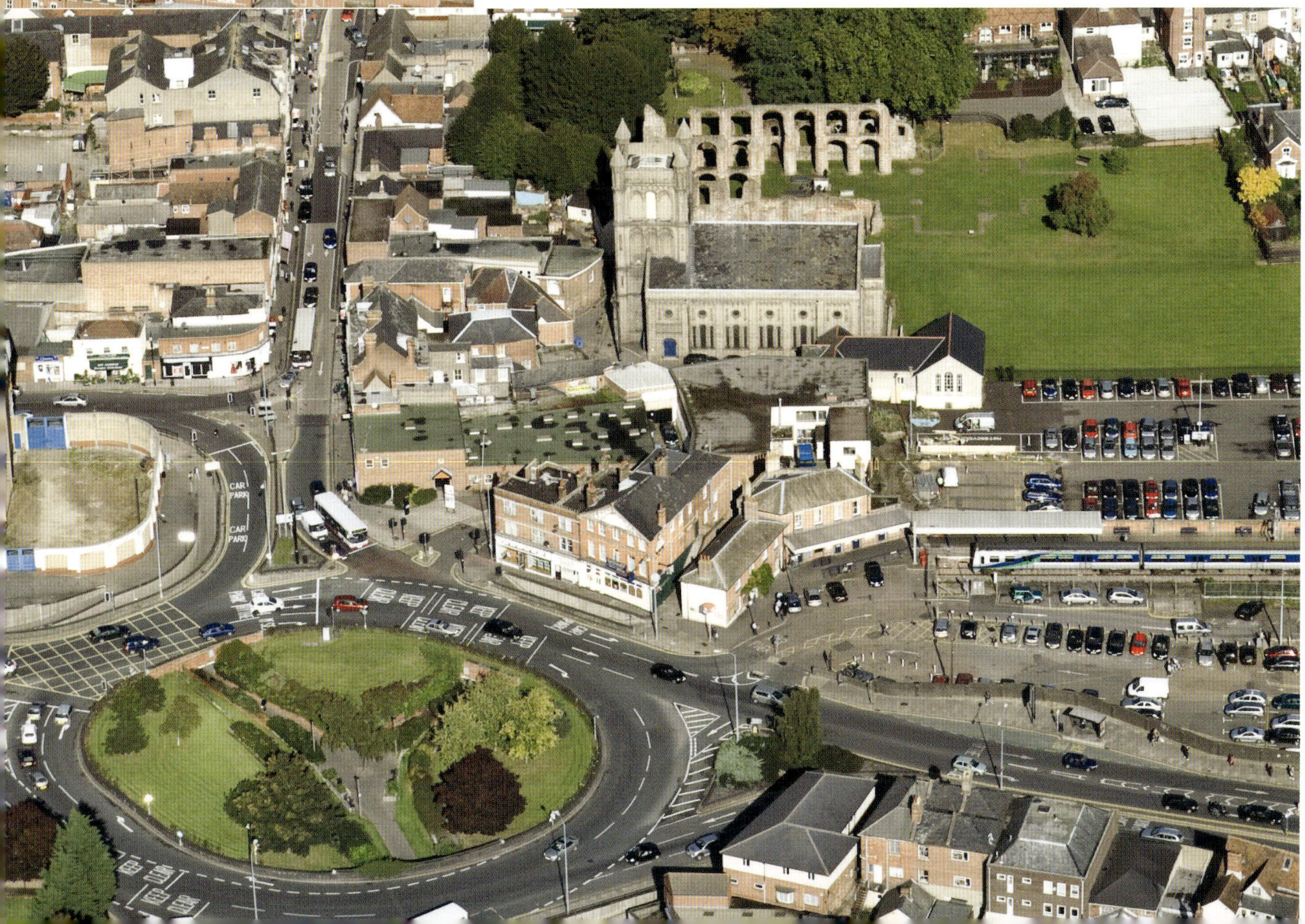

MILITARY TOWN

Ever since the Roman era, Colchester has been an important military garrison. Currently home to the 16th Air Assault Brigade, several battalions of Kitchener's Army were trained there during the First World War. Originally based in the centre of town, the barracks expanded rapidly during the Crimean War. During the Second World War Colchester and the surrounding district was home to a significant American presence with the establishment of a number of bases for the US Eighth Air Force. Recent redevelopment has moved the Colchester Garrison to the new and modern £560m Merville Barracks (above) outside the town centre, where each soldier has their own en-suite room.

The Essex coast

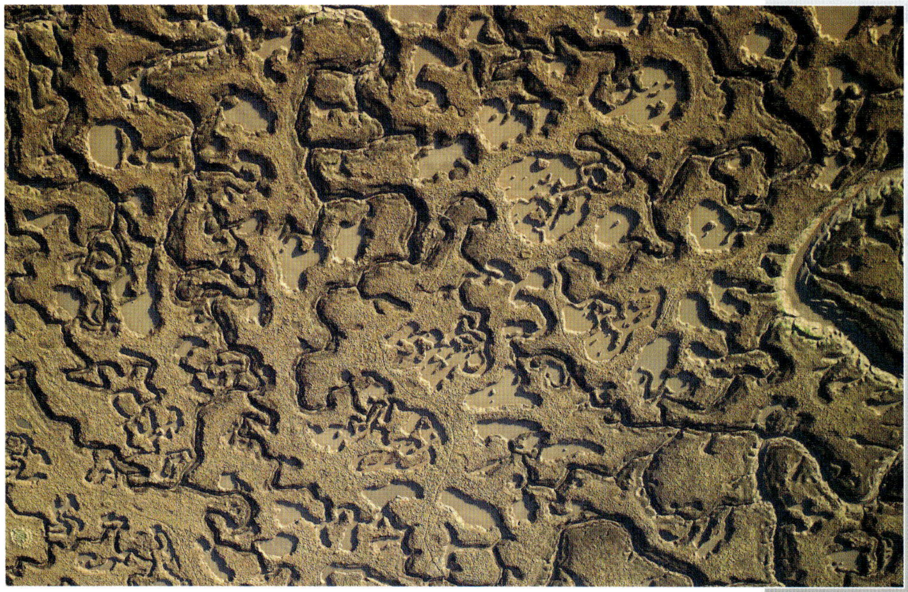

Just nine miles (14km) south of Colchester is an area of marshy coastline around the estuaries of the rivers Colne and Blackwater. At low tide, sailors must navigate the low-lying mudflats carefully as they reveal themselves in intricate patterns. The national nature reserve on the north bank of the Blackwater estuary is an important habitat for overwintering birds. The shallow creeks are ideal for the cultivation of oysters and nearby Brightlingsea has a renowned oyster fishery. Further around the coast lies Harwich (below), an international container port and cruise ship terminal. Based at the confluence of the Stour and Orwell river estuaries, it is the only safe anchorage between the Thames and Hull and provides regular ferry services to the Netherlands and Denmark. Bradwell-on-Sea (right) is best known as the site of a nuclear power station, but the village was once a Saxon Shore fort in Roman times. Built on the edge of a former Second World War airfield in 1957, the power station ceased generating electricity in 2002. Beyond and overlooking the sea lies the chapel of St Peter-on-the-Wall. Dating from 654 AD it is one of the oldest Christian churches in Britain.

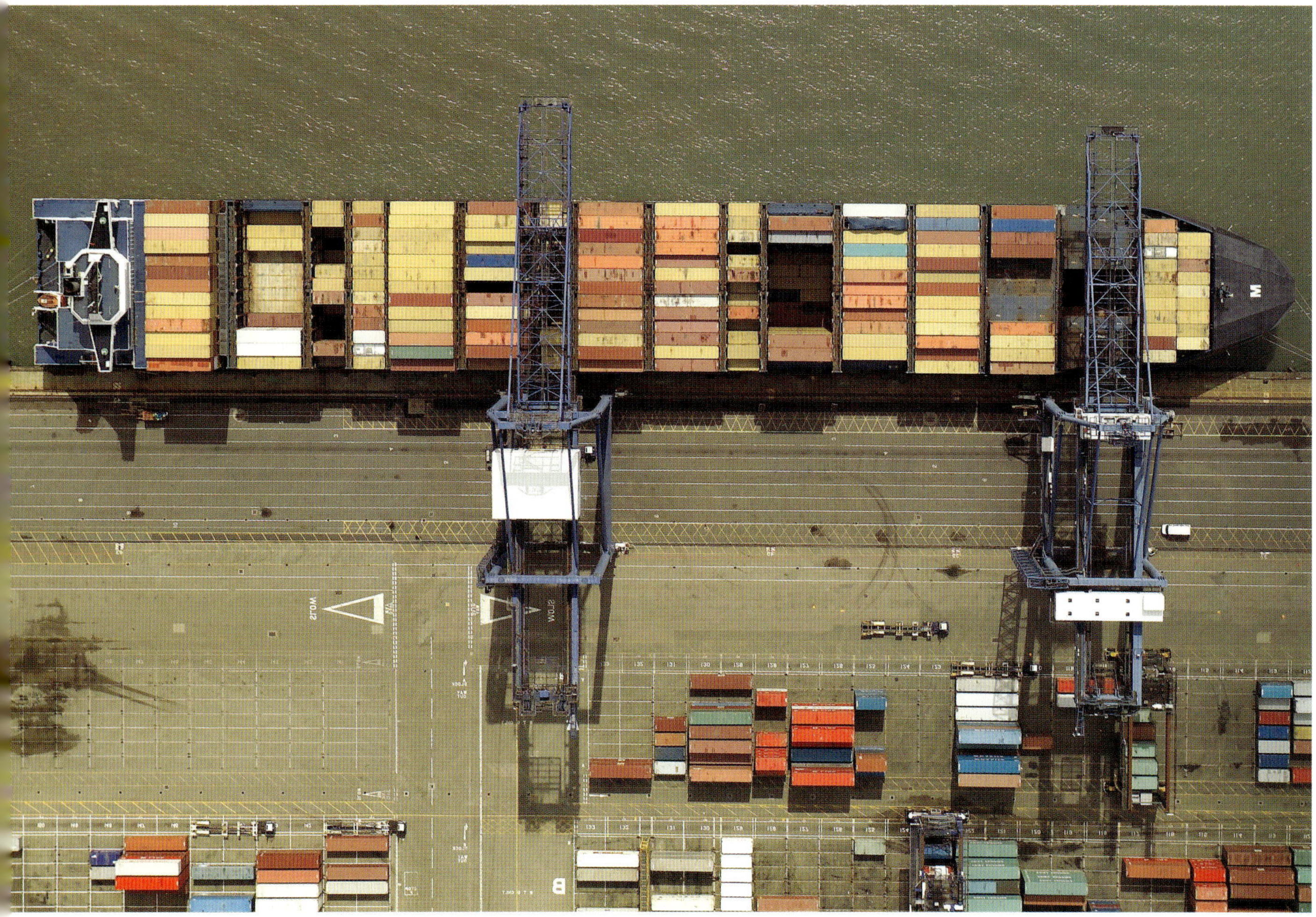

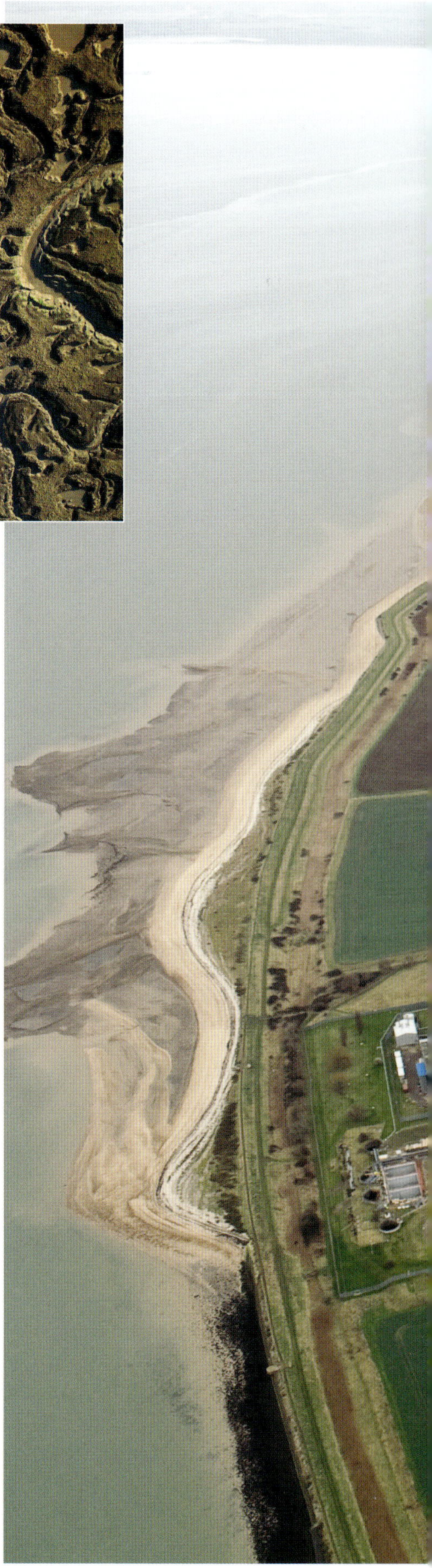

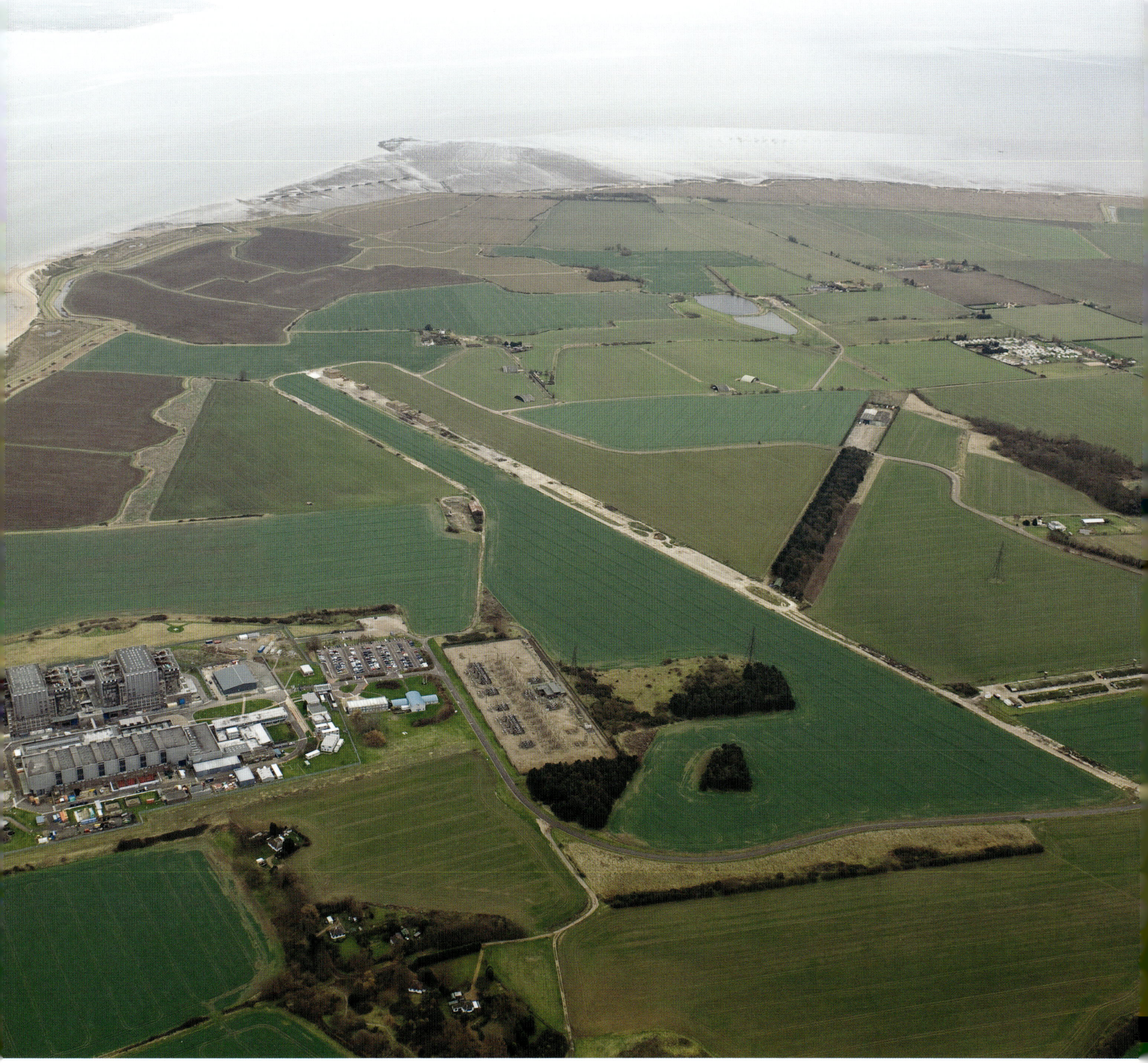

Southend

A popular seaside resort since the advent of the railways, Southend-on-Sea's pier (right) is the world's longest pleasure pier reaching 1.34 miles (2.15km) out to sea. Opened in stages between 1889 and 1929, the pier has survived a number of fires (including one in 2005), ship collisions, two world wars and plenty of stormy weather. A Grade II listed building, the pier has undergone significant renovation in recent years and now has a new lifeboat station and sundeck at the pier head, a permanent walkway and a new entrance at the shore end. Electric trains started running to the pier head in 1890 and, after the installation of new tracks and trains in 1986, visitors can still take the train to the restaurant and gift shop. Southend was home to the world's first theme park, the Kursaal (meaning a "cure house" or spa), which opened in 1894 at Marine Park in the east end of the town. The park boasted a scenic railway and dancing platform. This proved so popular that further attractions were added and the park rapidly expanded beyond its original boundary. In 1901 a grand building with a large silver dome was erected at its entrance complete with a circus, ballroom, an arcade with amusements, dining hall and billiard room. Later, fairground rides were added as well as a zoo and circus. By the 1930s the 26 acre site was the fairground of London's East End. However, by the 1970s the amusement park simply could not compete and in 1973 it closed. The site was developed for housing. Following many years of dereliction, the grand Kursaal building was restored and is now a prominent building on the seafront.

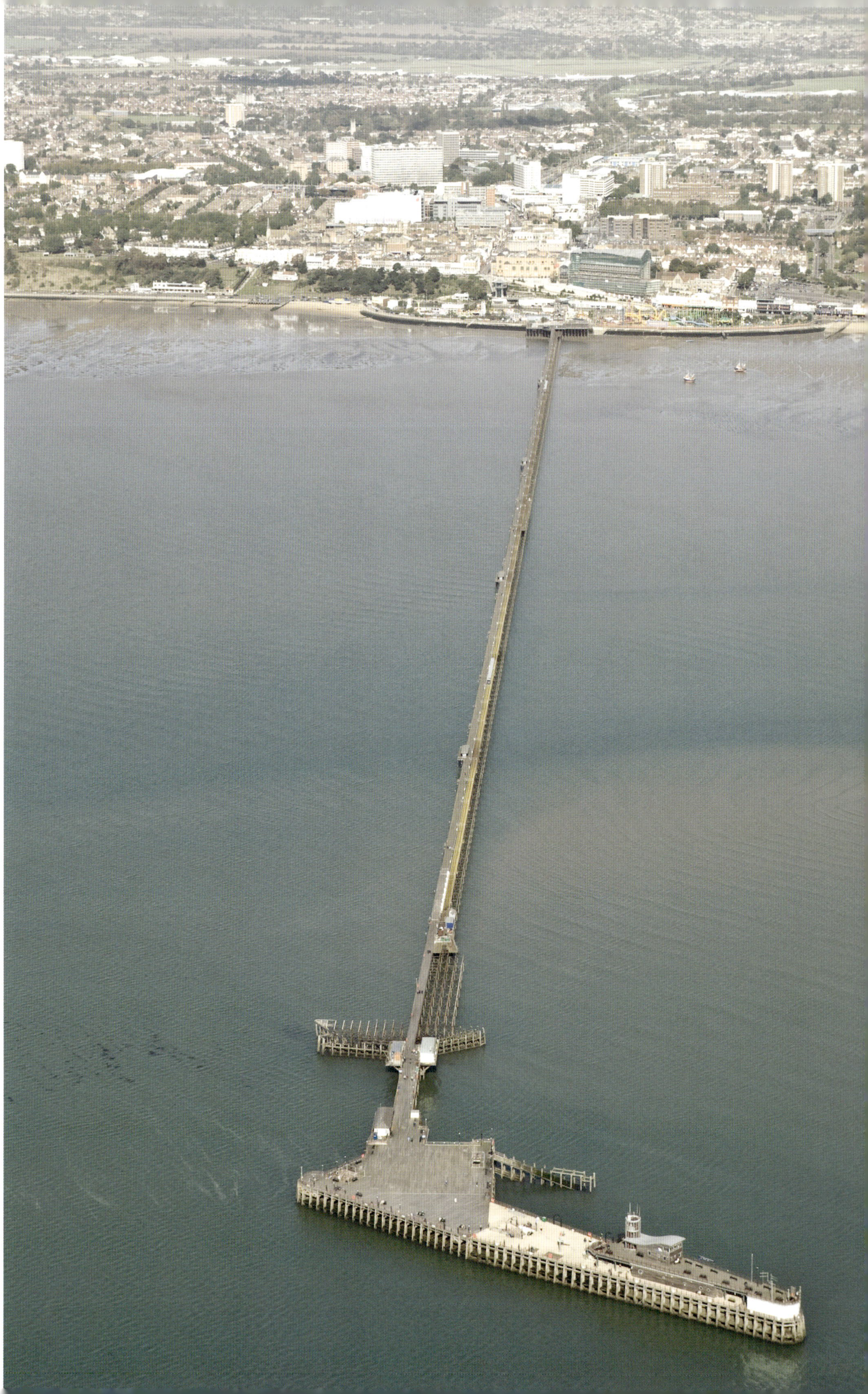

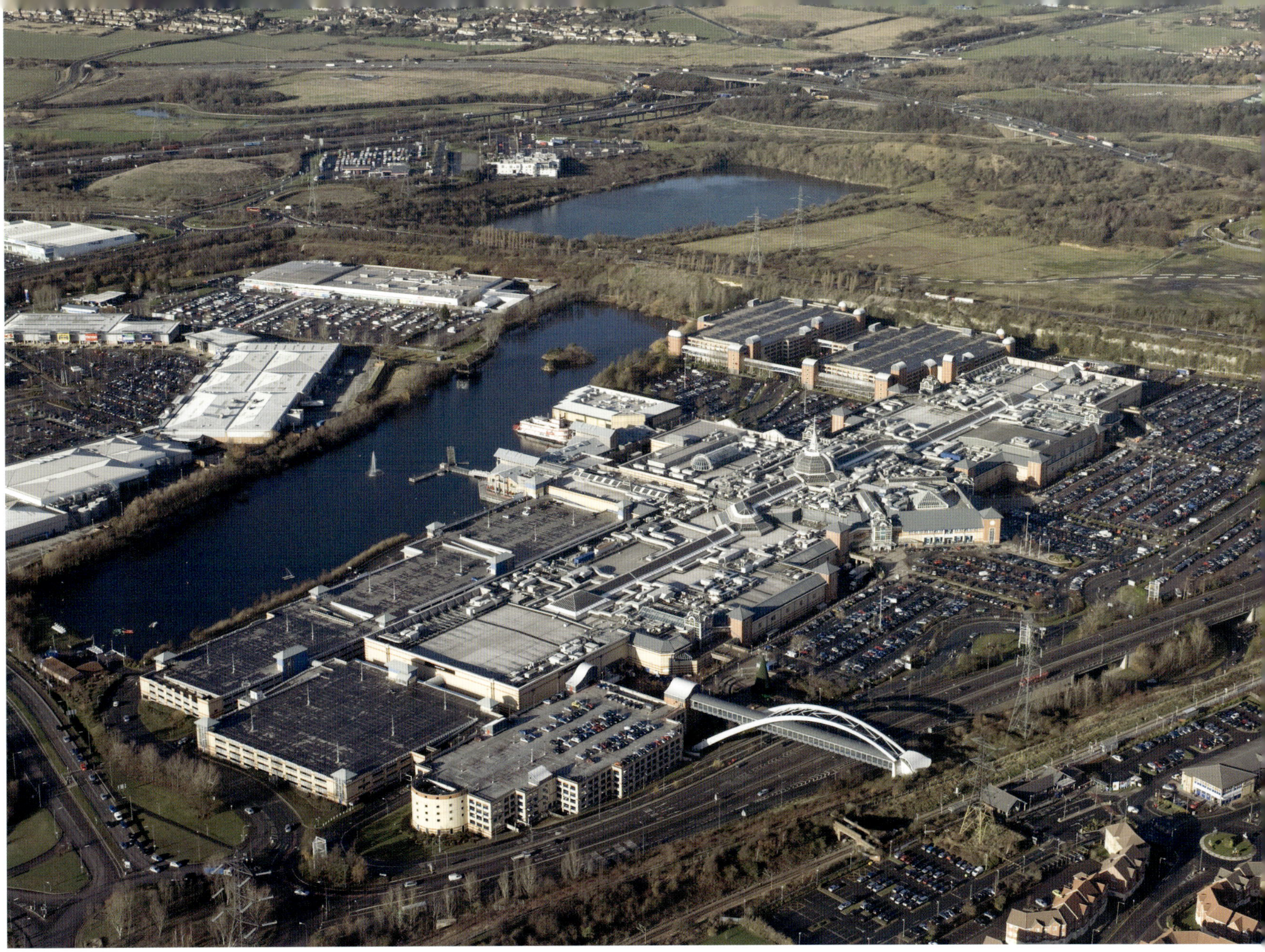

THURROCK

Lakeside Shopping Centre (above and right), based in West Thurrock, opened in 1990 and is Britain's seventh largest shopping centre with 1,402,537sq ft (130,300sq m) of available retail floorspace. Additional retail parks beside the shopping centre have created one of the largest shopping areas within Europe on a site of 200 acres. The shopping centre boasts 228 shops including three department stores, 33 cafes and restaurants, parking for 13,000 cars and a 26 acre width diving school. Recent refurbishment has added new glass roofs, lighting and porcelain flooring.

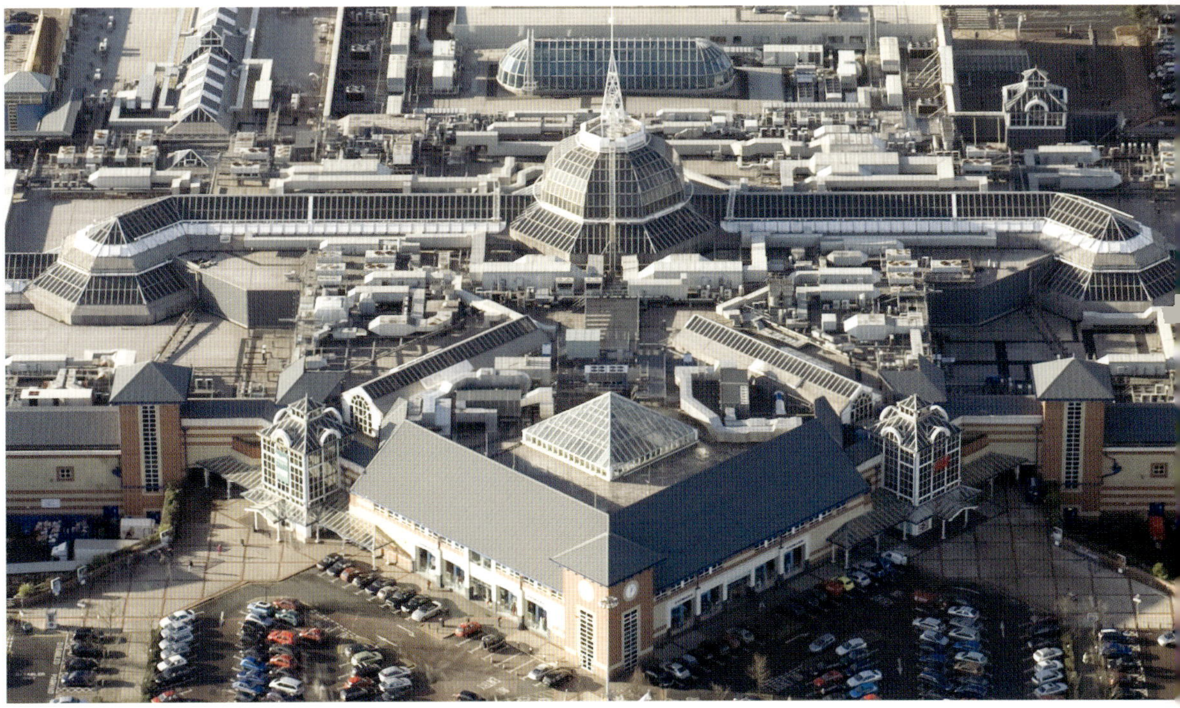

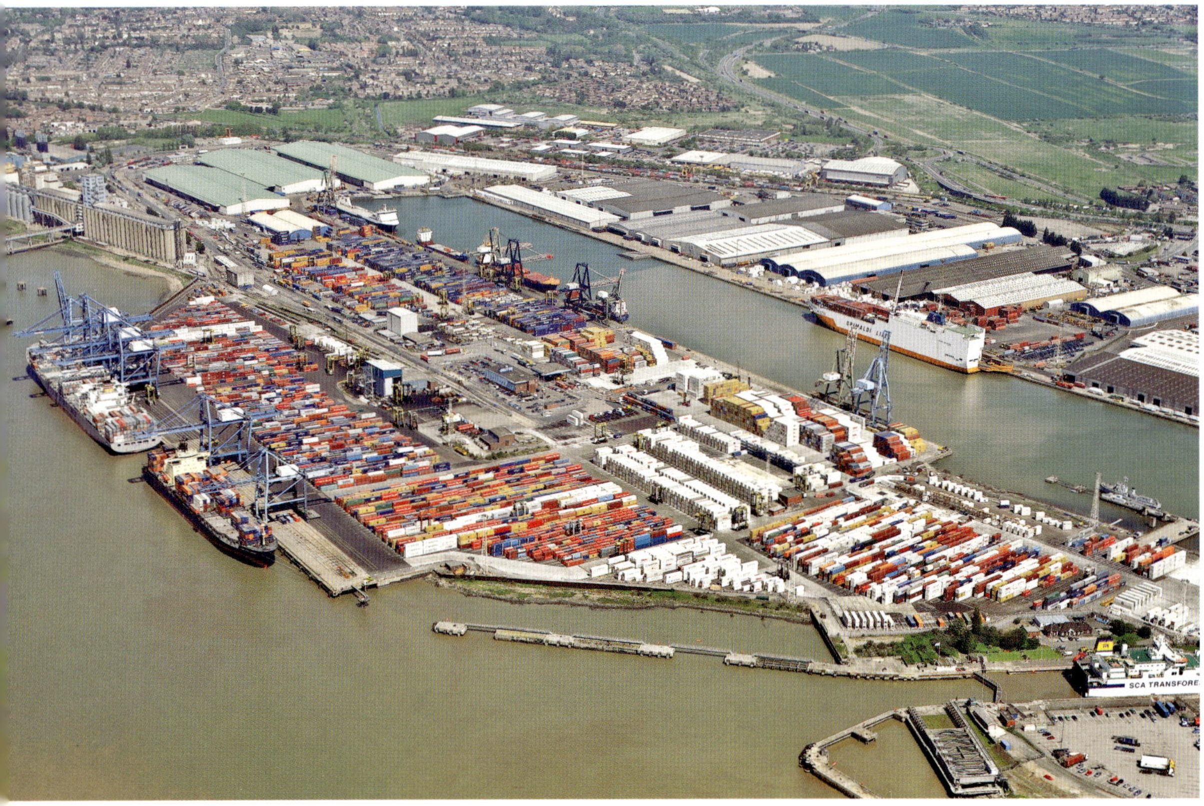

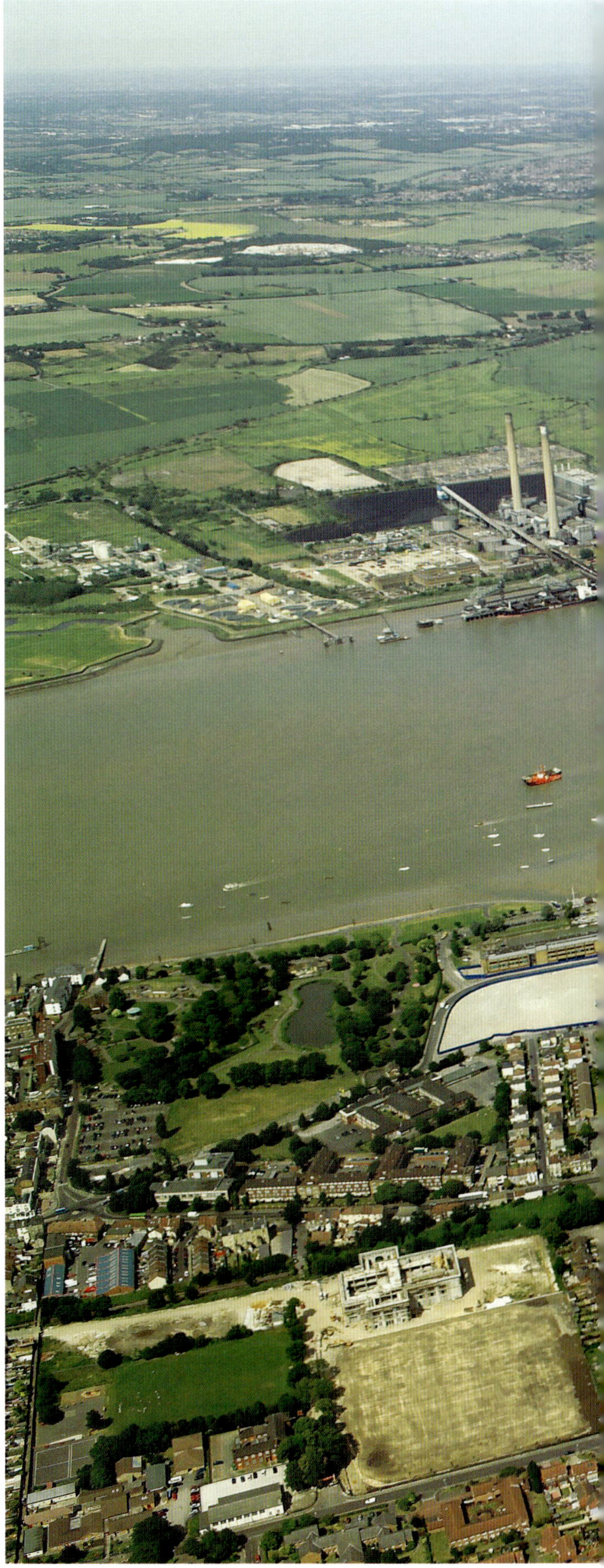

Tilbury

Tilbury (above) is situated on the north bank of the river Thames, east of the Dartford Crossing and across the river from Gravesend (right). Evidence suggests that a cross-river ferry ran between the two settlements from the 16th century, when a permanent D-shaped fort was also constructed by Henry VIII. The fort was reinforced during the Armada campaign and rebuilt by Charles II after the English Civil War as a pentagon. Tilbury Fort (below) saw military success during the First World War, gunning down a Zeppelin airship. After it was decommissioned in 1950, the fort was opened to the public. Tilbury grew mainly following construction of the docks from 1882 to 1886 as thousands of workers sought permanent housing. The Port of Tilbury is a deep-water port known for its importation of paper. It is London's principal port and one of Britain's three major container ports along with Southampton and Felixstowe.

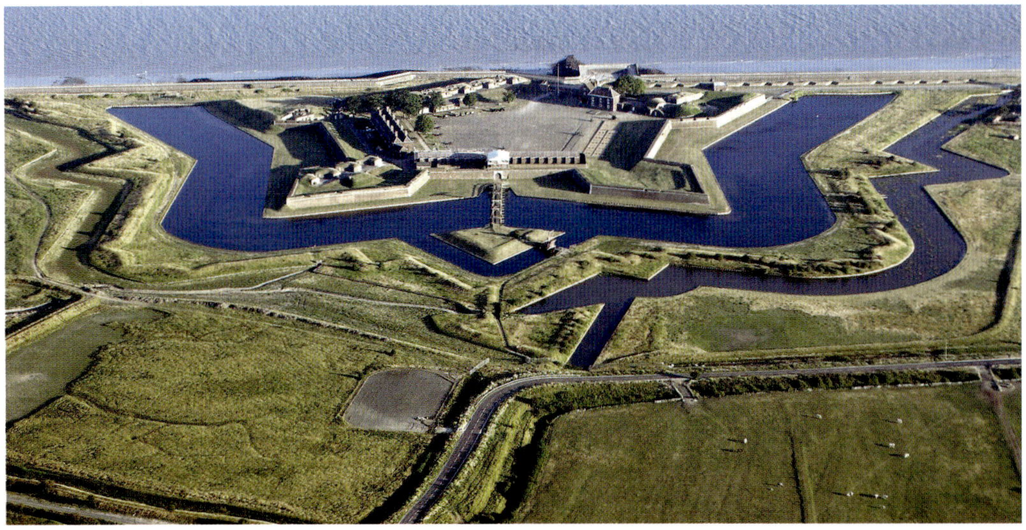

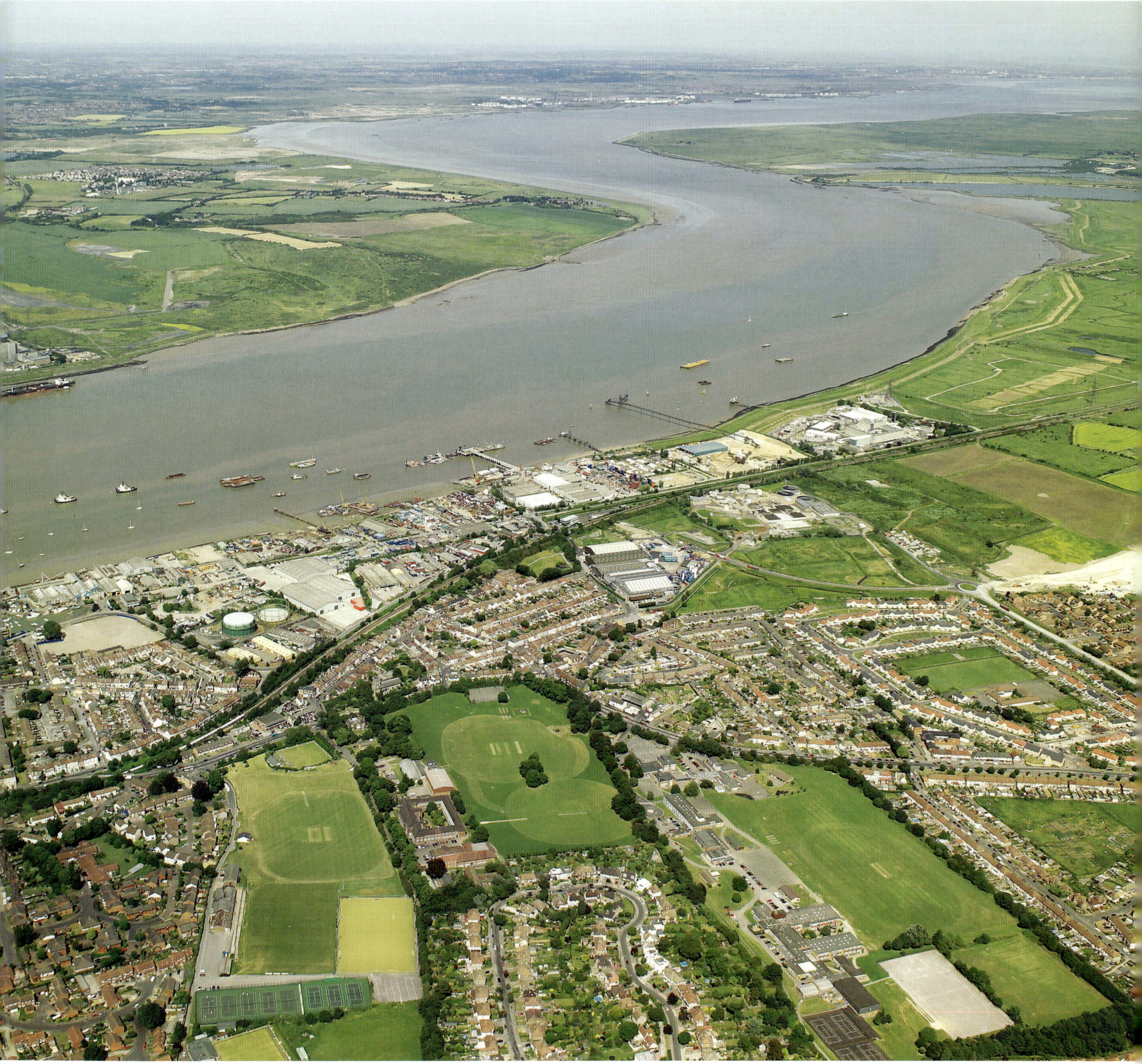

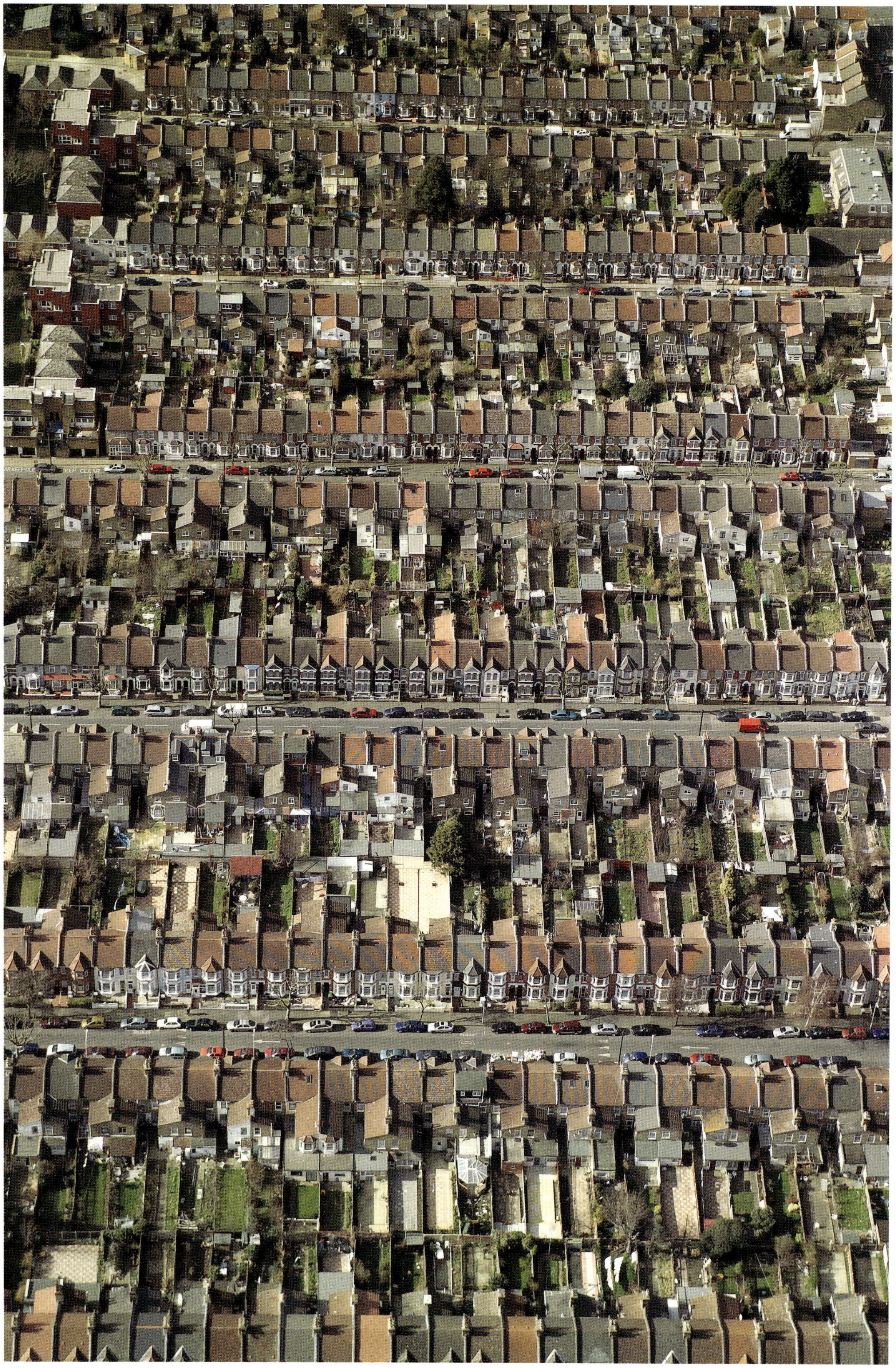

ILFORD

Between 1880 and 1910, Ilford's population grew from 10,000 to 78,000 and more than doubled again by 1938 due to the ease of access from London on the railway and the growth of the suburbs. Transport links were further improved with the arrival of the London Underground's Central Line in 1947. Ilford's first MP was Peter Griggs; he was instrumental in building housing to cope with the population boom. Parts of the Becontree housing estate, the largest public housing development in the world, were built in the 1920s and 1930s in Ilford. The estate has 27,000 homes and a population of over 100,000 people. Intended as "Homes for Heroes" after the First World War, the housing boasted indoor toilets and private gardens. Large firms that started in the town include the Ilford Photographic Company, now a large multinational company best known for their black and white film. Though Ilford was granted its Royal Charter as an Essex town in 1926, it has now been incorporated into the London Borough of Redbridge.
The famous philanthropist, Dr Barnardo, set up his Village Homes for Girls in Ilford in 1870 on a piece of rent-free land he was given as a wedding present. The home began with six girls but increased rapidly to 60. Today, Barnardo's has developed into one of Britain's leading children's charities; with its headquarters at Barkingside, Ilford, the charity retains its link with the town.